T0394626

Reading between the Lines

Library of the Written Word

The Handpress World

Reading between the Lines

Parish Libraries and Their Readers in Early Modern England, 1558–1709

By

Jessica G. Purdy

BRILL

LEIDEN | BOSTON

The Library of Congress Cataloging-in-Publication Data is available online at https://catalog.loc.gov

Typeface for the Latin, Greek, and Cyrillic scripts: "Brill". See and download: brill.com/brill-typeface.

ISSN 1874-4834
ISBN 978-90-04-36369-4 (hardback)
ISBN 978-90-04-36371-7 (e-book)

For my parents, Ian and Jillian

Contents

Acknowledgements XI
List of Figures and Table XII

Introduction 1

PART 1
Evolution

Introduction to Part 1 21

1 Pre-Reformation Clerical Libraries 24

2 Founders and Users of Post-Reformation Parish Libraries 31
　1 The Founders of Post-Reformation Parish Libraries 31
　2 The Users of Post-Reformation Parish Libraries 33
　3 Conclusion 35

3 Post-Reformation Parish Library Books 36
　1 Types of Books in Post-Reformation Parish Libraries 39
　2 Continental Books in Post-Reformation Parish Libraries
　　in England 41
　3 Conclusion 45

4 The Spread of Post-Reformation Parish Libraries 47
　1 The Chronological Spread of Parish Libraries in
　　Post-Reformation England 47
　2 The Geographical Spread of Parish Libraries in
　　Post-Reformation England 51
　3 Conclusion 52

PART 2
Establishment

Introduction to Part 2 55

5   The Parish Libraries of Grantham, Ripon, Gorton and Wimborne Minster   58
     1   The Francis Trigge Chained Library, Grantham, Lincolnshire   59
     2   Ripon Minster Parish Library, Ripon, Yorkshire   63
     3   The Gorton Chest Parish Library, Manchester, Lancashire   67
     4   The Wimborne Minster Chained Library, Wimborne Minster, Dorset   70

6   Parish Library Users and Usability   78
     1   Housing a Parish Library and Their Locations within Parish Churches   86
     2   Conclusion   90

7   Collecting Books and Compiling a Collection   91
     1   Establishing Libraries by Monetary Gift or Bequest   91
     2   Establishing Libraries by Gifting or Bequeathing Specific Books   100
     3   Later Augmentations   107
     4   The Cost of Early Modern Second-Hand Books   114
     5   Conclusion   120

8   Parsing the Collections of Early Modern Parish Libraries   121
     1   Authors' Confessional Identities   123
         1.1   *The Francis Trigge Chained Library*   124
         1.2   *Ripon Minster Parish Library*   126
         1.3   *The Gorton Chest Parish Library*   128
         1.4   *Wimborne Minster Chained Library*   130
     2   The Publication Dates of Parish Library Books   133
         2.1   *The Francis Trigge Chained Library*   133
         2.2   *Ripon Minster Parish Library*   135
         2.3   *The Gorton Chest Parish Library*   137
         2.4   *Wimborne Minster Chained Library*   139
     3   The Publication Locations of Parish Library Books and Links to the Continental Book Trade   141
         3.1   *The Francis Trigge Chained Library*   141
         3.2   *Ripon Minster Parish Library*   144
         3.3   *The Gorton Chest Parish Library*   147
         3.4   *Wimborne Minster Chained Library*   148

4 The Language of Books in Parish Libraries   151
   4.1 *The Francis Trigge Chained Library*   151
   4.2 *Ripon Minster Parish Library*   152
   4.3 *Wimborne Minster Chained Library*   154
5 Genres of Books in Early Modern Parish Libraries   156
   5.1 *The Francis Trigge Chained Library*   156
   5.2 *Ripon Minster Parish Library*   160
   5.3 *The Gorton Chest Parish Library*   163
   5.4 *Wimborne Minster Chained Library*   168
6 Conclusion   171

PART 3
Readership

Introduction to Part 3   175

9   Anti-Catholicism   180
   1 The Errors, Changes and Corruptions of the Catholic Church   182
   2 False Worship, Images and Idolatry in the Catholic Church   192
   3 Guidance for Identifying the True and Uncorrupted Church   196
   4 Conclusion   197

10   The Importance of Scripture   199
   1 Scripture as the Word of God   201
   2 Interpreting and Understanding Scripture   206
   3 Accessibility of the Scriptures   210
   4 Conclusion   212

11   Sin, Repentance and Salvation   213
   1 Sin   214
   2 Repentance and Salvation   218
   3 Conclusion   229

12   Godly Living and Death   230
   1 Godly Living in Early Modern Protestantism   232
   2 Godly Dying and Suicide in Early Modern Protestantism   245
   3 Conclusion   250

Conclusion   251

Appendix 1: List of Books in the Gorton Chest Parish Library   255

**Appendix 2: List of Books in the Turton and Walmsley
Parish Libraries**   265
  Turton   265
  Walmsley   266

**Appendix 3: List of Books in the Stone and Gillingham Donations to
Wimborne Minster Chained Library**   268
  William Stone's Donation   268
  Roger Gillingham's Donation   280

Bibliography   291
Index   328

Acknowledgements

This monograph is based on my PhD thesis, which I completed in 2021. That research, and this monograph, would not have been completed without the help and support of so many people. I would like to express my thanks to the kind and generous people associated with all four of the case study libraries in this monograph. Particular thanks must go to Judith Monds, who welcomed me to Wimborne Minster Chained Library and allowed me access to the collection, and Frank Tandy, the former librarian at Wimborne Minster, who was generous enough to meet with me and to share with me his research into the history of Wimborne Minster Chained Library and its founders. Special thanks must also go to Brian Stagg, who shared with me his knowledge of the Francis Trigge Chained Library, and to John and Barbara Manterfield, who were kind enough not only to share their knowledge of the library, but also to allow me to stay with them during my research visits to St Wulfram's church in Grantham. Finally, my heartfelt gratitude goes to the staff at Chetham's Library, whom I have had the pleasure to know for several years now. The Librarian, Fergus Wilde, and his wonderful predecessor, the late Michael Powell, were both on my PhD supervisory team and were always happy to chat and to answer any and all questions I had about Humphrey Chetham, his Library, and his parish libraries.

I am also extremely grateful to colleagues old at Manchester Metropolitan University and to colleagues new at the University of St Andrews, all of whom have been ready with words of support and encouragement, as well as practical assistance, when I needed it most. My PhD experience would have been far less enjoyable and fruitful without the guidance and inspiration of my supervisors, Dr Rosamund Oates and Dr Kathryn Hurlock. Adapting my PhD thesis into this monograph would have been far less enjoyable and far more difficult without the guidance of Professor Andrew Pettegree and Dr Arthur der Weduwen. Special thanks must also go to Professor Mark Towsey at the University of Liverpool, who examined my thesis in my *viva voce* and who has been a constant source of support and advice since then.

To my friends, old and new, particularly Dr Thomas McGrath and Dr Owen Rees, my heartfelt thanks. To my family, my sisters, Sophie and Molly, who were patient and supportive through all the ups and downs, and my parents, Ian and Jillian, who give me unconditional love and support, I love you.

Figures and Table

Figures

1   Parish libraries founded in England between 1558 and 1679   11
2   Parish libraries founded in England between 1558 and 1699   12
3   Surviving parish libraries possessing continental books   13
4   Parish libraries founded between 1558 and 1709   14
5a   Location types of parish libraries founded between 1558 and 1679   15
5b   Location types of parish libraries founded between 1680 and 1709   16
6   Locations of the four case study parish libraries   17
7   The residences and parish libraries of Humphrey Chetham   18
8   The founders of post-Reformation libraries, 1558–1709   32
9   Number of parish libraries founded by decade, 1558–1709   48
10   Quadripartite agreement establishing the Francis Trigge Chained Library   61
11   The Gorton Chest Parish Library   85
12   The list of books sent to Gorton Chapel for the parish library   116
13   The title page of Volume x of Saint Augustine's Works   119
14   Sizes of surviving parish library collections of books donated between 1558 and 1709   121
15   Confessional identities of authors in the Francis Trigge Chained Library   125
16   Confessional identities of authors in Ripon Minster Parish Library   127
17   Confessional identities of authors in the Gorton Chest Parish Library   129
18   Confessional identities of authors whose works were donated to Wimborne Minster Chained Library by William Stone and Roger Gillingham   131
19   Publication dates of books in the Francis Trigge Chained Library   134
20   Publication dates of surviving titles in Ripon Minster Parish Library   136
21   The publication dates of books in the Gorton Chest Parish Library by decade   138
22   Publication dates of the books donated by William Stone and Roger Gillingham by decade   139
23a   Publication locations of books in the Francis Trigge Chained Library by city   142
23b   Publication locations of books in the Francis Trigge Chained Library by country   142
24   Publication locations of books in Ripon Minster Parish Library by city   145
25   Publication locations of books in Wimborne Minster Chained Library by city   149

26   Languages of the surviving books in Ripon Minster Parish Library   153
27   Languages of the books donated by William Stone and Roger Gillingham to
      Wimborne Minster Chained Library   155
28   The genres of books in the Francis Trigge Chained Library Collection   157
29   Anthony Higgin's classifications of his theological works   161
30   Subject classifications of books in the Gorton Chest Parish Library   164
31   Genres of surviving books in the donations of William Stone and Roger
      Gillingham to Wimborne Minster Chained Library   169

Table

1   Books donated to Wimborne Minster Chained Library and their donors   113

Introduction

Parish libraries were a significant part of the intellectual and religious landscape of sixteenth- and seventeenth-century England as repositories of religious edification and theological and secular education, accessible to both the clergy and the laity. They evolved out of pre-Reformation collections of clerical texts in parish churches and were intended to provide the clergy and the local laity with an increased religious education. From the middle of the sixteenth century onwards, parish libraries were established by a mixture of both clerics and laymen, which was reflected in a wider and more inclusive clerical and lay readership of the books they contained. As the seventeenth century progressed, the number of parish libraries established in England increased and they began to appear in the country's more rural locales as well. At the same time, the range of genres of books in these collections broadened: they were still dominated by religious texts but they also diversified to include more secular works, books on history, philosophy, natural sciences and other liberal arts subjects. Extant marginalia and annotations still present in parish library books reveal a significant degree of reader interest in the topics of anti-Catholicism, the importance of Scripture, the related concepts of sin, repentance and salvation, and the need to live a godly life and prepare for death.

The study of parish libraries began in earnest in 1959 with *The Parochial Libraries of the Church of England* report prepared for the Central Council for the Care of Churches. This report provided a list of parish libraries in England, with a brief overview of their contents.[1] It also prompted a flurry of overview studies into individual parish libraries or groups of parish libraries in a particular geographical area. Much of the in-depth research on individual parish libraries began in the 1970s and continued into the 1980s; it outlined the details of a particular library's foundation and, in some cases, provided an overview of its surviving collection. Angela Roberts conducted research on the Francis Trigge Chained Library in Grantham in 1971, outlining the conditions of the library's establishment and arguing that even though the Latin nature of many of the books in the collection may have deterred general reading, the 'utilitarian rather than imaginative literature ... may well have attracted many of the educated people of Grantham'.[2] In 1982, Anne L. Herbert undertook similar research into Oakham parish library in Rutland. Herbert outlined

---

1   Central Council for the Care of Churches, *The Parochial Libraries of the Church of England* (London: Faith Press, 1959).
2   Angela Roberts, 'The Chained Library, Grantham', *Library History*, 2 (1971), pp. 75–90.

the circumstances of Oakham parish library's foundation and provided a catalogue of the books donated by the library's founder, Lady Anne Harington, in 1616.[3] In 1983, William Smith published his article on the parish library established at Steeple Ashton in Wiltshire – one of the first post-Reformation parish libraries to be founded – in 1568 and provided a select bibliography of surviving works from before 1828.[4] Sometimes, these studies of parish libraries focussed on a small number of repositories in a specific area or county, such as Nigel Yates's research on Kentish libraries or David Shaw's more recent research into the same area.[5] Shaw provided an overview of five parochial libraries in Kent, noting brief details about their founders as well as the surviving number of books in each collection.[6]

Other studies examined parish libraries more generally. Prominent amongst these early general studies of parish libraries are those by David Williams in the late 1970s. In his research, Williams noted broad patterns and trends in parish library foundation and development, arguing that parish libraries were subject to various access restrictions and that libraries were originally established in the urban areas of England until the late seventeenth century, after which founders' attention moved to the country's more rural locations.[7] One of the most wide-ranging studies of parish libraries came in 2004 when Michael Perkin published his *A Directory of the Parochial Libraries of the Church of England and the Church in Wales*. The *Directory* revised and expanded the scope of the 1959 report prepared for the Central Council for the Care of Churches by including brief details about all of the parish libraries established in England and Wales up to 1900, all of the chained libraries established in England and Wales from the mid-sixteenth century to the eighteenth century, and all of the diocesan and deanery libraries and other foundations established prior to 1850.[8]

3   Anne L. Herbert, 'Oakham Parish Library', *Library History*, 6:1 (1982), pp. 1–11.
4   William Smith, 'The Parochial Library of Steeple Ashton in Wiltshire', *Library History*, 6:4 (1983), pp. 97–113.
5   Nigel Yates, 'The Parochial Library of All Saints, Maidstone, and Other Kentish Parochial Libraries', *Archaeologia Cantiana*, 99 (1983), pp. 159–173; David Shaw, 'Parochial Libraries in Kent', *Library & Information History*, 27:4 (2011), pp. 239–245.
6   Shaw, 'Parochial Libraries in Kent', pp. 239–245.
7   David Williams, 'English Parochial Libraries: A History of Changing Attitudes', *Antiquarian Book Monthly Review*, 5:4 (1978), pp. 138–147; David Williams, 'The Use and Abuse of a Pious Intention: Changing Attitudes to Parochial Libraries', *The Library Association and Study School and National Conference Proceedings*, Nottingham, 1979, pp. 21–28.
8   Michael Perkin, *A Directory of the Parochial Libraries of the Church of England and the Church in Wales* (London: Bibliographical Society, 2004); Michael Perkin, 'The Parochial Libraries of the Church of England: a Revised Directory', *Library History*, 14 (1998), p. 13.

Most historians agree that post-Reformation parish libraries evolved out of their pre-Reformation counterparts. Some of the first in-depth studies into the book collections of pre-Reformation parish churches were those of John Shinners and Stacey Gee, in 1997 and 2003 respectively.[9] Gee argued that the donations of books to parish churches prior to the Reformation pre-empted and influenced the foundation of parish libraries in post-Reformation parish churches. Gee demonstrated similarities between the contents of pre-Reformation book collections of service books, commentaries and glosses on the Bible, pastoral manuals, grammar books and devotional texts that were housed in the parish church, and the collections of post-Reformation parish churches, which featured many of the same sorts of books.[10] Similarly, in 2008, Arnold Hunt argued in favour of a sense of continuity between pre-Reformation libraries in parish churches and their post-Reformation counterparts that manifested in the continued ownership of religious texts and theological works by parish churches. Hunt viewed this continued ownership as forming a bridge between medieval and early modern religious cultures.[11]

That the importance of post-Reformation parish libraries lay in their role as repositories of religious and spiritual education for both the clergy and the laity has been recognised by numerous historians. In 2008, Hunt asserted that 'the significance of these modest collections is that they gave parishioners access to the writings of some of the leading English and continental Reformed divines', thus spreading the Protestantism of the English Church. The presence of these texts in the reasonably accessible parish libraries of early modern England 'helped to disseminate the fruits' of Calvinism, and Protestantism more generally, 'to a wider readership'.[12] Hunt's argument was built on and broadened in 2011, when W. M. Jacob argued that 'books were an essential tool to promote a learned and godly clergy and godly laity for the reformed Church of England'.[13]

9   John Shinners, 'Parish Libraries in Medieval England' in Jacqueline Brown and William P. Stoneman (eds), *A Distinct Voice: Medieval Studies in Honor of Leonard E. Boyle* (Notre Dame, Ind.: University of Notre Dame Press, 1997), pp. 207–230; Stacey Gee, 'Parochial Libraries in Pre-Reformation England' in Sarah Rees Jones (ed.), *Learning and Literacy in Medieval England and Abroad* (Turnhout: Brepols, 2003), pp. 199–222.

10   Gee, 'Parochial Libraries in Pre-Reformation England', p. 220.

11   Arnold Hunt, 'Clerical and Parish Libraries' in Elisabeth Leedham-Green and Teresa Webber (eds), *The Cambridge History of Libraries, Volume I, to 1640* (Cambridge: Cambridge University Press, 2008), p. 401.

12   Hunt, 'Clerical and Parish Libraries', p. 416.

13   W. M. Jacob, 'Parochial Libraries and their Users', *Library and Information History*, 27:4 (2011), p. 211.

Post-Reformation parish libraries included books on a range of religious and secular subjects, which supports W. M. Jacob's 2006 assessment of parish library collections as having been 'mostly strong on theology, history and the classics', whilst also including 'books on agricultural topics ... and law, as well as ... travel, entomology, maths, science, theatre, poetry, and foreign languages'.[14] As will be demonstrated further in chapter 7, for the most part, the theological texts in sixteenth- and seventeenth-century parish libraries primarily discussed Protestant theology and included texts by key Protestant divines such as John Calvin, William Perkins and Peter Martyr. Some theological works in parish library collections also included Early Christian or patristic texts by the Church Fathers, or else were written by either medieval theologians or post-Reformation Catholics. The inclusion of medieval and post-Reformation Catholics supports Hunt's comments on continuity and David Pearson's argument from the early 1990s that the English Protestant clergy needed to be knowledgeable of opposing religions, so that they were better equipped to refute their claims.[15]

Many of the books in the corpuses of post-Reformation parish libraries demonstrate the strength of the European book trade in the early modern period, as considerable portions of some of their collections were comprised of books printed on the continent. Numerous historians – Andrew Pettegree, John Hinks and Joad Raymond perhaps foremost amongst them – have studied the early modern book trade and commented upon the nature of the relationship between the European and English book markets. All three scholars have argued that England's printing industry was under-developed in comparison to much of Europe in the early modern period, and that England continued to be reliant on the European book market into the seventeenth century, particularly for Latin texts. In 1996, David Pearson argued that the ownership of continental books was made possible in large part by 'the existence of a flourishing book trade, which organised the selling of new and second-hand books, [and] the importing of newly published books from London and abroad'.[16] In 2008, Andrew Pettegree's research into the relationship between centre and periphery in the early modern book trade placed England very much on the

---

14   W. M. Jacob, 'Libraries for the Parish: Individual Donors and Charitable Societies' in Giles Mandelbrote and K. A. Manley (eds), *The Cambridge History of Libraries in Britain and Ireland, Volume II: 1640–1850* (Cambridge: Cambridge University Press, 2006), p. 69.

15   David Pearson, 'The Libraries of English Bishops, 1600–1640', *The Library*, 14 (1992), p. 229.

16   David Pearson, 'Scholars and bibliophiles: book collectors in Oxford, 1550–1650' in Robin Myers and Michael Harris (eds), *Antiquaries, Book Collectors and the Circles of Learning* (Winchester: St Paul's Bibliographies, 1996), p. 4.

margins of the European book market. Pettegree described England in the late sixteenth and early seventeenth centuries as a 'secondary market' that 'relied for most scholarly and more expensive editions on imports, supplied through the long-established trade connections with the major centres of production elsewhere in Europe'.[17] In 2011, Joad Raymond demonstrated that at the same time, the English printing industry was gradually expanding. However, this was not necessarily commensurate with the European trade, as John Hinks noted in 2012 that even at the end of the seventeenth century, 'the growth of the book trade in Britain lagged behind many parts of Europe'.[18] Whilst it is true that several of the libraries considered in this book contained continental volumes, it is also the case that the percentage of the collection comprised by such works decreased over the time period considered here. For example, over ninety percent of the books in the Francis Trigge Chained Library in Grantham (founded in 1598) were printed on the continent whilst just thirty-seven percent of titles in the collection of Wimborne Minster Chained Library (founded in 1685) were printed on the continent. Such a decline supports Raymond's argument that the increasing rate of domestic book production 'gradually displaced' imported texts.[19]

Parish libraries were founded continuously throughout the period from 1558 to 1709, disproving research from the 1960s and the 1970s by historians such as Thomas Kelly and C. B. L. Barr arguing the opposite. The Interregnum from 1649 to 1660, a period to which both Kelly and Barr ascribed a dearth in parish library foundations, actually saw the establishment of ten libraries, with the highest number of parish library foundations to date within a single decade in the 1650s.[20] Further, the number of parish library foundations increased rapidly after the Restoration, with over 110 additional libraries established in the almost fifty years from 1660 to 1709.

---

17 Andrew Pettegree, 'Centre and Periphery in the European Book World', *Transactions of the Royal Historical Society*, 18 (2008), p. 106.

18 Joad Raymond, 'The Development of the Book Trade in Britain' in Joad Raymond (ed.), *The Oxford History of Popular Print Culture: Volume One: Cheap Print in Britain and Ireland to 1660* (Oxford: Oxford University Press, 2011), p. 61; John Hinks, 'The Book Trade in Early Modern Britain: Centres, Peripheries and Networks' in Benito Rial Costas (ed.), *Print Culture and Peripheries in Early Modern Europe: A Contribution to the History of Printing and the Book Trade in Small European and Spanish Cities* (Leiden: Brill, 2012), p. 114.

19 Raymond, 'The Development of the Book Trade in Britain', p. 61.

20 C. B. L. Barr, 'Parish Libraries in a Region: the Case of Yorkshire', *Proceedings of the Library Association Study School and National Conference*, Nottingham, 1979, p. 34; Thomas Kelly, *Early Public Libraries: a History of the Public Libraries in Great Britain before 1850* (London: Library Association, 1966), p. 76.

Since the mid-1960s, numerous historians including Thomas Kelly, David Williams, Sarah Gray and Chris Baggs, and W. M. Jacob, have argued that from 1680 onwards, there was a distinct shift in the preferred sites for establishing parish libraries from urban areas to more rural locations.[21] It is certainly true that between 1558 and 1679, a disproportionate number of parish libraries were established in urban areas when compared to rural locations, with almost twice as many urban foundations (thirty-eight) as there were rural (twenty). After 1680, largely thanks to the efforts of Reverend Thomas Bray and his associates in the Society for Promoting Christian Knowledge (SPCK), 'a large number of libraries were founded, principally in remote rural areas, for the benefit of those clergymen who were least likely to possess their own books'.[22] Urban foundations also continued unaffected: fifty parish libraries were established in urban areas after the 1680 watershed and before 1709, which is comparable with the fifty-four that were founded in rural areas in the same period. These fifty-four rural foundations established in the forty years between 1680 and 1709 constituted an almost three-fold increase in the number of rural parish libraries founded in the 120-year period from 1558 to 1679, demonstrating the continued and increasing significance of parish libraries to early modern people.

Increased parish library foundations brought educational opportunities to a wider range of people. In 1964, Lawrence Stone published a seminal article on educational provision in early modern England that sought to examine 'the scale of growth and the shifts in social distribution of education in England between 1560 and 1640'.[23] Stone followed this research five years later in 1969 with another examination of levels of literacy and education in early modern England, arguing that there were five different levels of literacy that ranged from the ability to 'read a little and to sign one's name' at the lowest level, to attendance at university and at the Inns of Court and the occupation of other elite positions at the highest level.[24] Stone also argued that because Protestantism was a religion of the book, centred around the Bible, that 'once this book ceased to be a closely guarded secret fit only to be read by the priests,

---

21   Jacob, 'Libraries for the Parish', pp. 67–68; Williams, 'The Use and Abuse of a Pious Intention', p. 22; Kelly, *Early Public Libraries*, p. 69; Sarah Gray and Chris Baggs, 'The English Parish Library: a Celebration of Diversity', *Libraries & Culture*, 35 (2000), p. 418.

22   Williams, 'The Use and Abuse of a Pious Intention', p. 22.

23   Lawrence Stone, 'The Educational Revolution in England, 1560–1640', *Past & Present*, 28 (1964), p. 41.

24   Lawrence Stone, 'Literacy and Education in England, 1640–1900', *Past & Present*, 42 (1969), p. 70.

it generated pressure for the creation of a literate society'.[25] This was arguably one of the first studies to consider the relationship between book availability and widespread literacy. David Cressy developed this argument more generally in the 1980s, stating that 'greater circulation of books may [have] create[d] more opportunities for people to learn to read them'.[26] It is possible that parish libraries provided their users with just such opportunities and that they may have positively affected literacy rates.

Rates of literacy in early modern England increased gradually over the sixteenth and seventeenth centuries. In 2004, Adam Fox argued that at the start of the sixteenth century, 'literacy was predictably highest among the gentry and professional groups, while merchants and craftsmen were proven to be more skilled in this respect than husbandmen and labourers'.[27] The increase in literacy rates as the century progressed came from amongst the ranks below the gentry, including yeomen, merchants and tradesmen. Ian Green has demonstrated that literacy rates amongst these middling sorts increased over the course of the sixteenth and seventeenth centuries. Literacy rates in the south of English increased by as much as ten or fifteen percent in the century after 1530 and by the same amount in the north of England by the end of the seventeenth century.[28] Stone argued that 'the average male literacy rate on the eve of the Civil War was probably not less than thirty percent', though there remained a north-south divide.[29]

Alongside the rising number of parish libraries being established between the middle of the sixteenth century and the end of the seventeenth century came a broadening geographical scope, which led to more repositories being founded in an increasing number of cities, towns and villages in early modern England. Figure 1 demonstrates the distribution of parish libraries across England between 1558 and 1679, whilst Figure 2 shows the distribution of early modern English parish libraries by 1699 and evidences a considerably higher number of northern and rural libraries.

Recent scholarship by Jennifer Richards has demonstrated that a higher proportion of literate people of middling social status may also have had a higher

---

25 *Ibid.*, pp. 76–77.
26 David Cressy, *Literacy and the Social Order: Reading and Writing in Tudor and Stuart England* (Cambridge: Cambridge University Press, 1980), p. 46.
27 Adam Fox, 'Religion and Popular Literature Culture in England', *Archiv fur Reformationsgeschichte-Archive for Reformation History*, 95 (2004), p. 266.
28 Ian Green, *Print and Protestantism in Early Modern England* (Oxford: Oxford University Press, 2000), p. 26.
29 Stone, 'Literacy and Education in England', p. 101.

degree of competency in Latin and some continental languages than previously thought by historians like Anna Bayman.[30] The language of a book naturally dictated its readership. Men with a grammar school education or better would have had some ability to read Latin whilst middling and gentry women received a 'parallel language-education', most commonly in French. Therefore, the 'learned works' referred to by Bayman may not have been as inaccessible as once thought.[31] The ability to read a book does not necessarily equate to the ability to understand it, particularly where the complex subject matter of many of the theological texts available in parish libraries is concerned. Richards' research, however, has interesting implications for broadening the prospective readership of parish library books, which is discussed more fully in chapter 8. Many of these were in Latin as well as English and other vernacular languages, meaning that they may have been more accessible to a wider range of people than previously thought.

In the mid-1990s, Roger Chartier became one of the first historians to acknowledge the notes made by readers in books as being the key to gaining an insight into how early modern texts were received and understood. He argued that the reading processes by which books took on different meanings for the individual reader were one of the most important elements of the history of the book.[32] This work acted as a catalyst for a deluge of studies into the reading practices of individual early modern readers, as well as several large-scale studies of early modern reading practices more generally. Many of these studies demonstrate reading to be purposeful, an activity that was usually undertaken for a specific reason. Sometimes reading was undertaken for political, social, or career advancement, or else for something more personal, as Lisa Jardine and Anthony Grafton demonstrated in their 1990 study of Gabriel Harvey's numerous rereadings of his copy of *Livy*.[33] The act of reading a book in the early modern period was thus often executed topically, rather than sequentially, as evidenced by the topical readings of Sir William Drake in the first half

---

30   Jennifer Richards, *Voices and Books in the English Renaissance: A New History of Reading* (Oxford: Oxford University Press, 2019), *passim*; Anna Bayman, 'Printing, Learning, and the Unlearned' in Joad Raymond (ed.), *The Oxford History of Popular Print Culture: Volume One: Cheap Print in Britain and Ireland to 1660* (Oxford: Oxford University Press, 2011), p. 81.

31   Richards, *Voices and Books in the English Renaissance*, pp. 76–79, 114–116.

32   Roger Chartier, *The Order of Books* (Cambridge: Polity Press, 1994), pp. 7–8.

33   Lisa Jardine and Anthony Grafton, '"Studied for Action": How Gabriel Harvey Read His Livy', *Past & Present*, 129 (1990), p. 30, *passim*.

of the seventeenth century, during which he 'frequently organised what he read under topic headings' in his commonplace books.[34]

Marginalia and other textual annotations acted primarily as aids to memory for early modern readers. In 2002, William H. Sherman observed that 'marginal annotations played a central role in pedagogical theory and practice' in the early modern period, and grammar school students were taught to make notes in their books as a way of 'making them more useful for their present and future needs'.[35] Making notes in the margin enabled the reader (and any later readers) to draw a direct link between the printed text and the written marginalia, making the connection between the two more explicit. Similarly, marginalia and other annotations may make the link between the text and the readers' own lives more explicit also. Many historians, including Sherman in 1995 and Kevin Sharpe in 2000, have argued that a reader's relationship with their texts was a reciprocal one. An individual's life experiences influenced the construction of different meanings by different readers, but likewise a text could inform a reader's worldview and sometimes even influence their 'specific responses to particular contemporary issues and events'.[36] Sharpe, for example, analysed the reading practices of Sir William Drake and argued that Drake's various readings of a small number of texts reflected 'a process by which the reader appropriates, consumes and reconstitutes the text'.[37] Mark Towsey developed this argument in his analysis of books and their readers in Scotland during the Enlightenment through his exploration of 'how far readers brought pre-existing values, beliefs and professional obligations to bear in appropriating books for their own ends'.[38]

These themes of the evolution, establishment, usage and growth of parish libraries in early modern England will be fully explored in Part 1 of this book in order to provide some contextual information for the origins of the parish

34   Kevin Sharpe, *Reading Revolutions: The Politics of Reading in Early Modern England* (London: Yale University Press, 2000), p. 180.

35   William H. Sherman, 'What Did Renaissance Readers Write in Their Books?' in Jennifer Andersen and Elizabeth Sauer (eds), *Books and Readers in Early Modern England: Material Studies* (Philadelphia: University of Pennsylvania Press, 2002), p. 121.

36   William H. Sherman, *John Dee: The Politics of Reading and Writing in the English Renaissance* (Amherst: University of Massachusetts Press, 1995), p. 59; Sharpe, *Reading Revolutions*, p. 74; Ann Blair, 'An Early Modernist's Perspective', *Isis*, 95:3 (2004), pp. 420, 423–424; Jardine and Grafton, 'Gabriel Harvey', p. 30; H. J. Jackson, *Marginalia: Readers Writing in Books* (New Haven; London: Yale University Press, 2001), pp. 82, 97.

37   Sharpe, *Reading Revolutions*, p. 182.

38   Mark Towsey, *Reading the Scottish Enlightenment: Books and the Readers in Provincial Scotland, 1750–1820* (Leiden: Brill, 2010), p. 18.

library as an institution. Part 2 will then build on this foundation to consider the parish libraries of early modern England through an analysis of their intended users, the ways in which their collections were compiled, and the nature of different libraries' collections. Finally, Part 3 of this book will examine in detail the collections of four individual parish libraries established between 1558 and 1709. Part 3 takes a thematic approach to the investigation of surviving marginalia and annotations in the books of these repositories to demonstrate the topics and themes in which early modern readers were most interested.

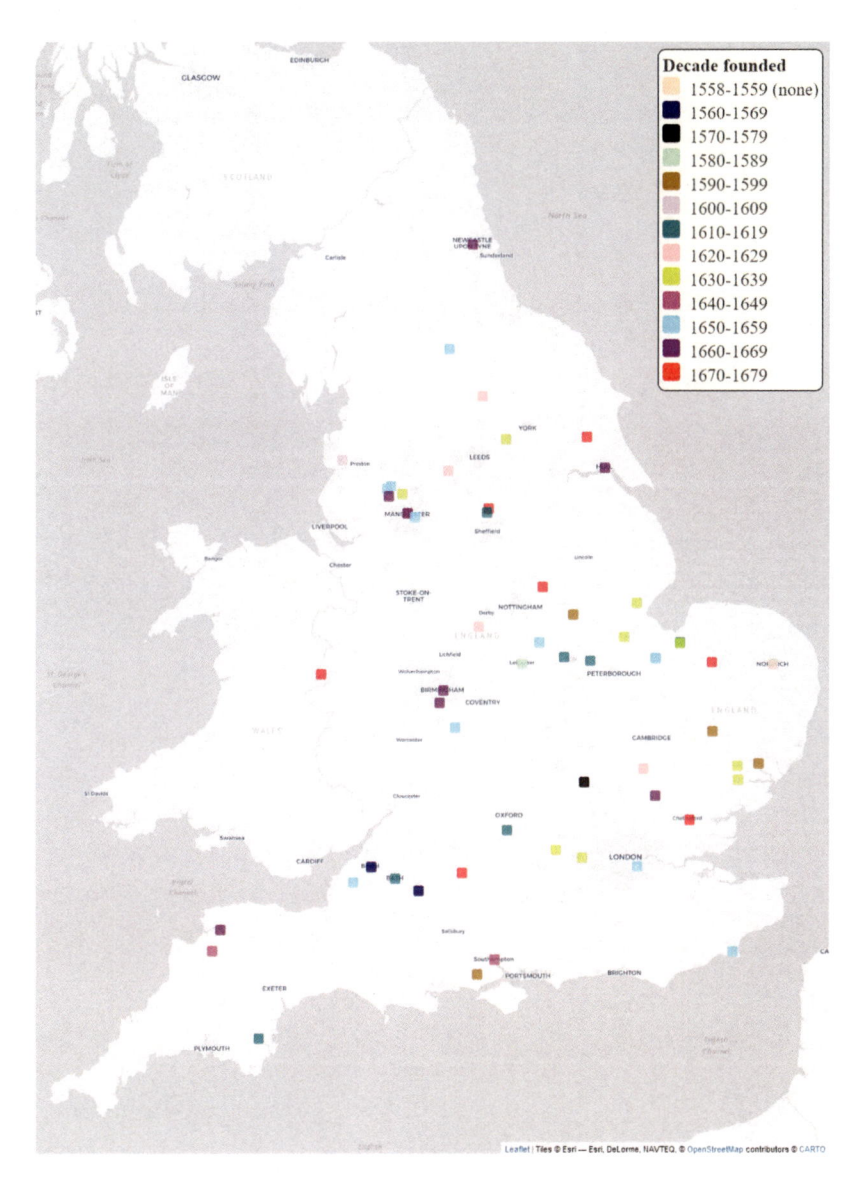

FIGURE 1   Parish libraries founded in England between 1558 and 1679

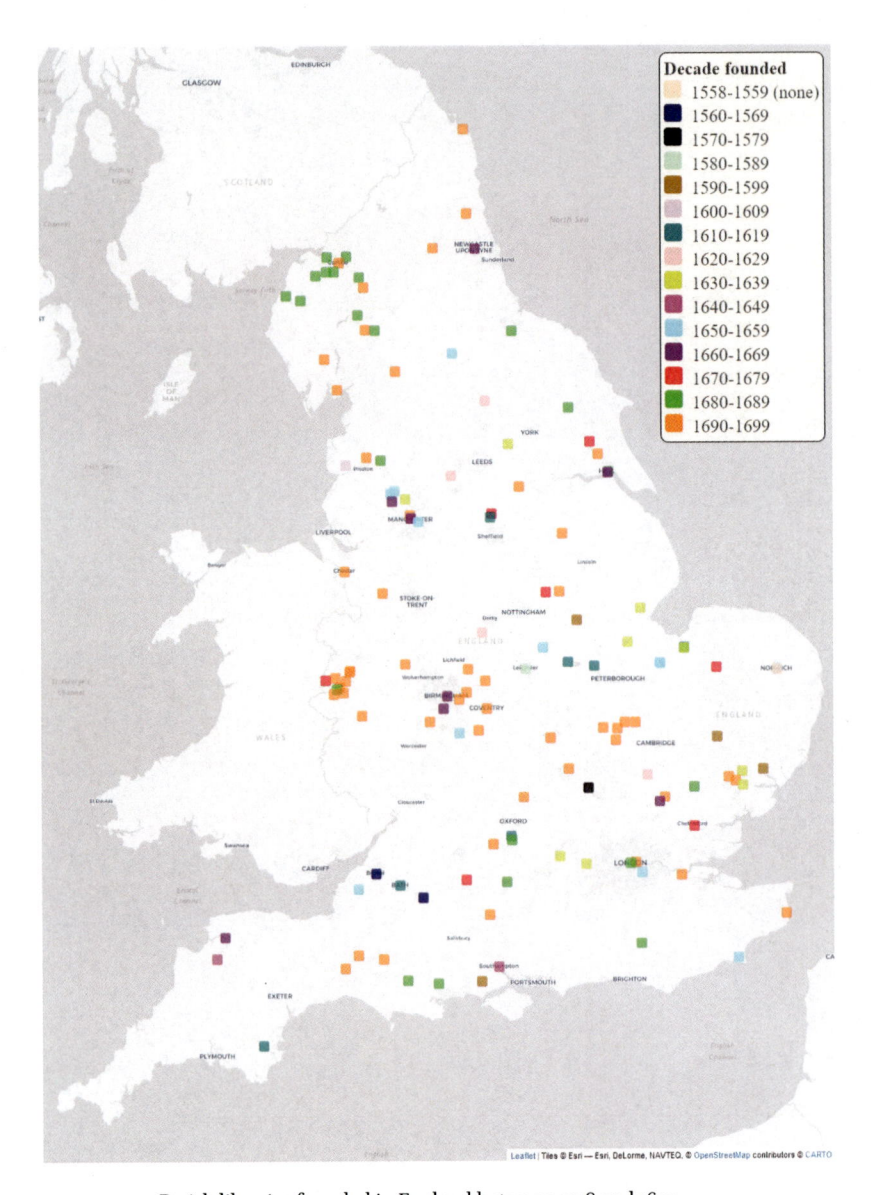

FIGURE 2   Parish libraries founded in England between 1558 and 1699

FIGURE 3   Surviving parish libraries possessing continental books

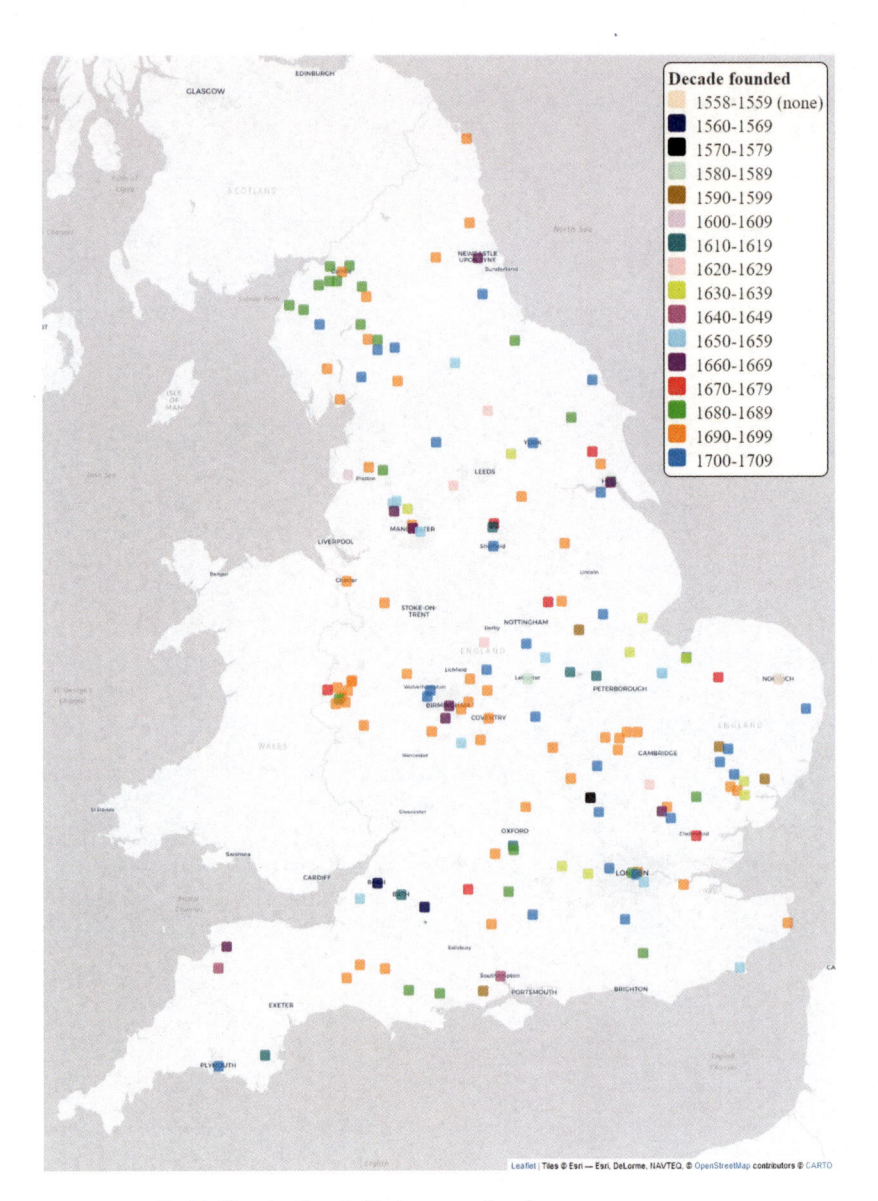

FIGURE 4   Parish libraries founded between 1558 and 1709

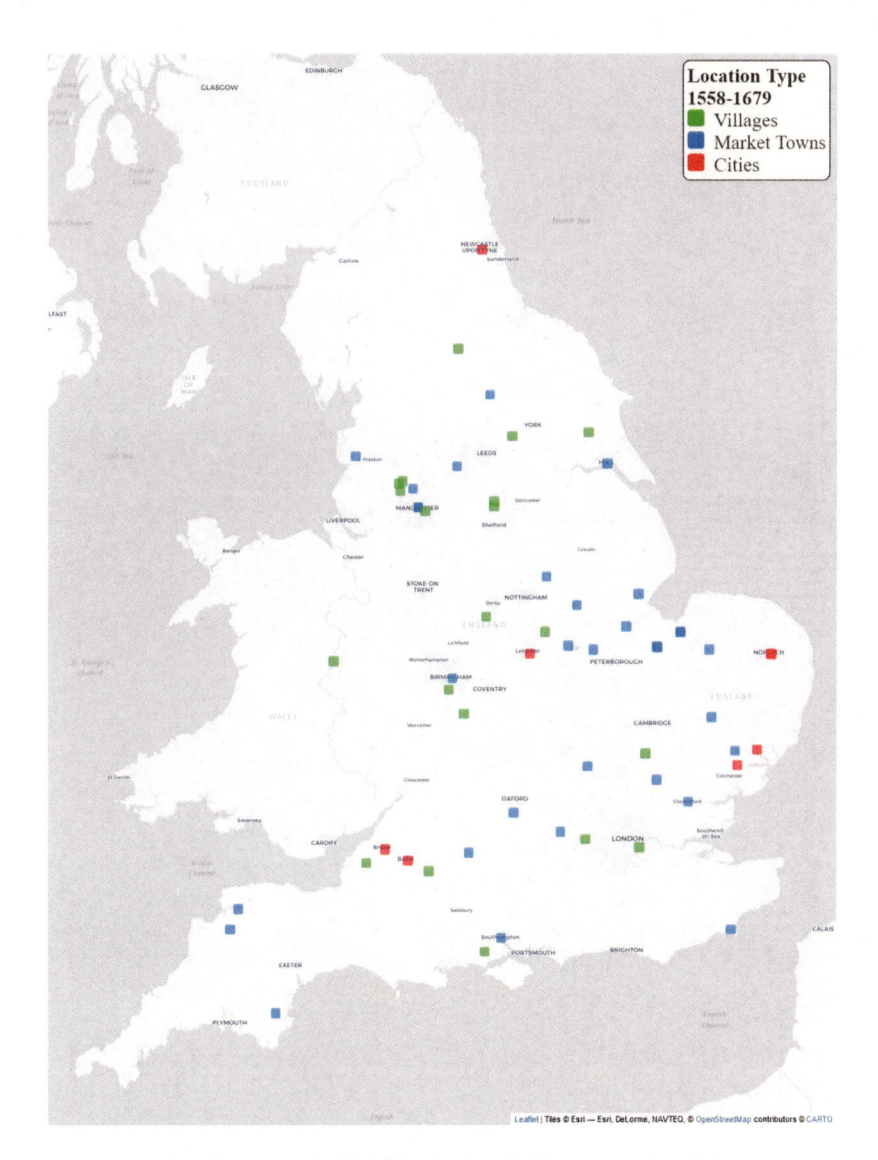

FIGURE 5A   Location types of parish libraries founded between 1558 and 1679

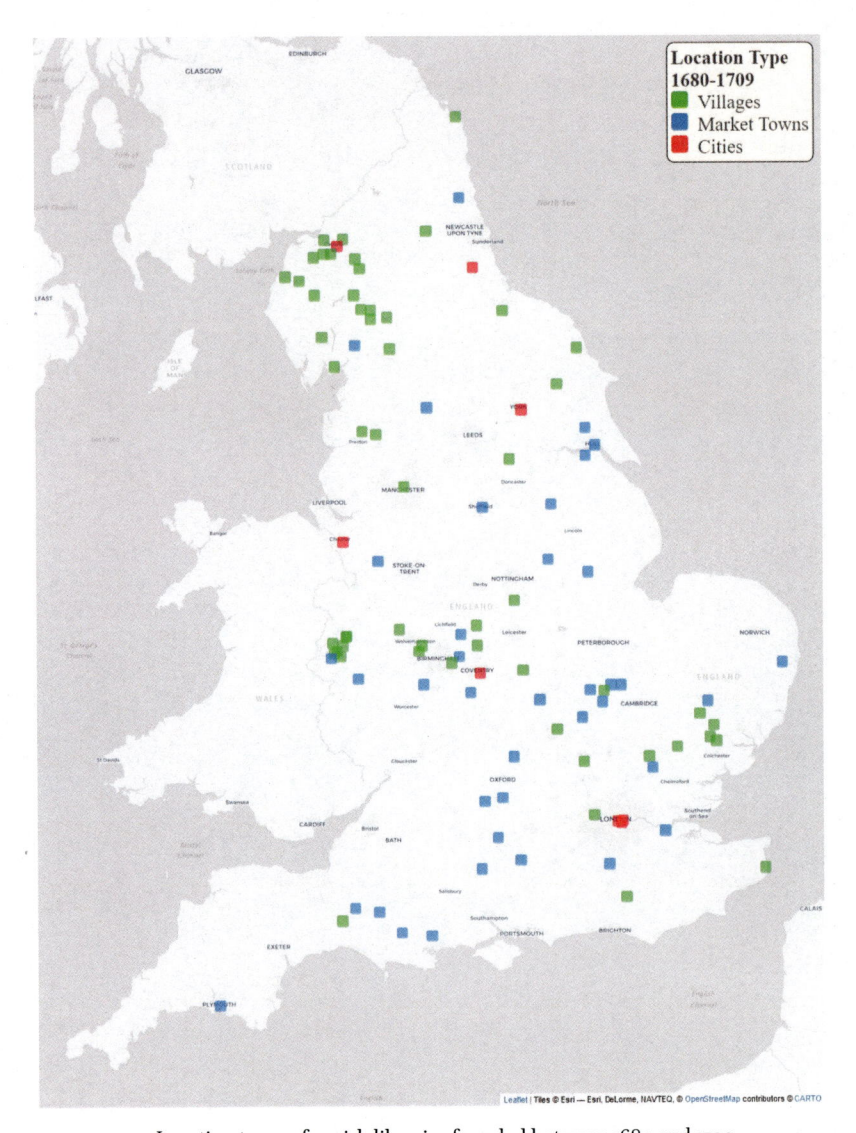

FIGURE 5B   Location types of parish libraries founded between 1680 and 1709

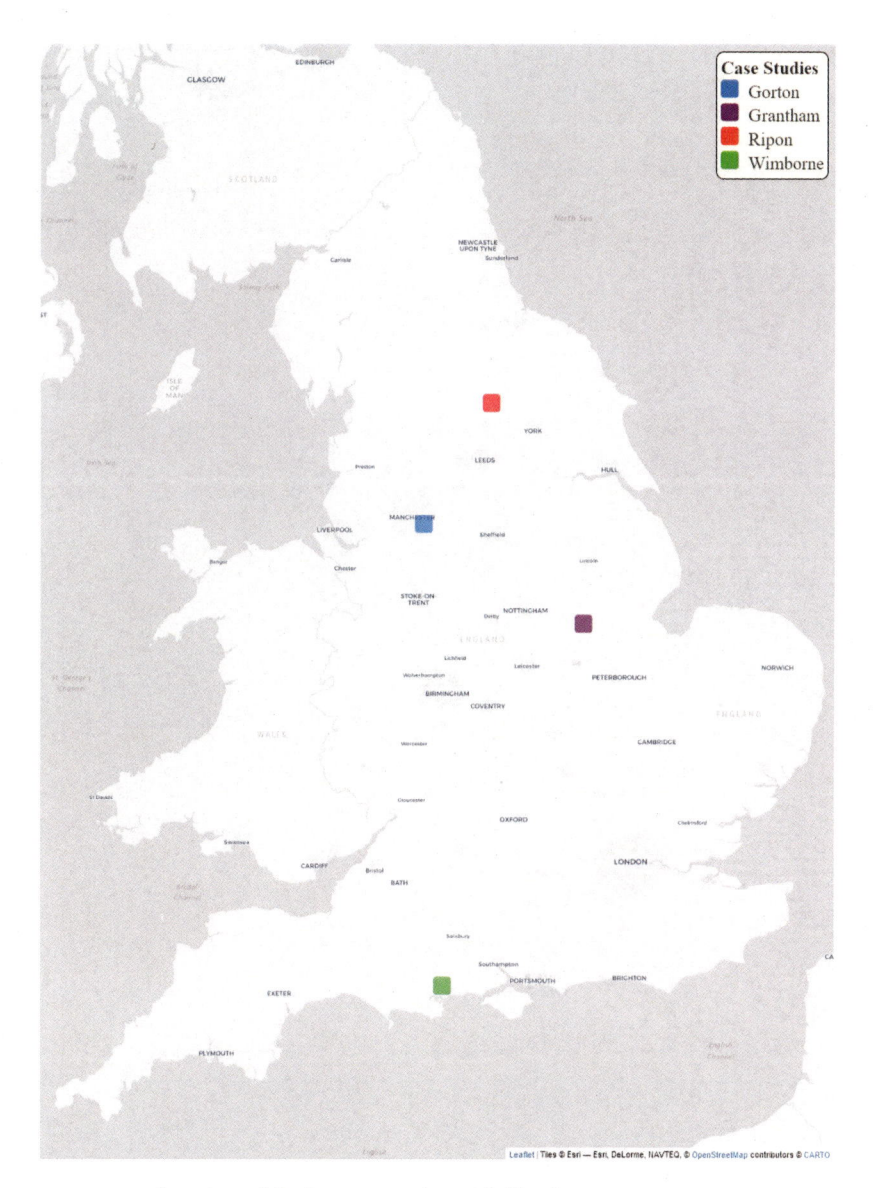

FIGURE 6   Locations of the four case study parish libraries

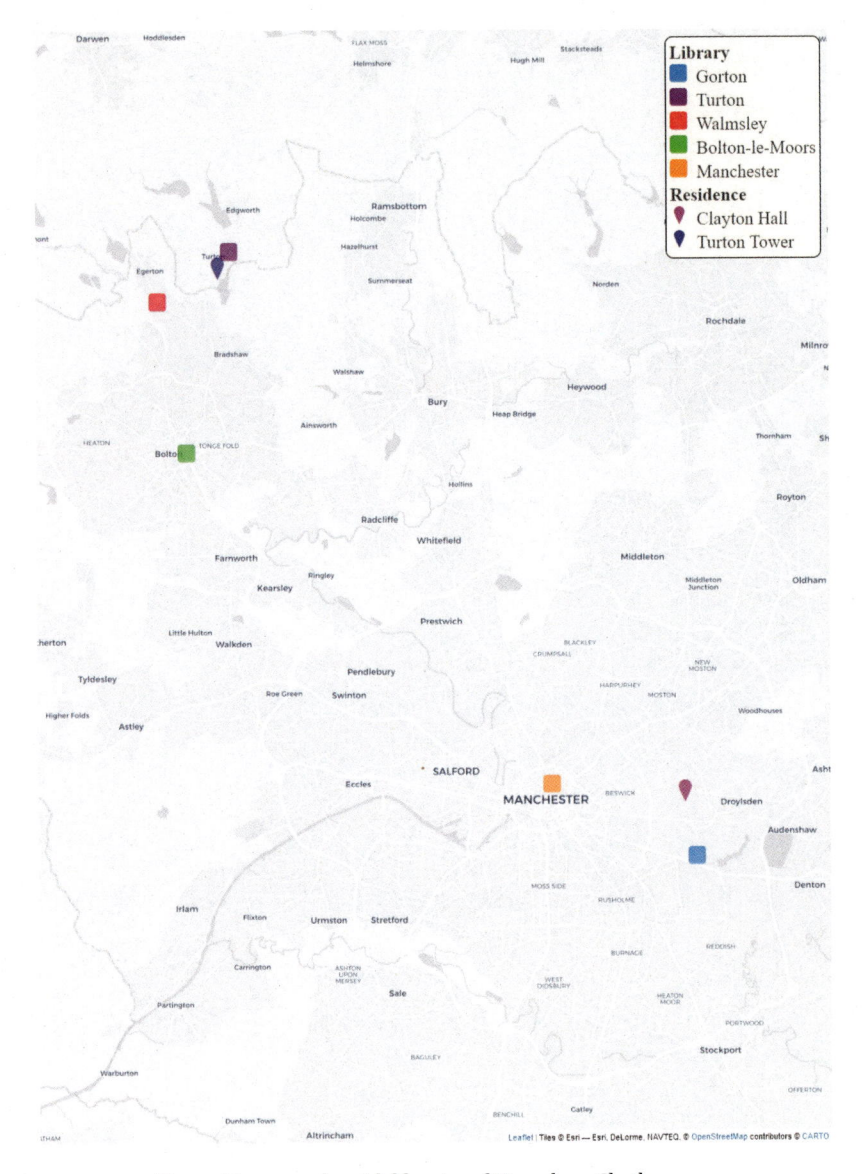

FIGURE 7   The residences and parish libraries of Humphrey Chetham

PART 1

Evolution

∴

Introduction to Part 1

Parish libraries were core elements of the intellectual and religious landscape of England from the second half of the sixteenth century to the early decades of the eighteenth century. Despite the 'series of reverberations' that stemmed from the Reformation of the 1530s and extended into the seventeenth and even into the early eighteenth centuries, they maintained a consistent level of importance in the shifting politico-religio-intellectual landscape of early modern England by providing both the clergy and the laity with spiritual edification and secular education.[1] Their continued significance was confirmed by the passing of the Parochial Libraries Act by Parliament under Queen Anne. The 1709 Act provided protection to parish libraries and prevented the removal of books from libraries without consent from the Ordinary, whose permission could only be given if there were duplicates of the book in the same collection.[2]

Post-Reformation parish libraries evolved out of the clerical libraries previously kept in pre-Reformation parish churches for the use of the clergy, and they built on the precedents set by those repositories. There was, however, a decided and demonstrable shift in the content, language and intended users of many post-Reformation libraries, as the repositories themselves were deliberately made accessible to a larger proportion of the population. Pre-Reformation book collections largely contained service books and liturgical works for use by the clergy in preparing their sermons and undertaking their pastoral and ministerial duties. Post-Reformation repositories comprised predominantly theoretical works of theology and some books of practical divinity for use by both the clergy and the literate laity. Pre-Reformation collections of books were housed in the holier, more private parts of the parish church such as the chancel, which before the Reformation was usually only accessible to the clergy. The shift in intended users led to post-Reformation parish libraries instead being housed in areas of the parish church that were more easily accessible to the laity, such as the nave or an upstairs room in the church. While

---

1   John Spurr, *The Post-Reformation: Religion, Politics and Society in Britain, 1603–1714* (Abingdon: Routledge, 2014), pp. 1–2; John Bossy, *Peace in the Post-Reformation* (Cambridge: Cambridge University Press, 1998), p. 3; Patrick Collinson and John Craig, 'Introduction' in Patrick Collinson and John Craig (eds), *The Reformation in English Towns, 1500–1640* (Basingstoke: Macmillan, 1998), p. 17.
2   Michael Perkin, *A Directory of the Parochial Libraries of the Church of England and the Church in Wales* (London: Bibliographical Society, 2004), p. 37. For a transcription of the Parochial Libraries Act of 1709, see Appendix A of Perkin's *Directory*, pp. 439–442.

distinctions between pre- and post-Reformation parish libraries are evident, they were nevertheless inherently linked by a pattern of sustained ownership of religious texts for educational purposes, connoting a high level of continuity. Parish libraries were constantly being established and used throughout the country by clergymen and the middling sorts of people in the early modern period, in search of a religious education.

Part 1 of this book provides an overview of the parish library's evolution as an institution. It opens with a chapter that describes the development of parish libraries from pre-Reformation collections of liturgical works and service books intended for practical use by the clergy to repositories of Protestant theoretical texts intended for the education of a literate clergy and laity. It argues that post-Reformation parish libraries had visible, tangible roots in their pre-Reformation counterparts. This chapter discusses the nature of the collections of pre-Reformation clerical libraries, their intended users and the location of these book collections within their parish churches. It also makes use of wills and other archival documents to consider the impetuses for the donations of books made to the parish churches of pre-Reformation England that formed these collections, showing that education was a prominent motivating factor for their establishment.

The second chapter considers the founders and users of post-Reformation parish libraries in general. It demonstrates that parish libraries in the post-Reformation period were established by a mixture of clerics and laymen and reveals that a small number of repositories were established by women. The second half of this chapter discusses the combined clerical and lay usage and readership of post-Reformation parish libraries and demonstrates the impact that this changed usage had on the location of the books within the parish church: namely, their removal from the more sacred spaces of the church into the more publicly accessible ones.

The third chapter shifts its focus to a broad examination of the types of books found in the parish libraries of early modern England, evidencing a shift in the religious nature of the collections as the sixteenth and seventeenth centuries progressed. It demonstrates that by the end of the seventeenth century, there was a substantial collection of secular volumes alongside the predominant religious and theological works in some parish library collections. Furthermore, this chapter provides a brief analysis of some of the continental books to be found in the collections of post-Reformation parish libraries and offers some suggestions as to the implications for, and the significance of, the continental book trade and the second-hand book trade in early modern England.

Finally, chapter 4 demonstrates that, despite previous research that argued the contrary, parish libraries in early modern England were established continually throughout the sixteenth and seventeenth centuries. There was no single decade between 1560 and 1710 in which no parish libraries were founded. Foundation rates were generally increasing slowly until the 1680s. In the 1680s, Barnabas Oley, bishop of Ely, founded ten libraries in various parish churches in the diocese of Carlisle. It was not until the 1690s, however, that the Church of England clergyman Thomas Bray and his associates in the Society for Promoting Christian Knowledge (SPCK) transformed the practice of parish library foundation from an individual pursuit into an educative programme on a nationwide scale. Moreover, the geographical spread of parish libraries expanded in the last quarter of the seventeenth century to include the more rural areas of England in addition to its urban ones.

CHAPTER 1

Pre-Reformation Clerical Libraries

Clerical libraries flourished in the parish churches of pre-Reformation England, with over 192 churches known to have possessed books in the period between 1350 and 1536.[1] Often overlooked by historians in favour of the larger and better-documented cathedral and monastic libraries, pre-Reformation book collections in parish churches were significant in their role as educational repositories for the clergy.[2] These collections of service books, liturgical texts and other religious volumes such as theologies, hagiographies and glosses and commentaries on the Bible aided medieval clerics in performing the rites and ceremonies of worship and in carrying out their pastoral duties. These pre-Reformation book collections were also important sources of inspiration for the post-Reformation repositories founded from the second half of the sixteenth century to the opening decade of the eighteenth century.

The clergy-focussed book collections in the parish churches of pre-Reformation England usually grew slowly, through gifts and bequests from both clergymen and laymen whose primary motivation was often to improve educational provision for the clergy. Evidence for their foundation is often scant because these pre-Reformation libraries were rarely formally established. Historians must therefore rely on 'inscriptions in extant manuscripts or printed books, the occasional church inventory or scattered references to parish churches in wills' for information on these repositories.[3] John Shinners has argued that in the century or two prior to the Reformation, small numbers of books were gifted or bequeathed in response to 'the obvious need for curates to have liturgical books', or for spiritual benefit.[4] The 1410 will of Richard

---

1   Stacey Gee, 'Parochial Libraries in Pre-Reformation England' in Sarah Rees Jones (ed.), *Learning and Literacy in Medieval England and Abroad* (Turnhout: Brepols, 2003), p. 200.

2   See for example, Charles C. Rozier, 'Durham Cathedral Priory and its Library of History, *c.* 1090–*c.* 1150' in Laura Cleaver and Andrea Worm (eds), *Writing History in the Anglo-Norman World: Manuscripts, Makers and Readers, c. 1066–c. 1250* (Suffolk: Boydell and Brewer, 2018), pp. 133–148; Mary P. Richards, 'Texts and their Traditions in the Medieval Library of Rochester Cathedral', *Transactions of the American Philosophical Society*, 78:3 (1988), pp. i–xii, 1–129; or Herman A. Peterson, 'The Genesis of Monastic Libraries', *Libraries & the Cultural Record*, 45:3 (2010), pp. 320–332.

3   Gee, 'Parochial Libraries in Pre-Reformation England', p. 200.

4   John Shinners, 'Parish Libraries in Medieval England' in Jacqueline Brown and William P. Stoneman (eds), *A Distinct Voice: Medieval Studies in Honor of Leonard E. Boyle* (Notre Dame, Ind.: University of Notre Dame Press, 1997), p. 208.

Tyttesbury, a canon of Exeter and reverend of Ermington parish church, for example, evidences Tyttesbury's bequest of one of his books, 'to be used by the ministers of [Ermington] Church for their learning'.[5] Medieval wills also provide evidence of where these book collections were situated within parish churches: in the more private areas of the church, like the 'chauncell', as indicated in the 1519 will of the chaplain Robert Same of Bury, or 'before the ferterers at the hygh aughter', as the priest John Hoore's 1509 will stated.[6]

Reasons for donations of books, plate and other gifts to parish churches were many and varied, though the hope of spiritual benefits such as reduced time in purgatory or the favourable answering of prayers seem to have been foremost amongst them. The 1435 will of the wealthy York merchant Richard Russel provides an illustrative example. It details Russel's donation of books, plate and vestments to his parish church and his request, in return, for the prayers of the chaplain and parishioners for his soul and the souls of his wife, family and benefactors.[7] Similarly, a Norwich vicar left a psalter to his church, asking that the anniversary of his death be commemorated annually for 'as long as the psalter lasts'.[8] It is possible that by bequeathing these items to their parish churches, these men were attempting to 'achieve a perpetual linkage of their own names with the corporate worship of the community', as Peter Marshall and others have suggested.[9]

In their studies of pre-Reformation parish libraries in the late 1990s and early 2000s, John Shinners and Stacey Gee used inventories and wills as their main sources of evidence to demonstrate that, in addition to the necessary service books and liturgical texts, the majority of libraries in parish churches appear to have had a small collection of other types of books by the mid-fifteenth century.[10] Shinners found that by the late medieval period 'there were fairly diverse collections of books (liturgical manuals, pastoral handbooks, synodal

5   F. C. Hingeston-Randolph (ed.), *The Register of Edmund Stafford, (A.D. 1396–1419)* (London: George Bell and Sons, 1886), pp. 394–395.

6   Samuel Tymms (ed.), *Wills and Inventories from the Registers of the Commissary of Bury St. Edmunds and the Archdeaconry of Sudbury* (London: Printed for the Camden Society, 1850), p. 253.

7   Borthwick Institute of Archives (BIA), University of York, (Probate Register 3, f. 439r–441r), Will of Richard Russell, York, 10 December 1435. The will is in Latin, translated in Shinners, 'Parish Libraries in Medieval England', pp. 210–211.

8   Shinners, 'Parish Libraries in Medieval England', p. 211.

9   Peter Marshall, *Beliefs and the Dead in Reformation England* (Oxford: Oxford University Press, 2002), p. 24; Eamon Duffy, *The Stripping of the Altars: Traditional Religion in England 1400–1580*, 2nd edition (New Haven and London: Yale University Press, 2005), p. 330.

10   Shinners, 'Parish Libraries in Medieval England', pp. 207–230; Gee, 'Parochial Libraries in Pre-Reformation England', pp. 199–222.

legislation, moral tracts) communally available to serve the needs of the curate and his assistants in most parishes – in effect, parish libraries'.[11] In addition to service books, liturgical texts and other clerical volumes, Gee's work highlighted the inclusion of 'reference' books such as legal and theological works, grammar books, clerical manuals and other works of religious edification and instruction in pre-Reformation clerical library collections.[12]

The service books in England's parish churches were cast out and brought back several times over the course of the sixteenth century as the religion of England changed with the royal injunctions of each successive monarch from Henry VIII to Elizabeth I. Unfortunately, the impossibility of knowing how many books survived or were lost during this period makes it difficult to know for sure how many parish churches possessed these liturgical texts, service books and reference works, and how many volumes each church owned prior to the Reformation and its concomitant religious upheaval. The fact that legal texts, theological works and other works of religious edification and instruction also formed the basis of many later post-Reformation parish libraries does, however, denote a significant degree of continuity in subject matter between pre- and post-Reformation collections. In turn, this suggests that the pre-Reformation repositories constituted at least partial inspiration for the post-Reformation collections.

The first attempt to systematically equip parish churches with relevant and necessary texts came towards the end of the thirteenth century when Robert Winchelsey, Archbishop of Canterbury (1293–1313), collated an unofficial list of books that each church should possess. The list included 'a missal, a lectionary, an antiphonary, a gradual, a psalter, a sequence book, an ordinal, and a manual', which parishioners themselves were supposed to purchase for their parish church. According to Shinners, the list was 'never formally issued', but he argued that 'it gained the stamp of officialdom through its wide circulation, and by the mid-fourteenth century it was treated as an official decree of the Canterbury archdiocese'.[13] In some dioceses, the laity endeavoured to provide these volumes for their church with decided enthusiasm: in Norwich, for example, over ninety-four percent of parishes owned all eight of these mandated texts by the time of the Norwich inventory in the mid-fourteenth

---

11   Shinners, 'Parish Libraries in Medieval England', p. 207.

12   Gee, 'Parochial Libraries in Pre-Reformation England', p. 199.

13   C. R. Cheney, 'The so-called Statues of John Pecham and Robert Winchelsey for the Province of Canterbury', *The Journal of Ecclesiastical History*, 12:1 (1961), p. 22.

century.[14] Whether the list was popular outside of the southeast and East Anglia is unclear.

At the same time, small numbers of additional books not on Winchelsey's list were also being given to parish churches, again seemingly for the improvement of the clergy. Thomas Daubtree, an ecclesiastical lawyer in York, for example, left a copy of John de Burgh's *Pupilla oculi* to Holy Trinity church, Goodramgate, York, in 1437, stating specifically that it was to be used by the chaplains of the church.[15] Copies of the *Pupilla oculi* were also given to Feltwell St Mary church in Norfolk by Thomas de Lexham in 1383 and to Ermington church in Devon by Richard Tyttesbury in 1410. Both bequests stipulated the use of the books by the chaplains and other clergy of the recipient churches.[16] In 1437, clerks John Crove of Wenlock and Thomas de Alta Ripa of York donated clerical manuals to their individual parish churches, and in 1471, layman Richard Willugby gifted the devotional book *Crede mihil* to the church of Wollaton in Nottinghamshire.[17] The commitment to improving the religious education of the clergy, demonstrated by the prominence of religious texts in the book collections of pre-Reformation parish churches, is similarly reflected in the dominance of such works in post-Reformation parish libraries, which, as will be shown in chapters 7 and 8, extended the scope of their pre-Reformation counterparts and were intended to develop the learning of a more general readership.

Despite survival rates of books once in pre-Reformation parish churches often not accurately reflecting their contemporary distribution, the books that do survive from parish churches from this period provide an insight into the types of books that were available to medieval readers. All pre-Reformation book collections included standard service books and liturgical texts including missals, manuals and psalters. In addition, many also included assortments of 'reference works', which variously comprised theological texts, hagiographies, pastoral works, glosses and commentaries on the Bible and many more. The surviving thirty-eight missals, twelve psalters and eight manuals, many of which are now in university library collections but were once in pre-Reformation parish churches, serve as testaments to their earlier prevalence.[18] As is perhaps to be expected, the Bible was almost ubiquitous in the parish churches

---

14 Shinners, 'Parish Libraries in Medieval England', p. 210.

15 C. B. L. Barr, 'Parish Libraries in a Region: the Case of Yorkshire', *Proceedings of the Library Association Study School and National Conference*, Nottingham, 1979, p. 33.

16 Gee, 'Parochial Libraries in Pre-Reformation England', pp. 201–202.

17 *Ibid.*, pp. 208–209.

18 N. R. Ker (ed.), *Medieval Libraries of Great Britain: A List of Surviving Books*, 2nd edition (London: Royal Historical Society, 1964), pp. 219–224.

of pre-Reformation England. However, few now survive, probably because, as William H. Sherman has suggested in relation to other titles, the Bible was used to destruction by many parish clergy.[19] A medieval Bible that was originally in the church of St John the Baptist in Newcastle-upon-Tyne is now held in the Bodleian Library. Manuscript copies of the Latin Vulgate Bible once belonging to the parish churches of Bredgar in Kent, Buckingham (given by John Rudyng in c.1481), and South Wingfield in Derbyshire also survive.[20] The survival rates of pastoral manuals such as the *Oculus sacerdotis* and the *Pupilla oculi* similarly do not reveal the level of popularity these volumes once enjoyed.[21] What seems to be the only extant parish church copy of the *Oculus sacerdotis* comes from the parish church of Halsall and is now housed in the John Rylands Library in Manchester, while only two parish church copies of John de Burgh's *Pupilla oculi* now survive from the churches of Albury in Surrey and Stanhope in County Durham.[22] It is possible that parish clergy also read and used volumes such as these to destruction, in addition to the Bible.[23]

Many of the same genres of books that were once housed in pre-Reformation parish churches – including calendars, dictionaries, hagiographies and martyrologies, Biblical commentaries and glosses, books on canon law, devotional texts and works on Christian life and morality – were included in the collections of post-Reformation parish libraries, evidencing the continuation in subject matter and educational intentions from pre- to post-Reformation institutions. Pre-Reformation parish churches often possessed, for example, glosses and commentaries on the Bible that assisted in the interpretation of Scripture, as parish priests found them 'invaluable for the well-informed practice of *cura animarum*' and often passed them on to their churches after their deaths.[24]

---

19   Margaret Deanesly, *The Lollard Bible: And Other Medieval Biblical Versions* (Cambridge: Cambridge University Press, 1920), p. 329; Peter Heath, *The English Parish Clergy on the Eve of the Reformation* (Abingdon: Routledge, 2007), p. 75; William H. Sherman, *Used Books: Marking Readers in Renaissance England* (Philadelphia: University of Pennsylvania Press, 2009), p. 5.

20   Ker, *Medieval Libraries of Great Britain*, p. 219, 221–224; Bodleian Library, Oxford, (MSS. Rawl. C. 258), New Testament (early Wycliffite version); for the donation of John Rudyng to the parish church of Buckingham see Michael Perkin, *A Directory of the Parochial Libraries of the Church of England and the Church in Wales* (London: Bibliographical Society, 2004), p. 159.

21   Gee, 'Parochial Libraries in Pre-Reformation England', pp. 213–214.

22   Ker, *Medieval Libraries of Great Britain*, pp. 220, 323; John Rylands Library, University of Manchester, (Latin MS 339), *Summa que vocatur sinistra pars oculi sacerdotum*; Ker, *Medieval Libraries of Great Britain*, pp. 219, 223.

23   Sherman, *Used Books*, p. 5.

24   Gee, 'Parochial Libraries in Pre-Reformation England', p. 211; Shinners, 'Parish Libraries in Medieval England', p. 209.

Commentaries on the Bible were also prevalent in post-Reformation parish libraries, as chapters 7 and 8 will show, and were studied in some detail by their readers. Whilst these commentaries were generally of a Protestant nature after the Reformation, there are also examples of post-Reformation Catholic Biblical commentaries in post-Reformation collections – the Francis Trigge Chained Library in Grantham, Lincolnshire provides a notable example. Other examples of similar works in both pre-Reformation clerical libraries and post-Reformation parish libraries included history books and the works of the Church Fathers. Pre-Reformation manuscript copies of the writings of Saint Augustine survive from the parish churches of Fenny Bentley in Derbyshire and Hardwick in Cambridgeshire and are now in the collections of the Bodleian Library and St John's College, Cambridge, respectively.[25] The works of the Church Fathers were common features of post-Reformation library collections as well – they were a dominant genre in the library of Wimborne Minster, for example – demonstrating again this pattern of continuity between book collections in pre- and post-Reformation parish churches.

The intrinsic link between the location of books in the parish church and their accessibility to potential readers is evident in both pre- and post-Reformation parish libraries; as elucidated in chapter 6, the intended users of these libraries determined their placement within their respective parish churches. The book collections kept in pre-Reformation parish churches were intended primarily for the use of the clergy and so books were usually located in the more private areas of the parish church that were only accessible by the clergy and perhaps a small number of wealthy and well-educated laity.[26] Before the Reformation, the usual locations in which collections of books were housed were those areas seen as the holiest and most sacred spaces in the parish church: the choir or the chancel which, as C. Pamela Graves pointed out, 'housed the main or High Altar and was almost exclusively associated with the clergy'.[27] In post-Reformation parish libraries, the intended audience of both clerical and lay readers often led to the books being placed in repurposed rooms that were (theoretically, at least) accessible by a much wider range of people. Interestingly, parish libraries established after the Reformation were rarely placed in the nave or the open hall of a church, which Graves called 'the locale of most lay participation'.[28]

---

25 Ker, *Medieval Libraries of Great Britain*, pp. 220–221.
26 Margaret Aston, 'Segregation in Church' in W. J. Sheils and D. Wood (eds), *Women in the Church* (Oxford: Blackwell, 1990), pp. 244–247.
27 C. Pamela Graves, 'Social space in the English medieval parish church', *Economy and Society*, 18:3 (1989), p. 301.
28 *Ibid.*

The continuity in content and practice between parish libraries in post-Reformation English parish churches and their pre-Reformation counterparts challenges the arguments made by historians such as C. B. L. Barr, who asserted that 'all these books, once in parish churches before the Reformation, are lost', and Michael Perkin, who stated that 'most books, whether manuscript or printed, together with service books, were cast out at the Reformation'.[29] Such an occurrence would suggest a high level of difference between the pre- and post-Reformation parish libraries, which may have prompted historians such as Sarah Gray and Chris Baggs to go so far as to suggest that 'nothing that could be described as a library is known to have existed in a parish church' for fifty years after the Reformation.[30] However, a continued educational intent between the two types of institution, and Arnold Hunt's argument that 'a continuous tradition of book-ownership can be seen as bridging the gap between medieval and early modern religious culture', are demonstrated by the evolution of pre-Reformation libraries of liturgies and service books aimed specifically at the clergy into more wide-ranging repositories of Protestant religious and secular education for both the clergy and the laity.[31] Libraries in parish churches in England after the Reformation continued to comprise predominantly religious texts, many of which were either officially mandated, or else donated to the church by associated clerical or lay individuals, as the following chapter will demonstrate. Thus, the continued possession of religious books by both pre- and post-Reformation churches was an important similarity between the two institutions and a significant element of stability amidst so many other changes to the fabric and worship in parish churches that occurred from the mid-sixteenth century.

---

29 Barr, 'Parish Libraries in a Region', p. 33; Michael Perkin, 'Parochial Libraries: Founders and Readers' in Peter Isaac and Barry McKay (eds), *The Reach of Print: Making, Selling and Using Books* (Winchester: St. Paul's Bibliographies, 1998), pp. 191–192.

30 Sarah Gray and Chris Baggs, 'The English Parish Library: a Celebration of Diversity', *Libraries & Culture*, 35 (2000), p. 417.

31 Arnold Hunt, 'Clerical and Parish Libraries' in Elisabeth Leedham-Green and Teresa Webber (eds), *The Cambridge History of Libraries, Volume I, to 1640* (Cambridge: Cambridge University Press, 2008), p. 401.

CHAPTER 2

Founders and Users of Post-Reformation Parish Libraries

Continuing the medieval tradition of clerical and lay book donations to parish churches, the parish libraries of the post-Reformation era were similarly established by different sorts of people, though this time in order to educate a varied audience. There was a distinct shift in this period from a primarily, if not exclusively, clerical audience for these volumes, to also include the laity as intended users of these repositories.

1 The Founders of Post-Reformation Parish Libraries

The 165 parish libraries established in England from 1558 to 1709 are a testament to the number of clergymen and laymen of means who pursued a purpose of educating people in matters of religion. Of the 165 parish libraries established in this period, 134 had known founders. Figure 8 below displays the various sorts of people who established parish libraries in the sixteenth and seventeenth centuries. It demonstrates the continuation of the precedent set by clerical and lay founders of the medieval period and reflects the sustained dominance of clerical founders in parish library foundation practices after the Reformation.[1]

---

1 John Shinners, 'Parish Libraries in Medieval England' in Jacqueline Brown and William P. Stoneman (eds), *A Distinct Voice: Medieval Studies in Honor of Leonard E. Boyle* (Notre Dame, Ind.: University of Notre Dame Press, 1997), pp. 210; Stacey Gee, 'Parochial Libraries in Pre-Reformation England' in Sarah Rees Jones (ed.), *Learning and Literacy in Medieval England and Abroad* (Turnhout: Brepols, 2003), pp. 201, 209–211.

© KONINKLIJKE BRILL NV, LEIDEN, 2024 | DOI:10.1163/9789004363717_005

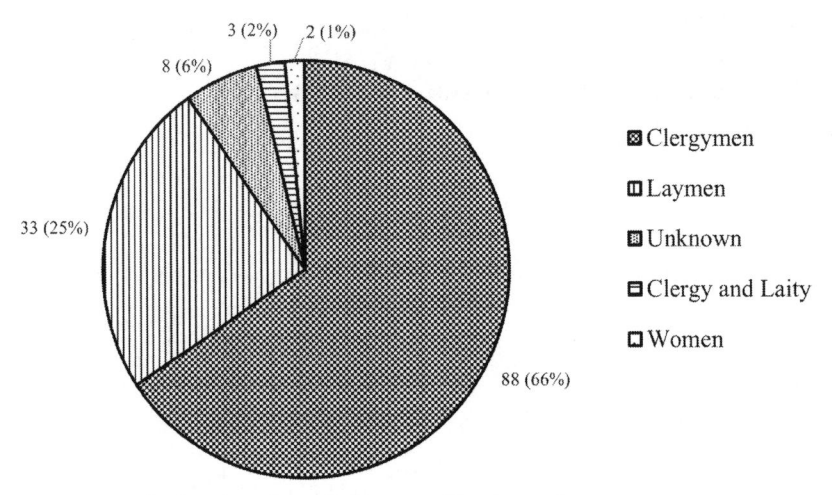

FIGURE 8   The founders of post-Reformation libraries, 1558–1709

Clergymen were responsible for the foundation of eighty-eight parish libraries between 1558 and 1709. The foundation rate of post-Reformation parish libraries by clergymen was relatively consistent until the 1680s. In each decade between 1558 and 1679, up to five individual clerics founded a library. From the 1680s onwards, the numbers are distorted by clerics founding multiple repositories, including the ten parish libraries established by Barnabas Oley, vicar of Great Gransden in Huntingdonshire and archdeacon of Ely, in Carlisle in 1685, and the three parish libraries established by Richard Busby, an Anglican priest who was headmaster of Westminster School, in 1695. Two of these libraries were established in Cudworth and Martock in Somerset and one in Willen in Buckinghamshire.[2]

Furthermore, between 1695 and 1705, the efforts of the Church of England clergyman Thomas Bray and his associates in the Society for Promoting Christian Knowledge (SPCK) resulted in the exponential growth of the overall number of parish libraries established in the late seventeenth and early eighteenth centuries. Thomas Bray has rightly been described by W. M. Jacob as 'the most significant figure in the promotion of parochial libraries' who 'offered practical advice about establishing and maintaining' parish libraries, which he

---

2   Elizabeth R. Clarke, 'Oley, Barnabas (bap. 1602, d. 1686)', *Oxford Dictionary of National Biography* (online, 2008); C. S. Knighton, 'Busby, Richard (1606–1695)', *Oxford Dictionary of National Biography* (online, 2004).

desired to see instituted in England on a national scale.[3] Bray and his associates were responsible for establishing thirty-eight parish libraries across the country in the space of ten years.[4] An additional ten clergymen were responsible for the foundation of the fourteen parish libraries established in England in the first decade of the eighteenth century.

Thirty-three libraries were established by laymen at a reasonably stable rate of foundation across the period. A further three libraries in Southwell in Nottinghamshire (1670), Sutton Courtenay in Berkshire (1686), and Bedford in Bedfordshire (1700), were collaboratively founded by laymen and clergymen together. Of particular note are the two libraries known to have been established by women between 1558 and 1709. Lady Anne Harington was responsible for the creation of the library in Oakham parish church in 1616 and a Mrs Eleanor Crowle gave three donations of £5 (1665), £20 (1666) and a further £5 (1667) for providing books for a library in Holy Trinity church in Hull, Yorkshire.[5] A further eight libraries were founded by known individuals of unknown professions in Devon, Lancashire, Berkshire, Yorkshire and other locations. Unknown donors in twenty counties established the remaining thirty-one of the 165 libraries founded between 1558 and 1709.

2   The Users of Post-Reformation Parish Libraries

Just as post-Reformation parish libraries were founded by diverse sorts of people, so too were they intended for use by them. Founders usually stipulated who the intended users of their books were in the foundation document, which was usually either a will, deed, or indenture. Some libraries, such as those established by Humphrey Chetham in the 1650s, were for use by the laity only; others, such as the libraries established at Oakham in Rutland or Ipswich in Suffolk, were for the exclusive use of the clergy. The parish library at Oakham was founded by Lady Anne Harington 'for the use of the Vicar of that Church,

---

3 W. M. Jacob, 'Libraries and Philanthropy, 1690–1740', *Bulletin of the Association of British Theological and Philosophical Libraries*, 4:2 (1997), pp. 8–9.

4 For more information on Thomas Bray and the efforts of the Society for Promoting Christian Knowledge, see Leonard W. Cowie, 'Bray, Thomas (*bap.* 1658, *d.* 1730)', *Oxford Dictionary of National Biography* (online, 2012); and Craig Rose 'The Origins and Ideals of the SPCK, 1699–1716' in John Walsh, Colin Haydon and Stephen Taylor (eds), *The Church of England, c. 1689–1833: From Toleration to Tractarianism* (Cambridge: Cambridge University Press, 1993), pp. 172–190.

5 Michael Perkin, *A Directory of the Parochial Libraries of the Church of England and the Church in Wales* (London: Bibliographical Society, 2004), pp. 245–246, 309–310.

and accommodation of the Neighbouring Clergy'.[6] The parish library in the church of St Mary-le-Tower in Ipswich was established by William Smarte (*d.* 1599), a draper, portman and burgess to Parliament for the borough of Ipswich. Smarte donated

> my latten printed books and written books in volume [velum] and p[ar]chmente ... which I gyve towards one librarye safelie to be keepte in the vestrye of the parishe church of St Mary Tower in Ipsw[i]ch ... to be used ther by the com[m]on preacher of the sayd towne for the tyme beinge or any other preacher mynded to preache in the saide p[ar]ishe church.[7]

Smarte's will also included instructions for the safekeeping of the books he donated, stipulating that they were to be kept locked in the vestry of the church and that the minister and the churchwardens were to hold the two keys used to open the door.[8] Restricting access to the books one donated to a parish church was a not-uncommon practice in early modern England. The library provided by Francis Trigge to St Wulfram's church in Grantham, Lincolnshire in 1598, for example, was also to be kept in a locked room above the south porch, to which only the alderman, the two vicars of the church and the schoolmaster of Grantham had the keys.[9]

For the vast majority of early modern English parish libraries after the Reformation, their intended users included the clergy and laity both. The library at More, founded by indenture in 1680 by Sir Richard More of Linley Hall in Shropshire, for example, was 'for the use and benefit of the inhabitants of the village and for the encouragement of a preaching minister'.[10] The library in the parish church of Newark-upon-Trent in Nottinghamshire, established in 1698 by the will of Thomas White, bishop of Peterborough, provides a similar example. White bequeathed

---

6   James Wright, *The History and Antiquities of the County of Rutland* (London: Printed for Bennet Griffin, 1684), p. 52. This edition not listed on the USTC.

7   The National Archives, Kew, (PROB 11/94/340), Will of William Smarte of Ipswich, Suffolk, 2 November 1599.

8   *Ibid.*

9   Lincolnshire Archives, Lincolnshire, (Grantham St Wulfram Par/23/1), Documents relating to the Trigge Library: Agreement.

10   Conal Condren, 'More Parish Library, Salop', *Library History*, 7:5 (1987), pp. 141–144; Shropshire Archives, Shropshire, (P193/S/1/1), More Church Library Trust Deeds with Rules.

to the maior aldermen and viccar of the Towne of Newarke upon Trent for the time being All my printed books to be a library at least a good beginning of a library for the use of them and the inhabitants of that towne and the Gentlemen and Clergy of the adjacent Countrey.[11]

All the inhabitants of the town of Newark were welcome to use White's books, but for users from the surrounding area, only the gentlemen and clergy were acceptable. Other founders who restricted lay access to books based on social standing included Roger Gillingham who, in 1695, significantly augmented the book collection given to the parish church of Wimborne Minster by William Stone a decade earlier. Gillingham's will asserted that his books were 'for the use of the clergy there but alsoe for the use of the Gent shopkeepers and better sort of Inhabitants in and about the Towne of Wimborne'.[12] Foundation documents for post-Reformation parish libraries make clear the educational incentives of those repositories. In the majority of cases, this education was extended to all literate members of the laity as well as the clergy.

3   Conclusion

Like their pre-Reformation ancestors, the majority of post-Reformation parish libraries continued to be established by clergymen, largely thanks to the efforts of men like Barnabas Oley and Thomas Bray and his associates in the SPCK. Laymen also contributed a significant percentage of library repositories throughout the sixteenth and seventeenth centuries. Perhaps the most striking difference elucidated in this chapter is the difference in intended audiences between pre-Reformation libraries intended primarily for a clerical audience and post-Reformation parish libraries intended for use by the laity and the clergy alike. The impact of this shift on the types of books found in these post-Reformation collections will be considered in the next chapter.

---

11   The National Archives, Kew, (PROB 11/446/372), Will of Reverend Thomas White, Bishop of Peterburgh, Doctor of Divinity, 19 July 1698.

12   The National Archives, Kew, (PROB 11/430/238), Will of Roger Gillingham of Middle Temple, Middlesex, 25 February 1696.

CHAPTER 3

Post-Reformation Parish Library Books

Books became increasingly more accessible throughout the sixteenth and seventeenth centuries. Various Henrician, Edwardian and Elizabethan injunctions evidence their educational intent through explicit instructions ordering religious texts written in English to be placed in locations within parish churches accessible to all. As part of the Henrician injunctions of 1536, for example, the Bible unsurprisingly became the first religious text officially ordered to be placed in the parish churches of England after the break with Rome:

> Every parson, or proprietary of any parish church within this realm, shall on this side of the feast of *S. Peter ad Vincula* [16 January] next coming, provide a book of the whole Bible, both in Latin, and also in English, and lay the same in the choir, for every man that will to look and read thereon, and shall discourage no man from the reading of any part of the Bible, either in Latin or in English.[1]

This was the only Tudor injunction regarding books in churches that explicitly stipulated where the books were to be placed: in the choir. In and of itself, this order speaks of the diminishing level of holiness associated with that space which, prior to the break with Rome, had been one of the most sacred spaces in the parish church. It also seems to support Arnold Hunt's argument in favour of lay access to the choir, at least from the sixteenth century onwards.[2]

The religious and educational benefits of lay access to books in parish churches continued to be recognised in later injunctions. An injunction of 1538, for example, ordered 'one book of the whole Bible of the largest volume in English, and the same set up in some convenient place within the said church ... whereas your parishioners may most commodiously resort to the same and read it'.[3] The stipulation of an unspecified 'convenient place' for the books that was accessible to parishioners evidences their general, unrestricted readership. The desire for books to be housed in convenient locations continued

---

1 Walter Howard Frere (ed.), *Visitation Articles and Injunctions of the Period of the Reformation, Volume II, 1536–1558* (London: Longmans, Green & Co., 1910), p. 9.

2 Arnold Hunt, 'Clerical and Parish Libraries' in Elisabeth Leedham-Green and Teresa Webber (eds), *The Cambridge History of Libraries, Volume I, to 1640* (Cambridge: Cambridge University Press, 2008), p. 412.

3 Frere, *Visitation Articles and Injunctions, Volume II*, pp. 34–35.

into the reign of Edward VI, who augmented the Henrician injunctions placing a Bible in every parish church to include a larger range of religious texts for reading by the clergy and the laity. In 1547, Edward's first set of injunctions ordered the provision not only of an English Bible, but also an English translation of Erasmus's *Paraphrases upon the Gospels*, suggesting that the scholarly merits of this work for Protestant readers and Erasmus's credentials as a humanist outweighed his Catholicism. Erasmus's *Paraphrases* were to be 'set up in some convenient place within the said church … whereas their parishioners may most commodiously resort unto the same, and read the same'.[4] Again, despite this 'convenient place' being left undetermined, public access to these texts was clearly of prime importance, a trait that would become a key feature of post-Reformation parish libraries.

Religious education remained a theme of the Marian regime in the 1550s, though it was distinctly oriented towards Catholicism. The regime was committed to promoting a renewed and revised form of Catholicism in England, promulgating its doctrine and the fundamentals of the faith, and encouraging the loyalty of the people to the traditions and rites of the Catholic Church.[5] Mary accordingly demanded the confiscation of all 'unlawful books' (i.e. Protestant religious works).[6] Further, in the injunctions Bishop Edmund Bonner set out for his London diocese in 1555, he stipulated that

> the churchwardens and parishioners of every parish, within the diocese and jurisdiction of London, shall of their own costs and charges, find, keep, and maintain … a legend, an antiphoner, a grail, a psalter, an ordinal to say or solemnize Divine Office, a missal, a manual, [and] a processional.[7]

The nature of the works Bonner ordered the London clergy to acquire reflected the Marian tendency towards clerical, as opposed to lay, religious education and the more clergy-centred religious practices of Catholicism. The volumes Bonner stipulated contained formularies of practical worship that were of little use or interest to the laity, explaining why these sorts of books are rarely found within the collections of post-Reformation parish libraries. Despite the large-scale shift in religion from Protestantism to Catholicism under the

---

4   *Ibid.*, pp. 117–118.
5   Eamon Duffy, *The Stripping of the Altars: Traditional Religion in England 1400–1580*, 2nd edition (New Haven and London: Yale University Press, 2005), p. 543.
6   Frere, *Visitation Articles and Injunctions, Volume II*, p. 326.
7   *Ibid.*, p. 365.

Marian regime, books in parish churches nevertheless retained their educational purposes.

When Elizabeth I acceded to the throne in November 1558, there was a renewed focus on providing Protestant religious reading material for the laity in England's parish churches. One injunction of the set issued by Elizabeth in 1559 stated that the clergy

> shall provide within three months next after this visitation at the charges of the parish one book of the whole Bible of the largest volume in English; and within one twelve months next after the said visitation, the Paraphrases of Erasmus, also in English, upon the Gospels, and the same set up in some convenient place within the said church that they have cure of, where as their parishioners may most commodiously resort unto the same and read the same.[8]

Whilst this injunction followed the form of those of Edward VI in omitting a specific location for these texts within parish churches, it may be that, considering these injunctions anticipated the reading of these volumes by ordinary parishioners, the books were placed in one of the areas where the 'common' people sat during services. Such places potentially included 'the back of the nave, in the belfry, in the aisles, or in the choir', emphasising again the accessibility of the latter area to the laity from the sixteenth century onwards.[9] Religious texts retained their popularity amongst the 'rural masses and urban lower classes' over the course of the sixteenth century and throughout the seventeenth century, even as the amount of secular material in parish libraries increased.[10] Over the course of the seventeenth century, post-Reformation repositories grew and evolved into wide-ranging collections of significant sizes that eventually mutated into the subscription and lending libraries that were an increasingly popular feature of the eighteenth century.[11]

This book argues that post-Reformation parish libraries were a significant part of the intellectual and religious environment of early modern England

---

8   Walter Howard Frere (ed.), *Visitation Articles and Injunctions of the Period of the Reformation, Volume III, 1559–1575* (London: Longmans, Green & Co., 1910), p. 10.

9   Christopher Marsh, 'Order and Place in England, 1580–1640: The View from the Pew', *Journal of British Studies*, 44: 1 (2005), p. 10.

10 R. A. Houston, *Literacy in Early Modern Europe: Culture and Education, 1500–1800*, 2nd edition (Harlow: Longman, 2002), p. 208.

11 James Raven, 'Libraries for Sociability: the Advance of the Subscription Library' in Giles Mandelbrote and K. A. Manley (eds), *The Cambridge History of Libraries in Britain and Ireland, Volume II: 1640–1850* (Cambridge: Cambridge University Press, 2006), pp. 239–263.

because of their purpose to educate both the clergy and the laity; that they had their roots in the collections of Catholic religious texts and liturgical works of pre-Reformation parish churches but developed into wide-ranging repositories to fulfil the spiritual and educational needs of parishioners. As Arnold Hunt has stated,

> the significance of these modest collections is that they gave parishioners access to the writings of some of the leading English and continental Reformed divines – Calvin, Peter Martyr, William Perkins, Samuel Hieron – which, in theological terms, went considerably beyond the official doctrine of the Church of England.[12]

This educational impetus for establishing post-Reformation parish libraries is evident in the foundation documents for several repositories. Humphrey Chetham's will, for example, provided for five parish libraries to be established in and around Manchester in the 1650s, specifically 'for the edificac[i]on of the common people'.[13] Many of the authors Hunt identified were included in Chetham's and other parish libraries, including those in Grantham, Ripon and Wimborne Minster, whose collections will be explored more thoroughly in Part 2 of this book. These and other institutions educated their users and promoted a '"Calvinist consensus" to a wider readership' within the intellectual and religious landscape of early modern England.[14]

1 Types of Books in Post-Reformation Parish Libraries

The sorts of books available to readers in the collections of post-Reformation parish libraries were varied and wide-ranging. Most repositories were strong on theology, history and the classics, works that provided readers with a theoretical education. Many collections also included numerous genres of works that often reflected either the specific interests, occupations, or intentions of the donor. Such texts usually offered a secular, more practical education. In Roger Gillingham's donation to Wimborne Minster church, for example, there were works on agriculture, gardening and winemaking, some of which may have already been in Gillingham's collection before they were given to the church.

---

12   Hunt, 'Clerical and Parish Libraries', p. 416.
13   Chetham's Library, Manchester, (Uncatalogued), Last Will and Testament of Humphrey Chetham.
14   Hunt, 'Clerical and Parish Libraries', p. 416.

Similarly, books on topics such as travel, science, poetry, grammar and mathematics were also included in early modern parish libraries and can be taken as a reflection of the interests of the donors.[15] Sir Richard More, for example, who founded More parish library in Shropshire in 1680, gifted books on these and other, comparable subjects from his own collection to the parish library. Thus, the donation provides a clear insight into More's own religious, academic and more general interests. Taken from More's collection of poetry, theology, history and geography, the parish library included works by classical authors such as Cicero, Isocrates and Euripides, as well as early medieval writers like Bede. Like many other libraries of the seventeenth century, the theological texts in More parish library 'suggest the continuing importance of older thought in the structure of seventeenth-century intellectual life'. They comprised works by authors ranging from 'evangelical to Jesuit and embracing a considerable range of subtle ecclesiastical distinctions'.[16] Texts by John Calvin, Theodore Beza, Jacob Arminius, Martin Luther, William Perkins and Philipp Melanchthon sat alongside the works of men such as Martin Becanus, the Jesuit priest, theologian and controversialist.[17] Such a combination suggests that Richard More believed in the importance of providing a broad theological education for his readers, supplying them with books he thought most appropriate to facilitate this.

In a similar way, the 'two hundred English and Greek Folio's, consisting chiefly of Fathers, Councils, School-men, and Divines' that Lady Anne Harington donated to the parish church of Oakham in 1616 were appropriate for her audience of 'the vicar of that Church, and ... the Neighbouring Clergy'.[18] These books also reflected the reading interests of Lady Anne, her husband, or her son: the volumes seem to have been taken from the Haringtons' personal collection and many of the books were 'curiously bound, the Covers adorn'd with several guilded Frets (commonly call'd the *Harington* Knots) and *Ex Dono Domine* Annæ Haringtonæ *Baronesse*. Printed and pasted in the Title Pages'.[19]

After their original foundation, some parish library collections were augmented by later donations, meaning that those collections were amalgamations reflective of the reading interests of various donors. The library collection

---

15   W. M. Jacob, 'Libraries for the Parish: Individual Donors and Charitable Societies' in Giles Mandelbrote and K. A. Manley (eds), *The Cambridge History of Libraries in Britain and Ireland, Volume II: 1640–1850* (Cambridge: Cambridge University Press, 2006), p. 69.

16   Conal Condren, 'More Parish Library, Salop', *Library History*, 7:5 (1987), p. 146.

17   *Ibid.*, pp. 150–158.

18   James Wright, *The History and Antiquities of the County of Rutland* (London: Printed for Bennet Griffin, 1684), p. 52. This edition not listed on the USTC.

19   *Ibid.*

in Wimborne Minster church, which was augmented in 1695, ten years after its initial establishment in 1685, will be discussed in more detail in chapters 7 and 8. The Cranston Library in the parish church of St Mary Magdalene in Reigate in Surrey, offers another example of a library that was significantly augmented after its original foundation. The Reigate library was founded in 1701 by Andrew Cranston, vicar of Reigate. Cranston began the collection with seventy of his own books and later donated a further 116 volumes, to bring the total to 186 books. He also sought additional donations from the wealthier inhabitants of Reigate and received gifts from a wide range of people, including merchants, M P s, clergy and lawyers, as well as weavers, shopkeepers and widows. Such a diverse range of donors naturally led to a diverse range of books that reflected their individual interests, in addition to those books Cranston felt it necessary for his readers to be able to access. The Reigate collection included books on 'history, the Classics, biography, reference works, science, topography, philosophy, medicine, mathematics, and law', reflecting Cranston's desire to 'bring the widest possible range of knowledge to his flock'. The Reigate library also demonstrates Cranston's belief in the necessity of knowing the religious arguments of opponents in order to refute them: it includes, amongst the predominantly Anglican texts, works by Catholic, Puritan and Quaker authors as well.[20]

2   Continental Books in Post-Reformation Parish Libraries in England

Books printed on the continent are found in at least twenty-seven of the 102 parish libraries established between 1558 and 1709 that still contain surviving books. Such figures by themselves are suggestive of the extent of the continental book trade in post-Reformation England, but it is highly probable – though not necessarily provable – that this number would increase significantly if there were more libraries with surviving books from the period 1558 to 1709. The twenty-seven parish libraries that contain continental books equate to approximately twenty-six and a half percent of the 102 libraries with surviving books, and sixteen percent of the 165 parish libraries founded from 1558 to 1709. These are reasonably small percentages, but ones that are possibly distorted by the need for further close research into surviving parish library collections and an unfortunate lack of knowledge regarding what was in the parish library collections that no longer survive. The geographic spread of the surviving libraries that possessed continental books, as displayed in Figure 3, demonstrates

---

20   Andrea Thomas and Hilary Ely, 'The Cranston Library, Reigate: The First Three Hundred Years', *Library and Information History*, 27:4 (2011), pp. 246–248.

the reach of the continental book trade in the early modern period, evidencing that these works were available to and accessible by people in areas of England that extended far beyond London and the southeast.

The foundation dates of these twenty-seven parish libraries demonstrate both the increased physical accessibility and financial affordability of books as the seventeenth century progressed. Just two of the libraries with surviving continental books date from before 1600; seven were founded between 1601 and 1650; the remaining eighteen were established between 1651 and 1709. That only sixteen percent of the parish libraries founded between 1558 and 1709 still contain continental books does not reflect existing scholarship on the European book trade in England in the sixteenth century and suggests the possibility of the loss or removal of continental books that may once have been in the collections of these parish libraries. Continental books were seemingly readily available in England in the sixteenth century: as Andrew Pettegree has noted, 'English libraries and collectors availed themselves freely of the easy and long-established connections with the continent to obtain the best books that continental suppliers had to offer'.[21] The widespread preference for continental volumes remained into the second half of the sixteenth century as well, as demonstrated by the library of Bishop Richard Cox, over ninety percent of whose collection was comprised of continental imprints at his death in 1581.[22] There was a marked increase in the number of texts printed in England and texts printed in English on the continent by the mid-seventeenth century. Joad Raymond has demonstrated that this was the result of a combination of factors, including the increased demand for books fuelled by contemporary events from the 1640s onwards and the shift towards the printing of 'cheap works of controversy and polemic' that were utilised by those involved in the Civil War and who were attempting to enlist public opinion in their favour.[23]

In this context, the relative paucity of surviving continental books in parish library collections is attributable to several factors. Firstly, the survival of any library was in part a matter of chance, and there may be numerous libraries that once contained continental books that have since been disbanded. Secondly, the likelihood of a parish library containing books printed on the continent was significantly impacted by its proximity to a market town and the logistics

---

21   Andrew Pettegree, 'Centre and Periphery in the European Book World', *Transactions of the Royal Historical Society*, 18 (2008), p. 118.

22   Alan B. Farmer, 'Cosmopolitanism and Foreign Books in Early Modern England', *Shakespeare Studies*, 35 (2007), p. 59.

23   Joad Raymond, 'The Development of the Book Trade in Britain' in Joad Raymond (ed.), *The Oxford History of Popular Print Culture: Volume One: Cheap Print in Britain and Ireland to 1660* (Oxford: Oxford University Press, 2011), pp. 60–61.

of transportation between the two. Finally, the inclusion of continental books in parish libraries was in some instances dependent upon the library's founder having European connections or sufficient finances that enabled the provision of continental books.

Most of the parish libraries with surviving continental books, as shown in Figure 3, were market towns, or else were in close proximity to a market town that provided opportunities for acquiring books. The number of northern and East Anglian libraries that possessed continental books evidences the strength of the provincial book trade, which was practiced by notable booksellers in and around York, such as John Foster in the early seventeenth century, and Norwich by men like Robert Scott in the second half of the sixteenth century.[24] Perhaps most surprising is the relatively few surviving parish libraries in the southeast, in and around London, that still possess surviving continental books. Numerous early modern booksellers congregated in a relatively small area of London centred on St Paul's Churchyard, Fleet Street and Paternoster Row, where they would have had easy access to the books imported from the continent. Such a dearth of continental books in the southeast suggests the distorting impact of book loss on modern analyses of continental imprints in surviving parish libraries.

The English book trade was unique in Europe in its concentration on a single city – London – as its central hub. John Taylor's *The Carriers Cosmographie* (1637) details all of the carriers and wagons that journeyed between London and diverse parts of England in order to facilitate trade, and demonstrates the city's dominance of England's domestic and international book trade. The *Cosmographie* lists the trading journeys between London and over 200 English and Scottish towns, highlighting the importance of trade routes along the road networks of England in explaining how continental books came to be in parish libraries in all corners of the country, some in locations very far distant from London.[25]

It is almost impossible to say with any certainty where all of the continental books in the libraries depicted in Figure 3 were purchased from, but it is likely

24   John Barnard and Maureen Bell, *The Early Seventeenth-Century York Book Trade and John Foster's Inventory of 1616* (Leeds: The Leeds Philosophical and Literary Society Ltd, 1994), p. 4; Jennifer Winters, 'The English Provincial Book Trade: Bookseller Stock-Lists, c. 1520–1640', Volume I (Unpublished PhD thesis, University of St Andrews, 2012), p. 40.

25   John Taylor, *The Carriers Cosmographie* (London: Printed by A. G. [Anne Griffin], 1637). USTC 3019285; James Raven, *The Business of Books: Booksellers and the English Book Trade, 1450–1850* (New Haven: Yale University Press, 2007), p. 61.

that most originally came from London before being sold by provincial book-sellers. According to *The Carriers Cosmographie*, the city of York sent carriers to London on a weekly basis.[26] The numerous booksellers who congregated in the area around York Minster – so densely populated by tradesmen that the south side of the Minster became known as 'booksellers alley' – probably took considerable advantage of the goods brought from London on those weekly journeys. John Foster is one of the most well-documented York booksellers of the early seventeenth century, when he and at least six other booksellers prac-ticed their trade in service to an increasingly literate local population.[27] The inventory of Foster's shop, made at the time of his death in 1616, shows that just over fifteen percent of his stock (equating to 102 individual titles) was printed on the continent or elsewhere outside of England. Foster's continental stock came from Germany, Switzerland, France, the Netherlands and Dublin.[28] The range of countries from which Foster's stock originated, and the breadth of subjects that stock covered in order to appeal to the clergy, gentry and profes-sionals, in addition to students and literate townspeople, clearly demonstrate the wide reach of the provincial book trade in England.[29] It is possible that the continental books in the Yorkshire parish libraries were purchased from Foster and his fellow York booksellers.

The long reach of the continental book trade in England and the resultant access to continental texts in its provincial localities is similarly demonstrated by the continental texts found in parish libraries in East Anglia. The booksell-ers of East Anglia may have drawn on the weekly trade link between the two cities of Norwich and London to procure foreign books.[30] Robert Scott was one of four booksellers operating in Norwich in the 1570s, along with John Clifford, Thomas Gilbert and Leonard Delyson. All four men had shops reasonably close together in the parish of St Andrew's.[31] The printing locations for about half of Robert Scott's stock are unidentifiable. Only nineteen of the 152 titles with identifiable imprints were printed on the continent, in Antwerp, Cologne, Frankfurt, or Zurich, though it must be remembered that this may be a mis-leadingly small proportion of the entire stock.[32] Even accounting for a degree of variation between the booksellers' businesses and stockholdings, it can

26   Taylor, *The Carriers Cosmographie*, sig. C3r. USTC 3019285.
27   Barnard and Bell, *The Early Seventeenth-Century York Book Trade*, *passim*; D. M. Palliser, *Tudor York* (Oxford: Oxford University Press, 1979), pp. 173–174.
28   Winters, 'The English Provincial Book Trade', Volume I, pp. 70–71.
29   *Ibid.*, pp. 72–73.
30   Taylor, *The Carriers Cosmographie*, sig. B4v. USTC 3019285.
31   Winters, 'The English Provincial Book Trade', Volume I, p. 40.
32   *Ibid.*, pp. 45–46.

be reasonably assumed that the founders of parish libraries in Norwich and East Anglia more widely were able to purchase both English and continental imprints from one or more of these sellers to give to their libraries.

Some parish libraries possessed continental books that were initially bought by their founders and held in their personal collections. Though the evidence is circumstantial, the parish library of Swaffham, established in 1679, seems to provide a good example. Founded at the bequest of Clement Spelman, Swaffham library consisted of Clement Spelman's collection combined with those of his father, Sir Henry, and his elder brother, Sir John Spelman. It is possible that the Spelmans' various continental trips and connections were responsible for the continental volumes contained within Swaffham library. Clement Spelman appears to have had no connections with the continent himself, but both his father and brother did. Sir Henry Spelman was an antiquarian in London who, during the course of publishing one of his works, *Archaeologus*, was known to be in contact with European scholars. Furthermore, his eldest son, Sir John, made several trips abroad, notably to Paris in 1619 and Italy in 1628–1629. During these trips, Sir John was in contact with numerous European scholars. It may be, therefore, that visits to the continent or a relationship with continental scholars led to the inclusion of several continental books in their personal collections and thus, later, in Swaffham parish library.[33]

3 Conclusion

The increasing importance of books, and general lay access to religious texts in the vernacular specifically, is demonstrated by the plethora of royal injunctions in the sixteenth century ordering their placement in accessible parts of every parish church in England. The increasingly varied genres of religious and secular volumes within post-Reformation parish libraries testifies to their continued significance on the religious and educational landscape of early modern England and simultaneously demonstrates their continued use by readers. The number of parish libraries holding continental books, which at first glance seems almost insignificant, is probably merely indicative of the numbers of now-lost collections that also housed continental books before their dispersal.

---

33   Michael Perkin, *A Directory of the Parochial Libraries of the Church of England and the Church in Wales* (London: Bibliographical Society, 2004), pp. 364–365; William Carr and Stuart Handley, 'Spelman, Clement (bap. 1598, d. 1679)', *Oxford Dictionary of National Biography* (online, 2004); Stuart Handley, 'Spelman, Sir Henry (1563/4–1641)', *Oxford Dictionary of National Biography* (online, 2005); David L. Smith, 'Spelman, Sir John (1594–1643)', *Oxford Dictionary of National Biography* (online, 2008).

The remaining continental books in surviving parish library collections reflect the dominance of books imported into England via the Latin trade. Their proliferation across the hinterlands of England highlights the trade and road networks active in this period that made it possible for these books to be found in parish libraries far distant from the centre of the English book trade in London. The geographical scope of English parish libraries, along with their establishment across the entirety of the period between 1558 and 1709, will be discussed in the following chapter.

CHAPTER 4

The Spread of Post-Reformation Parish Libraries

The trade and road networks that spread across England meant that, despite London's place at the centre of the English book trade, books could be transported to all parts of the country. It is therefore unsurprising that the vast majority of English counties had at least four parish libraries between 1558 and 1709, with some having many more. Parish libraries were founded continually across the period 1558 to 1709 without interruption, despite the upheavals of the English Civil War and the Interregnum. Having been established primarily in England's more urban areas before 1679, the last quarter of the seventeenth century onwards saw a marked increase in rural parish library foundations. The proliferation of repositories after 1680 was largely thanks to the efforts of Reverend Thomas Bray and his associates in the Society for Promoting Christian Knowledge (SPCK), who were keen to ensure that there was a parish library in every parish in early modern England.

1 The Chronological Spread of Parish Libraries in Post-Reformation England

In the 1970s, historians Thomas Kelly and C. B. L. Barr argued that parish library foundation in the early modern period was disrupted in the mid-seventeenth century by the English Civil War and the Interregnum.[1] Disruption, however, did not equate to the dearth ascribed to the middle decades of the seventeenth century by these historians. In fact, as is shown in this chapter, there was not a single decade between 1560 and 1709 when there were no parish libraries established. The rate of parish library foundation in the period from 1558 to 1679 was characterised by a slow growth. As was shown in chapter 2, the subsequent dramatic increase in the number of parish libraries founded between 1680 and 1709 was partly the result of Barnabas Oley's efforts in the 1680s and the involvement of Thomas Bray and the SPCK in the 1690s and early 1700s.

---

1 C. B. L. Barr, 'Parish Libraries in a Region: the Case of Yorkshire', *Proceedings of the Library Association Study School and National Conference*, Nottingham, 1979, p. 34; Thomas Kelly, *Early Public Libraries: a History of the Public Libraries in Great Britain before 1850* (London: Library Association, 1966), p. 76.

In addition to the combined forty-eight libraries established by Oley and Bray and the SPCK, other donors established a further fifty-four parish libraries between 1680 and 1709. Figure 9 below demonstrates the number of parish libraries founded in England per decade between 1558 and 1709.

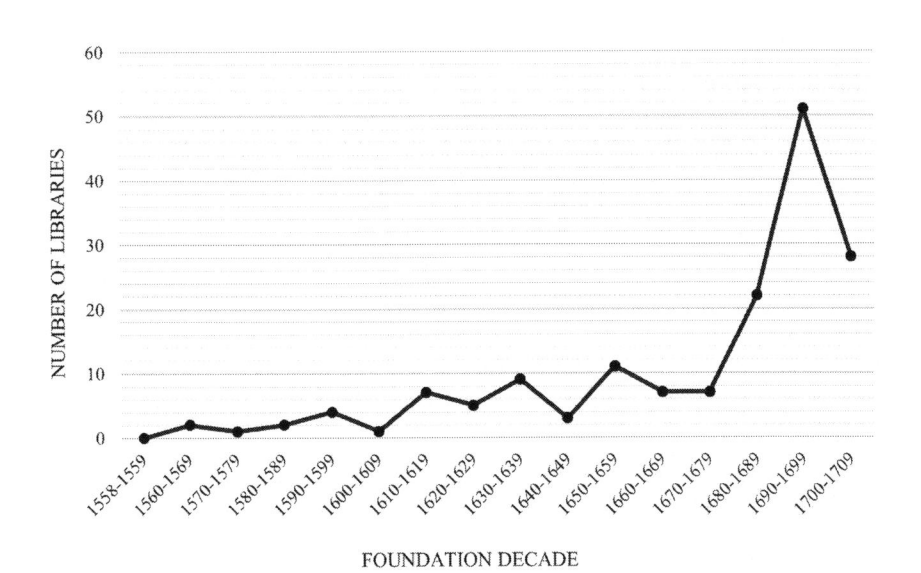

FOUNDATION DECADE

FIGURE 9   Number of parish libraries founded by decade, 1558–1709

Foundation rates for parish libraries established between the accession of Elizabeth I in 1558 and 1709, when the Parochial Libraries Act was passed by Parliament, began slowly: ten parish libraries were established in total in England in the fifty-one years between 1558 and 1609. The numbers saw a comparative increase from 1610 to 1639, with between five and nine parish libraries established per decade. During the Civil War years from 1640 to 1649, there was, evidently, a drop in the foundation rate to just three libraries. However, during the Interregnum in the following decade, the rate increased again, and ten libraries were founded in England in the 1650s. Seven libraries were established between 1660 and 1669, and a further seven from 1670 to 1679. In total, fifty-nine parish libraries were founded between 1558 and 1679. The year 1680 proved to be a watershed in the establishment of English parish libraries: 106 were founded in the thirty years between 1680 and 1709. The achievements of individual founders of parish libraries before the 1680s (perhaps with the exception of Barnabas Oley) were somewhat eclipsed by the accomplishments of the Church of England clergyman Thomas Bray and his associates from the SPCK, who were responsible for founding thirty-three (approximately sixty-five percent) of the fifty-one parish libraries established in the 1690s.[2] Between 1700 and 1709, a further twenty-two parish libraries were established in England. All 165 parish libraries established in England between 1558 and 1709 can be seen on the map in Figure 4.

Historians Sarah Gray and Chris Baggs have argued that nothing like a parish library existed for fifty years after the English Reformation.[3] The five institutions recognisable as parish libraries that were established in the first fifty years after the beginning of the Reformation in the 1530s up to the mid-1580s, shown above in Figures 4 and 9 (above), challenge that assertion. The first post-Reformation parish libraries appeared in Bristol (1567) and Steeple Ashton in Wiltshire (1568). A library in Toddington in Bedfordshire followed in 1570, as did two foundations in 1586 in Leicester and Norwich.

Furthermore, the arguments of C. B. L. Barr and Thomas Kelly, who separately asserted that few parish libraries were founded during the Civil War and Interregnum, are also disputable.[4] It was indeed the case during the Civil War that few parish libraries were founded: only three were established between 1640 and 1649. Very little is known about these three institutions – located in Manchester, Great Torrington in Devon, and Southampton – beyond the information found in the testamentary instructions of their founders. Neither the Manchester nor the Great Torrington libraries survive; seven books survive in the library at Southampton, but none are the original two works donated by John Clungeon, a London haberdasher, in 1646.[5] However, ten parish libraries were founded during the Interregnum in the 1650s, signifying what was at that point the highest rate of parish library foundation in any decade since their inception in the 1560s. The foundation of these parish libraries may reflect the relative freedom of religious expression and the freedom of the press from censorship that were a feature of these years.[6]

2   For more information on the efforts of Thomas Bray and the Society for Promoting Christian Knowledge in founding parish libraries, see Michael Perkin, *A Directory of the Parochial Libraries of the Church of England and the Church in Wales* (London: Bibliographical Society, 2004), pp. 35–37, 444–452. See also Leonard W. Cowie, 'Bray, Thomas (bap. 1658, d. 1730)', *Oxford Dictionary of National Biography* (online, 2012).

3   Sarah Gray and Chris Baggs, 'The English Parish Library: a Celebration of Diversity', *Libraries & Culture*, 35 (2000), p. 417.

4   Barr, 'Parish Libraries in a Region', p. 34; Kelly, *Early Public Libraries*, p. 76.

5   The National Archives, Kew, (PROB 11/198/73), Will of John Clungeon, Haberdasher of London, 9 November 1646; Perkin, *A Directory of the Parochial Libraries*, pp. 349–350.

6   Andrew Bradstock, *Radical Religion in Cromwell's England: A Concise History from the English Civil War to the End of the Commonwealth* (London; New York: I. B. Tauris, 2011), p. xiii.

The ten libraries established in the Interregnum were founded by a mixture of clergymen and laymen, mirroring the general pattern in parish library establishment in the sixteenth and seventeenth centuries. They included a library founded in St Peter and St Paul church in Wisbech in Cambridgeshire in 1651 by William Coldwell, rector of the church. This library was augmented twice in 1654: firstly, by William Fisher, who was elected Sheriff of Cambridge and Huntingdon for 1653, and secondly – and more substantially – by John Thurloe, Secretary of State to Oliver Cromwell from 1652 until Cromwell's death in 1658.[7] In addition, two of the libraries founded in the Manchester area by the merchant Humphrey Chetham were also completed in the 1650s.[8] A library was established in the parish church of Wootton Wawen in Warwickshire by its rector George Dunscomb (d. 1652), and Francis Roberts, the Presbyterian rector of All Saints church in Wrington, Somerset founded a library in the church by donating several volumes in 1659.[9] In Yorkshire, familial connections led Matthew Hutton, an antiquary and rector of two benefices at Aynho (from 1677) and Croughton (from 1689) in Northamptonshire, to donate books to St Edmund's church in Marske, for the use of his nephew, Thomas Hutton, when Thomas was appointed as rector of that church in 1659.[10] Not only do these libraries demonstrate the multiplicity of repositories established in the 1650s, they also serve to reinforce the involvement of both clerics and laymen in the establishment of parish libraries. This level of shared participation evidences the continued significance of these institutions in the tumultuous politico-religious landscape of the decade.

7   Edmund Carter, *The History of the County of Cambridge from the Earliest Account to the Present Time* (London, 1819), p. 359; Perkin, *A Directory of the Parochial Libraries*, p. 395; Timothy Venning, 'Thurloe, John (bap. 1616, d.1668)', *Oxford Dictionary of National Biography* (online, 2008).

8   Chetham's Library, Manchester, (Uncatalogued), Last Will and Testament of Humphrey Chetham.

9   Perkin, *A Directory of the Parochial Libraries*, pp. 400, 402–403; William Blades, *Books in Chains and Other Bibliographical Papers*, (London: Elliot Stock, 1892), p. 80; Burnett Hillman Streeter, *The Chained Library: A Survey of Four Centuries in the Evolution of the English Library* (New York: Burt Franklin, 1931), p. 292.

10   Perkin, *A Directory of the Parochial Libraries*, p. 282; Jan Broadway, 'Hutton, Matthew (1638/9–1711)', *Oxford Dictionary of National Biography* (online, 2008); Joseph Foster (ed.), *Alumni Oxonienses: The Members of the University of Oxford, 1500–1714, Volume II – Early Series* (Oxford: Parker & Co., 1891), pp. 779–780.

2   The Geographical Spread of Parish Libraries in Post-Reformation England

Before 1680, post-Reformation parish libraries were established primarily in towns. Thereafter, there was a shift in focus to England's more rural areas, as W. M. Jacob rightly argued. At the same time, there was a threefold increase in the number of parish libraries founded between 1680 and 1709 compared to between 1558 and 1679.[11] *The Theatre of the Empire of Great Britaine*, the atlas published by the English cartographer and historian, John Speed in 1611 or 1612, used different symbols to distinguish between villages, market towns and cities, which were characterised by their increasing levels of urbanity. Working on the basis of these symbols, Speed's maps have been used in order to determine the type of area – city, market town, or village – in which each parish library founded between 1558 and 1709 was established, as shown in Figures 5a and 5b.[12] Thirty-nine of the fifty-four parish libraries established before 1680 were founded in cities, such as Bristol, Norwich, or Bath, or else in market towns and ports, such as Halifax, Boston in Lincolnshire, or Southampton. The remaining twenty parish libraries of the pre-1680 period were founded in rural locations. Post-1680 rural foundations, it is important to note, did not come at the expense of urban library foundations, which continued and, in fact, doubled in number themselves between 1680 and 1709.

Of the 106 parish libraries established in England between 1680 and 1709, fifty-seven were in rural localities. Barnabas Oley, archdeacon of Ely, endowed ten parish churches in the diocese of Carlisle with a donation of sixteen books each in his will of 1685.[13] Further, motivated by their belief that the parish clergy needed to be well educated in order to fulfil their ministerial and pastoral duties, and desirous to improve Christian teaching as a way of increasing religious devotion in the localities of post-Restoration England, Thomas Bray and his associates in the SPCK instigated the establishment of almost forty parish

---

11   W. M. Jacob, 'Libraries for the Parish: Individual Donors and Charitable Societies' in Giles Mandelbrote and K. A. Manley (eds), *The Cambridge History of Libraries in Britain and Ireland, Volume II: 1640–1850* (Cambridge: Cambridge University Press, 2006), p. 67; David Williams, 'The Use and Abuse of a Pious Intention: Changing Attitudes to Parochial Libraries', *The Library Association and Study School and National Conference Proceedings*, Nottingham, 1979, p. 22; Gray and Baggs, 'The English Parish Library', p. 418; Perkin, *A Directory of the Parochial Libraries*, p. 33.

12   Sarah Bendall, 'Speed, John (1551/2–1629)', *Oxford Dictionary of National Biography* (online, 2008).

13   The National Archives, Kew, (PROB 11/383/4), Will of Barnabas Oley, Vicar of Great Gransden, Huntingdonshire, 15 March 1686.

libraries across England between 1695 and 1709.[14] The remaining forty-nine libraries founded after 1680 were established in cities such as Chester, Carlisle, or Coventry, or in market towns such as Bishop's Castle in Shropshire or Bromsgrove in Worcestershire. Thus, in many counties, post-1680 rural foundations did not come at the expense of continuing urban parish library establishment, though it is important to note that the characteristics of urban and rural are, as John Patten has suggested, subject to regional variations, particularly along the divisional lines between the uplands and lowlands of England.[15] However, when considered on a countrywide basis, Figures 5a and 5b demonstrate that the pattern of foundation supports the theory propounded by historians that a growing trend for rural parish libraries can be seen in the last decades of the seventeenth century.

3   Conclusion

Despite previous research to the contrary, the English Civil War and the subsequent decade of the Interregnum did not impede parish library establishment to a considerable degree. In fact, it is possible that the relative religious freedom of the Interregnum encouraged parish library foundation, with the most repositories of any decade thus far being established in the 1650s. Moreover, the geographical spread of post-Reformation parish libraries demonstrates that their establishment was indeed concentrated in England's urban centres prior to 1680, whereafter increased numbers of parish libraries established in rural areas followed.

Some of the elements of parish libraries considered here in general terms – the users of parish libraries, collecting practices and the nature of parish library collections will be discussed in more detail in Part 2, with specific reference to the four case study parish libraries of Grantham, Ripon, Gorton and Wimborne Minster. The analysis of these libraries will elucidate in finer detail the conclusions drawn here and demonstrate that these parish libraries were placed in generally accessible locations; that these libraries were established by either gifts of money or books; and that the nature of these collections were influenced both by their donors and by their intended users.

---

14   Gray and Baggs, 'The English Parish Library', p. 419.
15   John Patten, *English Towns, 1500–1700* (Folkestone: Dawson, 1978), pp. 27–28.

PART 2

Establishment

∴

Introduction to Part 2

Parish libraries in post-Reformation England were established with the education of both the clergy and the laity in mind, a combined readership that is reflected in both the foundation documents of parish libraries as well as in their locations within their individual churches. The parish libraries that continued to be established mainly for the clergy were often housed in areas of the church accessed almost exclusively by the clergy and sometimes by the elite laity. The parish libraries intended for a mixed audience were often more accessible, but were sometimes secured either by being kept in a locked room, by chaining the books to their shelves, or by the implementation of both of these measures. Parish library collections were often compiled by the donors themselves, or by people acting on their behalf, whether posthumously or during the donor's lifetime. Parish libraries were commonly dominated by religious texts primarily written in Latin, but many repositories also had increasing numbers of secular volumes written in English as the seventeenth century progressed. The places of publication and publication dates of the books in parish libraries across this period attest to the common practice of purchasing second-hand volumes, to the prevalence of the continental book trade in England, and to the growing English domestic book trade.

The first chapter of Part 2 of this book, chapter 5, consists of an overview of four specific parish libraries established in early modern England: the Francis Trigge Chained Library in Grantham, Lincolnshire (1598); the Ripon Minster parish library in Ripon, Yorkshire (1624); the Gorton Chest parish library in Manchester, Lancashire (1653); and the Wimborne Minster Chained Library in Wimborne Minster, Dorset (1685, augmented 1695). These parish libraries will be analysed in detail in this volume as they are representative both of the disparate geographical locations and chronological distribution of parish library establishment between 1558 and 1709. By choosing these parish libraries, it is intended that comparisons will be drawn and similarities and differences noted between parish library foundations at the beginning of this period and at the end.

Chapter 6 begins a deeper exploration than has hitherto been offered of the different users of the various parish libraries established in post-Reformation England. This chapter makes extensive use of wills, which provide information regarding founders' instructions for the location of a library within a parish church, their directives regarding the intended users of those libraries and, occasionally, their directions for ensuring the security of the books after donation, either by chaining or by their placement in a lockable room. They also occasionally reveal the amount of money given by the donor to found and purchase books for the library. Following the pattern established in the pre-Reformation era, there continued to be a number of parish libraries from the sixteenth century onwards that were almost exclusively the purview of the clergy. At the same time, there was an increasing tendency towards establishing parish libraries with a definite mixed clerical and lay readership. In addition, there were even a small number of libraries – those established by Humphrey Chetham in and around Manchester, for instance – that were intended for the sole use of the 'common people'. In its final section, chapter 6 considers the impact of these different intended readerships on the location of post-Reformation parish libraries within their parish churches.

Chapter 7 again makes use of wills as well as churchwardens' account books, purchase invoices and other archival material such as probate records, to examine the collecting practices of various parish library founders between 1558 and 1709. Churchwardens' account books often include details about transport costs for transferring books from their place of purchase to the parish church, itemised payment information for the purchasing of wood for shelves or bookcases, funds paid to local craftsmen for services rendered in building the bookcases, chests, or cupboards to house the books, and to blacksmiths for the making and attaching of chains to the books. In addition, purchase invoices provide information regarding the cost of individual books, the date on which certain books were purchased and also, on occasion, detail packing, transport and chaining costs, in a similar manner to churchwardens' account books. These account books and invoices both provide important circumstantial evidence regarding the physicality of parish libraries in the sixteenth and seventeenth centuries and the practical costs of their foundation. This chapter evidences the different ways in which collections were established, either by a gift or bequest of money or books, and compiled, through the auspices of the donors themselves, or their representatives. It demonstrates that the libraries established by gifts or bequests of books were naturally more strongly linked to and influenced by the donor's own vision for the collection and for the repository more generally, whilst those established by gifts or bequests of money were less so. This chapter also offers a consideration of the impact of later augmentations to parish library collections and ends with a brief discussion of the cost of early modern books as demonstrated on title pages and purchase invoices.

The final chapter of Part 2, chapter 8, provides an in-depth analysis of the collections of the four parish libraries of Grantham, Ripon, Gorton and Wimborne Minster. It examines the confessional identities of the authors whose works comprise each collection, the languages of the works in these collections, the publication dates and places of their volumes and the implications of these for the English and continental book trades, and finishes by examining the various genres of the works in each of these libraries. Through this close analysis, this chapter demonstrates that these collections were filled with volumes by authors of extremely wide-ranging confessional identities, from Church Fathers to medieval Catholics, to post-Reformation Catholics and Protestants of all sorts. It demonstrates that the Latin language of many of the volumes may not have been as prohibitive to a wide readership as was once thought and that therefore the messages contained within these volumes could be understood by a larger number of readers. This analysis also demonstrates that the second-hand book trade was thriving across England throughout the period from 1558 to 1709 and that the Latin continental trade was of critical significance to the provision of books in three of the four repositories under analysis. Finally, this chapter argues that the predominance of religious volumes in early modern parish libraries persisted right across the sixteenth and seventeenth centuries. This predominance continued despite an increasing number of secular works also being included in parish library collections, as evidenced by the analysis of the Francis Trigge Chained Library (1598), which contained only a small number of secular works, and the Wimborne Minster Chained Library (1685/1695), of which a significant proportion was secular books.

CHAPTER 5

The Parish Libraries of Grantham, Ripon, Gorton and Wimborne Minster

The four case study parish libraries at the core of the analysis in the remainder of this volume are the Francis Trigge Chained Library in Grantham, Lincolnshire (1598); Ripon Minster parish library in Ripon, Yorkshire (1624); the Gorton Chest parish library in Manchester, Lancashire (1653); and Wimborne Minster Chained Library in Wimborne Minster, Dorset (1685, augm. 1695). These libraries were selected for close analysis for several reasons. Firstly, these collections vary in size from fifty to around 750 volumes, a range that enabled the examination of the variety of texts and subjects found in each collection and whether that was broader or narrower based on the number of books in the collection. Secondly, these libraries were all established in English counties reasonably remote from one another, as shown in Figure 6, which enabled consideration of whether similarities and differences of belief could be ascertained in different geographical areas. Finally, all four parish libraries were established at different points in time between 1558 and 1709: two before the Civil War, one during the Interregnum and one after the Restoration. The establishment of these libraries at different points in time enabled an analysis of whether the religious beliefs of the people at a parish level who were reading these books changed over time.

In 1598, Francis Trigge, a Church of England clergyman with godly leanings, founded a library in St Wulfram's church in Grantham to provide the people of the surrounding area with an education in divinity and the liberal sciences.[1] Ripon Minster parish library was founded in 1624 by Anthony Higgin, whose will stipulated that his collection of some 2,000 books was to be used by two of his relatives before being donated to the Minster for a library.[2] Approximately 750 of these 2,000 volumes were theological texts, and these will form the basis of the analysis in the following chapters. Manchester-based merchant and philanthropist, Humphrey Chetham, established the Gorton Chest parish library in 1653. Chetham's will stated that the Gorton Chest and the four other parish

---

1 Lincolnshire Archives, Lincolnshire, (Grantham St Wulfram Par/23/1), Documents relating to the Trigge Library: Agreement.

2 Borthwick Institute of Archives (BIA), University of York, (Archbishop Register 31, f. 238v–239r), Will of Anthony Higgin, 12 November 1624.

© KONINKLIJKE BRILL NV, LEIDEN, 2024 | DOI:10.1163/9789004363717_009

libraries his will provided for were for the religious education of the 'common people' of the surrounding areas.[3] Wimborne Minster Chained Library was established in 1685 after the Church of England clergyman, William Stone, sent his collection of patristic and theological works to Wimborne Minster church. Roger Gillingham, a local gentleman, significantly augmented the collection in 1695 by bequeathing a range of religious and secular volumes to Wimborne Minster church for the clergy, gentry and merchants of Wimborne Minster and the surrounding areas.[4]

1   The Francis Trigge Chained Library, Grantham, Lincolnshire

Francis Trigge was born in Lincolnshire in around 1547. Very little is known about Trigge's early life until 1564, when he matriculated to University College, Oxford. Trigge earned his BA in February 1569 and proceeded MA in May 1572.[5] How Trigge spent the next years of his life is unclear, but by 1589 he had taken orders and had been appointed as the rector of Welbourn in Lincolnshire, a post that Trigge held until his death in 1606.[6] The town of Welbourn, where Trigge was rector for over twenty-five years, was less than twelve miles from Grantham. It is evident from the title of Trigge's published sermon, *A Godly and Fruitfull Sermon Preached at Grantham 1592*, that he visited the town at least once and preached in St Wulfram's church.[7] If this was a regular occurrence, the connection that Trigge developed with the town may have provided the justification for such a substantial gift to the area in the form of a sizeable library.

Trigge was a popular author of at least eight different titles written in either English or Latin. Trigge's writings suggest he was a Calvinist, whose belief in the importance of Scripture as the primary source of religious authority, along

3   Chetham's Library, Manchester, (Uncatalogued), Last Will and Testament of Humphrey Chetham.
4   The National Archives, Kew, (C8/446/3), Attorney General v Fry, 1695; The National Archives, Kew, (PROB 11/430/238), Will of Roger Gillingham of Middle Temple, Middlesex, 25 February 1696.
5   E. I. Carlyle and A. McRae, 'Trigge, Francis (1547?–1606)', *Oxford Dictionary of National Biography* (online, 2004); Joseph Foster (ed.), *Alumni Oxoniensis: the Members of the University of Oxford, 1500–1714: Volume IV – Early Series* (Oxford: James Parker & Co., 1891), p. 1510.
6   Carlyle and McRae, 'Trigge, Francis', ODNB; Foster, *Alumni Oxonienses, Volume IV – Early Series*, p. 1510.
7   Francis Trigge, *A Godly and Fruitfull Sermon Preached at Grantham 1592* (Oxford: Joseph Barnes, 1594). USTC 512686.

with the importance of preaching, intimates moderate Puritan sympathies. In his *An apologie, or defence of our dayes, against the vaine murmurings & complaints of manie* ... (1589), for example, Trigge defended the Elizabethan Settlement, describing Reformed religion as a light that

> when Calvin, Bucer, and Bullinger preached was ... spread farre and wyde. But nowe truly, all darkenes being dispersed, it hath filled all the worlde, it hath entred into every chinke, it hath lightned all the ayre. And it encreaseth everye daye, and is more brighter and clearer.[8]

Trigge was seemingly aware, however, that Reformed religion had not 'filled all the world' and 'entred into every chinke', as he frequently used his works to attempt to inspire his readers to convert to Protestantism: in his *A Godly and Fruitfull Sermon Preached at Grantham 1592*, which was first printed in 1594, Trigge stated that he hoped to 'pul some out of the fire of sinne and wickednes'.[9] He further demonstrated his desire to convert Catholics to Protestantism in his *A touchstone, whereby may be easilie discerned, which is the true Catholike faith, of all them that professe the name of Catholiques in the Church of Englande*.[10] In his epistle to the reader, Trigge stated his wish 'by the handes of our writings, or by any other meanes whatsoever, [to] drawe such as bee obstinate from the flame and fire of heresie'.[11]

In October 1598, Francis Trigge provided £100 by indenture for the foundation of a library in Grantham. The indenture was a quadripartite agreement, seen in Figure 10 below, made on 'the twentieth daie of October in the fortieth yeare of the raign of our Soveraign Lady Elizabeth [1598]'. The four parties between whom this agreement was made were Francis Trigge; the Alderman of Grantham, John Gibbard (or Gibson) and his two burgesses; two prebendaries

---

8   Francis Trigge, *An apologie, or defence of our dayes, against the vaine murmurings & complaints of manie wherein is plainly proved, that our dayes are more happie & blessed than the dayes of our forefathers* (London: John Wolfe, 1589), p. 4. USTC 511333.

9   Trigge, *A Godly and Fruitfull Sermon*, sig. A4v. USTC 512686.

10   Francis Trigge, *A touchstone, whereby may easilie be discerned, which is the true Catholike faith, of all them that professe the name of Catholiques in the Church of Englande, that they bee not deceived taken out of the Catholike Epistle of S. Jude* (London: Peter Short, 1599). USTC 514096; Francis Trigge, *A touchstone, whereby may easilie be discerned, which is the true Catholike faith, of all them that professe the name of Catholiques in the Church of Englande, that they bee not deceived taken out of the Catholike Epistle of S. Jude*, 2nd edition (London: Peter Short, 1600). USTC 514973.

11   Trigge, *A touchstone, whereby may easilie be discerned, which is the true Catholike faith*, 2nd edition, sig. A2r. USTC 514973.

of Salisbury Cathedral, Abraham Conham and William Barkesdale; and Robert Bryan and Stephen Loddington, two vicars of Grantham.[12] The positions of authority these men enjoyed within Grantham and its surrounding areas are evident in this agreement. They were all men of considerable financial means with influence in the local community, who were 'well devoted to further[ing] the said enterprise [the establishment of the library] beinge so good & commendable'.[13]

FIGURE 10   Quadripartite agreement establishing the Francis Trigge Chained Library
             © LINCOLNSHIRE ARCHIVES (GRANTHAM ST WULFRAM PAR/23/1)
             DOCUMENTS RELATING TO THE TRIGGE LIBRARY: AGREEMENT

---

12   Lincolnshire Archives, Lincolnshire, (Grantham St Wulfram Par/23/1), Documents relating to the Trigge Library: Agreement.

13   *Ibid.*

In the agreement, Trigge promised to 'have a lybrary erected in the said towne of Grantham' and to provide 'books of divinitie and other learninge to the value of one hundreth poundes'. The library's role was to promote access to a collection that would facilitate the 'better encreasinge of learninge and knowledge in divinitie and other liberall sciences' for the clergy and laity of Grantham and its surrounding areas, thus evidencing Trigge's educational motives.[14] The foundation indenture also stated that Trigge had 'devised good orders & constitucions' for the security of the library, to which his co-signatories were avowedly committed. The alderman and burgesses enjoined to uphold the orders and constitutions by doing 'what in them shall reasonably lye not onely to endeavour to have the said orders on their partes observed but also to cause the failures & offences of such as shall breake the said orders to be presented or otherwise complained of ... to the Bychop of the diocese of Lincoln'.[15] Had Trigge's co-signatories not been men of substance in the local community, they would not have had the power, authority or influence to carry out Trigge's penalties for transgressors, nor to contact the bishop of Lincoln directly to ask for his involvement and assistance. This would have opened the library up to having its books wrongfully removed or poorly treated, or else taken out of St Wulfram's church in its entirety. Trigge seems to have been confident in his colleagues' commitment to the library and its security, so much so that he bequeathed a further seven books 'to the librarye at Grantham' in his will of 1606.[16] Perhaps he felt that these volumes – which included works by Andrew Willett, Duns Scotus and John Foxe, amongst others – filled what he perceived to be a hole in the religious education provided by the original collection.

Trigge's death and testamentary bequest of further books to the collection in 1606 may have prompted the compilation of the library's *Catalogus Librorum* in 1608. The *Catalogus Librorum* demonstrates that the collection was largely comprised of second-hand religious texts, including commentaries on the Bible, works of general theology and religious or Church histories. The majority of these were published after the Reformation and therefore reflected the new Protestant teachings, but post-Reformation Catholic works by authors such as Hector Pintus and Robert Bellarmine were also included, making this library a repository of a more general religious education.

Through its theological makeup, the Francis Trigge Chained Library allows historians an insight into the intellectual and religious life of Grantham at

---

14   *Ibid.*
15   *Ibid.*
16   Lincolnshire Archives, Lincolnshire, (LCC Wills/1606), Wills proved in the Lincoln Consistory Court, number 252.

the end of the sixteenth century and the beginning of the seventeenth century. Protestantism had gained a strong foothold in Lincolnshire by the end of Elizabeth's reign but, as R. B. Walker has argued, it was 'not numbered among the most Protestant counties of the kingdom; its allegiance was divided'.[17] As such, the repository included works by Catholic authors to enable the local clergy to improve their knowledge of Catholicism in order to better refute its arguments to their parishioners. In its inclusion of Catholic volumes in a largely Protestant book collection, the Francis Trigge Chained Library was broadly similar not only to the personal libraries of late sixteenth- and early seventeenth-century archbishops and bishops, such as Samuel Harsnett, Lancelot Andrewes and Arthur Lake, whose private collections were dominated by Protestant volumes but intentionally included numerous Catholic texts as well, but also to other, later parish library collections, as will be shown in chapters 7 and 8.[18]

2   Ripon Minster Parish Library, Ripon, Yorkshire

Anthony Higgin, the founder of the parish library at Ripon Minster in Yorkshire, was born in Manchester, the second son of Thomas Higgin and his wife, Elizabeth Birch of Birch.[19] His birth date is unknown, but assuming Higgin was seventeen or eighteen years of age when he matriculated to St John's College, Cambridge in 1568, he was probably born in the early 1550s. Higgin gained his BA from St John's College in 1571–1572, received ordination as a priest in 1572 and became a Fellow of St John's in 1574. He was awarded his MA in 1575, before being appointed as a prebendary of Gloucester Cathedral in 1578 and receiving his Bachelor of Divinity degree in 1582.[20] His studies for his MA and BD degrees coincided with his tenure as vicar of Kempsford in Gloucestershire from 1572 to 1578, though Higgin did not reside in the town.[21] Presumably, he maintained his residence in Cambridge. Higgin was a university preacher in 1581 and was for a short time in 1582 a tutor to

17   R. B. Walker, 'The Growth of Puritanism in the County of Lincoln in the Reign of Queen Elizabeth I', *Journal of Religious History*, 1:3 (1961), p. 157.

18   David Pearson, 'The Libraries of English Bishops, 1600–1640', *The Library*, 14 (1992), pp. 223, 229.

19   Jean E. Mortimer, *The Library Catalogue of Anthony Higgin: Dean of Ripon (1608–1624)* (Leeds: Chorley and Pickersgill, 1962), p. 2.

20   John Venn and J. A. Venn (eds), *Alumni Cantabrigienses, Part I, Volume II* (Cambridge: Cambridge University Press, 1922), p. 367.

21   A. B. Mynors, 'Kempsford', *Transactions of the Bristol and Gloucestershire Archaeological Society*, 57 (1935), p. 217.

Thomas Morton, later Bishop of Durham. In 1583, Higgin was 'called out of the College [St John's] to other more weighty imployments in the Church' and was presented with the rectorship of Kirk Deighton, near Harrogate in North Yorkshire, in that year.[22] Higgin was master of St Michael's Hospital in Well in the North Riding of Yorkshire from 1605, but seems to have remained at Kirk Deighton until 1608, when he was appointed by King James I to succeed Moses Fowler as dean of Ripon.[23] Higgin held the two positions at Kirk Deighton and Ripon in plurality until his death. He died in Well in North Yorkshire, on 17 November 1624 and was buried the next day.[24]

In August 1604, four years before Anthony Higgin became dean, James I had issued letters patent to reconstitute the Collegiate Church of Ripon.[25] The letters patent setting out the refoundation of the collegiate church were detailed and comprehensive, outlining the purpose of the church in the local community and in Yorkshire more generally, and stipulating how it was to be organised.[26] In the letters patent, James I asserted that in refounding the collegiate church, he was

> desiring above all thing to promote and so spread abroad the Glory and the Honour of Almighty God, and that the said inhabitants [the parishioners of Ripon] henceforth may be piously and religiously in a better manner instructed, trained, and informed to the true worship of God.[27]

---

22   John Barwick, *Hieronikēs, or The Fight, Victory, and Triumph of S. Paul. Accommodated to the Right Reverend Father in God Thomas Late L. Bishop of Duresme ... Together with the Life of the Said Bishop* (London: Printed for R. Royston, 1660), p. 64. This edition not listed in the USTC.

23   Mortimer, *The Library Catalogue of Anthony Higgin*, p. 2; Venn and Venn, *Alumni Cantabrigienses, Part I, Volume II*, p. 367; Joseph Thomas Fowler (ed.), *Memorials of the Church of SS. Peter and Wilfrid, Ripon, Volume II* (Durham: Andrews & Co. for the Surtees Society, 1886), p. 260.

24   J. T. Fowler, 'Ripon Minster and its Founder', *The Yorkshire Archaeological and Topographical Journal*, 2 (1873), p. 373.

25   University of Leeds Brotherton Special Collections Library, Leeds, (MS Dep 1980/1/1.0), Letters Patent of James I (known as 1st Letters Patent), re-constituting the collegiate church of Ripon, 2nd August 1604; University of Leeds Brotherton Special Collections Library, Leeds, (MS Dep 1980/1/1.1), Copy of 1st Letters Patent. With Translation (1916) by J. T. Fowler.

26   Brotherton Special Collections Library, Leeds, (MS Dep 1980/1/1.0), Letters Patent of James I, re-constituting the collegiate church of Ripon, 2nd August 1604; Brotherton Special Collections Library, Leeds, (MS Dep 1980/1/1.1), Copy of 1st Letters Patent. With Translation (1916) by J. T. Fowler.

27   Brotherton Special Collections Library, Leeds, (MS Dep 1980/1/1.0), Letters Patent of James I, re-constituting the collegiate church of Ripon, 2nd August 1604; Brotherton Special Collections Library, Leeds, (MS Dep 1980/1/1.1), Copy of 1st Letters Patent. With Translation (1916) by J. T. Fowler.

After 1604, the newly refounded Ripon Minster became an important centre for preaching and the religious education of the clergy and laity in Yorkshire and the north of England in the early Stuart period. To ensure that the people of Ripon and its surrounding area were properly instructed in religion, James I decreed that

> from henceforth and forever there may be and shall be in the said Church, one learned and erudite man, a Doctor in Theology or at least a Bachelor in Theology who shall be a first-man of the same Church and shall be called Dean of the same Church of Rippon, and that likewise hereafter may be and shall be in the same Church six other persons learned and erudite, and admitted ministers and preachers of the Word of God, who shall be the Chapter of the same Church, subject to and assisting the same Dean, and shall be called the prebendaries of the same church.[28]

The aims and objectives of the dean and chapter of the newly reconstituted collegiate church were clear: the promulgation of doctrine and theology according to the Church of England. James I appointed

> Christopher Lyndall, William Crashaw, William Barker, Robert Cooke, George Proctor, and William Bowe, learned and erudite men and ministers and preachers of the Word of God, to be in future and to be now the first and for the time being prebendaries of the Collegiate Church of Ripon aforesaid.[29]

William Crashawe, one of Ripon Minster's new prebendaries, himself owned a large library of books that numbered around 4,000 volumes.[30] These learned men constituted the chapter of Ripon Minster and worked closely with Anthony Higgin after his appointment as dean in 1608 and with his predecessor, Moses Fowler. The Charter of Refoundation made no provision for the continued education of those learned men it appointed. It is possible that Anthony Higgin

---

28   Brotherton Special Collections Library, Leeds, (MS Dep 1980/1/1.0), Letters Patent of James I, re-constituting the collegiate church of Ripon, 2nd August 1604; Brotherton Special Collections Library, Leeds, (MS Dep 1980/1/1.1), Copy of 1st Letters Patent. With Translation (1916) by J. T. Fowler.

29   Brotherton Special Collections Library, Leeds, (MS Dep 1980/1/1.0), Letters Patent of James I, re-constituting the collegiate church of Ripon, 2nd August 1604; Brotherton Special Collections Library, Leeds, (MS Dep 1980/1/1.1), Copy of 1st Letters Patent. With Translation (1916) by J. T. Fowler.

30   R. M. Fisher, 'William Crashawe and the Middle Temple Globes, 1605–15', *The Geographical Journal*, 140:1 (1974), p. 105.

bequeathed his library to the church in order to fulfil its purpose in instructing, training and informing the inhabitants of Ripon and the surrounding areas about 'the true worship of God', by providing access to his own collection of Protestant-dominated religious texts to parishioners and clergymen.

It is probable that Anthony Higgin began to collect books around the time of his arrival at the University of Cambridge in the 1570s. He seems, however, to have had little notion in the beginning of their ever becoming a collection for general use, despite his later testamentary instructions. During his time in Cambridge, first as a student and then as a preacher, Higgin purchased new and second-hand books from booksellers both in Cambridge and in London. After his appointment as rector of Kirk Deighton in Yorkshire in 1583, when Higgin moved north from Cambridge, he seems to have made regular visits to York, purchasing books from the city's booksellers during his trips. Throughout his tenure as dean of Ripon, Higgin continued to acquire books in large quantities, educating himself on theology and a wide range of other subjects that could then be passed on to his parishioners through his sermons and ministerial and pastoral activities.

Anthony Higgin wrote his final will on 12 November 1624, five days prior to his death. In it he bequeathed his books to two members of his family:

> To my cosen [William] Cleaburne and my nephew Mr [William] Lumley I give all my bookes upon condicion that they, when they die, shall give them to the Church of Rippon for a liberarie.[31]

The will gives no indication as to how many books Higgin had in his collection at the time of his death but later estimates suggest that Higgin's complete collection once numbered around 2,000 volumes.[32] As the working collection of an active preacher and clergyman, Higgin's library included a large number of Protestant works by authors of various denominations alongside works by medieval theological writers, Early Christians and

---

31   Borthwick Institute of Archives (BIA), University of York, (Archbishop Register 31, f. 238v–239r), Will of Anthony Higgin, 12 November 1624.

32   Rosamund Oates, '"Far Off from the Well's Head": The Production and Circulation of Books in Early Modern Yorkshire' in Rosamund Oates and Jessica G. Purdy (eds), *Communities of Print: Readers and their Books in Early Modern Europe* (Leiden: Brill, 2021), p. 77; Mortimer, *The Library Catalogue of Anthony Higgin*, pp. 6, 8; University of Leeds Brotherton Special Collections Library, Leeds, (Ripon Cathedral MS 35), *Catalogus librorum*, compiled by Anthony Higgin, followed by Latin exercises and commentaries on Ovid's *Heroides and Tristia*, written by Roger Phillips.

post-Reformation Catholics. It thus bears remarkable similarities to Francis Trigge's library in Grantham and suggests that readers of the two collections received a comparable education.

3 The Gorton Chest Parish Library, Manchester, Lancashire

Humphrey Chetham, the founder of five parish libraries, including the Gorton Chest, was born at Crumpsall Hall in Manchester in 1580, the sixth child of Henry and Jane Chetham.[33] A member of a relatively wealthy mercantile family, Chetham was raised in a godly household and educated at Manchester Grammar School until the age of seventeen. At school, Chetham came into contact with the sons of other wealthy merchants, with whom he began to establish the social and business networks that would serve him so well in adulthood.[34] During his lifetime, Chetham held various administrative positions that brought him considerable authority, but little financial gain. Chetham was appointed as High Sheriff of the County Palatine of Lancaster in 1634 and again in 1648, and he was named the High Collector of Subsidies granted to the king by Parliament in 1641. From the beginning of the English Civil War in 1642, Chetham established himself firmly in favour of the Parliamentarians by providing the army with substantial sums of money, as well as food and other provisions for the entirety of the war.[35] In 1643, he was appointed Treasurer of the county and given responsibility for collecting money to maintain the army, before he was appointed receiver-general of assessments in Lancashire in 1647.[36] By the time of his death in September 1653, Chetham had amassed a vast fortune, primarily accumulated through his business dealings as both a cloth merchant and a moneylender, which he charged at an interest rate of eight percent.[37]

In his will, written in 1651 and proved after his death in 1653, Chetham's large fortune was divided between three charitable endeavours. Chetham already

---

33 Alan G. Crosby, 'Chetham, Humphrey (bap. 1580, d. 1653)', *Oxford Dictionary of National Biography* (online, 2008).

34 S. J. Guscott, *Humphrey Chetham, 1580–1653: Fortune, Politics and Mercantile Culture in Seventeenth-century England* (Manchester: The Chetham Society, 2003), pp. 15, 169.

35 *Ibid.*, pp. 221–222, 237.

36 Francis Robert Raines and Charles William Sutton, *Life of Humphrey Chetham, founder of the Chetham Hospital and Library, Manchester, Volume I*, printed for the Chetham Society (Manchester: James Stewart, 1903), pp. 72–74, 132, 137–138, 158; Crosby, 'Chetham, Humphrey', *ODNB*.

37 Raines and Sutton, *Life of Humphrey Chetham, Volume I*, p. 113.

maintained twenty-two poor boys from in and around Manchester, providing them with apprenticeships, as stated in an earlier draft of Chetham's will from 1642.[38] His final will of 1651 provided for a further eighteen boys to be taken care of and educated until they were eighteen years of age. In order to facilitate this, Chetham requested that his trustees use his fortune to purchase 'the great howse, with the buildings, outhouses, courts, yards, gardens and appurtenances ... called the colledge or the colledge house' to be 'an hospitall for the habitac[i]on of the said forty poore boyes'. In addition, Chetham also bequeathed £1,000 to establish a public library, which was to be placed in 'some convenient part or place thereof or therein' the College House as well. Whilst ostensibly a 'publick librarie', this repository was restricted 'for the use of schollars and others well affected to resort unto', thus limiting the sense of publicness. Both the school and the public library are still in existence today: the school evolved into what is now Chetham's School of Music in Manchester, whilst the public library that Chetham founded in his will has remained true to its origins and is now known as Chetham's Library, Manchester. The final charitable endeavour Chetham financed was the establishment of the five parish libraries, separate from the public library, to religiously educate the 'common people' of Manchester and its surrounding areas.

The £200 that Chetham bequeathed in his will for the parish libraries was to be divided by Chetham's trustees into five portions to provide a parish library to five churches and chapels in different areas of Lancashire, with which Chetham had a personal connection. Chetham named the Collegiate Church of St Mary in Manchester (now the Cathedral), to which his family had been connected for generations, and St Peter's church in Bolton, a town where he conducted much of his business, to receive parish libraries. In addition, the chapels of Gorton, Turton and Walmsley, all three of which were in reasonably close proximity to two of Chetham's properties, were also gifted libraries by Chetham in his will.[39] The locations of these properties and the five parish libraries Chetham established can be seen in Figure 7.

Only two of the original five parish libraries founded by Humphrey Chetham survive: the Gorton Chest parish library and the Turton parish library. The library that was in Manchester Collegiate Church from 1665 was removed from the church in the 1830s and booksellers in Manchester's Shudehill area subsequently dispersed its books in the mid-nineteenth century. The current

38   Chetham's Library, Manchester, (ChetDeeds/5/12), Draft of the Last Will and Testament of Humphrey Chetham of Turton, Lancashire, Esq.
39   Chetham's Library, Manchester, (Uncatalogued), Last Will and Testament of Humphrey Chetham.

whereabouts and survival rates of the books are unknown.[40] The parish library in St Peter's church in Bolton was also disbanded in the nineteenth century. It was still in the church when Edward Baines compiled his *History of Lancashire* in 1833, but had disappeared by 1855 when Gilbert J. French published his *Bibliographical Notices*.[41] Some of the volumes from the Bolton parish library are now contained in the almery-style chest at Bolton School, which was donated to the school by James Leaver in the 1690s; how Chetham's books came to be included in the collection is unclear.[42] The library intended for the chapel at Walmsley seems never to have reached completion; its fifteen allocated books were amalgamated into the library at Turton instead.[43] The Turton parish library itself was originally in St Anne's church but is now in Turton Tower, Bolton. It is well-preserved, and a large number of books from the original collection are extant. A manuscript list of the books originally sent to the Turton library survives in the archives at Chetham's Library in Manchester.[44]

This book focuses on the Gorton Chest parish library because the original collection survives almost in its entirety and is in extremely good condition. Chetham chose to establish a library in Gorton chapel because of its proximity to his home at Clayton Hall and because he was closely connected to Richard Johnson, the chapel's godly minister. Gorton was situated less than two miles from the Clayton Hall estate that Chetham purchased with his brother George in 1620 and which Chetham made his permanent home after George's death in 1627.[45] The Clayton Hall estate had no chapel of its own and so Humphrey Chetham attended parish churches in the surrounding area, including Gorton, and became friendly with their ministers, including Johnson. The friendship between Chetham and Johnson lasted until Chetham's death. Its strength lead Chetham to describe Johnson as 'my loveinge friend' in his will and likely

---

40 Michael Perkin, *A Directory of the Parochial Libraries of the Church of England and the Church in Wales* (London: Bibliographical Society, 2004), p. 280.

41 Edward Baines, *History of the County Palatine and Duchy of Lancaster, Volume III* (London: Fisher, Son & Co., 1836), p. 64; Gilbert J. French (ed.), *Bibliographical Notices of the Church Libraries at Turton and Gorton, bequeathed by Humphrey Chetham*, printed for the Chetham Society (Manchester: Charles Simms and Co., 1855), p. 4.

42 Perkin, *A Directory of the Parochial Libraries*, pp. 143–144; Richard Copley Christie, *The Old Church and School Libraries of Lancashire* (Manchester: Charles E. Simms for the Chetham Society, New Series, 7, 1885), p. 56.

43 Perkin, *A Directory of the Parochial Libraries*, pp. 376–379.

44 Chetham's Library, Manchester, (Chet/4/5/2), Invoices of Books, 1655–1685, f. 58r.

45 Raines and Sutton, *Life of Humphrey Chetham, Volume I*, pp. 19, 22, 30; Guscott, *Humphrey Chetham, 1580–1653*, p. xiii.

prompted Chetham's request that his friend preached his funeral sermon.[46] Chetham's frequent visits to Gorton, his friendship with Johnson and Johnson's skill as a preacher and affiliation to Gorton played instrumental roles in Chetham's naming of the parish in his will as one of the areas in which he wanted to establish a library.[47]

Johnson was one of three trustees named in Chetham's will. All three men were personally connected to Chetham and they were all Protestants from Calvinist and Presbyterian confessional backgrounds, seemingly selected to foster a shared sense of religion in post-Civil War Lancashire.[48] Richard Johnson was a Calvinist with Puritan tendencies and Richard Hollinworth and John Tildsley, Chetham's other trustees, were both staunch Presbyterians. Chetham knew Richard Hollinworth through their mutual connection to Manchester Collegiate Church. The third man, John Tildsley, was married to Chetham's niece, Margaret. In collaboration with two London-based booksellers, John Rothwell and Robert Littlebury, Johnson, Hollinworth and Tildsley selected books for the five parish libraries that mirrored their own religiosity and that together promoted a Reformed Protestantism that was broadly Calvinist and Presbyterian in nature to educate the readers of Chetham's parish libraries.[49]

4　The Wimborne Minster Chained Library, Wimborne Minster, Dorset

William Stone, the man responsible for the initial donation of books to Wimborne Minster church, was the son of another William Stone, who was a schoolmaster in the town of Wimborne Minster from 1601 to 1639. The younger William Stone was born either in the last months of 1614 or in the first half of 1615; his tombstone, which provides the only surviving information about the date and place of his birth, states that Stone was in his seventieth year at the time of his death in 1685. Stone received his early education from his

---

46　Guscott, *Humphrey Chetham, 1580–1653*, p. 185; for examples of surviving correspondence between Chetham and Johnson see Chetham's Library, Manchester, (CPP/3/72, 73, 88, 95–99); Chetham's Library, Manchester, (Uncatalogued), Last Will and Testament of Humphrey Chetham.

47　Guscott, *Humphrey Chetham, 1580–1653*, pp. 184–185.

48　Matthew Yeo, *The Acquisition of Books by Chetham's Library, 1655–1700* (Leiden: Brill, 2011), p. 33; *Ibid.*, p. 266.

49　Chetham's Library, Manchester, (CPP/2/141), Letter from John Tildsley to Rev. Hollinworth at Manchester; Yeo, *The Acquisition of Books by Chetham's Library*, p. 86.

father at the grammar school in Wimborne Minster before he proceeded to St Edmund's Hall at the University of Oxford.[50] In December 1639, Stone, then a deacon, subscribed to the Thirty-Nine Articles, signing himself 'Guilelmus Stone LL Bacc:'.[51] Despite this reference to the possession of a Law degree, there is no record of William Stone ever having entered an Inn of Court. He does not appear in the Admissions Register for Gray's Inn, Lincoln's Inn, the Inner Temple, or the Middle Temple.[52] As such, the details of William Stone's legal career – if, indeed, he pursued one – remain obscure.

In a Latin indenture dated 24 December 1641, Stone was appointed by the governors of Wimborne Minster Grammar School as one of three ministers who were conjointly in charge of Wimborne Minster church. Stone retained his position until March 1645, when he was forcibly ejected from his living by Parliamentarian forces under the command of Colonel John Bingham.[53] The *Mercurius Academicus*, a Royalist newspaper, described Bingham and his officers as having 'expelled the Doctor [Stone] out of his living and banished him out of the county'.[54] Over the next sixteen years, William Stone travelled. In the early 1650s, he was in Padua, where the admissions register at the University of Padua recorded his admission *'aegrotus'* on 26 September 1652.[55] The nature and duration of his stay are unclear.

By the summer of 1660, Stone had returned to England. While in London on 11 July, Stone wrote to the governors of Wimborne Minster Grammar School, who also controlled ministerial appointments, to accept their request that he return to Wimborne and resume his duties as minister.[56] The appointment

50   J. M. J. Fletcher, *A Dorset Worthy, William Stone, Royalist and Divine (1615–1685)* (Dorchester: Dorset County Chronicle Printing Works, 1915), p. 2.

51   Oxfordshire Record Office, Oxford, (Oxf dioc, pp. e 13, p. 441), Subscription to the 39 Articles by William Stone.

52   Joseph Foster, *The Register of Admissions to Gray's Inn, 1521–1889* (London: the Hansard Publishing Union, Limited, 1889); The Society of Lincoln's Inn, *The Records of the Honourable Society of Lincoln's Inn, Volume I: Admissions from A.D. 1420–A.D. 1799* (London: Lincoln's Inn, 1896); The Inner Temple, 'The Inner Temple Admissions', *The Inner Temple Admissions Database*, (online); Henry F. MacGeagh and H. A. C. Sturgess (eds), *Register of Admissions to the Honourable Society of the Middle Temple: From the Fifteenth Century to the Year 1944, Volume I: Fifteenth Century to 1781* (London: Butterworth & Co. Ltd., 1949).

53   Dorset History Centre, Dorset, (PE-WM/GN/2/2/7), Appointments of Ministers, 1633–1665; Joseph Foster (ed.), *Alumni Oxonienses: The Members of the University of Oxford, 1500–1714, Volume I – Early Series* (Oxford: Parker & Co., 1891), p. 124; Fletcher, *A Dorset Worthy*, p. 3.

54   *Mercurius Academicus*, 2 March 1645, pp. 109–110.

55   Biblioteca del Seminario Vescovile, Padua, (ms. 634), *Registro in cui dal 1614 fino all'anno 1765 moltissimi inglesi, scozzesi e irlandesi scrissero i loro nomi e cognomi.*

56   Dorset History Centre, Dorset, (PE-WM/GN/2/2/4), Appointments of Schoolmasters with recommendations of suitable candidates, 1600–1760.

was confirmed by indenture on 1 February 1661, but was relatively short-lived.[57] On 6 July 1663, Stone was appointed Principal of New Inn Hall at the University of Oxford. This appointment necessitated his resignation as minister of Wimborne Minster church, as one of the requirements of the minister was a continual residence in Wimborne.[58] New Inn Hall was strongly associated with Puritanism from the mid-seventeenth century and several clergymen who were ejected after the Restoration had previously studied there: the *Oxford Dictionary of National Biography* lists nine such men, including the brothers Richard and William Alleine, Samuel Fisher and William Bartlet.[59] Stone's tenure there, in light of the college's strong Puritan tone, is surprising: he was in Europe throughout the Interregnum and only returned at the Restoration, which does not suggest strong Puritan inclinations or tendencies on Stone's part.

In 1684, William Stone resigned as Principal of New Inn Hall and briefly returned to Dorset, perhaps to live with his sisters. By April 1685, however, Stone had returned to Oxford.[60] He died there in June 1685 and was buried in the College chancel of St Michael's church.[61] The town of Wimborne Minster featured heavily in his will, demonstrating Stone's connection to the area. He provided two shillings apiece to one hundred poor people residing in the parish, and he stated that after the death of his siblings, to whom Stone left his lands in Wimborne Minster, the profits of those lands were to benefit the poor living in St Margaret's Hospital in Wimborne Minster. The remainder of Stone's wealth was to be 'bestowed on some charitable uses as Mr [Obadiah] Walker now Master of University Colledge shall direct'.[62]

Before his death, Stone gave verbal instructions for his collection of patristic texts and other religious volumes to be sent to the church of Wimborne

57   Dorset History Centre, Dorset, (PE-WM/GN/2/2/7), Appointments of Ministers, 1633–1665.
58   Andrew Clark (ed.), *The Life and Times of Anthony Wood, antiquary, of Oxford, 1632–1695, described by Himself, Volume I: 1632–1663* (Oxford: Clarendon Press, 1891), p. 478; Fletcher, *A Dorset Worthy*, p. 6.
59   H. E. Salter and Mary D. Lobel (eds), 'St. Peter's Hall' in *The Victoria History of the County of Oxford: Volume 3, the University of Oxford* (London: Victoria County History, 1954), pp. 336–338; Stephen Wright, 'Alleine, Richard (1610/11–1681)', *Oxford Dictionary of National Biography* (online, 2008); Stephen Wright, 'Alleine, William (1613/14–1677)', *Oxford Dictionary of National Biography* (online, 2008); Stephen Wright, 'Fisher, Samuel (1605/6–1681)', *Oxford Dictionary of National Biography* (online, 2008); Stephen Wright, 'Bartlet, William (1609/10–1682)', *Oxford Dictionary of National Biography* (online, 2008).
60   Andrew Clark (ed.), *The Life and Times of Anthony Wood, antiquary, of Oxford, 1632–1695, described by Himself, Volume III: 1664–1681* (Oxford: Clarendon Press, 1892), pp. 108–109.
61   *Ibid.*, p. 144.
62   The National Archives, Kew, (PROB 11/380/483), Will of William Stone, Clerk of Oxford, Oxfordshire, 27 July 1685.

Minster. His will makes no specific mention of his books, but an inventory drawn up in the immediate aftermath of his death demonstrates that Stone was a wealthy man when he died. His books, most of which were religious, were estimated to be worth £120 in total – the volumes that had been sent to Wimborne Minster church already were valued at £43 7s. 4d.[63] They included fifty-one volumes by Early Christians, twenty-three by Protestant authors (including Calvinists and Presbyterians), six by medieval theological writers and three by post-Reformation Catholics. They were likely originally purchased for his own personal and professional use as they were written almost exclusively in Latin.

These patristic texts and other religious works arrived at Wimborne Minster church in 1685. A court case against Dr Stephen Fry, the executor of Stone's will, was brought before the Attorney General in 1695 because Dr Fry was not perceived to be executing Stone's will in a timely manner. Fry's answer to the Attorney General stated that Stone's patristic texts were sent to the church by verbal agreement between Stone and an unknown second party: Stone 'did before credible witnesses declare that the Church of Wimborne in the county of Dorsett should have all the Fathers & Commentators whereof he should dye possessed'.[64] How Stone intended for the books to be kept and used by the church is unclear. There is no mention either in Stone's will or in the court case of an explicit intention, or indeed any intention whatsoever, to create a library. Nor is there a discussion in either document of why the books were sent to the church in the first place, making it difficult to ascribe an educational impetus to this donation. Instead, it may be inferred that despite the amount of time that Stone spent in Oxford during his career, he had a personal attachment to his hometown of Wimborne Minster, which may have influenced his decision to endow its church with part of his library.

Ten years later, in 1695, local gentleman Roger Gillingham augmented the book collection given to Wimborne Minster by Stone, donating a total of eighty-two volumes comprised of a combination of over thirty volumes purchased specifically for inclusion in the parish library and books from his own personal library collection. Gillingham's will shows that he and William Stone knew one another, though the origins of their acquaintance are unclear, especially as it appears that Stone did not enter any of London's Inns of Court. In his will, Gillingham referred to Stone as 'my late good friend' and it is possible (though not provable) that Stone and Gillingham discussed the possibility of founding a library in Wimborne Minster church before Stone's death. Their

---

63   The National Archives, Kew, (C8/446/3), Attorney General v Fry, 1695.
64   *Ibid.*

friendship, combined with Gillingham's ownership of property in the town of Wimborne Minster, may have influenced Gillingham's decision to add his books to Stone's patristic collection and augment the library in the church. In bequeathing his own books to the church in 1695, Gillingham made it plain that he perceived Stone's books as a library already and that he intended to enlarge the collection of books 'given to that Library by my late good friend Mr William Stone'.[65]

Roger Gillingham was born in approximately 1626, the second son of Richard Gillingham, a gentleman, in either Pamphill or Cowgrove in Dorset, both of which are situated less than three kilometres west of the town of Wimborne Minster.[66] Roger Gillingham matriculated to All Souls' College, Oxford at the age of fourteen in 1640 and on 27 November 1654, at the age of approximately twenty-eight, he was admitted to The Middle Temple Inn of Court.[67] After being called to the Bar in June 1662, Gillingham was later promoted first to Bencher of the Inn on 26 November 1680, where he sat as a member of the Inn's governing body, or parliament, and then to the position of Reader in autumn 1686.[68] Gillingham reached the apogee of his career at the Inn when he was appointed as the Temple's Treasurer for 1694, during which he presided over the parliaments of the Inn.[69] Gillingham's rise through the Middle Temple provided him with the means to purchase large numbers of books and build a sizeable personal library, part of which was donated after his death to the church in Wimborne Minster. Roger Gillingham died in late 1695 and requested that his body 'be decently interred with the least charge and trouble and vain solemnity as it may conveniently be done in the Temple Church there to expect the joyfull resurrection'.[70] He was buried in the Temple Church vault on 3 January 1696.[71]

---

65   The National Archives, Kew, (PROB 11/430/238), Will of Roger Gillingham of Middle Temple, Middlesex, 25 February 1696.

66   In his will dated 1695, Roger Gillingham refers to himself as having been born in both Cowgrove and Pamphill, *Ibid.*; Joseph Foster (ed.), *Alumni Oxonienses: The Members of the University of Oxford, 1500–1714, Volume II – Early Series* (Oxford: Parker & Co., 1891), p. 568.

67   Charles Trice Martin (ed.), *Minutes of Parliament of the Middle Temple, Volume III: 1650–1703* (London: Butterworth & Co. Ltd., 1905), p. 1071.

68   J. Bruce Williamson, *The Middle Temple Bench Book*, 2nd edition (London: Chancery Lane Press, 1937), pp. xix–xx, 18.

69   MacGeagh and Sturgess, *Register of Admissions to the Honourable Society of the Middle Temple*, p. 155; Williamson, *The Middle Temple Bench Book*, p. xxiii.

70   The National Archives, Kew, (PROB 11/430/238), Will of Roger Gillingham of Middle Temple, Middlesex, 25 February 1696.

71   Williamson, *The Middle Temple Bench Book*, p. 139; Foster, *Alumni Oxonienses, Volume II – Early Series*, p. 568.

Roger Gillingham's will demonstrates his wealth at the time of his death and indicates the depth and strength of his connection to the town of Wimborne Minster. Gillingham held stocks in the East India Company, the Royal Africa Company and Lechmere's saltpetre works, in addition to having extensive holdings in Bedfordshire, Dorset and Middlesex, including several houses in and around London.[72] Gillingham provided funds for several charitable endeavours that included money for the building of a school at Pamphill Green (one of his two prospective birthplaces slightly west of the town of Wimborne Minster) and lodgings for a Schoolmaster there. Gillingham also left funds for the erection of four almshouses adjacent to the school for 'poor indigent men who shall be widowers or single persons never married' and another four almshouses for 'poor indigent women who shall be widows or single persons never married to live in and inhabit'. Finally, Gillingham bequeathed money to be distributed as alms to the general poor of the town of Wimborne Minster.[73] A clear focus on providing for the education and wellbeing of the town and inhabitants of Wimborne Minster and its surrounding areas was evident in Gillingham's will.

Such philanthropic endeavours suggest that the library in Wimborne Minster church was another way in which Gillingham desired to improve the intellectual and religious landscape of Dorset in the last years of the seventeenth century. He bequeathed the books to the church 'for the use of the now erected Library of Wimborne Minster' in an undated codicil to his will of 2 July 1695.[74] Gillingham left to the library in Wimborne Minster church 'all the books I lately bought for that purpose', as well as 'soe many of my best folio 4to and 8vo Bookes which are not Law Bookes as are fittest and most usefull for that Library as my said Executors shall estimate and Judge', up to the value of £10.[75] The bequest of eighty-two volumes included works by authors including Anabaptists, Latitudinarians, post-Reformation Catholics, Protestants of various confessional identities, classical writers and even some post-Restoration Anglicans, perhaps suggesting that he wished to provide himself and his readers with a broad-based knowledge of Protestantism. In his will, Gillingham listed thirty-four volumes by sixteen different authors that he bought specifically for the library. They included Walton's Polyglot Bible; Arthur Lake's *Sermons with some religious and divine meditations*; two volumes

---

72 London Metropolitan Archives, London, (P93/DUN/267), Register of Marriages October 1653–August 1656; City of Westminster Archives, Westminster, (SML/PR/3/2), Marriages 16 October 1653–29 May 1669.

73 The National Archives, Kew, (PROB 11/430/238), Will of Roger Gillingham of Middle Temple, Middlesex, 25 February 1696.

74 *Ibid.*

75 *Ibid.*

of Gilbert Burnet's *History of the Reformation*, which defended the English Reformation and earned Burnet the gratitude of both Houses of Parliament; Sir Walter Raleigh's *History of the World*; and Archbishop Laud's *A Relation of the Conference between William Laud and Mr Fisher, the Jesuit*, an attempt by Laud to refute the allegations of popery being levelled against him.[76] Other books purchased by Gillingham specifically for the library included the extant works of Plutarch, in two volumes, and those of Plato, also in two volumes. Further, the three volumes of William Howell's *An Institution of General History* and the royalist cleric Henry Hammond's *Works* in four volumes were also listed.[77] The books that Gillingham purchased specifically for the library thus had a strong religious and historical focus, whilst also featuring works by classical authors.

Additional books for the library in Wimborne Minster Chained Library were drawn from Gillingham's own collection and placed into the library after his death. These volumes evidence Gillingham's personal reading interests and included Edward Herbert's *The Life and Raigne of King Henry the Eighth*, Thomas Fuller's *The Church-History of Britain* and the extant works of Cicero.[78]

---

76 Brian Walton, *Biblia Sacra, Polyglotta, Volumes I–V* (London: Thomas Roycroft, 1653–1657), Wimborne Minster Chained Library, shelfmarks I11–I17. These editions not listed on the USTC; Arthur Lake, *Sermons with some religious and divine meditations* (London: William Stansby for Nathaniel Butter, 1629). Wimborne Minster Chained Library, shelfmark D14. USTC 3014201; Gilbert Burnet, *History of the Reformation of the Church of England, Volumes I and II* (London: T. H. for Richard Chiswell, 1679 and 1681). Wimborne Minster Chained Library, shelfmarks D10 and D11. These editions not listed in the USTC; Walter Raleigh, *The History of the World* (London: George Lathum and Robert Young, 1634). Wimborne Minster Chained Library, shelfmark K4. USTC 3017553; William Laud, *A Relation of the Conference between William Laud and Mr Fisher, the Jesuit* (London: Richard Badger, 1639). Wimborne Minster Chained Library, shelfmark D16. USTC 3020501 and 3020493.

77 Plutarch, *Quae extant omnia* (Frankfurt: Daniel and David Aubry and Clemens Schleich, 1620). Wimborne Minster Chained Library, shelfmarks I3 and I4. These editions not listed in the USTC; Plato, *Opera quae extant omnia* (Lausanne: Henr. Stephanus, 1578). Wimborne Minster Chained Library, shelfmarks I1 and I2. These editions not listed in the USTC; William Howell, *An Institution of General History, Volume I* (London: Printed for Henry Herringman et al., 1680). Wimborne Minster Chained Library, shelfmark D1. This edition not listed in the USTC; William Howell, *An Institution of General History, Volume II* (London: Printed for Thomas Bassett et al., 1680). Wimborne Minster Chained Library, shelfmark D2. This edition not listed in the USTC; William Howell, *An Institution of General History, Volume III* (London: Miles Flesher, 1685). Wimborne Minster Chained Library, shelfmark D3. This edition not listed in the USTC; Henry Hammond, *The Works of the Reverend and Learned Henry Hammond, Volumes I–IV* (London: Printed for R. Royston, 1684). Wimborne Minster Chained Library, shelfmarks D4 and D5. These editions not listed in the USTC.

78 Edward Herbert, *The Life and Raigne of King Henry VIII* (London: Printed by E. G. for Thomas Whitaker, 1649). Annotated copy in Wimborne Minster Chained Library, shelfmark D15. USTC 3047333; Thomas Fuller, *The Church-History of Britain* (London: Printed

Other works taken from Gillingham's personal library included William Chillingworth's *The Religion of the Protestants, A Safe Way to Salvation*, Thomas Rogers' *Treatise upon Sundry Matters Contained in the 39 Articles* and Robert Sanderson's *The Obligation of Conscience to Attend the School of Theology at Oxford*.[79] Again, a religious and historical leaning can be detected amongst these titles, suggesting that Gillingham believed them to be appropriate reading for his intended library users and that he found these genres of personal interest as well. Together, they demonstrate a clear royalist and Anglican persuasion.

Many of the books that Stone and Gillingham donated to Wimborne Minster church were common in other scholarly libraries of the late seventeenth century. The works of Eusebius, Saint Augustine and Saint Clement of Alexandria in Stone's collection, for example, could also be found in the libraries of five seventeenth-century clergymen and laymen surveyed by David Pearson, including William Bassett (an Anglican clergyman), Stephen Charnock (a nonconformist clergyman) and Sir Norton Knatchbull (an MP, private scholar and member of a gentry family). Similarly, authors such as Walter Charleton, Jeremy Taylor, James Ussher, Henry Hammond, William Camden, William Dugdale and Thomas Fuller, all of whom feature in Gillingham's donation to the library, are also in the collections of several of the men Pearson examined, demonstrating the popularity of these authors in the second half of the seventeenth century.[80]

---

for John Williams, 1655). Wimborne Minster Chained Library, shelfmark I7. This edition not listed in the USTC; Marcus Tullius Cicero, *Opera quae extant omnia, Volumes I–IV* (London: J. Dunmore, 1681). Wimborne Minster Chained Library, shelfmarks I5 and I6. These editions not listed in the USTC.

79 William Chillingworth, *The Religion of the Protestants, A Safe Way to Salvation* (Oxford: Leonard Lichfield, 1638). Wimborne Minster Chained Library, shelfmark K19. USTC 3019801; Thomas Rogers, *Treatise upon Sundry Matters Contained in the 39 Articles* (London: William Hunt, 1658). Wimborne Minster Chained Library, shelfmark unknown. This edition not listed in the USTC; Robert Sanderson, *The Obligation of Conscience to Attend the School of Theology at Oxford* (London: Robert Littlebury, 1686). Wimborne Minster Chained Library, shelfmark M7. This edition not listed on the USTC.

80 David Pearson, 'Patterns of Book Ownership in Late Seventeenth-Century England', *The Library*, 11 (2010), pp. 141–153.

CHAPTER 6

Parish Library Users and Usability

The vast majority of early modern parish libraries founded in England between 1558 and 1709 were established for use by a mixed clerical and lay readership. Repositories were sometimes founded exclusively for use by the clergy, but only rarely were they established with the 'common people' solely in mind. A library's intended audience often impacted its placement in its parish church. A library intended for use by the laity, or a mixed clerical and lay readership, was more likely to be placed in the more public parts of a parish church: the nave, for example, or an upper room in the church. Collections intended primarily for the use of the clergy, on the other hand, could be kept in parts of the church with stricter access restrictions, such as the vestry, or even, occasionally, in the vicarage or parsonage attached to the church. Thus, even where intended users are not explicitly stated in a library's foundation documents, it may be possible to infer who a collection was supposed to be read by based on its location.

In 1693, the Cambridge historian Thomas Baker noted in his papers that George Dunscomb, rector of St Peter's church in Wooton Wawen, 'gave some good books for the use of the parishioners' upon his death in 1652.[1] Dunscomb's stipulation that the books were for the use of the laity, with no mention of the incumbent minister or local clergy, was unusual. The only other notable case of parish libraries established for lay users were those founded by Humphrey Chetham in Manchester by his will of 1653. As mentioned in the previous chapter, Chetham's intended users of his parish libraries were 'the common people'. Chetham himself used this phrase to describe his intended audience, in order to distinguish the parish libraries' readership from the 'schollars and others well affected' that were the intended users of the public library also established by his will.[2] These intended users were reflected in the 'godly English Bookes, such as Calvins, Prestons, and Perkins workes' that Chetham's will stipulated were to be included in the parish libraries, and that will be explored in greater detail in chapter 8. The surviving invoices for the books sent to the Manchester,

---

1 Burnett Hillman Streeter, *The Chained Library: A Survey of Four Centuries in the Evolution of the English Library* (New York: Burt Franklin, 1931), p. 292.
2 Chetham's Library, Manchester, (Uncatalogued), Last Will and Testament of Humphrey Chetham.

© KONINKLIJKE BRILL NV, LEIDEN, 2024 | DOI:10.1163/9789004363717_010

Bolton, Gorton, Turton and Walmsley parish libraries demonstrate that a range of works that would have held significant appeal to the 'common' readers of Chetham's parish libraries were included in each collection.[3] Commentaries upon the Bible, copies of sermons given by eminent preachers and the 'collections of prayers and handbooks on godly living and godly dying' that Ian Green has demonstrated common people were interested in, formed the basis of these collections.[4] The books in all five of the parish libraries Chetham established were written exclusively in the vernacular, making them accessible to all literate people and not limiting their usage to those with the grammar school education required for reading Latin volumes.

Several parish libraries established across the period 1558 to 1709 had a contrasting intended readership comprised exclusively of clerics, irrespective of whether their founders were clergymen or laymen. The library at Ipswich provides an early example of a parish library established exclusively for the use of the clergy. In 1599, William Smarte, a draper, bequeathed both his printed and his manuscript books to his local church as part of a library 'to be used ther by the com[m]on preacher of the sayd towne for the tyme beinge or any other precher mynded to preache in the saide p[ar]ishe church'.[5] Smarte's intended clerical readers are thereby evident, as are those of Lady Anne Harington, who established a library in the parish church of Oakham in Rutland. According to the seventeenth-century antiquary and author James Wright, Lady Anne Harington, widow of the staunchly Protestant John Harington, first Baron Harington of Exton, gave approximately 200 volumes to All Saints church in 1616, 'for the use of the Vicar of that Church, and accommodation of the Neighbouring Clergy'.[6] Wright's assertion is supported by a wooden board in the vestry of the church that states that 'Lady Harington gave a small library for the use of the vicar'.[7]

The practice of donating books for the incumbent, local and visiting clergy continued later in the seventeenth century as well, as evidenced by

---

3   Chetham's Library, Manchester, (Chet/4/5/2), Invoices of Books, 1655–1685, f. 55r, f. 55v, f. 58r, f. 59r.

4   Ian Green, *Print and Protestantism in Early Modern England* (Oxford: Oxford University Press, 2000), p. 36.

5   The National Archives, Kew, (PROB 11/94/340), Will of William Smarte of Ipswich, Suffolk, 2 November 1599.

6   James Wright, *The History and Antiquities of the County of Rutland* (London: Printed for Bennet Griffin, 1684), p. 52. This edition not listed on the USTC.

7   Michael Perkin, *A Directory of the Parochial Libraries of the Church of England and the Church in Wales* (London: Bibliographical Society, 2004), p. 309.

the elaborately decorated parish library in St Mary the Virgin church in Langley Marish, Buckinghamshire. In his will of 1631, Sir John Kedermister of Langley Park bequeathed 'for the benefit as well of ministers of the said towne [Langley Marish] and such other in the Countie of Bucks ... those books which I have already prepared ... together with soe many more as shall amount to the summe of Twenty pounds'.[8]

Clerical parish libraries were also founded by both clergymen and laymen in the last decades of the seventeenth century. In the 1670s, William White, a Church of England clergyman who served as Master of Magdalen College from 1632 until his ejection by parliamentary commissioners in 1648, bequeathed 'all my Bookes and Papers' to St Mary the Virgin church in Marlborough, Wiltshire. White's will, proved July 1678, stated that his collection was 'for the use of Mr Yate Vicar of St Maries in that Towne [Marlborough] and of his Successore forever'.[9] The library established in St Peter's church in the town of More in Shropshire in 1680 by Sir Richard More was given to the churchwardens 'for their better instruction and the increase of their learning and knowledge and for the encouragement of a good orthodox and preaching ministry of Gods word in the sayd parish'.[10]

The libraries of Assington, Milden and Lawshall were all founded by clergymen in the fifteen years from 1690 to 1704. Assington parish library was established in St Edmund's church according to the will of the Reverend Thomas Alston in 1690. Alston's will gave his books 'unto the vicar incumbent of Assington ... and to his successors in the said vicaridge for ever for and towards a standing library'.[11] Just after the turn of the eighteenth century, the libraries of Milden (1703) and Lawshall (1704) were established in Suffolk by clergymen. In his will of 1703, William Burkitt, rector of Milden from 1678 to his death, gave 'my library Books ... for the benefit of succeeding Incumbents'.[12] Burkitt's donation comprised approximately 2,000 volumes, which Perkin has described as being 'easily the largest of the Suffolk libraries'.[13] Just three

8   The National Archives, Kew, (PROB 11/159/567), Will of Sir John Kidderminster of Langley Marish, Buckinghamshire, 7 May 1631.

9   Hugh de Quehen, 'White, William (*bap.* 1604, *d.* 1678)', *Oxford Dictionary of National Biography* (online, 2008); The National Archives, Kew, (PROB 11/357/182), Will of William White, Clerk of Pusey, Berkshire, 1 July 1678.

10   Shropshire Archives, Shropshire, (P193/S/1/1), More Church Library Trust Deed with rules; Perkin, *A Directory of the Parochial Libraries*, p. 287.

11   The National Archives, Kew, (PROB 11/403/170), Will of Thomas Alston, Clerk of Assington, Suffolk, 31 January 1691.

12   The National Archives, Kew, (PROB 11/473/499), Will of William Burkitt, Vicar and Lecturer of Dedham, Essex, 18 December 1703.

13   Perkin, *A Directory of the Parochial Libraries*, p. 284.

months later, Burkitt's contemporary Stephen Camborne, rector of Lawshall from 1681 until his death in 1704, bequeathed his books to his church of All Saints. His will gave 'all my Library of Bookes to my Successor in this living of Lawshall to continue here forever'.[14]

What can be seen from the various libraries established by a combination of clergymen and laymen is that parish libraries for the sole use of the clergy continued throughout the period and were not always restricted to men who shared the same profession as their intended users. It may be possible to infer that, like the parish library established in More in 1680, the men who founded parish libraries for the exclusive use of the clergy were hoping to improve the religious education of incumbent ministers, who would then disseminate the messages of their books to their parishioners through their preached sermons and pastoral activities.

Other early modern parish library founders evidently desired to reach as broad an audience as possible with the books they gave to their local parish churches. At the very end of the sixteenth century, the library established by Francis Trigge in St Wulfram's church in Grantham, Lincolnshire was, according to its foundation indenture, for the use of the 'cleargie and others beinge inhabitants in or nere Grantham and the souke thereof'.[15] There are no user registers for many early modern parish libraries, which makes tracing actual users virtually impossible. The Francis Trigge Chained Library is no exception and so it is difficult to know who actually used the collection in its earliest years. However, the Hall Book of Grantham, 'the earliest surviving book of minutes recording the discussions and decisions of the alderman's Court of the Corporation of Grantham', demonstrates that the library was still in use in the mid-seventeenth century.[16] In December 1642, it was recorded that Edward Skipwith, a Grantham-born merchant, gave fifty shillings to the town of Grantham. Skipwith gave the annual interest on these fifty shillings, which amounted to four shillings, to the upkeep of the library:

---

14   The National Archives, Kew, (PROB 11/473/499), Will of Stephen Camborne, Rector of Lawshall, Suffolk, 29 March 1704.

15   Lincolnshire Archives, Lincolnshire, (Grantham St Wulfram Par/23/1), Documents relating to the Trigge Library: Agreement. For a brief description and discussion of the surrounding area of Grantham, the 'Soke', see Edmund Turnor, *Collections for the History of the Town and Soke of Grantham* (London: W. Bulmer and Co. for William Miller, 1806), p. ix.

16   John B. Manterfield, *Newton's Grantham: The Hall Book and Life in a Puritan Town* (Grantham: Grantham Civic Society, 2014), p. 9.

> Out of his love and well wishing to learning, and the better to make &
> incourage the viccars of Grantham (in the winter & colde tyme of the
> yeare to follow theire studies) ... I will that ytt [the four shillings] ... be
> allowed yearlie for the maintaineing of a fire within the librarie'.[17]

Such a donation makes clear that the library was still in use almost fifty years
after its foundation. It also suggests that the library was more popular with
clerical users than lay ones, though Skipwith's wording implies that even the
clergy needed prompting in the winter months.

The intended users of some early modern parish library foundations were
less clear. It seems that Anthony Higgin had a similar intended audience of
both clergymen and laymen in mind for the collection he donated to Ripon
Minster in 1624. Higgin's will stated that his cousin, William Cleaburne, and
Higgin's nephew, William Lumley, could use the books before they were given
to Ripon Minster.[18] A large proportion of Higgin's complete collection of
around 2,000 volumes was theological and, as both his cousin and his nephew
were clergymen, it is probable that Higgin thought his books would be of some
use to his relatives. Considering his long incumbency as dean of Ripon, the
church's educational objectives set out in James I's letters patent and the seem-
ing lack of books for the clergy to educate themselves with, it is probable that
Higgin intended for his books to serve as religiously instructive for clerical and
lay readers after his relatives were finished with them. It is likely that, once
in the Minster, the collection that had once been a working library for Higgin
became an important resource for the Yorkshire clergy and educated members
of the laity – those with a grammar school education or better – in a similar
way to Tobie Matthew's collection at York Minster.[19]

The intended users of the library collection at Swaffham in Norfolk,
donated in 1679 after the testamentary bequest of Clement Spelman, are similarly obscure, but they seem to suggest a varied clerical and lay readership.
In his will, Spelman gave 'to the Towne of Swaffham all my Bookes to the end
a Librarie may be constantly kept there'.[20] Considering Spelman stipulated

---

17   Bill Couth, *Grantham During the Interregnum: The Hallbook of Grantham, 1641–1649*
      (Woodbridge: The Boydell Press for Lincoln Record Society, 1995), p. 21.

18   Borthwick Institute of Archives (BIA), University of York, (Archbishop Register 31,
      f. 238v–239r), Will of Anthony Higgin, 12 November 1624.

19   Rosamund Oates, *Moderate Radical: Tobie Matthew and the English Reformation* (Oxford:
      Oxford University Press, 2018), p. 169; Jennifer Richards, *Voices and Books in the English
      Renaissance: A New History of Reading* (Oxford: Oxford University Press, 2019), p. 76.

20   The National Archives, Kew, (PROB 11/363/68), Will of Clement Spelman of Saint Mary
      Magdalene, Norfolk, 15 May 1680.

that his books were to be given to the town, it seems unlikely that he intended to restrict his readership merely to either clerics or laymen, and that he was instead keen to enable a more general access to his collection.

Like the Ripon Minster and Swaffham corpuses, William Stone's intended users for his collection of patristic texts and other religious volumes that he gave to Wimborne Minster church in its namesake town in Dorset are unclear. Roger Gillingham, who augmented Stone's collection, provided an explicit statement in his will as to who he intended to use the books in the library collection. They were to be used and read by 'the clergy ... but alsoe ... the Gent shopkeepers and better sort of Inhabitants in and about the Towne of Wimborne'.[21] Unfortunately, as is the case for most parish libraries of this period, there are no surviving records documenting by whom, or even whether, the books were used after their placement in the library of Wimborne Minster church.

The intended users of early modern parish libraries sometimes impacted upon the usage and security restrictions that founders placed on their collections. These restrictions tended to manifest in the form of instructions for the library to be kept in a locked room or for the books to be chained to their shelves. In some cases, such as the Francis Trigge Chained Library, both of these things happened. Theoretically, the declaration in the library's foundation indenture that the 'cleargie and others beinge inhabitants in or nere Grantham and the souke thereof' could use the books should have made the library at St Wulfram's easily accessible by the vast majority of the literate locality.[22] However, the stipulation in the same document that the door to the library was to be kept locked significantly reduced the physical accessibility of the books. Only four men (the alderman, the two vicars of the church and the schoolmaster of Grantham) were permitted keys and if none of them could be found when a reader wished to consult the library, then it could not be used.[23] Access to the library was therefore by *de facto* permission of one of the four men who held a key. Trigge was not the only library founder to make these kinds of stipulations: William Smarte's library, founded at Ipswich a year after Trigge's collection at Grantham, was also ordered to be kept in a locked room. Smarte's will, proved 2 November 1599, instructed that 'the doore [was] to have two sufficiente lockes and keyes there to remayne in the Custodye of

21   The National Archives, Kew, (PROB 11/430/238), Will of Roger Gillingham of Middle Temple, Middlesex, 25 February 1696.

22   Lincolnshire Archives, Lincolnshire, (Grantham St Wulfram Par/23/1), Documents relating to the Trigge Library: Agreement.

23   *Ibid.*

the minister of the parishe for the time beinge and the other to be kepte by the churchwardens'.[24]

A locked library door was not the only way in which founders sought to safeguard the security of their books. Chaining books to their shelves was a not-uncommon practice. In total, Perkin noted twenty-five libraries established between 1558 and 1709 that have been recorded as containing chained books at some point within this period.[25] In addition to being kept in a locked room, the orders and constitutions put in place by Francis Trigge for the maintenance of the library after its establishment stipulated that 'the bookes be kept continually bownd with convenient chaines to the staples devised', increasing the security of the books to prevent them from being removed from the library.[26] In 1593–1594, the parish library established in St Martin's church (now the Cathedral) in Leicester 'receaved 7 bookes that were chaynedd in the Church and geven by Symon Craftes', as recorded in the churchwardens' accounts.[27]

The practice was still in use fifty years later in the mid-seventeenth century. The library John Clungeon established at Southampton in 1640 was also to be 'chaned with iron chanes and kepte in an iron grate' for security purposes.[28] The volumes in the Gorton Chest parish library established by Chetham and compiled by his trustees in the 1650s were likewise all chained to an iron rod that ran horizontally between the two levels of shelves within the almery book chest, discussed in more detail in the second half of this chapter, following Chetham's testamentary instructions.[29]

---

24   The National Archives, Kew, (PROB 11/94/340), Will of William Smarte of Ipswich, Suffolk, 2 November 1599.

25   Perkin, *A Directory of the Parochial Libraries*, pp. 83–107.

26   Lincolnshire Archives, Lincolnshire, (Grantham St Wulfram Par/23/3), Documents relating to the Trigge Library: Schedule of Orders and Constitutions.

27   Thomas North (ed.), *The Accounts of the Churchwardens of S. Martin's, Leicester, 1489–1844* (Leicester: Samuel Clarke, 1884), p. 137.

28   The National Archives, Kew, (PROB 11/198/73), Will of John Clungeon, Haberdasher of London, 9 November 1646.

29   Chetham's Library, Manchester, (Uncatalogued), Last Will and Testament of Humphrey Chetham.

FIGURE 11   The Gorton Chest Parish Library
REPRODUCED WITH THE KIND PERMISSION OF CHETHAM'S LIBRARY,
MANCHESTER

Even at the end of the seventeenth century and into the beginning of the eighteenth century, parish library founders were still ordering their books to be chained to the shelves for their security and preservation. In 1695, Roger Gillingham's will instructed that the books he bequeathed to the Library were not to be given to the church until Stone's books 'be chained to their places as is usefull in other public Libraryes and chaines and places be provided for such Bookes as I hereby give'. For this purpose, Gillingham bequeathed £10 to the churchwardens of the Minster 'towards the provideing [of] the said chaines for the bookes'.[30] The volumes remain chained to their shelves in Wimborne Minster church today, though the chains themselves are more recent replacements.

In 1703, Edward Smith, vicar of Sleaford in Lincolnshire, gave to his parish church a small collection of approximately fifteen books. The chaining of these

---

30   The National Archives, Kew, (PROB 11/430/238), Will of Roger Gillingham of Middle Temple, Middlesex, 25 February 1696.

books to their desk was recorded by the antiquarian Edward Trollope in 1872. Trollope noted that

> in the passage leading from the chancel to the vestry [in the church of St Denys] is a curious old oak reading desk, containing a collection of books of Divinity, each of which is fastened to a rod by a chain sliding upon it, long enough to allow of its being placed on any part of the desk above, but intended to prevent its abstraction.[31]

This method of securing books had, by the beginning of the eighteenth century, been in use for over two hundred years, demonstrating not only the value of the books themselves, but also the value that founders placed on their library collections and thus, implicitly, their importance in the local community as repositories of religious education.

1   Housing a Parish Library and Their Locations within Parish Churches

The method of storing the books of a parish library collection often depended on its size. Larger collections of more than approximately fifty volumes were likely to be housed on bookshelves. Smaller collections of less than approximately fifty volumes could be stored in book chests or cupboards in the body of the church. The Gorton Chest parish library provides one of the best surviving examples of early modern chest libraries in England, despite some later alterations (see Figure 11 above). Built in the almery style of a book cupboard on wooden legs, the chest was altered in the mid-nineteenth century: its reading ledge was removed sometime between 1865 and 1885, meaning that the hinges on the doors needed to be moved from the sides to the bottom, so that they could open out horizontally to form a makeshift reading desk. The legs were also shortened to increase comfort for sitting and reading.[32] Although not a parish library in any sense, the slightly later example of an almery book chest that was given to Bolton School by James Leaver in the 1690s remains *in situ* and largely unaltered; it 'reproduces in essentials the older model of Gorton'.[33]

Post-Reformation parish libraries were often housed in one of four locations within or adjacent to a parish church: in the body of the church, in an upper

---

31   Edward Trollope, *Sleaford, and the Wapentakes of Flaxwell and Aswardhurn, in the County of Lincoln* (London: Kent and Co.; Sleaford: William Fawcett, 1872), p. 165.

32   Hillman Streeter, *The Chained Library*, pp. 302–303.

33   *Ibid.*, p. 46.

room of the church, in the vestry, or in the parsonage. There was a somewhat symbiotic relationship between a library's intended audience and its location with a parish church, meaning that the placement of a library collection within its church was influenced by its prospective users and affected its accessibility. The libraries intended primarily for the clergy tended to be less easily accessible than those intended for a combined clerical and lay readership.

The clerical parish libraries of Langley Marish (1613), Assington (1690), Milden (1703) and Lawshall (1704) provide excellent examples of collections that were the sole purview of the clergy and thus were all housed either in purpose-built rooms or else in a separate building to the parish church itself, to which only the clergy had access. Langley Marish parish library, for example, is situated in a room built adjacent to the parish church of St Mary the Virgin, specifically for the purpose of housing Kedermister's book collection.[34] The room itself is perhaps the most singularly impressive library room of the early modern period, having been described by E. Clive Rouse in the 1940s as 'the most remarkable seventeenth-century parish library in England'.[35] Lavishly decorated with ornate Jacobean panelling and paintings of the library's founder, Sir John Kedermister and his family that hide the books from view and prevented their clerical readers from forgetting to whom they were indebted for the use of this collection, this room holds a library that was to be used by ministers in the town of Langley Marish and the county of Buckinghamshire more generally. This limited readership explains the lack of need for a more publicly accessible space to house the collection.[36]

It seems to have become more common for parish libraries intended for use by clerics to be housed in a parsonage, vicarage, or rectory, at the end of the seventeenth century and at the beginning of the eighteenth century. Examples of such collections include those of Assington (1690), which was housed in the vicarage; Milden (1703), which was located in the parsonage; and Lawshall (1704), which was situated in the rectory.[37] Examined from a purely logistical point of view, the placement of these libraries within the incumbent's residence is unsurprising, as it would have allowed ministers uninhibited access to the collection within their own home and prevented its use by other members of the clergy or lay parishioners.

---

34   Jane Francis, 'The Kedermister Library: an Account of its Origins and a Reconstruction of its Contents and Arrangement', *Records of Buckinghamshire*, 36 (1994), pp. 62–85; E. Clive Rouse, 'The Kederminster Library', *Records of Buckinghamshire*, 14 (1941–6), pp. 50–66; Perkin, *A Directory of the Parochial Libraries*, pp. 259–262.

35   Rouse, 'The Kederminster Library', p. 66.

36   The National Archives, Kew, (PROB 11/159/567), Will of Sir John Kidderminster of Langley Marish, Buckinghamshire, 7 May 1631.

37   Perkin, *A Directory of the Parochial Libraries*, pp. 124, 263, 284.

The repositories founded for clergy and laity alike were usually in the more public spaces of a parish church. This wasn't, however, always the case, as the library established in Swaffham suggests. Despite being given to the town seemingly for use by both the clergy and the laity, the collection was housed first in the Priest's Chamber above the church vestry before being moved to the vestry itself early in the eighteenth century, making public access potentially problematic.[38] Nevertheless, an examination of the locations of other parish libraries within their churches does more positively reflect the relationship between intended users and library placement. Despite its security measures, the Francis Trigge Chained Library was ostensibly intended for a combined readership, its foundation indenture explicitly stated that the library was to be placed in 'a verie convenient place in a chamber over the Sowth porch' of St Wulfram's church.[39] This room was nominally accessible to all. Construction on the south porch of the church was completed sometime after 1300, slightly later than the church itself, and seems at some point in its history to have served as accommodation for the vicar of the church.[40] The Bishop of Lincoln's consent to use this room for the library was granted on 8 November 1599 and preparations to convert it into a suitable space for the library were undertaken at the cost of the Alderman and clergy, as set out in the indenture.[41] That Trigge and his co-founders were willing to spend their own money on the building work and the effort required to transform the room into a suitable space for the library demonstrates the level of importance they placed on the library and their commitment to providing the people of Grantham with a useable and accessible educational repository.

The library appears to have fallen into disrepair sometime after the mid-seventeenth century and its restoration in the nineteenth century demonstrates the renewed sense of importance that was attached to the library by its then-custodians as something of cultural value, despite the books by then being less topically relevant than they had once been. When Thomas Frognall Dibdin visited the library in the late 1830s, he found it a 'desolate and deserted spot. The windows were yet broken; the floor was yet cracked; the chains ... yet

---

38   *Ibid.*, p. 365.

39   Lincolnshire Archives, Lincolnshire, (Grantham St Wulfram Par/23/1), Documents relating to the Trigge Library: Agreement.

40   Nikolaus Pevsner and John Harris, *The Buildings of England: Lincolnshire*, 2nd edition (New Haven and London: Yale University Press, 1989), pp. 316–317; Angela Roberts, 'The Chained Library, Grantham', *Library History*, 2 (1971), p. 89.

41   Lincolnshire Archives, Lincolnshire, (Grantham St Wulfram Par/23/2), Documents relating to the Trigge Library: Consent of the Bishop of Lincoln; Lincolnshire Archives, Lincolnshire, (Grantham St Wulfram Par/23/1), Documents relating to the Trigge Library: Agreement.

dangling about the books'.[42] The damaged floor and leaking roof were repaired by Samuel Rudd in 1881 and the library was given a 'thorough restoration' in 1894. As part of this restoration, a local bookbinder in Grantham rebound numerous books, many of the chains were repaired and the bookshelves that still hold the books today were partially reconstructed from the original library furniture.[43] Today, the library remains in its original room over the south porch, accessible only via a narrow spiral staircase.

Similarly, the books 'for the com[m]on use of the said parrish' that the Manchester-based clerk Henry Bury bequeathed £10 to purchase in 1640 were to be housed in 'a convenient place of their owne' within the collegiate church.[44] Originally intended to establish a parish library in the collegiate church in Manchester, this library seems never to have come to fruition, possibly as a result of the English Civil War that consumed the 1640s. The failure to establish this library may have partially prompted Humphrey Chetham to bequeath one of his five parish libraries to the collegiate church just over a decade later, in 1653. Chetham's libraries were to be 'chained uppon deskes, or to bee fixed to the pillars or in other convenient places' within their parish churches, their publicly accessible location reflecting their intended use by the 'common people'.[45]

Like the Francis Trigge Chained Library in Lincolnshire, the Wimborne Minster church library in Dorset was also housed in a re-purposed upper room of the parish church. The churchwardens set about making the former Treasury above the fourteenth-century sacristy a suitable space for the library almost immediately upon the arrival of William Stone's collection of patristic texts at the church in 1685.[46] The substantial sums of money paid to various individuals for the conversion of the former Treasury and the construction of the library space demonstrates again a considerable level of commitment

42   Thomas Frognall Dibdin, *A Bibliographical Antiquarian and Picturesque Tour in the Northern Counties of England and in Scotland, Volume 1* (London: C. Richards, 1838), pp. 48–49.

43   John Glenn, 'A Sixteenth-Century Library: the Francis Trigge Chained Library of St Wulfram's Church, Grantham' in Daniel Williams (ed.), *Early Tudor England: Proceedings of the 1987 Harlaxton Symposium* (Woodbridge: The Boydell Press, 1989), p. x; Hillman Streeter, *The Chained Library*, pp. 297–298.

44   The National Archives, Kew, (PROB 11/171/190), Will of Henry Bury, Clerk of Bury, Lancashire, 24 May 1636.

45   Chetham's Library, Manchester, (Uncatalogued), Last Will and Testament of Humphrey Chetham.

46   Charles Mayo, *A History of Wimborne Minster* (London: Bell and Daldy, 1860), p. 56; Thomas Perkins, *Wimborne Minster and Christchurch Priory* (London: George Bell & Sons, 1902), p. 54; John Newman and Nikolaus Pevsner, *The Buildings of England: Dorset* (London: Yale University Press, 2002), p. 462.

to the prospective educational purpose and usability of the collection. The churchwardens' accounts for Wimborne Minster church listed charges including £6 15s. paid to Dennis Smith 'for one hundred of Deal boards for ye Library', suggesting that the wardens may have been constructing bookshelves on which to house Stone's collection. The accounts also included charges such as £2 4s. 4d. paid 'for bringing the books from Oxford' and £5 5s. 9d. paid to John Mackrill 'for timber and work about the Library'.[47] In total, the conveyance of Stone's books from Oxford and the construction and cleaning of the Library cost the churchwardens £34 13s. 6d., a not inconsiderable sum. The location of the books in the former Treasury made its usage by clergy and laity alike possible, and Roger Gillingham, who augmented the collection in the 1690s for a broad lay and clerical audience, was happy to add his books to the pre-existing collection with no requirement for them to be moved beforehand.

2   Conclusion

A mixed clerical and lay readership was intended by the founders of the vast majority of post-Reformation parish libraries in early modern England from the second half of the sixteenth century through to the beginning of the eighteenth century. This had a direct impact on the location of these book collections within their resident parish church: they were removed from the more spiritual locations that had housed their pre-Reformation religious counterparts and placed in the more secular, more accessible parts of the church instead, areas like upper rooms or purpose-built add-ons to the church structure. However, those collections that continued to be established solely for the use of the clergy could still be housed in less accessible areas: the vestry, the vicarage or the parsonage, for example. How the books for a parish library were chosen and how their collections were compiled will be examined in the following chapter.

---

47   Dorset History Centre, Dorset, (PE-WM/CW/1/42), Account Book, 1640–1696.

CHAPTER 7

Collecting Books and Compiling a Collection

Collecting practices and purposes had a significant impact on the nature of a collection. Books found their way into parish libraries through various means in the early modern period: libraries could be established by monetary gift or by the bequest of specific books, and some were subsequently augmented by later gifts of money or donations of certain volumes. The nature of a library's foundation often dictated who was responsible for selecting the books that comprised a library's collection. If a library was established through the gift or bequest of books from an individual donor, for example, the collection would be chosen *de facto* by the donor. Thus, the collection was more likely to closely resemble their reading interests or educative aims. If a library was founded by a gift of money to purchase books for a collection, the books would likely be selected and bought by a third party, meaning that the original donor had less control over the volumes that went into their collections and were reliant upon their chosen executors to carry out their wishes. There are numerous examples of both of these types of library foundations amongst the surviving parish libraries of early modern England.

1 Establishing Libraries by Monetary Gift or Bequest

Libraries founded by a gift or bequest of money were less common than those established by a gift of books. In such cases, the alignment between the donor's vision and the final library collection was often dependent upon the degree to which the donor's proxies adhered to the donor's intentions.

The Francis Trigge Chained Library in Grantham, founded in 1598, provides an early example of a parish library established by financial gift. The theologically diverse collection of this library was purchased from Cambridge, using the donation of £100 from Trigge himself, with the confessionally divided people of Grantham and its surrounding areas in mind. The books were intended for use by the clergy, in the preparation of their sermons and publications in defence of the established religion, and by the laity in search of an education. Prior to the re-discovery of the foundation documents for this library in the Borough archives in 1957, many nineteenth-century historians assumed that the library

© KONINKLIJKE BRILL NV, LEIDEN, 2024 | DOI:10.1163/9789004363717_011

collection was a portion of Trigge's personal collection of books.[1] The agreement that provided for the library's establishment stated that Francis Trigge 'hath provided or intendeth to provide at his like costs ... books of divinitie and other learninge to the value of one hundreth poundes or thereaboutes', which suggests that Trigge provided the money for the books, as opposed to the books themselves from his own collection.[2]

Evidence for the compilation of the original Francis Trigge library collection is at best circumstantial, but an examination of the collection (to be conducted more thoroughly in the following chapter) reveals that Trigge's vision of a repository useful to both the clergy and the laity was somewhat observed. In the 1980s, John Glenn asserted that the Trigge library collection was bulk-bought from Cambridge by Francis Trigge's agent, who selected and purchased the books for this repository 'without much discernment'.[3] Glenn concluded that the resulting corpus was not 'an attempt to bring together a library as useful and comprehensive as possible for the provincial clergy who would be its main users'.[4] This is not, in fact, the case. The provenance of the books themselves certainly speaks to them having been bought in Cambridge and possibly in London, many of them second-hand. The bindings of several books in the collection are identifiable as the work of known Cambridge binders, such as the Dutchman Garrett Godfrey, who was appointed one of three University stationers in 1534, and Thomas Thomas, who was a Cambridge scholar and binder also appointed Printer to the University in 1583.[5] Books bound by other Cambridge or London-based binders, who are known only by their initials, are also in the Francis Trigge Chained Library collection.[6] However, there is no direct evidence for the involvement of an agent in the purchasing of books for the library and the foundation indenture makes no mention of how the books were to be purchased or where they were to be purchased from.

Nor does the diversity of the collection likewise suggest that it was compiled without conscious thought given to its prospective readers, when considered

---

1   John Glenn, 'A Sixteenth-Century Library: the Francis Trigge Chained Library of St Wulfram's Church, Grantham' in Daniel Williams (ed.), *Early Tudor England: Proceedings of the 1987 Harlaxton Symposium* (Woodbridge: The Boydell Press, 1989), pp. 61, 63.

2   Lincolnshire Archives, Lincolnshire, (Grantham St Wulfram Par/23/1), Documents relating to the Trigge Library: Agreement.

3   Glenn, 'A Sixteenth-Century Library', p. 66.

4   *Ibid.*, p. 65.

5   *Ibid.*, p. 64; R. B. McKerrow (ed.), *A Dictionary of Printers and Booksellers in England, Scotland and Ireland, and of Foreign Printers of English Books 1557–1640* (London: Blades, East & Blades, 1910), pp. 264–265; E. Gordon Duff, *A Century of the English Book Trade* (London: Blades, East & Blades, 1905), pp. 56–57.

6   Glenn, 'A Sixteenth-Century Library', p. 64.

in comparison to other parish library and clerical library collections. On the contrary, the multiplicity of book topics and of authors' confessional identities in the collection of the Trigge library was reflective of the religiously disparate populace in Grantham, its surrounding areas and Lincolnshire more generally. Further, it also represented the acknowledgement by Trigge and his associates of the need to provide the local clergy with the necessary information to refute Catholicism and promote the Church of England. Such an argument contradicts that made by Glenn, that there was no clear purchasing agenda and no attempt to provide a coherent and useful selection of books intended specifically for educating the clergy and laity of Grantham.

The collection was primarily comprised of theological works by Protestant authors that included Calvinist sermons, Lutheran propaganda and an array of Protestant Biblical commentaries, all of which were useful for improving the religious knowledge of the clergy, as well as any lay readers. The inclusion of multiple different commentaries on some Books of the Bible – the inclusion of five different commentaries on both the Psalms and Genesis in the collection, for example, was cited by Glenn as evidence of disinterested collecting practices – perhaps reflected instead the 'fascination' that these books held for people in the last years of the sixteenth century.[7] Similar duplications of different commentaries on the Bible can be seen in Ripon Minster parish library, which included several commentaries on the Book of Revelation and the Book of Psalms, for example.

These volumes of Reformed theology sat alongside works by medieval and post-Reformation Catholic authors that were also of use to the parish clergy. Such works included Catholic canon law written in the late fifteenth and early sixteenth centuries and Biblical commentaries and doctrinal works by post-Reformation Catholics. This combination of Protestant and Catholic works was prominent in many other contemporary and later collections.[8] The library of Archbishop Tobie Matthew, for instance, contained works by various Reformers including John Calvin, Theodore Beza, Martin Bucer and Heinrich Bullinger alongside the works of notable post-Reformation Catholics such as Robert Bellarmine, Hector Pintus and William Allen, an English Catholic cardinal. These and other, similar works provided the archbishop with a broad religious understanding. Such variation in the context of late Elizabethan and early Jacobean Lincolnshire suggests a heightened religious awareness on the part of Trigge and his associates. This awareness may have influenced them and

---

7   *Ibid.*, p. 65; Ian Green, *Print and Protestantism in Early Modern England* (Oxford: Oxford University Press, 2000), p. 116.
8   David Pearson, 'The Libraries of English Bishops, 1600–1640', *The Library*, 14 (1992), p. 229.

their book-buying agent to provide a theologically diverse collection for use by the clergy in rejecting Catholicism and promoting established religion, as was the case elsewhere. That the material collection of the Trigge library reflects this religious awareness is evidence of a strong alignment between Trigge's vision and the final corpus of books.

The vagueness that surrounds the person (or persons) responsible for compiling the Francis Trigge Chained Library collection was not always present in library foundations. Humphrey Chetham's will, for example, in which he provided for the establishment of five parish libraries in and around Manchester, was meticulous in its detail. In his will, Chetham named a total of twenty-four men as his trustees. Three of those trustees, Richard Johnson, Richard Hollinworth and John Tildsley, all of whom were clerics, were also nominated to have particular responsibility for selecting the books for both the five parish libraries and for the public library Chetham founded, which survives today as Chetham's Library in Manchester. Richard Johnson was a Calvinist with puritan inclinations and Richard Hollinworth and John Tildsley were both 'very zealous' Presbyterians. In selecting men of different theological outlooks as his trustees, Matthew Yeo has argued that Chetham had a 'plan for religious and political reconciliation' in post-Civil War Lancashire that he hoped to see spread across England in the 1650s, after the political and religious upheaval of the 1640s.[9] Whilst there is no explicit evidence to support this, what is clear is that Chetham had a desire to spread godly religion to the readers of the parish libraries and deliberately chose men who had previously been in conflict to work together to establish those libraries. This may suggest a desire to encourage the kind of cooperation Yeo asserted was Chetham's goal, but what cannot be doubted was Chetham's intention, brought to fruition by his trustees, to create libraries for the 'common people' that had widespread appeal to Protestants of different denominations.

Chetham was clear in his will that the parish libraries were to contain 'godly English Bookes, such as Calvins, Prestons, and Perkins works, comments of annotac[i]ons uppon the bible or some parts thereof, or such other bookes as the said Richard Johnson, John Tildsley, and Maister Hollinworth ... thinke most proper for the edificac[i]on of the common people'.[10] Despite their differing confessional identities, Johnson, Hollinworth and Tildsley worked together to fill the parish libraries with religious books of various genres, the overwhelming majority of which were by authors of Protestant confessional identities.

---

9   Matthew Yeo, *The Acquisition of Books by Chetham's Library, 1655–1700* (Leiden: Brill, 2011), pp. 33–34; S. J. Guscott, *Humphrey Chetham, 1580–1653: Fortune, Politics and Mercantile Culture in Seventeenth-century England* (Manchester: The Chetham Society, 2003), p. 266.
10   Chetham's Library, Manchester, (Uncatalogued), Last Will and Testament of Humphrey Chetham.

As such, the three men brought Chetham's vision of the parish libraries as providers of a Reformed religious education to the laity of Manchester to completion.

In order to get a sense of the scale of this achievement, it is necessary to consider the deep divisions between Chetham's appointed trustees in a little more detail. Richard Johnson, 'Chetham's closest friend', was 'a sound doctrinal Calvinist'. Yeo has noted that 'Calvinism was a strong influence on both Humphrey Chetham's and Richard Johnson's faiths'.[11] Johnson's Puritan inclinations were attested to by his refusal to wear a surplice and by various other offences, with correspondence between Johnson and Chetham demonstrating the latter's sympathies with Johnson's protestations.[12] As a Calvinist, 'zealous royalist and cavalier', Johnson was deprived of both his fellowship of Manchester Collegiate Church and his living at Gorton and subsequently imprisoned during the attempt to establish Presbyterian government in Lancashire in 1646, an effort in which Johnson's co-trustees Richard Hollinworth and John Tildsley were instrumental.[13] Upon his release, Johnson moved to London and later became Master of the Temple Church until 1659, when he returned to Manchester to take up a position as the first librarian of Chetham's public library.[14]

Richard Hollinworth was a noted religious author and leading Presbyterian who was acquainted with Chetham through his role as an influential divine in the area and by virtue of his position as Chaplain and Fellow of Manchester Collegiate Church from 1643.[15] Hollinworth was described by the seventeenth-century nonconformist minister Adam Martindale as one of the 'very zealous (usually called Rigid) Presbyterians' who were intrinsically involved in the implementation of a Scottish-style Presbyterianism in Lancashire.[16] A member of the Bolton *classis* from 1646 and later the Manchester

---

11   Yeo, *The Acquisition of Books by Chetham's Library*, p. 39.

12   Francis Robert Raines and Charles William Sutton, *Life of Humphrey Chetham, founder of the Chetham Hospital and Library, Manchester, Volume I*, printed for the Chetham Society (Manchester: James Stewart, 1903), p. 39; for examples of surviving correspondence between Chetham and Johnson see Chetham's Library, Manchester, (CPP/3/72, 73, 88, 95–99).

13   James Crossley (ed.), *The Diary and Correspondence of Dr. John Worthington, Volume II, Part I* (Manchester: Charles Simms and Co. for the Chetham Society, 1855), p. 239 n. 1.

14   Charles Trice Martin (ed.), *Minutes of Parliament of the Middle Temple, Volume III: 1650–1703* (London: Butterworth & Co. Ltd., 1905), p. 1138; Yeo, *The Acquisition of Books by Chetham's Library*, p. 38.

15   John Venn and J. A. Venn (eds), *Alumni Cantabrigienses, Part I, Volume II* (Cambridge: Cambridge University Press, 1922), p. 396.

16   Richard Parkinson (ed.), *The Life of Adam Martindale* (Manchester: Charles Simms and Co. for the Chetham Society, 1845), pp. 62–63.

classis, Hollinworth was a constant advocate for Presbyterianism in Lancashire even after the failure of the Presbyterian experiment. He produced numerous favourable tracts on the subject and played a central role in the composition of various statements by Lancashire Presbyterian ministers in the 1650s. In 1654, two years before his death, Hollinworth was appointed as a commissioner for ejecting 'scandalous and ignorant ministers and schoolmasters in Lancashire' in the parliamentary ordinance of 29 August.[17]

John Tildsley was the husband of Humphrey Chetham's niece, Margaret, and another of Lancashire's highly influential Presbyterians. Tildsley, like Hollinworth, was heavily involved in the attempt to establish Presbyterian government in the area in 1646. In 1648, Tildsley signed the 'Harmonious Consent' of the ministers of Lancashire, to which Hollinworth also subscribed.[18] Written in support of the Westminster Assembly and Presbyterian government in England, the 'Harmonious Consent' condemned toleration as something akin to the 'puting of a sword into a mad man's hand', and praised the Assembly's Confession of Faith as 'orthodox, sound, solid, substantial, and pious, but also to be very ful, and in especial maner useful for these times'.[19] Tildsley's dedication to 'the utter extirpation of Independencie, root and branch', as asserted by Martindale, is reflected in a surviving letter that Tildsley wrote to his co-religionist Richard Hollinworth in April 1655. In the letter, Tildsley was careful to stress his desire to avoid 'erroneous' and 'Independent' authors in the parish library collections.[20]

Considering the prominent role both men played in the Presbyterian experiment of 1646 that lost Johnson his livelihood, working with Tildsley and Hollinworth cannot have been easy for Johnson; the disagreements in correspondence between the trustees, preserved in the Accessions Registers for Chetham's libraries, certainly suggest that the cooperation was not always harmonious.[21] One particular example of these disagreements is centred on the portion of the £200 provided by Chetham allotted to each parish library collection. At a meeting of the trustees in October 1654, over a year after

17   Yeo, *The Acquisition of Books by Chetham's Library*, p. 36.

18   John Tildsley, *The True Relation of the Taking of the Town of Preston, by Colonell Seatons Forces from Manchester* (London: J. R. for Luke Fawn, 1642). USTC 3052212.

19   Unknown author, *The Harmonious Consent of the Ministers of the Province within the County Palatine of Lancaster* (London: printed for Luke Fawne, 1648), pp. 6, 12. USTC 3046480; Hollinworth and Tildsley's names can be seen on p. 26.

20   Parkinson, *Life of Adam Martindale*, p. 63; Chetham's Library, Manchester, (CPP/2/141), Letter from John Tildsley to Rev. Hollinworth at Manchester.

21   Yeo, *The Acquisition of Books by Chetham's Library*, p. 34; Chetham's Library, Manchester, (Chet/4/11/1), Accession Register, 1655–1880.

Chetham's death, the trustees in attendance apportioned the money left by Chetham, who had given no instructions as to how the money was to be divided. The trustees seem to have allocated funds to the different parish libraries according to the size of the town in which the library was to be located: the bigger the area, the more money apportioned to that particular library. The trustees allocated £70 to purchase books for Manchester parish library, £50 for books for Bolton parish library, £30 each for Gorton and Turton and £20 for the library at Walmsley.[22]

John Tildsley, whose position as the vicar of Deane in Bolton led to him being given responsibility for the Bolton, Turton and Walmsley parish libraries, was absent from the meeting, which may account for his outrage at what he deemed to be the insufficient funds allocated to the three parish libraries in his charge. Tildsley seemingly felt that the sums allocated to these libraries, and to Bolton in particular, would not be sufficient to provide adequate books to the libraries. In the letter he wrote to Hollinworth in April 1655, Tildsley asserted that he had 'little stomach to meddle at all in the business' if the sums allocated to Bolton, Turton and Walmsley were to stand. Tildsley even went so far as to state that 'if I die without a son I should be willing to add to it [the library] at my decease'.[23] Hollinworth's reply to Tildsley's letter, if he ever wrote one, does not survive, and the funds apportioned to each library remained the same despite Tildsley's protestations. Tildsley's displeasure at what he perceived to be such a small sum being allocated to the three libraries he was charged with likely related to his desire to eradicate Independency. His indignation at not being able to supply as many Protestant texts for the parish libraries as he wished demonstrates his commitment to the provision of edifying and educational books for the people of Bolton, Turton and Walmsley.

Whilst Chetham was extremely specific in naming the people responsible for buying the books for his libraries, he left no testamentary instructions as to where or from whom the books for either the public library or the parish libraries were to be purchased. The books that went into the parish libraries were primarily purchased between the mid-1650s and the mid-1660s from Robert Littlebury and John Rothwell, two London-based booksellers. Littlebury's print shop was located at the Unicorn in Little Britain.[24] Rothwell specialised in theological texts, with print shops located first in St Paul's Churchyard and then in

---

22   Chetham's Library, Manchester, (Chet/1/2/1), Minute Book, 6 Dec 1653–16 Apr 1752.
23   Chetham's Library, Manchester, (CPP/2/141), Letter from John Tildsley to Rev. Hollinworth at Manchester.
24   Simon Bradley and Nikolaus Pevsner, *London 1: The City of London* (London: Yale University Press, 2002), p. 534.

Goldsmith's Row, Cheapside.[25] The Temple Church, where Johnson was Master in the late 1650s, was in reasonably close proximity to Little Britain, Cheapside and St Paul's Churchyard, three areas of London in which numerous booksellers had shops. Therefore, Johnson, at least, was likely to have had knowledge of both Littlebury and Rothwell prior to being appointed as one of Chetham's trustees, which may be why he used these booksellers to provide texts for both the public library and the parish libraries.[26] The precise roles of Littlebury and Rothwell in the selection processes for the parish libraries is unclear. Only one delivery of English books for the parish libraries from Rothwell's bookshop was recorded, in May 1657; Littlebury provided the rest, in addition to the vast majority of the works now in the public library.[27] Matthew Yeo, in his analysis of the public library collection that is now Chetham's Library, argued that Littlebury was given a large amount of freedom in choosing to provide the public library with whichever books he deemed fit and appropriate, and with the best of what was available in the new and second-hand book markets.[28] It is possible that Littlebury was afforded a similar level of autonomy in suggesting and supplying books for the parish libraries, though the closeness with which the confessional nature of the parish library collections reflected the confessional identities of the trustees implies that they had a considerable influence over them.

Certainly the books for the five parish libraries were selected with the precise intention of achieving Chetham's vision of facilitating the 'edificac[i]on of the common people'.[29] The focus on Protestant theology demonstrated by the surviving invoices of books purchased for all five parish libraries is clear: the works of Protestant authors of different confessional identities dominated and works that opposed Protestantism were notable by their omission. The broad exclusion of Catholic works in the collections of the five parish libraries appears to have been a conscious decision on the part of Johnson, Hollinworth and Tildsley. The reasons for this are unclear. Likely, it was a combination of factors, including the lack of mention of these books in Chetham's will, their desire to adhere to Chetham's testamentary wishes, their mindfulness of their intended audience of 'common people' and the relatively small amount of money they were working with for the parish libraries, though there is no firm

25   Henry R. Plomer, *A Dictionary of the Booksellers and Printers who were at work in England,
      Scotland and Ireland from 1641 to 1667* (London: Blades, East and Blades, 1907), pp. 157–158.
26   Yeo, *The Acquisition of Books by Chetham's Library*, pp. 84–85.
27   Chetham's Library, Manchester, (Chet/4/5/2), Invoices of Books, 1655–1685, f. 17r.
28   Yeo, *The Acquisition of Books by Chetham's Library*, pp. 49–50.
29   Chetham's Library, Manchester, (Uncatalogued), Last Will and Testament of Humphrey
      Chetham.

evidence to support this. For the parish libraries, the trustees focussed on vernacular religious works by prominent Protestant authors of primarily Calvinist and Presbyterian confessional identities. These books included expository works of doctrine, general theology, books of practical divinity and printed sermons, in addition to Biblical commentaries and Church histories, thus fulfilling Chetham's instructions.

The delivery dates of books to Manchester for the five parish libraries demonstrate how long it took for these libraries to be compiled and placed in their respective churches. Deliveries of English religious books from London to Manchester began in August 1655, almost two years after Chetham's death in September 1653. Because Littlebury, at least, was providing books for the public library and the five parish libraries at the same time, he often combined deliveries for the two different types of libraries, as indicated on the relevant invoices.[30] English books were delivered to the trustees on 2 August and 20 September 1655, 7 May and 28 July 1657, 30 June 1659 and 1 October 1666.[31] As books were still being delivered in 1666, this must mean that at least one of the parish libraries (in this case, that at Bolton) was yet to be finalised by that date. The books do not seem to have been collected on a library-by-library basis: invoices for the books list the titles sent by date and separate manuscript lists were made of which titles were sent to which parish libraries.[32] The Gorton Chest parish library was the first of Chetham's parish libraries to be placed in its intended church in 1655, followed by Turton (with some of the books originally intended for Walmsley included) in 1659. A parish library was placed in Manchester Collegiate Church in 1665 and Bolton-le-Moors was the last location to receive its library in 1668, fifteen years after Chetham's death.[33] The reasons for the length of time taken are not clear, though it could have been the result of the trustees' desire to source precisely the right books to align with Chetham's intentions.

The library established at the behest of a Mrs Eleanor Crowle in Hull in Yorkshire in the 1660s provides another example of a parish library founded by monetary gift from the second half of the seventeenth century. Eleanor Crowle

---

30 Chetham's Library, Manchester, (Chet/4/5/2), Invoices of Books, 1655–1685, f. 6r, f. 8r, f. 17r, f. 19r.

31 *Ibid.*, f. 6r, f. 8r, f. 17r, f. 19r, f. 58r, f. 58v.

32 See Chetham's Library, Manchester, (Chet/4/5/2), Invoices of Books, 1655–1685, for the full selection of invoices for books delivered and for the lists of books sent to each parish library.

33 Michael Perkin, *A Directory of the Parochial Libraries of the Church of England and the Church in Wales* (London: Bibliographical Society, 2004), pp. 60–61, 143–144, 216–217, 280, 376, 378–379.

was the wife of George Crowle, who was the mayor of Kingston-Upon-Hull. The Crowle family appear to have played a prominent role in the administration of the town in the East Riding of Yorkshire in the sixteenth and seventeenth centuries. In 1661, George and Eleanor Crowle founded a hospital for the poor in Kingston-Upon-Hull. Despite having a large family of their own, the Crowles provided money for the hospital in their will, 'as a standing revenue for its future support'.[34] In addition, Eleanor Crowle gave money to the church of Holy Trinity on three separate occasions for the purchasing of books for a library. Her first donation was in 1665, when she gave £5 to the church 'to be disposed of in books for ye use of the Church'. This was followed by a donation of £20 in 1666 and a further donation of £5 in 1667.[35] Eleanor Crowle, it seems, also provided books of her own, in addition to the sums of money she gave to the church. Her name is listed as one of the first donors of books to the library and Latin verses in praise of Eleanor as 'the first and greatest benefactress to this library' were in the church in the late eighteenth century.[36]

2   Establishing Libraries by Gifting or Bequeathing Specific Books

It was far more common for parish libraries in early modern England to be established with either a gift or testamentary bequest of books than it was for them to be founded by financial donations. Examples of libraries established with specific texts can be found across the sixteenth and seventeenth centuries. In these instances, the donor and their collecting practices evidently had a bigger impact on the nature of the collection than when the library was established by monetary gift, irrespective of how closely their proxies attempted to align instructions with purchases of books.

In 1616, Lady Anne Harington, widow of John, 1st Baron Harington of Exton in Rutland, gifted a collection of books to All Saints church in Oakham, establishing a library. The books Lady Harington gave to the parish church of Oakham had probably previously formed part of the collection of books owned by her son, John (d. 1613/1614), the rest of whose collection was given to Sidney Sussex College, Cambridge, by Lady Harington.[37] John Harington's collection in its entirety mirrored his academic pursuits and strengths and his

34   John Tickell, *A History of the Town and County of Kingston upon Hull, From its Foundation in the Reign of Edward the First to the Present Time* (Hull: Thomas Lee & Co., 1798), pp. 760–761, *passim*.

35   Perkin, *A Directory of the Parochial Libraries*, p. 245.

36   Tickell, *A History of the Town and County of Kingston upon Hull*, p. 793.

37   Anne L. Herbert, 'Oakham Parish Library', *Library History*, 6:1 (1982), pp. 1, 6.

religious interests. John, who was particularly proficient in languages and had a strong grasp of logic, philosophy and mathematics, had spent time studying at Cambridge before improving his education in France and Italy at his father's instigation.[38] As such, Anne Herbert has shown, the collection of books that Lady Anne Harington donated to both Oakham parish church and Sidney Sussex College in 1616 were accumulated by John during his time studying in Cambridge and in the course of his travels on the continent. Many of John's academic texts were donated to Sidney Sussex College. These included works of history, mathematics, grammar and criticism and poetry, amongst others. The vast majority of the volumes gifted to Oakham parish church were theological texts in Greek and Latin, indicating John's proficiency in those languages.[39] The seventeenth-century antiquary and author, James Wright, described the collection given to Oakham parish church as 'consisting chiefly of Fathers, Councils, School-men, and Divines', indicating conscientious collecting practices on John Harington's part, and the deliberate selection of appropriate texts from his collection for Oakham parish church and its vicar by John's mother, Lady Anne.[40]

In a similar manner, the collection of theology books bequeathed to Ripon Minster in Yorkshire by its dean, Anthony Higgin, constituted just part of Higgin's complete collection, which numbered around 2,000 volumes at the time of his death in 1624. Included within this collection were 758 theological works that were catalogued by Higgin himself prior to his death, ostensibly in preparation for their eventual donation to Ripon Minster as a library.[41] The collection as a whole was varied and wide-ranging, encompassing histories and chronicles, bibliographical works such as Conrad Gesner's *Bibliotheca Universalis* and medical books by authors as diverse as Hippocrates and Timothy Bright, the sixteenth-century physician turned clergyman. In addition, there were numerous books on geography and astronomy as well as several law books in English and Latin.[42] The scope for the practical application of the vast majority of these volumes reinforces Higgin's deliberate collecting practices. His decision to donate such a significant number of religious and theological works to the Minster signals his intention for the collection to

---

38   Herbert, 'Oakham Parish Library', p. 6; Richard Stocke, *The Churches Lamentation for the Losse of the Godly* (London: John Beale, 1614), pp. 67–68. USTC 3006143 and 3006141.
39   Herbert, 'Oakham Parish Library', pp. 6–11.
40   James Wright, *The History and Antiquities of the County of Rutland* (London: Printed for Bennet Griffin, 1684), p. 52. This edition not listed on the USTC.
41   Jean E. Mortimer, *The Library Catalogue of Anthony Higgin: Dean of Ripon (1608–1624)* (Leeds: Chorley and Pickersgill, 1962), pp. 6, 8.
42   *Ibid.*

function as a working clerical library, employed to educate its readers for their personal improvement and for the development of their preaching and ministerial occupations. The diverse character of the theology section of Higgin's collection may be accounted for by the variety of sources from which Higgin acquired his books. They not only reflected Higgin's interests as a collector, but also the interests of those friends and colleagues who gifted Higgin their own books and from whom Higgin occasionally purchased books.

Higgin frequently travelled to York, London and Cambridge, the main centres of book production and distribution in England, and purchased the volumes he desired whilst there. During several trips to York in the 1580s and 1590s, Higgin purchased numerous volumes that later formed part of the theology collection he gave to Ripon Minster. In 1585, for example, he purchased a copy of Saint Athanasius's *Opera* and in 1589, he bought Willem van der Lindt's *Panoplia Evangelica* in York. Higgin again travelled to York in 1590 and whilst there purchased a copy of Conrad Kling's *Loci communes theologici*, the title page of which he inscribed with the note, '*Anth: Higgin empt. Ebor. Aprilis 16. 1590*'.[43] After his appointment as dean of Ripon in 1608, Higgin made numerous visits to London. On a visit in 1593, Higgin purchased Bishop Theodoret of Cyrus's *De providentia sermones x* and on a 1609 visit, he bought Francisco de Toledo's *In sacrosanctum Ioannis Evangelium commentarii ....*[44] Higgin also visited London in January and December 1622. During his January visit, Higgin purchased Nicolaus de Gorran's *In Acta Apostolorum*, inscribing it '*Ant: Higgin Londini 8 solidi, Januarii 20 1622*'. During his December visit, Higgin bought

---

43   Saint Athanasius, *Athanasii magni Alexandrini episcopi, graviss. scriptoris, et sanctiss. martyris, opera, in quatuor tomos distributa* (Basel, 1564). Annotated copy in University of Leeds Brotherton Special Collections Library, shelfmark Ripon Cathedral Library XIII.C.17/q. USTC 613803; Willem Van der Lindt, *Panoplia evangelica: sive De verbo Dei evangelico libri quinque ...* (Paris: Jean Le Blanc, Guillaume Julian and Michel Julian, 1564). Annotated copy in University of Leeds Brotherton Special Collections Library, shelfmark Ripon Cathedral Library XII.G.10. USTC 153579; Conrad Kling, *Loci communes theologici* (Paris: Nicolas Chesneau, 1563). Annotated copy in University of Leeds Brotherton Special Collections Library, shelfmark Ripon Cathedral Library XII.G.1. USTC 198658.

44   Theodoret, Bishop of Cyrus, *Theodoreti Episcopi Cyri De providential sermones x. Nunc primum in lucem editi* (Rome: Antonio Blado, 1545). Annotated copy in University of Leeds Brotherton Special Collections Library, shelfmark Ripon Cathedral Library XVIII.E.3. USTC 858943; Francisco de Toledo, *In sacrosanctum Ioannis Evangelium commentarii ...* (Cologne: in officina Birckmannica, 1599). Annotated copy in University of Leeds Brotherton Special Collections Library, shelfmark Ripon Cathedral Library XVI.B.16/q. USTC 626093.

Willem Hesselszoon van Est's *Annotationes aureæ in præcipua ac difficiliora Sacræ Scripturæ loca*, a newly-printed title for which Higgin paid 10s. 6d.[45]

In addition to purchasing volumes from city booksellers, Higgin also acquired works by purchasing them from friends and colleagues, such as Griffin Briskin, a prebendary of York. Others he received as gifts from other friends and local collectors, including Richard Cox, bishop of Ely, John Favour, vicar of Halifax, and Sir Henry Savile of Bank, the noted antiquarian book collector.[46] Moreover, Higgin received at least one work as a gift from the author himself. Thomas Bell gave Higgin a copy of his *The Survey of Popish Religion*, as noted by Higgin on the book's title page: *'Liber Anthony Higgin ex dono autoriis'*.[47] Such volumes may reflect Higgin's friends' reading interests more than his own, but his decision to retain them in the corpus for the Minster library suggests Higgin perceived the importance of these works as being sufficiently high to make them worthy of inclusion.

The works that Higgin purchased himself from Cambridge, York and London demonstrate similar collecting practices to his contemporaries. The signatures and notes on the title pages of various volumes show that Higgin was actively collecting books for a period of at least forty years: the first recorded purchase date on a title page is 1582 and the last recorded purchase date is 1622. The collection included works by medieval theological writers, post-Reformation

45   Nicolaus de Gorran, *In Acta Apostolorum* ... (Antwerp: n. p., 1620). Annotated copy in University of Leeds Brotherton Special Collections Library, shelfmark Ripon Cathedral Library XVI.C.12/q. USTC 112708; Willem Hesselszoon van Est, *Annotationes aureæ in præcipua ac difficiliora Sacræ Scripturæ loca* (Cologne: widow of Johann Crith, 1622). Annotated copy in University of Leeds Brotherton Special Collections Library, shelfmark Ripon Cathedral Library I.B.15. USTC 2019159.

46   'Richardus Cox Eliensis Anth: Higgino dedit' is inscribed on the title page of Walter Haddon, *Contra Hieron. Osorium, eiusq[ue] odiosas infectationes pro Evangelicae veritatis necessaria Defensione, Responsio Apologetica* (London: John Day, 1577). Annotated copy in University of Leeds Brotherton Special Collections Library, shelfmark Ripon Cathedral Library XVII.A.17. USTC 508369; *'Librum hunc Mr Guil.* [actually John] *Favor ... ecclesiae Halifaxiensis Vicarius A. Higgin dono dedit'* inscribed on the title page of Theodoret, Bishop of Cyrus, *De selectis scripturae divinae quaestionibus ambiguis* (Paris: Jacques du Puys, 1558). Annotated copy in University of Leeds Brotherton Special Collections Library, shelfmark Ripon Cathedral Library XII.D.1. USTC 152441; *'Liber Antonii Higgin ex dono Mr Henrici Savill, totius antiquitatis studiosissimi. Novembris. 17. 1593'* is inscribed on the title page of Johann Beckenhub, *Index alphabeticus sive Reptorium domini Johannis Beckenhaub Moguntini in scripta divi Bonaventure super quattuor libris sententiarum* (Paris: n. p., 1510?). Annotated copy in University of Leeds Brotherton Special Collections Library, shelfmark Ripon Cathedral Library XVIII.E.21. This edition not listed in the USTC.

47   Thomas Bell, *The Survey of Popish Religion* (London: Valentine Sims, 1596). Annotated copy in University of Leeds Brotherton Special Collections Library, shelfmark Ripon Cathedral Library XVII.F.13 USTC 513050.

Catholic authors and Protestants of different denominations, a combination necessitated by Higgin's profession as a clergyman committed to the promotion and furtherance of the Church of England. His position, like those of his clerical colleagues, required an awareness of the arguments made against the Church of England by Catholic polemicists, in order to refute them comprehensively. The catechisms, works of Protestant theology, Biblical commentaries and texts on Christian life not only shaped clerical ministries, but also provided spiritual support and inspiration in the face of the everyday difficulties of leading a godly life and advocating Protestantism.[48] Higgin's collecting practices clearly demonstrate the need for comprehensive religious knowledge that fuelled his deliberate selection of books intended to help him fulfil his ministerial duties and which, in turn, influenced the nature of the collection given to the Minster after Higgin's death in 1624.

The parish libraries of More, Wimborne Minster and Reigate were also established by a gift of books from the donors' personal collections. Wimborne Minster and Reigate additionally provide excellent examples of parish library collections that were substantially augmented by later donations from benefactors who also gifted or bequeathed parts of their own personal book collections. More parish library was established in 1680 by Richard More of Linley Hall. Richard More gifted St Peter's church in the parish of More, near Bishop's Castle in Shropshire, 350 books from his own collection, meaning that Richard More had complete control over which books were given to the church. The nature of the collection given to the church suggests purposive selecting practices on Richard More's part. More intended the collection he gifted to the church to encourage and educate a new preaching minister, who would then disseminate the messages of the texts More donated to the parishioners.[49] The corpus of texts extracted from More's own collection to be gifted to the church as a parish library included works of poetry, theology, history and geography.[50] Such works reflect not only More's personal reading interests, but also what works he thought would be appropriate and useful for the parish of More's preaching minister to read and disseminate to the congregation. As such, the impact of this library being gifted by the donor during his lifetime on the nature of the collection is clear: More oversaw the selection of

---

48   Rosamund Oates, '"Far Off from the Well's Head": The Production and Circulation of Books in Early Modern Yorkshire' in Rosamund Oates and Jessica G. Purdy (eds), *Communities of Print: Readers and their Books in Early Modern Europe* (Leiden: Brill, 2021), pp. 76–77; Pearson, 'The Libraries of English Bishops', p. 223.

49   Shropshire Archives, Shropshire, (P193/S/1/1), More Church Library Trust Deeds with Rules.

50   Conal Condren, 'More Parish Library, Salop', *Library History*, 7:5 (1987), p. 146.

titles from his collection that would best work to complete his vision for the parish library as a religiously educational repository.

Wimborne Minster Chained Library was established in 1685, when William Stone gifted the church his collection of around ninety patristic and theological texts, which was only a part of his larger personal library. Why Stone sent these works to Wimborne Minster church is unclear. Stone was born in Wimborne Minster and was briefly a minister of the church in the early 1660s, so it may be that this personal connections to the town served as the impetus behind the gift. The patristic texts and other religious books that Stone gave to Wimborne Minster church reflected his position as an Anglican conformist clergyman with royalist sympathies, but the lack of clarity surrounding his motivations for donation make it difficult to ascribe any educational intentions to the gift. In his capacity as Principal of New Inn Hall at the University of Oxford, Stone lived in Oxford from the early 1660s until his death in 1685, a place and time that Jean-Louis Quantin has described as 'the heyday of English patristic scholarship'. Because of his residence in Oxford and his large collection of patristic volumes, it is reasonable to suggest that Stone was one of those restoration divines, identified by Quantin, who 'valued antiquity all the more as they were confident, to a higher degree than ever before, that they could argue from it much more effectively than ever before' in order to effectually 'express and promote the confessional identity of the Restoration Church'.[51]

Stone's access to books was facilitated by his proximity to the book trade in both Oxford and Cambridge, which 'was on a larger scale than anywhere else outside London'.[52] It was driven primarily by the needs and interests of the students and senior members of the universities, resulting in local booksellers holding a significantly increased number of Latin volumes, many of which were printed on the continent.[53] As Principal of New Inn Hall, Stone had easy and almost immediate access to numerous Oxford booksellers, who were themselves reliant on the London-based book trade to provide them with continental works.[54] It is perhaps unsurprising, therefore, that Stone was able

---

51   Jean-Louis Quantin, *The Church of England and Christian Antiquity: The Construction of a Confessional Identity in the 17th Century* (Oxford: Oxford University Press, 2009), p. 312.

52   John Barnard and Maureen Bell, 'The English Provinces' in John Barnard, D. F. McKenzie and Maureen Bell (eds), *The Cambridge History of the Book in Britain, Volume IV: 1557–1695* (Cambridge: Cambridge University Press, 2002), p. 668.

53   *Ibid.*, p. 669.

54   Julian Roberts, 'The Latin Trade' in John Barnard, D. F. McKenzie and Maureen Bell (eds), *The Cambridge History of the Book in Britain, Volume IV: 1557–1695* (Cambridge: Cambridge University Press, 2002), p. 146.

to compile such a large collection between 1663 and his death in 1685, which by then was worth over £120.[55]

The patristic texts and other theological books that Stone donated to the church in Wimborne Minster demonstrate his scholarly interests and it can be speculated that he thought they would prove instructive to his Dorset-based colleagues. An overwhelming majority of works written by Protestant and Early Christian authors were included in the collection Stone sent to Wimborne Minster. He also owned numerous texts by prominent humanists and Reformers including Desiderius Erasmus, John Calvin and Theodore Beza. Moreover, the works of John Prideaux, a notable Oxford Calvinist of the early seventeenth century and rector of Exeter College, whose lectures Stone may have attended, were also in the collection.[56] All ten volumes of the Restoration Anglican churchman John Pearson's *Critici Sacri* are present in Stone's corpus, reinforcing Stone's position as a royalist conformist. The collection also included a small number of works by medieval theological writers and post-Reformation Catholic authors. Anthony Milton has argued that both the Catholic Church and the Church of England maintained some orthodox doctrines in the early modern period. They differed on Catholic additions, which the English Church argued touched on fundamentals that, from their perspective, rendered the institution corrupt.[57] Ostensibly, the presence of post-Reformation Catholic authors in Stone's collection of religious texts that he gifted to Wimborne Minster church showed a willingness on Stone's part to purchase books by those on the opposite side of the religious divide. However, Stone's ownership of these Catholic texts may also suggest that he was interested in determining the extent of the Church of England's similarities to and differences from the Church of Rome and recognised the inspirational role the Catholic Church played in the formulation of the doctrines and practices of the Church of England. Stone's collecting practices appear to have been purposeful; he purchased books that would aid him in his religious education and in his career as Principal of New Inn Hall. That he gifted these books to the church of Wimborne Minster means that – whether deliberately or inadvertently – Stone had ultimate control over the nature of this library collection that may have proved educational for later clerics.

55   The National Archives, Kew, (C8/446/3), Attorney General v Fry, 1695.

56   A. J. Hegarty, 'Prideaux, John (1578–1650)', *Oxford Dictionary of National Biography* (online, 2008); M. N. E. Tiffany, *The History of the Rev. Mr. William Stone and his Hospital together with that of other Almshouses in Oxford* (Headington: Tiffany Arts, 2000), pp. 3–4.

57   Anthony Milton, *Catholic and Reformed: The Roman and Protestant Churches in English Protestant Thought, 1600–1640* (Cambridge: Cambridge University Press, 1995), pp. 176–181.

The library at Reigate is another prominent example of an early eighteenth-century gift of specific volumes to a parish church for the purpose of creating a library. The Reigate library was established in 1701 in St Mary Magdalene church by its vicar, Andrew Cranston. Cranston's original donation of books included seventy volumes, which was later increased, meaning that Cranston's entire donation to the library totalled 186 volumes.[58] Cranston not only gifted his own books, he also encouraged his vast network of personal and professional connections to follow his example. These included members of the local clergy, lawyers, MPs, merchants and apothecaries, as well as weavers, shopkeepers and others of similar professions.[59] The benefactors' book that was begun in 1700 lists 365 donors, including Cranston himself, who together donated approximately 1,400 books to the collection.[60] Cranston exercised close control of the library's earliest donations and stipulated the kinds of genres of books that he wanted to include in the collection. Andrea Thomas and Hilary Ely have asserted that Cranston was eager to bring together a varied and wide-ranging collection, at the centre of which were works of divinity, liturgy and ecclesiastical history, supplemented by more secular volumes on history, science, philosophy, mathematics and other subjects.[61] As these books were gifted in their donors' lifetimes, the donors would have had complete control over which books they donated and what works went into the collection, within the constraints of Cranston's thematic stipulations. These stipulations provided not only the basis for the library, but also the guidelines for its development and augmentation. Later donations to and augmentations of parish library collections was an uncommon but not unheard of occurrence. Later additions of books to established parish library collections evidence the continued importance of a parish library to its clergy and local community.

3   Later Augmentations

When considering additions to parish library collections, the physicality of the library itself must be taken into account. Many parish libraries did not constitute the traditional arrangement of books on shelves that are so familiar today; they were contained within book chests or cupboards, sometimes referred to

---

58   Andrea Thomas and Hilary Ely, 'The Cranston Library, Reigate: The First Three Hundred Years', *Library and Information History*, 27:4 (2011), p. 247.
59   *Ibid.*, p. 247.
60   Perkin, *A Directory of the Parochial Libraries*, p. 327.
61   Thomas and Ely, 'The Cranston Library, Reigate', p. 248.

as desk libraries, that did not invite augmentation and supplementation by their very nature. The five parish libraries established by Humphrey Chetham, all of which were in chests or almery-style cupboards, were never augmented because there was no space in which to store the additional volumes. The parish libraries established by the Church of England clergyman Thomas Bray and his associates in the Society for Promoting Christian Knowledge (SPCK) also provide good examples of parish libraries contained in book cupboards that did not invite or allow augmentation. Similar examples of these desk libraries, housed in book cupboards or chests, were established in the parish churches of Abingdon in Berkshire (1618), Wootton Wawen in Warwickshire (1652) and Wrington in Somerset (1659), amongst others.[62]

Both the Cranston library in Reigate and the Trigge library in Grantham are examples of parish libraries that were housed on traditional bookshelves and thus allowed augmentation. The library at Reigate continued to expand after its foundation and the initial flurry of gifts and benefactions. Unfortunately (though perhaps unsurprisingly) donations to the library continued at a much slower rate after Cranston's death in late 1708. They did, however, continue, and they did so into the late nineteenth century, shaping the nature of the collection according to the decisions and desires of the various later donors.[63] Those donations are outside of the chronological scope of this study, but it is worth noting that two of the largest donations to the collection were made in the 1840s and the 1880s by John Newman Harrison, who was then the vicar of Reigate. Donations continue to trickle into the library even into the twenty-first century.[64]

Numerous donations and bequests throughout the seventeenth century added to the initial *en masse* purchase of books for the Francis Trigge Chained Library, emphasising its continued importance to the local community. The first post-foundation bequest to the library came from Francis Trigge himself in his will proved in 1606 and may well have prompted the compilation of the *Catalogus Librorum* library catalogue in 1608.[65] Trigge bequeathed several books to the library at St Wulfram's church, including the three-volume *Historia Venerabilis Antonini* of Saint Antoninus of Florence, Johannes Balbus's *Summa que Catholicon appellatur*, six volumes of Caesar Baronius's *Annales ecclesiastici*, the *Eicasmi seu meditations in sacram Apocalypsin* by John Foxe, Blasio Viegas's *Commentaria exergetici in Apocalypsim Joannis apostoli*,

---

62   Perkin, *A Directory of the Parochial Libraries*, pp. 83–112, 115, 400, 402–403.
63   Thomas and Ely, 'The Cranston Library, Reigate', p. 249.
64   *Ibid.*, p. 249.
65   Glenn, 'A Sixteenth-Century Library', p. 67.

Andrew Willett's *Synopsis Papismi, that is a general view of Papistry* and the four volumes of Theodor Zwinger's *Theatrum humanae vitae*.[66] Trigge's testamentary instructions on which books to give to the library were clear:

> My Theatru[m] vitae humanae, and Scotus his works, and all Antoninus, and my great Pagnen his lexicon, Concordantiae grecae Phillippus de dies his postill with that p[ar]te wh[ich] Mr Pontell of Carleton hath of it, Vigeas upon the Revelation, Fox upon the Revelation and Catholicon.[67]

The books bequeathed by Trigge were listed together in the *Catalogus Librorum* of 1608.[68] All of these works are still in the library, except the lexicon of 'Pagnen' (the Italian Dominican friar, Sante Pagnini), which has since been lost.[69] These volumes may represent Trigge's attempts to fill a perceived gap in the collection, or may have been volumes that he had in his personal collection that he felt would be beneficial for the people of Grantham to have access to.

Later in the seventeenth century, the theologian Henry More donated several of his own works to the collection. More was born in Grantham in 1614, attended Christ's College, Cambridge, achieving his BA in 1636 and his MA in 1639, and was ordained and presented with the living of Ingoldsby, approximately six miles east of Grantham, which he held from 1641 to 1666.[70] More donated eight titles of his own works in ten volumes to the Francis Trigge Chained Library between 1662 and 1681. Three volumes of More's works bear the Latin phrase

---

66   Antoninus Forciglione, *Historia Venerabilis Antonini, Volumes I–III* (Basel: Nicolaus Kasler, 1502). Francis Trigge Chained Library, shelfmarks I12–I14. These editions not listed in the USTC; Johannes Balbus, *Summa que Catholicon appellatur* (Lyon: Nicolaus Wolff, 1503). Francis Trigge Chained Library, shelfmark H10. USTC 142905; Caesar Baronius, *Annales ecclesiastici*, in six volumes (Mainz: Balthasar Lippi, 1601–1603). Francis Trigge Chained Library, shelfmarks J19–J24. These editions not listed in the USTC; John Foxe, *Eicasmi seu meditationes in sacram Apocalypsin* (London: T. Dawson for George Bishop, 1587). Francis Trigge Chained Library, shelfmark H1. USTC 510753; Andrew Willett, *Synopsis Papismi, that is a general view of Papistry* (London: Felix Kingston for Thomas Man, 1600). Francis Trigge Chained Library, no shelfmark. USTC 515024; Theodor Zwinger, *Theatrum humanae vitae*, in four volumes (Basel: ex officina Episcopiorum, 1586–1587). Francis Trigge Chained Library, shelfmarks J15–J18. USTC 606252.

67   Lincolnshire Archives, Lincolnshire, (LCC Wills/1606), Wills proved in the Lincoln Consistory Court, number 252.

68   Lincolnshire Archives, Lincolnshire, (Grantham St Wulfram Par/23/4), Documents relating to the Trigge Library: Catalogue of Books Given by Francis Trigge.

69   B. Roussel and R. E. Shillenn (trans.), 'Pagnini, Sante (1470–1536)', *The Oxford Encyclopedia of the Reformation* (online, 2005).

70   Sarah Hutton, 'More, Henry (1614–1687)', *Oxford Dictionary of National Biography* (online, 2008).

'*ex dono auctoris*' at the beginning of the book.[71] The books were seemingly given in a series of different donations, as some were gifted before the last were published. The number of donation points is unclear. The location of More's living at Ingoldsby, in relatively close proximity to Grantham, makes it possible that More used the library for his own purposes. This, his association with the church's clergy (two of the volumes More authored and donated bear the inscription 'Sep 20 1679 *Ex dono reverend auctoris* / in the years of John Smyth church warden'), and the town as his birthplace may therefore be accounted amongst the reasons for his gifts.[72]

In the mid-eighteenth century, John Newcome, another Grantham-born man who was Dean of Rochester as well as Master of St John's College and Lady Margaret Professor of Divinity at the University of Cambridge, also donated books to the Francis Trigge Chained Library. The donation of these books over 150 years after the library's original foundation suggests that it had not yet begun to fall into the deplorable state in which it was found in the nineteenth century. A second codicil to Newcome's will, dated 18 September 1764, stated that,

> To the parish library in the church of Grantham ... I give so many usefull Books as will fill the three Book cases in my Gallery such as Books of morality, Christian divinity, proper Commentation on the Bible or any part thereof, English history, chronology, geography, sermons.[73]

Presumably, the users were to remain 'the clergy and gentlemen of the neighbourhood', as described in Newcome's first codicil to his will on 27 July 1763.[74] The selection of books Newcome deemed 'usefull' for the clergy and gentlemen

---

71   Henry More, *An explanation of the grand mystery of godliness* (London: J. Flesher, 1660). Francis Trigge Chained Library, shelfmark D9. This edition not listed in the USTC; Henry More, *Enchiridion ethicum praecipua moralis philosophiae rudimenta complectens* (London: J. Flesher, 1669). Francis Trigge Chained Library, shelfmark B13. This edition not listed in the USTC; Henry More, *Enchiridion metaphysicum. Pars prima* (London: E. Flesher, 1671). Francis Trigge Chained Library, shelfmark B14. This edition not listed in the USTC.

72   Henry More, *Opera philosophica tum quae Latine tum quae Anglice primitus scripta sunt ... Volumes I and II* (London: printed by J. Macock for J. Martyn and Gualt. Kettilby, 1679). Francis Trigge Chained Library, shelfmarks D10 and D11. These editions not listed in the USTC.

73   The National Archives, Kew, (PROB 11/907/118), Will of Reverend John Newcome, Doctor of Divinity, Master of Saint John's College University of Cambridge, 12 March 1765.

74   *Ibid.*

of Grantham – works that were religiously edifying as well as a number of secular volumes – suggests that he wished the educational nature of the Francis Trigge library to be retained and furthered, not altered by his augmentation. However, the books that Newcome donated to the church were never merged with the existing collection, for reasons unknown. It may be that there was no space for an additional three bookcases in the room over the south porch of the church; it may suggest that popular interest in the library was beginning to wane and its usage was beginning to dwindle; or it may be for other reasons entirely. Instead of being housed with the Trigge library, Newcome's books were kept in the South chancel of the church until 1806 and then in the vestry until 1878, before being moved to the bottom of the belfry stairs.[75]

Like the Francis Trigge Chained Library, the Wimborne Minster Chained Library was also housed on traditional bookshelves and able to expand its collection. The first major augmentation of the corpus occurred ten years after Stone's original gift in 1685. In 1695, the gentleman Roger Gillingham bequeathed books to Wimborne Minster church to be added to the collection previously gifted by Stone. The books donated by Roger Gillingham constituted a combination of religious and secular volumes, heavily weighted in favour of the latter, and reflected the books that he and his executors deemed appropriate and necessary for reading by a combined clerical and lay intended readership, as stated in Gillingham's will.[76] Some of the volumes were purchased specifically for the library, whilst others were drawn from Gillingham's personal library collection by his executors after his death. Thus, the donation is a combination of the books that Gillingham thought important and the books that Gillingham's executors deemed likewise, as Gillingham's will made no specific mention of which additional works or genres of texts were to be donated.[77]

As a complete collection, the books Gillingham donated included secular works by authors including Samuel Hartlib, Sir William Dugdale, Edward Chamberlayne and Edward Grimeston, alongside the texts of religious writers such as James Ussher, Arthur Lake, William Chillingworth and the German Lutheran, Christoph Scheibler. When collecting some of the secular volumes that Gillingham purchased for his collection, he seems to have taken

---

75   Unknown Author, 'Local Notes and Queries, Replies: Libraries', *Grantham Journal*, Saturday 26 October 1878, p. 3.

76   The National Archives, Kew, (PROB 11/430/238), Will of Roger Gillingham of Middle Temple, Middlesex, 25 February 1696.

77   *Ibid.*

inspiration from his copy of William Ramesey's *The Gentleman's Companion: or, a Character of True Nobility, and Gentility* (1672), which itself Gillingham subsequently donated to Wimborne Minster Chained Library.[78] The works of Plutarch, Henry Hammond, William Laud and Walter Raleigh were all listed by Ramesey as being 'requisite' reading and of sufficient 'substance' for the seventeenth-century gentleman to better his education. Works by all of these men were mentioned in Gillingham's will as having been purchased by him for donation to the library in Wimborne Minster church, suggesting that Gillingham used his own copy of Ramesey's work to guide his collecting practices.[79] More broadly, Gillingham's donated collection of secular works on topics including history, agriculture, hygiene, health and melancholy indicate his interest in the liberal sciences. The preponderance of Anglican and Protestant religious works, which far outweigh the works by medieval theological writers and post-Reformation Roman Catholics, reflect the influence of Gillingham's confessional identity on his collecting practices and on the nature of the collection given to Wimborne Minster church at the end of the seventeenth century.

In addition to the gifts of Stone and Gillingham, the library in Wimborne Minster church received gifts of books from numerous other donors. The catalogue compiled in 1725 by William Russell, then Presbyter of the Minster, showed that twenty-three known benefactors donated 284 books to Wimborne Minster Library between 1685 and the catalogue of 1725. A further five books were given to the library in the same time period by unknown donors.

---

78   William Ramesey, *The Gentleman's Companion: or, a Character of True Nobility, and Gentility* (London: E. Okes, for Rowland Reynolds, 1672). Wimborne Minster Chained Library, shelfmark J23. This edition is not listed in the USTC.

79   Ramesey, *The Gentleman's Companion*, pp. 127–129. Wimborne Minster Chained Library, shelfmark J23. This edition is not listed in the USTC; Henry Hammond, *The Works of the Reverend and Learned Henry Hammond, Volumes I–IV* (London: Printed for R. Royston, 1684). Wimborne Minster Chained Library, shelfmarks D4 and D5. These editions not listed in the USTC; William Laud, *A Relation of the Conference between William Laud and Mr Fisher, the Jesuit* (London: Richard Badger, 1639). Wimborne Minster Chained Library, shelfmark D16. USTC 3020501 and 3020493; Walter Raleigh, *The History of the World* (London: George Lathum and Robert Young, 1634). Wimborne Minster Chained Library, shelfmark K4. USTC 3017553; Plutarch, *Quae extant omnia* (Frankfurt: Daniel and David Aubry and Clemens Schleich, 1620). Wimborne Minster Chained Library, shelfmarks I3 and I4. These editions not listed in the USTC.

TABLE 1   Books donated to Wimborne Minster Chained Library and their donors

Donor	Number of books	Donor	Number of books
William Stone	90	Henry Lewen	3
Roger Gillingham	88	Aldrich Swann	3
Thomas Ansty	27	John Webb, baronet	3
Samuel Conant	21	Minster	2
Richard Goodridge	8	J. Cole	1
Richard Gillingham	6	John Corbett	1
Thomas Holway	5	John Grene	1
Richard Lloyd	5	John Moyle	1
Philip Traherne	5	George Mullens	1
Churchill	4	John Talbot	1
Dewey	3	Anonymous	5

The wills of several of these donors to Wimborne Minster Chained Library survive, though as many of them do not include specific information about the testators' books nor instructions for their donation to Wimborne Minster church, it is difficult to ascribe an educational motive to the gifts. It is more likely that the donations were prompted by an affinity with the town itself and a desire to leave something to the parish church as the centre of community life. The surviving wills of Thomas Ansty, a minister, Richard Gillingham, a priest, Richard Lloyd, a clerk and headmaster of Wimborne Minster School, and Thomas Holway, a joiner, demonstrate their connections to the town.

Thomas Ansty was born in Wimborne Minster and died in 1669. His will made no mention of books specifically, but he bequeathed 10s. to the church and 'the rest of my goods chattells [and] household stuffe' – including the books, presumably – to his son, also named Thomas.[80] It was probably the younger Thomas Ansty who donated the twenty-seven volumes now in the Wimborne Minster collection, meaning that the elder Thomas Ansty had no control over which books were selected to be given to the church, if indeed these volumes were part of a larger collection.

Similar circumstances surround the donation of books in Richard Gillingham's name. Richard Gillingham was born in the town of Wimborne

---

80   The National Archives, Kew, (PROB 11/331/257), Will of Thomas Anstye, Clerk of Wimborne Minster, Dorset, 2 November 1669.

Minster and died in 1680. In his will, Gillingham gave 'to my Grandson Richard Fidkins ... all my Books, except some to be reserved for his Sister Elizabeth'.[81] Fidkins likely donated the books to the church in Wimborne Minster sometime after his grandfather's death and in his name, though when this donation took place is unclear.

Richard Lloyd (*d.* 1738), a clerk of Wimborne Minster and headmaster of Wimborne School, was another donor to the library. He donated five volumes to the church in his hometown of Wimborne Minster. This must have been a considerable number of years before his death as the catalogue was made thirteen years prior to his will being proved and the books are therefore not mentioned in his will.[82] Thus, Richard Lloyd would have had complete control over which volumes were donated.

Likewise, Thomas Holway, a joiner, was also born in the town of Wimborne Minster. Precisely when Holway donated five books to the library in the church is unclear, but it must have been a significant amount of time before his death: the books were listed in the 1725 catalogue but Holway's will is dated 1742.[83] The books were therefore not mentioned in Holway's will and he had complete control over his donation. The donations to the library in Wimborne Minster church continued through the first half of the eighteenth century, reflecting the library's continued importance in the local religious and intellectual landscape of England.

4   The Cost of Early Modern Second-Hand Books

The cost of early modern books was influenced by numerous factors: the quality of materials used to produce a volume, its size and format, and the public demand for either a particular author or a specific title.[84] James Raven has comprehensively demonstrated the difficulties of reconstructing the early modern second-hand book trade, describing it as a 'diverse business, much of it irrevocable for the historian', as books were sold by people and businesses

81   The National Archives, Kew, (PROB 11/365/283), Will of Richard Gillingham of Wimborne Minster, Dorset, 19 February 1681.

82   The National Archives, Kew, (PROB 11/693/256), Will of Richard Lloyd, Clerk of Wimborne Minster, Dorset, 12 December 1738.

83   The National Archives, Kew, (PROB 11/720/99), Will of Thomas Holway, Joiner of Wimborne Minster, Dorset, 11 August 1742.

84   Leah Orr, 'Prices of English Books at Auction *c.* 1680', *The Library*, 20 (2019), p. 502.

as disparate as pedlars of cheap print and chapmen, small shops (which were not always specialised bookshops), and the great auction houses and 'finely printed catalogues of famous stockists [who] offered for sale distinguished libraries of recently deceased or impoverished scholars, clerics, and gentlemen'.[85] However, there are some tools at the historian's disposal that provide an insight into the cost of some early modern second-hand books in relation to early modern parish libraries: the usefulness of booksellers' and auction catalogues has been widely discussed elsewhere and is not particularly relevant here, as benefactors of parish libraries do not seem to have referred to them often.[86] However, purchase invoices kept by those acquiring books for parish libraries, the title pages of the books themselves, a donor's will, or the foundation documents of a library, can all be used to discern how much (some of) the books in parish libraries cost when they were purchased second hand.

Purchase invoices, for example, are of particular use in calculating the cost of books for the five libraries bestowed by Humphrey Chetham on various Manchester parishes. Numerous invoices kept by Johnson, Tildsley and Hollinworth survive, listing the cost of each individual title that went into both the parish libraries and the public library. The invoice seen in Figure 12 below lists the books that comprised the Gorton Chest parish library and the prices paid for them. It demonstrates that the trustees spent exactly the £30 they had previously allocated to this collection in their meeting in October 1654.

85   James Raven, *The Business of Books: Booksellers and the English Book Trade, 1450–1850* (New Haven: Yale University Press, 2007), pp. 193–194.

86   For some examples of discussions of booksellers' and auction catalogues and their various uses, see: Andrew Pettegree and Arthur der Weduwen, *The Library: A Fragile History* (London: Profile Books, 2021), *passim*; Orr, 'Prices of English Books at Auction *c.* 1680', pp. 501–526; Michael F. Suarez, S. J., 'English Book Sale Catalogues as Bibliographical Evidence: Methodological Considerations Illustrated by a Case Study in the Provenance and Distribution of Dodsley's Collection of Poems, 1750–1795', *The Library*, 6–21 (1999), pp. 321–360.

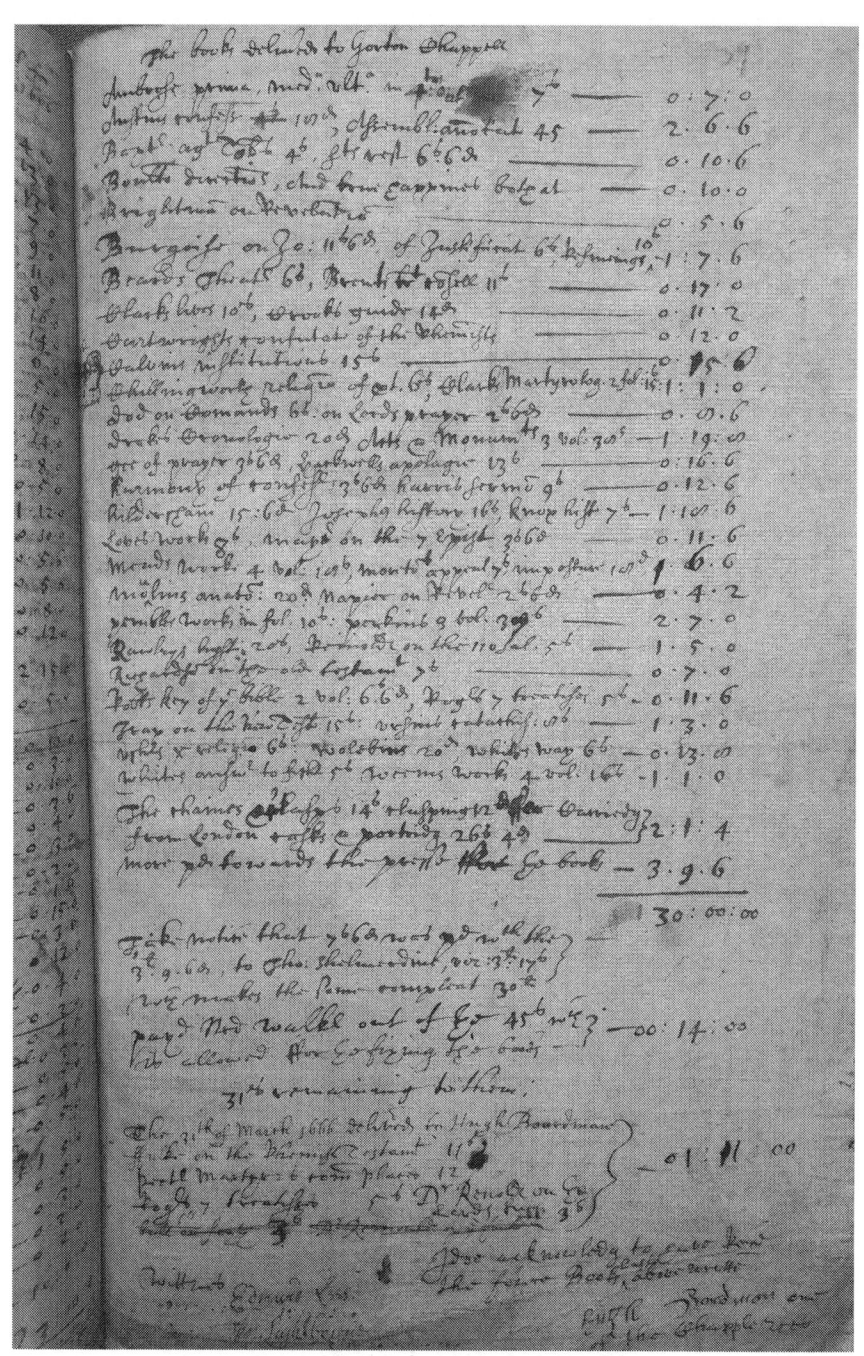

FIGURE 12 The list of books sent to Gorton Chapel for the parish library
© CHETHAM'S LIBRARY, MANCHESTER (CHET/4/5/2) INVOICES OF
BOOKS, 1655–1685, F. 59R. REPRODUCED WITH THE KIND PERMISSION OF
CHETHAM'S LIBRARY, MANCHESTER

In addition to recording how much they paid for each individual volume, the invoices kept by Chetham's trustees occasionally detailed other pieces of information that help historians reconstruct why the books cost the amount they did. For example, an invoice dated 20 September 1655 listing numerous volumes intended for the parish library details a second-hand copy of John Foxe's *Acts and Monuments*, listed on the invoice as the '*Booke of Martyrs*', which was 'bound in Fillets', meaning that its binding had been impressed with a line or parallel lines made by the binder's tool known as a fillet, 'a revolving wheel with one or more raised bands on its circumference'.[87] This decorated binding may partially account for the book's cost of £1 18s., in addition to its popularity as a title in high-demand, written by a well-known author.[88] The trustees' invoices also occasionally recorded the size of each book, the number of copies purchased of each work and, on the invoices of 2 August 1655 and 30 June 1659, for example, the costs for packing and transporting the books from London to Manchester. The dates of the various invoices also indicate just how long it took for the parish libraries to be completed after Chetham's death in September 1653.[89]

In other collections, such as the Francis Trigge and Ripon Minster corpuses, the costs of several books are recorded on their title pages. In 1986, J. M. Blatchly published an article on Ipswich Town Library in which he offered a breakdown of the price codes employed by booksellers in the sixteenth century. For example, Blatchly referred to the letter 'e' as being noted on the title pages of the first five volumes of the *Councils* of Binius, which cost the buyer £5. Blatchly therefore suggested that the letter 'e' stood for '5'.[90] Sixty books in the Francis Trigge library collection (equal to around one quarter of the original corpus) contain booksellers' price codes written on their title pages, in a manner akin to that identified by Blatchly. In his work on the Trigge collection, John Glenn applied Blatchly's work on the price codes in the books of Ipswich Town Library to the letters on the title pages of the books in the Trigge collection. The sixty books (or the quarter of the collection) that contained price codes on their title pages cost approximately £25 in total, equivalent to one quarter of the total sum of £100 Trigge gave. Glenn therefore estimated that the original library would have been relatively close to being completed within its original budget.[91] The cost of the individually priced volumes ranged from between £2 10s. for an eight-volume set of the Magdeburg Centuriators' *Ecclesiastica*

---

87   John Carter, *ABC for Book Collectors*, 7th edition (New Castle, Delaware: Oak Knoll Press, 1995), p. 99.

88   Chetham's Library, Manchester, (Chet/4/5/2), Invoices of Books, 1655–1685, f. 8r.

89   *Ibid.*, f. 6v, f. 58r.

90   J. M. Blatchly, 'Ipswich Town Library', *The Book Collector*, 32:2 (1986), p. 194.

91   Glenn, 'A Sixteenth-Century Library', pp. 69–70.

Historia (1560–1574), down to Hieronymus Zanchius's *In D. Pauli epistolam ad Ephesios, commentarius* (1594) at 10s. Danaeus's *Vetustissimarum primi mundi antiquitatum sections* (1596) was the lowest priced book of the sixty coded volumes, priced at just 1s. 6d.[92] Again, such differences in cost may be attributable to variations in the demand for these authors and/or their works, the material quality of the physical books, their age, or their condition at the time of purchase.

Similarly, Anthony Higgin noted the prices he paid for ten of the books in the collection he eventually bequeathed to Ripon Minster on their title pages. Again, these prices may be indicative of the influence of authorship, subject matter and edition on the cost of a book. For example, Higgin purchased the eight volumes of Saint Augustine's collected works in 1596 for £4 (see Figure 13 below).[93] Edited by Erasmus in the 1520s and printed in 1569–1570 on the Froben press in Basel in Switzerland, the volumes were at least twenty-five years old when Higgin purchased them. The high regard in which this edition was held, in respect of its Erasmian scholarship and its faithfulness to Augustine's original ideas and writings, account for its high price in spite of the age of the work.[94] In 1595, Higgin paid 10s. for a copy of the New Testament printed forty-five years earlier in 1550 and in 1585, he purchased a volume of Saint Athanasius's works from 1564 for 10s. 6d. The lowest recorded price that Higgin paid for a text was just 2s. 6d., for which Higgin purchased a 1564 copy of Willem van der Lindt's interpretation of the New Testament in 1589.[95]

---

92 For the full list of price-marked books in the Francis Trigge Library, see John Glenn and David Walsh, *Catalogue of the Francis Trigge Chained Library, St Wulfram's Church, Grantham* (Cambridge: D. S. Brewer, 1988), pp. 81–82.

93 Saint Augustine, *D. Aurelii Augustini Hipponensis Episcopi, cuius praestantissima in omni genere monimenta ...*, Vols. I–VIII (Basel: Froben Press, 1569–1570). Annotation appears on the title page of Book X, University of Leeds Brotherton Special Collections Library, shelfmark Ripon Cathedral Library XIII.E.14/q. USTC 686573.

94 Arnoud S. Q. Visser, *Reading Augustine in the Reformation: The Flexibility of Intellectual Authority in Europe, 1500–1620* (Oxford: Oxford University Press, 2011), pp. 30–31; Forrest C. Strickland, 'Teachers of Christ's Church: Protestant Ministers as Readers of the Church Fathers in the Dutch Golden Age' in Rosamund Oates and Jessica G. Purdy (eds), *Communities of Print: Readers and their Books in Early Modern Europe* (Leiden: Brill, 2021), pp. 123, 125.

95 Unknown Author, [*Novum Testamentum*] (s. l.: 1550). Annotated copy in University of Leeds Brotherton Special Collections Library, shelfmark Ripon Cathedral Library X.B.7. This edition not listed in the USTC; Saint Athanasius, *Athanasii magni Alexandrini episcopi.* Annotated copy in Brotherton Special Collections Library, shelfmark Ripon Cathedral Library XIII.C.17/q. USTC 613803; Van der Lindt, *Panoplia evangelica.* Annotated copy in Brotherton Special Collections Library, shelfmark Ripon Cathedral Library XII.G.10. USTC 153579.

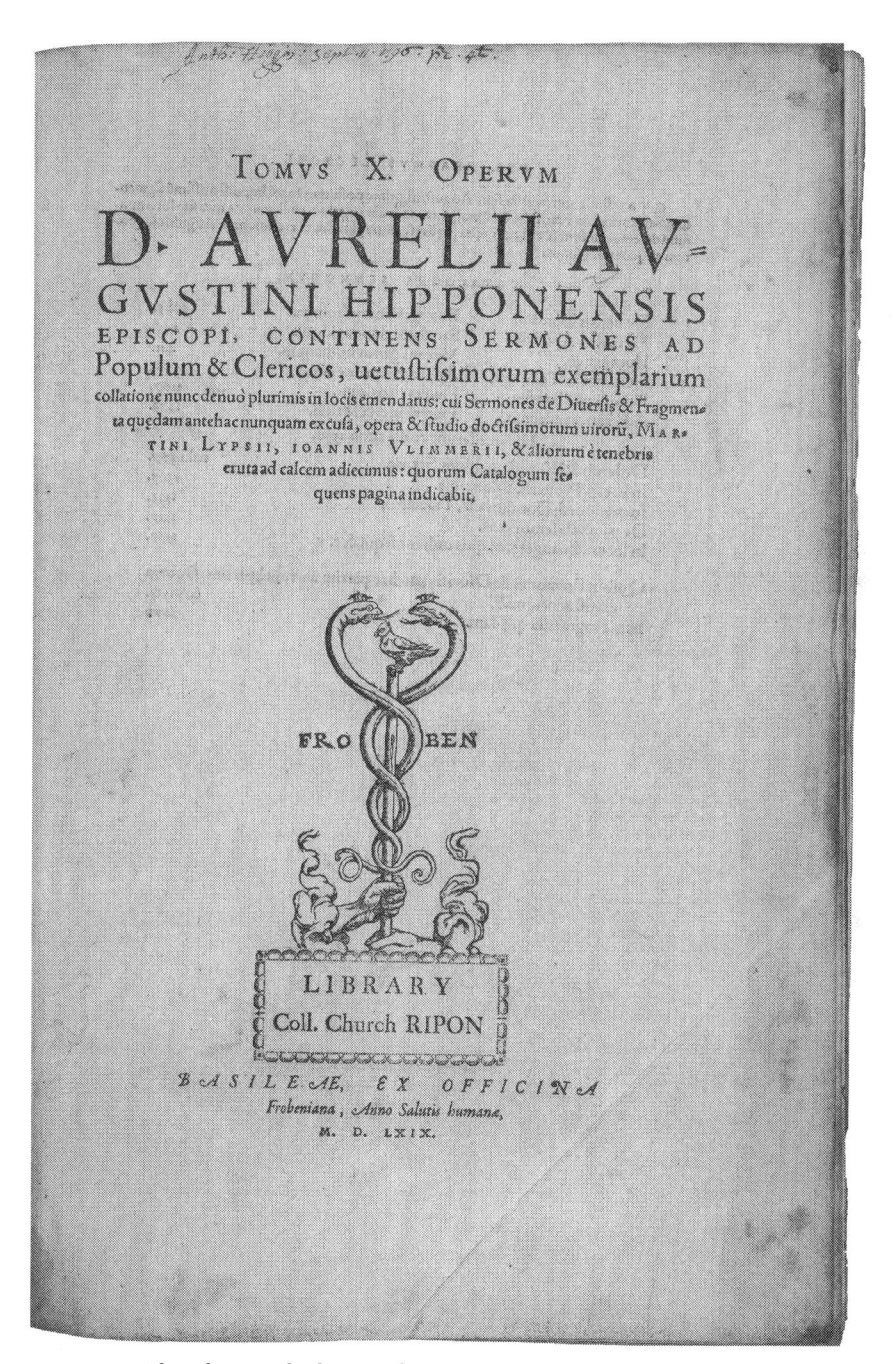

FIGURE 13   The title page of Volume x of Saint Augustine's *Cuius praestantissima in omni genere monimenta* ... showing Anthony Higgin's signature and the purchase price of all ten volumes

© REPRODUCED WITH THE PERMISSION OF SPECIAL COLLECTIONS, LEEDS UNIVERSITY LIBRARY (RIPON CATHEDRAL LIBRARY XIII.E.14/Q)

In determining the value of numerous early modern books in the library of Wimborne Minster church, the donors' wills and other parish library foundation documents are of only limited usefulness, due to the vagueness of their wording. A codicil to the will of Roger Gillingham in 1695, for example, includes a comprehensive list of individual titles to be given to the library that he 'lately bought for that purpose'. In addition to listing the titles, Gillingham also includes the number of volumes in the title and the size of the books themselves – the vast majority are folios. In addition, Gillingham also bequeathed 'soe many of my best folio 4to and 8vo Bookes which ... my said Executors shall estimate and Judge to be worth tenn pounds' to the library in Wimborne Minster church.[96] As illustrated in Table 1 above, Gillingham donated a total of eighty-eight volumes to the collection and only thirty-four of those were named in the codicil to his will. Therefore, whilst it can be logically concluded that the remaining fifty-four volumes Gillingham gave to the library were those deemed by his executors to be worth £10, how this was split between the volumes is difficult to ascertain. Gillingham's will also does not reveal how much money he spent on the thirty-four named volumes. The valuation of William Stone's estate after his death in 1685 demonstrates that the patristic and other theological volumes that he gave to Wimborne Minster church in that year were worth £43 7s. 4d. Again, how that figure is broken down and applied to the ninety volumes donated by Stone is difficult to determine, though it seems likely that these volumes were deemed more valuable than those given by Gillingham, possibly as a result of their subject matter, material condition and their authors.

5   Conclusion

The nature of a collection was significantly impacted by the circumstances of its establishment. If, for example, a library was established by a financial gift or bequest, the donor likely had less direct influence over the final collection than those donors who established their repositories by gifting or bequeathing specific books. The same can be said for later donors to existing collections. In these instances, it is interesting to note that these later donors often tried to align with the initial donors' impetus or vision for the library, as opposed to changing or updating its purpose. The consideration of the cost of books in the sixteenth and seventeenth centuries has provided an interesting insight into the second-hand book trade in early modern England, evidencing how much books could cost in this period and how their value was influenced and, in some cases, determined by their authorship or the quality of materials used to produce the physical volume.

---

96   The National Archives, Kew, (PROB 11/430/238), Will of Roger Gillingham of Middle Temple, Middlesex, 25 February 1696.

Parsing the Collections of Early Modern Parish Libraries

Of the 165 parish libraries established in England between 1558 and 1709, 102 still have at least one surviving book. The vast majority have many more. Forty-six of these 102 repositories (approximately forty-five percent) contain books that can be said with certainty to have been donated between 1558 and 1709. These libraries will form the basis of the introductory analysis in this chapter, before it moves on to a detailed examination of the collections of the Grantham, Ripon, Gorton and Wimborne Minster parish libraries. It must be noted that the surviving numbers of books is, in almost every library, lower than the number originally donated. Surviving collection sizes of English parish libraries established between 1558 and 1709 range from just one or two books, to 200 or 300 volumes, to over a thousand books, as shown in Figure 14 below.

The size of a library's original collection appears to be in no way linked to the date of its foundation: surviving library collections do not suggest a consistent, gradual increase in size as time progressed, books became more easily available and parish libraries became more institutionalised. Nor does the

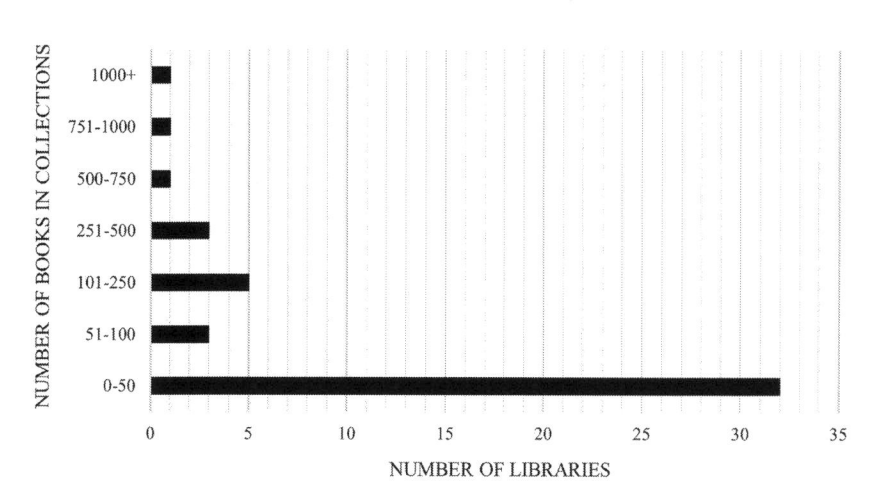

FIGURE 14   Sizes of surviving parish library collections of books donated between 1558 and 1709

© KONINKLIJKE BRILL NV, LEIDEN, 2024 | DOI:10.1163/9789004363717_012

date of a library's foundation necessarily correlate to the number of surviving books. The libraries of Coniston in Lancashire and Milden in Suffolk, for
example, were founded late in the period, in 1699 and 1703 respectively, and
just one book survives in each collection. Conversely, the libraries of Oakham
(1616) and Ripon (1624) were founded much earlier in the period. Oakham has
150 volumes remaining and Ripon has a staggering minimum of 750 surviving
books, the second largest surviving collection from the period.[1] Book survival
appears in large part to be a matter of chance. The library at Coniston was
reported in 1885 as containing approximately a hundred volumes that had
been purchased using the money originally donated by the library's founder,
Roger Fleming, but Michael Perkin reported them as having been destroyed,
'probably in 1957, as being dirty and unread', in his 2004 *Directory of the
Parochial Libraries*.[2] Similarly, the library at Milden survived in numbers in
excess of 2,000 books until the early twentieth century when the books were
sold to raise funds to buy more modern volumes. Unfortunately, no catalogue
of the parish library was made prior to this event.[3] The libraries of Oakham
and Ripon have survived relatively well intact, again seemingly by chance, as
no specific instructions for the maintenance and retaining of the books formed
part of either donation.[4]

The following analysis will focus primarily on the four case study parish
libraries outlined in chapter 5: the Francis Trigge Chained Library in Grantham,
Lincolnshire (1598), the Ripon Minster parish library in Ripon, Yorkshire
(1624), the Gorton Chest parish library in Manchester, Lancashire (1655) and
the Wimborne Minster Chained Library in Wimborne Minster, Dorset (1685,
augmented 1695). The Francis Trigge Chained Library currently has 263 volumes remaining; the Ripon Minster parish library has 486 surviving theological books, which will be the focus here; the Gorton Chest parish library still
contains fifty-one volumes; and the combined Stone and Gillingham donations to the Wimborne Minster Chained Library has 151 volumes remaining.

1 Michael Perkin, *A Directory of the Parochial Libraries of the Church of England and the Church
   in Wales* (London: Bibliographical Society, 2004), pp. 309, 331.
2 Richard Copley Christie, *The Old Church and School Libraries of Lancashire* (Manchester:
   Charles E. Simms for the Chetham Society, New Series, 7, 1885), pp. 95–96; Perkin, *A Directory
   of the Parochial Libraries*, p. 180.
3 Perkin, *A Directory of the Parochial Libraries*, p. 284.
4 Anne L. Herbert, 'Oakham Parish Library', *Library History*, 6:1 (1982), pp. 1–11; Jean E. Mortimer,
   The Library Catalogue of Anthony Higgin: Dean of Ripon (1608–1624) (Leeds: Chorley and
   Pickersgill, 1962), pp. 1–10.

Various elements of these four parish libraries will be examined in this chapter. Firstly, the array of confessional identities held by the authors of the volumes within these collections will be demonstrated, to illustrate that a wide range of confessions remained evident throughout the second half of the sixteenth century and the entirety of the seventeenth century. Secondly, this chapter will examine the age of the books through close analysis of their publication dates, to suggest that the vast majority of volumes in all four of these case study parish libraries were published at least a decade prior to their placement in the library and thus were potentially purchased on the second-hand book market. Thirdly, the publication locations of the volumes in each of these four collections will be analysed and the implications of this for the continental book trade considered. This analysis demonstrates that the continental book trade remained a strong and integral part of not only the English book trade, but also the provincial book trade in England. An examination of the language of the books in these collections will then show that the implications for readers were not as limiting as previously thought, and that the Latin nature of many of these books was not as prohibitive as has been suggested in the past. Finally, this analysis will examine the genres of the books contained in these library repositories in order to evince that they remained largely the same over time: dominated by religious and theological texts and supplemented by secular works of various genres.

1   Authors' Confessional Identities

The Grantham, Ripon and Wimborne Minster parish libraries all included works by authors of diverse confessional identities. All three of these repositories contained texts by Protestant authors of various denominations, post-Reformation Catholics, medieval theologians, patristic writers and other Early Christians.[5] As such, they each represent 'a cross section of the writings of the men who brought about the Reformation and of those who sought to oppose it'.[6] For Anthony Higgin, who compiled the Ripon Minster

---

5   Patristic writers, Early Christian and Late Antiquity authors have all been conflated under the umbrella term 'Early Christians' for the sake of clarity throughout. Authors from the Middle Ages to the Reformation in the 1520s have been classified throughout as medieval theological writers, whilst post-Reformation authors have been categorised according to their Catholic or Protestant denominational confessional identity.

6   John Glenn, 'A Sixteenth-Century Library: the Francis Trigge Chained Library of St Wulfram's Church, Grantham' in Daniel Williams (ed.), *Early Tudor England: Proceedings of the 1987 Harlaxton Symposium* (Woodbridge: The Boydell Press, 1989), p. 65.

parish library, his works were intended to aid him in his preaching and to support the efforts of Tobie Matthew, Archbishop of York, and other clerics in combatting the increase in recusancy in Jacobean Yorkshire. For clerical readers of these and other collections more broadly, and for sixteenth- and seventeenth-century readers in general, this range of texts can have been no bad thing, as a thorough knowledge of one's religious opponents was of paramount importance when refuting them, or attempting to effect conversions in parishioners.[7] The exception to this was the Gorton Chest parish library which, in accordance with its founder Humphrey Chetham's wishes, was comprised almost entirely of Protestant authors of varying denominations. Sitting alongside such volumes was a text written by the sole Catholic author in the collection, *The History of the Council of Trent* by Paolo Sarpi.

1.1 The Francis Trigge Chained Library

The 263 surviving volumes in the original collection of the Francis Trigge library were written by 114 individual named authors. This number excludes the numerous different versions of the Bible in the 1608 *Catalogus Librorum* and the multi-volume *Historia Ecclesiastica*, which was written by a group of authors known collectively as the Magdeburg Centuriators. The religious affiliations of the known authors included in the Trigge library include patristic and other Early Christian writers; medieval theological authors; and Catholics and Protestants at each end of the confessional spectrum, from committed Jesuits such as Robert Bellarmine or Francis Ribera, to the English Puritan clergyman John Rainolds. In addition, there were several classical authors like Seneca and Pliny the Elder, who were part of the canon of classical authors included in many libraries in the sixteenth and seventeenth centuries. As discussed in chapter 7, Glenn argued that the mixture of Catholic and Protestant authors was probably attributable to happenstance resulting from indiscriminate selection practices by an agent who paid little care and attention to the books he was purchasing.[8] However, it is far more likely the result of a conscious acknowledgement of the need to understand both sides of the confessional debate that pervaded Elizabethan and Jacobean religious society in general, and which was particularly relevant in a religiously-divided Lincolnshire. Figure 15 below demonstrates the different confessional identities found within the Francis Trigge Chained Library and the number of authors who held these religious convictions.

---

7   David Pearson, 'The Libraries of English Bishops, 1600–1640', *The Library*, 14 (1992), p. 229.
8   Glenn, 'A Sixteenth-Century Library', p. 65.

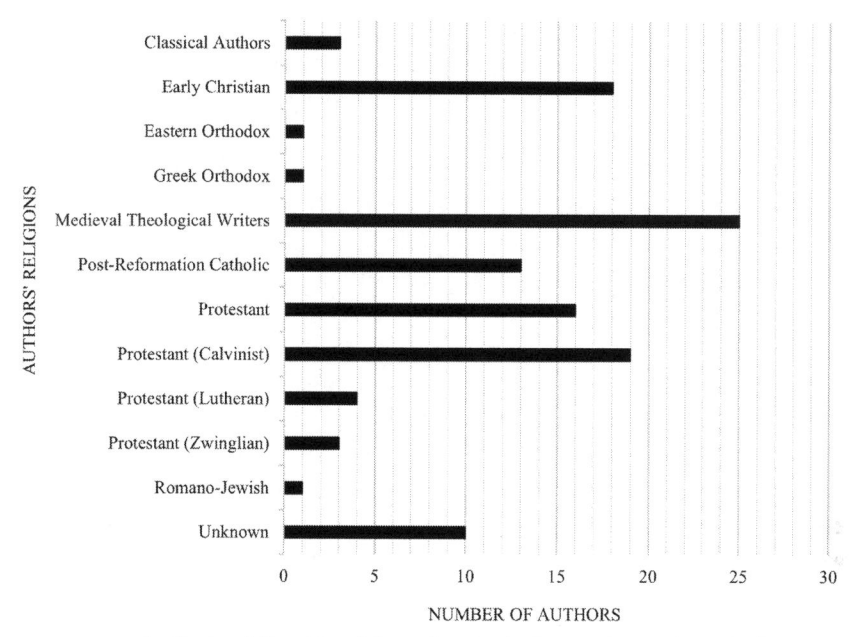

FIGURE 15   Confessional identities of the authors in the Francis Trigge Chained Library

Within the Francis Trigge library collection, the cumulative number of Protestant authors of any denomination far outweighed the number of post-Reformation Catholic authors. This weighting was similarly reflected in the split between the number of Protestant and Catholic titles. Protestant authors of all denominations account for thirty-six percent of the total number of authors in the collection, compared to post-Reformation Catholic authors who represent just eleven percent of the collection. This suggests that whilst Trigge was keen to provide Catholic reading material for bettering the knowledge of the local clergy in their refutation of Catholic religious arguments, he was far keener to promote the Protestant religion, as shown in his own printed works. The relatively high number of medieval theologians whose works were included in this repository is interesting, as they account for twenty-two percent of the entire corpus of named authors. This is a higher percentage than any of the other four collections included here and may be attributable to this collection being the first of the four repositories established.

1.2   *Ripon Minster Parish Library*

A total of 263 individual named authors wrote 465 of the surviving titles in the theology collection now in Ripon Minster parish library. The remaining twenty-one titles (totalling 486 surviving titles, as previously stated) have no known authors recorded in either the original manuscript catalogue, the printed catalogue of 1962 by Jean Mortimer, who was then a librarian at the University of Leeds, or the current University of Leeds Brotherton Special Collections Library online catalogue.[9] The various confessional identities of the authors whose works were included in this collection provide an insight into which authors Anthony Higgin was both interested in reading and found to be useful in his defence of the Church of England, and that he felt would be useful to later readers of the Minster library.

Higgin put the vast majority of volumes in his collection to use in attempting to counter the increasing levels of Catholic recusancy in late Elizabethan Yorkshire. He may have undertaken this practice with the encouragement and support of Archbishop Tobie Matthew, when Higgin was appointed as dean of Ripon in 1608. Ripon had 120 recorded recusants in 1604 and, as Rosamund Oates has argued, that number 'only increased as James's reign progressed'. Consequently, Archbishop Matthew encouraged the 'use [of] Ripon Minster as a centre for preaching and education for the clergy' in the northern Church, a scheme that Higgin supported and which may have factored into his decision to leave his theological works to the Minster after his death.[10]

Figure 16 below demonstrates the different confessional identities of those 263 named authors in the Ripon Minster collection. The inclusion of works by post-Reformation European Catholic theologians like Hector Pintus, Peter Binsfield, Robert Bellarmine and Martin Becanus, as well as a relatively large number of English Catholic theologians from the post-Reformation period in the collection, is unsurprising. English Catholic theologians in the collection included Thomas Dorman, Thomas Harding, Nicholas Harpsfield and William Watson, in whose works Higgin perhaps recognised the continued importance amongst Catholics of religious instruction and education for the people.[11] Together, this corpus of Catholic works provided Higgin and his

---

9   University of Leeds Brotherton Special Collections Library, Leeds, (Ripon Cathedral MS 35), *Catalogus librorum*, compiled by Anthony Higgin, followed by Latin exercises and commentaries on Ovid's *Heroides and Tristia*, written by Roger Phillips; Mortimer, *The Library Catalogue of Anthony Higgin*.

10   Rosamund Oates, *Moderate Radical: Tobie Matthew and the English Reformation* (Oxford: Oxford University Press, 2018), p. 213.

11   Lucy E. C. Wooding, *Rethinking Catholicism in Reformation England* (Oxford: Clarendon Press, 2000), p. 152.

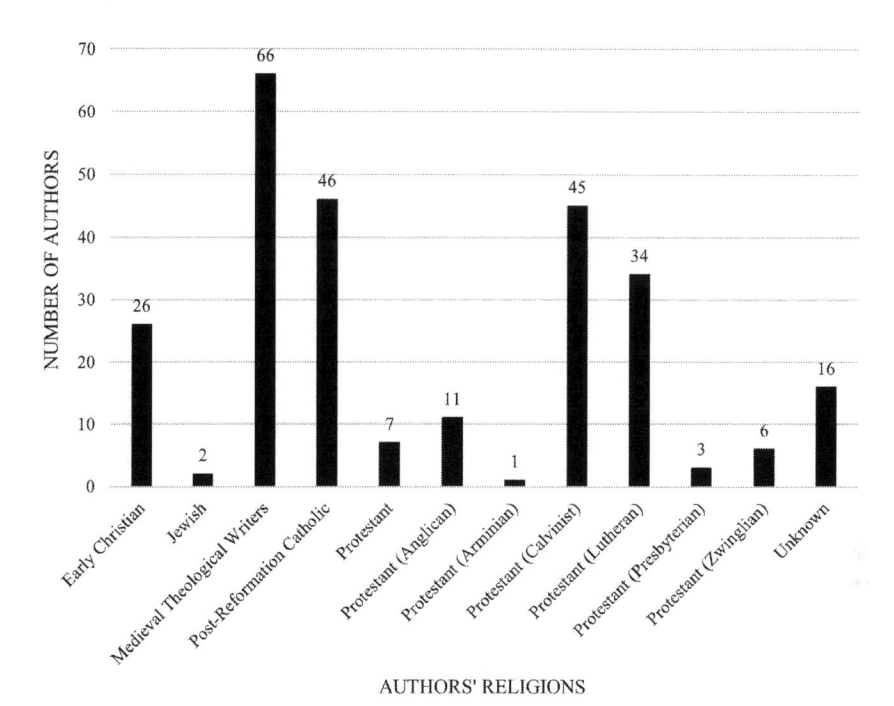

AUTHORS' RELIGIONS

FIGURE 16   Confessional identities of authors in Ripon Minster Parish Library

contemporaries, as well as later readers, with an insight into Catholic religious arguments that could be appropriately refuted in their own sermons or anti-Catholic polemical writings.[12] These sermons and Protestant polemics were likely bolstered by the information found in books by the 101 combined Protestant authors that this collection also contained.

Notably for an early seventeenth-century clergyman, Higgin did not own works by many patristic authors. The texts of just eight Church Fathers of the Eastern and Western Churches were included in the collection: Saint Ambrose, Saint Basil of Caesarea, Saint Athanasius, Saint Augustine, Pope Clement I, Saint Epiphanius, Saint Gregory of Nyssa and Saint John Chrysostom. In total, Higgin owned forty volumes of patristic works by these eight authors, five of whom were included in the Erasmian and Calvinist canon of Greek and Latin Fathers identified by Irena Backus, their perceived importance a reflection of the

12   Oates, *Moderate Radical*, p. 158.

quality of their scholarship.[13] The writings of the Church Fathers were widely held in high regard amongst Protestants: Saint Augustine's writings were of central importance in Protestant doctrines, as was Saint John Chrysostom, on account of his 'capacity to communicate God's mysteries to the common people' and his opinions on the value of Scripture being read by all.[14] However, the popularity of the Church Fathers waxed and waned in the first three decades of the seventeenth century as tensions arose between Church of England divines and Calvinist conformists. While Church of England divines like Lancelot Andrewes, John Overall and Richard Montagu emphasised the importance of the Fathers in the interpretation of Scripture, Calvinist conformists such as Gabriel Powel, Robert Abbot and George Downame questioned the Fathers' authority and stressed the self-interpreting nature of Scripture.[15] In the midst of this controversy, it is perhaps not surprising that Higgin's collection of works by the Church Fathers focussed on those authors endorsed by both Erasmus and Calvin. The relative lack of patristic volumes in Higgin's collection compared to that of William Stone in Wimborne Minster, for example, suggests that Higgin may have been of a similar mind to Powel, Abbot and Downame.

1.3   The Gorton Chest Parish Library

Thirty-six individual named authors were responsible for writing forty-nine of the fifty-one remaining volumes in the Gorton Chest parish library. The remaining two volumes are annotations on the Old and New Testaments by an unknown author. The majority of authors whose works were included in the Gorton Chest collection were either Calvinists or Presbyterians, reflecting the confessional identities of the trustees, Johnson (a Calvinist) and Hollinworth and Tildsley (both Presbyterians). The inclusion of authors of other Protestant confessional identities again suggests an attempt to reflect within the collection the breadth of English Protestantism. Whilst there is no explicit evidence to support Yeo's argument in favour of Chetham and the trustees' attempts to promote reconciliation and unity through the Gorton Chest and the other parish

---

13   Irena Backus, *Historical Method and Confessional Identity in the Era of the Reformation (1378–1615)* (Leiden: Brill, 2003), p. 102; see pp. 102–106 for a general discussion on the merits of the Fathers' works.

14   *Ibid.*, p. 102; Nicholas Hardy, 'The Septuagint and the Transformation of Biblical Scholarship in England, from the King James Bible (1611) to the London Polyglot (1657)' in Kevin Killeen, Helen Smith and Rachel Willie (eds.), *The Oxford Handbook of the Bible in Early Modern England, c.1530–1700* (Oxford: Oxford University Press, 2018), p. 120.

15   Anthony Milton, *Catholic and Reformed: The Roman and Protestant Churches in English Protestant Thought, 1600–1640* (Cambridge: Cambridge University Press, 1995), pp. 274–275.

library collections, there are clear parallels between the authors' confessional identities and those of the people with whom Chetham associated. Francis Raines and Charles Sutton have asserted that Chetham 'was not so blindly hostile to the Roman Catholics as to have no dealings with them ... he had certainly no hostility to their persons, and extended to several members of that community a wide and generous benevolence', whilst S. J. Guscott has demonstrated, through an examination of the legacies in Chetham's numerous wills, that Chetham was not afraid to associate with Manchester's 'more aggressively godly'.[16] Figure 17 below demonstrates the distribution of confessional identities amongst the authors in the Gorton Chest parish library.

The percentage of Catholic authors in this collection is significantly lower than in the other three corpuses examined here: Johnson, Hollinworth and Tildsley included just one Catholic author in the Gorton Chest parish library collection, the Venetian friar, Paolo Sarpi, whose religion placed him in obvious juxtaposition to the other authors represented in this library. However, Sarpi's most famous work, *The History of the Council of Trent*, a translation of which

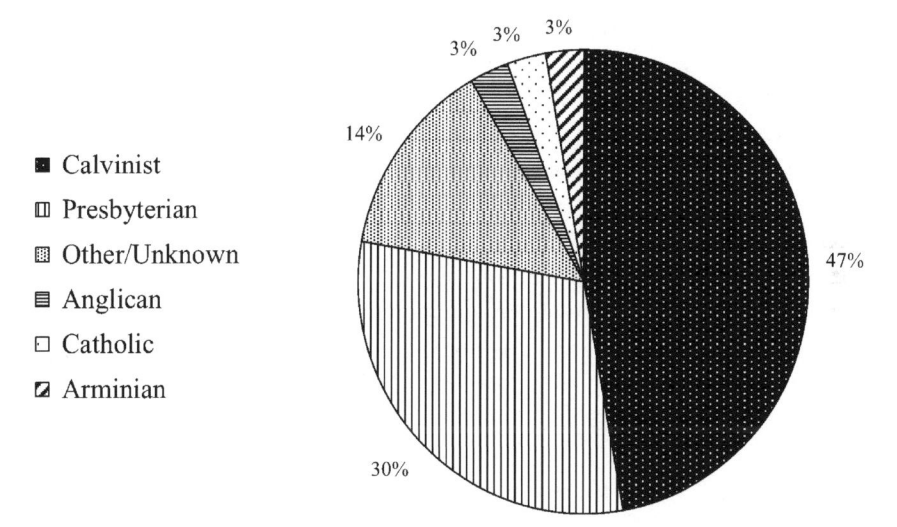

■ Calvinist

▥ Presbyterian

▤ Other/Unknown

▤ Anglican

☐ Catholic

▨ Arminian

FIGURE 17   Confessional identities of authors in the Gorton Chest Parish Library

---

16   Francis Robert Raines and Charles William Sutton, *Life of Humphrey Chetham, founder of the Chetham Hospital and Library, Manchester, Volume I*, printed for the Chetham Society (Manchester: James Stewart, 1903), pp. 32–35, 135; S. J. Guscott, *Humphrey Chetham, 1580–1653: Fortune, Politics and Mercantile Culture in Seventeenth-century England* (Manchester: The Chetham Society, 2003), pp. 172–173.

was included in the Gorton Chest, outlined Sarpi's strong opposition to the papacy, its policies and its practices in the second half of the sixteenth century. In *The History of the Council of Trent*, Sarpi asserted that 'ecclesiastical councils had become mere manifestations of papal power'; he denounced the supremacy of the Roman Catholic Church and denied its claim that it had reverted to a purer form of Christianity, after the conclusion of the Council of Trent in 1563.[17] Despite his Catholicism, Sarpi's vocal opposition of the papacy was in alignment with the anti-papist stance of the trustees, and the volume itself was popular in Protestant countries throughout Europe.[18] In England, over thirty copies of the edition included in the Gorton chest survive. The inclusion of Sarpi's *History* in the Gorton Chest parish library suggests that it was highly valued by Protestants for its anti-papal tone and demonstrates that works by Catholic authors could be – and were – used to promote Protestant ends.

1.4   *Wimborne Minster Chained Library*

The 154 titles in 151 surviving volumes donated by Stone and Gillingham to the library in Wimborne Minster church were written by 109 individual authors from a range of confessional identities.[19] Figure 18 below demonstrates this diversity, evidencing works by Early Christians, including several Church Fathers, medieval theological authors, post-Reformation Catholics, Protestants of various denominations and post-Restoration Anglicans. The multiplicity of confessional identities displayed in Stone's and Gillingham's collections was not unusual, as the collections already discussed have shown. Within the Wimborne Minster collection, as in the Grantham and Ripon libraries, there was a clear focus on works by Protestant authors, with varying proportions of Early Christian texts as well, demonstrating their continued (or renewed) importance in early modern England, after the Commonwealth and the Restoration of the monarchy.[20]

---

17   Nicla Riverso, 'Paolo Sarpi: the Hunted Friar and his Popularity in England', *Annali d'Italianistica*, 34 (2016), pp. 302–303; Jaska Kainulainen, *Paolo Sarpi: A Servant of God and State* (Leiden: Brill, 2014), p. 173.

18   K. Brinkmann Brown, 'Sarpi, Paolo (1552–1623)', *The Oxford Encyclopedia of the Reformation* (online, 2005); Kainulainen, *Paolo Sarpi*, p. 173.

19   The various Bibles and liturgical works with no known authors have been excluded from these figures. Those volumes with more than one author, such as the *Biblia Polyglotta*, have been included on the basis of the first-named authors.

20   Jean-Louis Quantin, *The Church of England and Christian Antiquity: The Construction of a Confessional Identity in the 17th Century* (Oxford: Oxford University Press, 2009), pp. 24–31, 327.

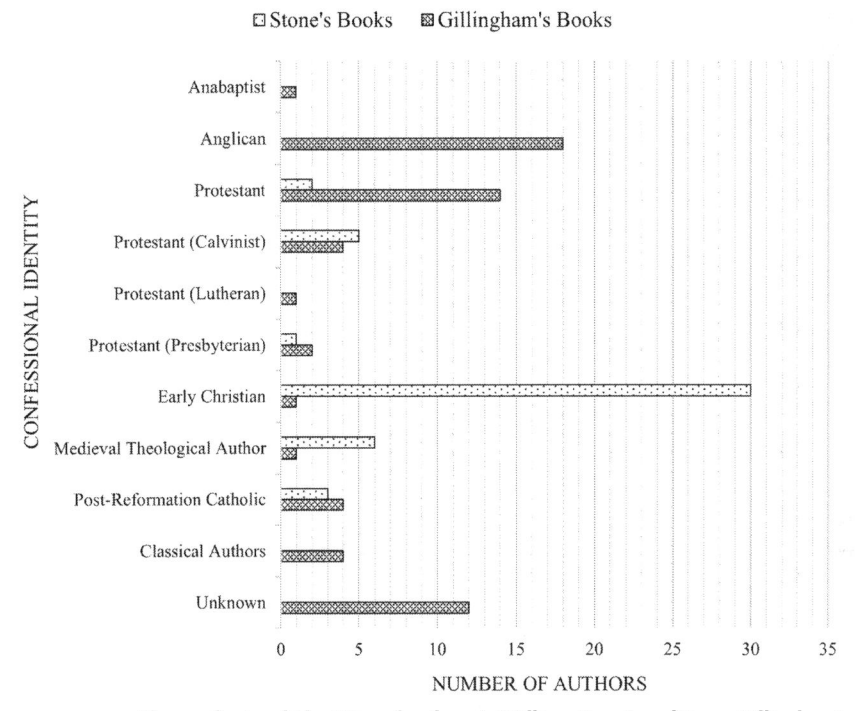

FIGURE 18 The confessional identities of authors in William Stone's and Roger Gillingham's donations to Wimborne Minster Chained Library

By separating out Stone's and Gillingham's individual donations, it becomes clear that both corpuses included works by authors from a range of confessional identities. Unsurprisingly, given the prominence and popularity of works by the Church Fathers in Oxford in the 1670s and 1680s, Stone's collection was largely comprised of books by Early Christians, whilst Gillingham's was predominantly comprised of Protestant authors of various denominations.[21] When considered together, the two collections of books donated by Stone and Gillingham to the church of Wimborne Minster were dominated by works by Protestants of all denominations, including Anglicans, which together accounted for forty-two percent of the collection, and by works by Early Christian writers, which accounted for twenty-eight percent of the collection.

---

21   *Ibid.*, p. 312.

Medieval theological writers and post-Reformation Catholics each totalled five percent of the collection. The remaining eighteen percent of the collection was comprised of authors of other or unknown confessional identities. Such a wide array of confessional identities amongst the authors in these collections demonstrates Stone's and Gillingham's commitment to acquiring the best and most learned scholarship.

William Stone's collection was originally part of a working library for use in his clerical and academic occupations: his 'learning, knowledge, and probity' and his abilities as a preacher were much talked of in contemporary Oxford.[22] Forty-seven different authors were responsible for the eighty-nine volumes in Stone's donation and Early Christian authors accounted for just over half of those (fifty-one percent). The Church Fathers formed a canon of sacred texts that were so popular they can be found in almost every episcopal library in seventeenth-century England; they were esteemed particularly highly in the years after the Restoration, when Stone was employed at New Inn Hall, Oxford.[23] In addition to their value as Scriptural interpretations, Protestants of all denominations also employed the works of the Church Fathers to demonstrate the antiquity of Protestantism and refute Catholic claims to the same.[24] Stone's former position as a clergyman may account for his interest in, and thus the prominence of, works by the Church Fathers in his collection. After their donation to Wimborne Minster church, the books would likely have been of most value and interest to the library's clerical users as well as those members of the laity who were able to read Latin and had a particular interest in reading patristic Biblical commentaries.

The donation of Roger Gillingham, a gentleman, included a combination of books that he purchased specifically for the library in Wimborne Minster church and those taken from Gillingham's personal library collection by his executors after his death. His bequest was primarily comprised of works by Protestant authors of various denominations that together accounted for around thirty-four percent of the total. However, the collection as a whole was wider ranging than Stone's in its representation of authors of different confessional identities, and also included a number of works by medieval theological writers and post-Reformation Catholics. There were several additional

22　　Philip Bliss, *Reliquiae Hearnianae: The Remains of Thomas Hearne, M.A., of Edmund Hall* (London: John Russell Smith, 1869), pp. 185–186; J. M. J. Fletcher, *A Dorset Worthy, William Stone, Royalist and Divine (1615–1685)* (Dorchester: Dorset County Chronicle Printing Works, 1915), p. 8.

23　　David Pearson, 'Patterns of Book Ownership in Late Seventeenth-Century England', *The Library*, 11 (2010), p. 139.

24　　Quantin, *The Church of England and Christian Antiquity*, p. 68.

volumes by authors of unclear confessional identities as well. The collection of books Gillingham gave to the library reflects the sorts of books that a seventeenth-century gentleman was interested in reading, and exemplifies the kinds of books that Gillingham and his executors thought most appropriate for the library's clerical and lay readers.

2 The Publication Dates of Parish Library Books

The publication dates for the vast majority of books in all four parish library collections of Grantham, Ripon, Gorton and Wimborne Minster, suggest that the books were second-hand at the time of their purchase, evincing the strength of this trade in the second half of the sixteenth century and throughout the seventeenth century. In the foundation indenture for the library he established by monetary gift, Francis Trigge did not stipulate that the desired 'encreasinge of learninge and knowledge in divinitie' in the library's users should come exclusively from contemporary texts.[25] The majority of works in this collection were printed after the Henrician Reformation of the 1530s but before the 1590s, when the library was founded. Similarly, the greater part of Anthony Higgin's theology collection that he gave to Ripon Minster as a library was printed in the century prior to the library's establishment in Higgin's will of 1624. Less than thirty percent of the books in the Gorton Chest parish library were published in the 1650s, the decade of its foundation, with most of the books being published in the preceding seventy-year period between the 1580s and the 1640s. The chronological distribution of publication dates for the Stone and Gillingham donations to Wimborne Minster Chained Library is wide-ranging, though perhaps a greater relative proportion of these collections were printed in the decade preceding and the decade of the donations than in the other library collections. Nevertheless, these corpuses also include a large percentage of second-hand books. All four library collections are therefore reflective of the importance of the second-hand book trade and the strength of the relationship between the centre and the peripheries of the trade in the sixteenth and seventeenth centuries.

2.1 *The Francis Trigge Chained Library*
The books in the Francis Trigge Chained Library were printed over a period of 130 years, which suggests a thriving second-hand book market in late

---

25 Lincolnshire Archives, Lincolnshire, (Grantham St Wulfram Par/23/1), Documents relating to the Trigge Library: Agreement.

Elizabethan England. Seventy of the 263 surviving volumes were published in the 1590s or the first decade of the 1600s, while the remaining 193 volumes were published prior to 1590. The seventy volumes printed between 1590 and the compilation of the *Catalogus Librorum* in 1608 are the most likely to have been new at the time of their purchase and placement in the collection. The books published before 1590, on the other hand, were a decade old or more when they were purchased, meaning they were probably at least second-hand at the time of their inclusion in the Trigge collection.

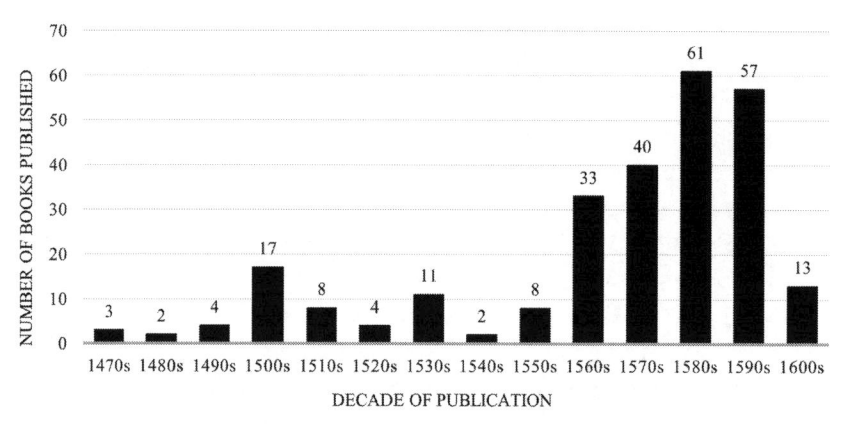

FIGURE 19   Publication dates of books in the Francis Trigge Chained Library

Figure 19 above demonstrates the chronological publication pattern of the books in the Francis Trigge Chained Library. The publication dates of the books in the Trigge library suggest that around three quarters of the books were bought second-hand, meaning that just a quarter of the collection was likely to have been new at the time of its purchase in Cambridge for the library collection. The 193 volumes published before 1590 account for seventy-four percent of the total collection. Even if this figure was lowered in order to take into consideration the time spent in booksellers' warehouses or back rooms and err on the side of caution, it is clear that a much higher proportion of the books were purchased second-hand than previously thought. In the 1980s, John Glenn asserted that just a quarter of the collection was purchased second-hand, based on the surviving 'signatures and marginalia in sixteenth-century hands'.[26] However, if the publication dates of these volumes are also considered, the proportion

---

26   Glenn, 'A Sixteenth-Century Library', p. 65.

of second-hand books rises significantly. This has important implications for the annotations in these volumes, which will be discussed in detail in Part 3 of this book. It is possible, considering the age of the books, that previous, private owners of the books (as opposed to library users) were responsible for any surviving marks of readership. In such cases, the library users read these books in conjunction with the surrounding marginalia, which shaped their reading experience and ultimately influenced the messages they took away from these texts, many of which went 'considerably beyond the official doctrine of the Church of England' in their theology.[27]

2.2   *Ripon Minster Parish Library*

The publication dates of the titles in Higgin's theology collection spanned 150 years, from the 1470s to the 1620s. There were forty-four volumes in the collection that included handwritten notes detailing when Higgin purchased the books, which demonstrate how old the books were at the time of their purchase. Over half of the books in the corpus (251 volumes equating to around fifty-six percent) were printed prior to 1570, meaning that they were most likely second-hand when Higgin purchased them for his library. Precisely when Higgin began to collect books is unknown, but it is plausible that he began to purchase volumes when he matriculated to the University of Cambridge in the early 1570s. The earliest purchase date Higgin recorded on the title page of one of his books is 1582, though it is unlikely that Higgin would have spent the better part of a decade in Cambridge, a key centre of the English book trade, without purchasing a single volume.[28] The second-hand nature of many of these books, like those in the other three collections discussed in detail here, again has significant implications for any surviving annotations. Figure 20 below demonstrates the decades in which the books of Ripon Minster's theology collection, donated by Higgin, were printed.

Much of the evidence for Higgin's purchase of specifically second-hand books is circumstantial because the date of purchase is unknown. However, the forty-four volumes in the theology collection of Ripon Minster parish library that included purchase information on their title pages evidence that

---

27   Arnold Hunt, 'Clerical and Parish Libraries' in Elisabeth Leedham-Green and Teresa Webber (eds), *The Cambridge History of Libraries, Volume 1, to 1640* (Cambridge: Cambridge University Press, 2008), p. 416.

28   The date of 1582 is noted on the title page of Saint Augustine, *D. Aurelii Augustini Hipponensis Episcopi Confessionum libri xiii. Opera theologorum Lovaniensium ex manuscriptis codicibus multum emendati. Eiusdem Confessio theologica tripartite* (Louvain: Hieronymus Welleus, 1573). Annotated copy in University of Leeds Brotherton Special Collections Library, shelfmark Ripon Cathedral Library xiii.A.33. USTC 406004.

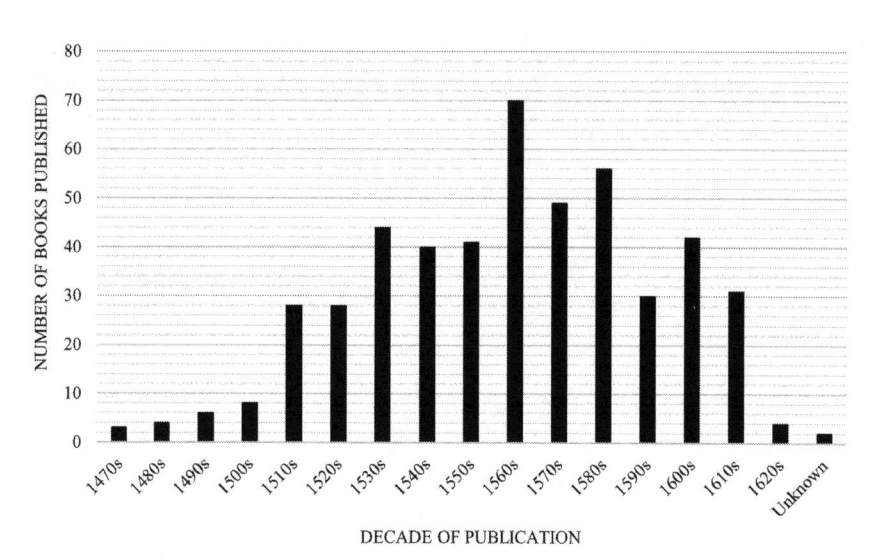

DECADE OF PUBLICATION

FIGURE 20   Publication dates of surviving titles in Ripon Minster Parish Library

the ages of these books at the time of their purchase ranged from brand new to 103 years old. Higgin purchased just three volumes in the year of their publication: Joannes Drusius the Elder's *Joh. Drusii ad loca difficiliora Josuæ, Judicum, & Samuelem commentaries liber* ... (1618), Willem Hesselszoon van Est's *Annotationes aureæ in præcipua ac difficiliora Sacræ Scripturæ loca* (1622) and Theodore Beza's *Ad acta Colloquii Montisbelgardensis Tubingae edita* (1588).[29] Archbishop Theodoret of Cyrus's *Theodoreti Episcopi Cyri De providential sermones X. Nunc primum in lucem editi* was published in 1545 and purchased by Higgin in London in 1593, making it almost fifty years old at the time.[30] In 1596,

29   Joannes Drusius the Elder, *Joh. Drusii ad loca difficiliora Josuæ, Judicum, & Samuelem commentaries liber* ... (Franeker: Fredericus Heynsius, 1618). Annotated copy in University of Leeds Brotherton Special Collections Library, shelfmark Ripon Cathedral Library I.B.8. USTC 1018085; Willem Hesselszoon van Est, *Annotationes aureæ in præcipua* (Cologne: widow of Johann Crith, 1622). Annotated copy in Brotherton Special Collections Library, shelfmark Ripon Cathedral Library I.B.15. USTC 2019159; Theodore Beza, *Ad acta Colloquii Montisbelgardensis Tubingae edita* (Geneva: Joannes Le Preux, 1588). Annotated copy in University of Leeds Brotherton Special Collections Library, shelfmark Ripon Cathedral Library II.C.10. USTC 451142.

30   Theodoret, Bishop of Cyrus, *Theodoreti Episcopi Cyri De providential sermones X. Nunc primum in lucem editi* (Rome: Antonio Blado, 1545). Annotated copy in University of Leeds Brotherton Special Collections Library, shelfmark Ripon Cathedral Library XVIII.E.3. USTC 858943.

Higgin bought a copy of the medieval writer Astesano's *Summa Astensis.*
Clarissimi sacre theologie eximii professoris fratris Astesani de Ast ... Summa de
casibus amenissimam complectens disciplinarum divinarum & ecclesiasticarum
sanctionem ....[31] Astesano's text was published in just one edition, in 1519, leav-
ing Higgin no choice but to purchase such an old copy if he wanted to read
this work of moral theology.[32] The oldest volume in Higgin's collection with
a purchase date noted on the title page was a 1488 imprint of the first volume
of Guillaume Durand's *Rationale divinorum officiorum* that Higgin bought in
1591, making the book 103 years old at the time of its purchase.[33] Higgin's purchasing of such old books was not unusual. Many of his contemporaries and
earlier clerics purchased second-hand versions of texts they could not otherwise obtain, and the practice is replicated in the other libraries analysed here.
It demonstrates an acknowledgement of the fact that the most recent edition
of a work was not always the best edition.[34] This desire for the best works of
scholarship available demonstrates the significance of these parish libraries on
the intellectual and religious landscape of early modern England as repositories of education that consisted of the highest-quality information available.

2.3   *The Gorton Chest Parish Library*

The vast majority of titles in the Gorton Chest parish library were published
over a seventy-year period between the 1580s and the 1640s. Less than a third of
the titles were published in the 1650s, the same decade as the library was placed
in the church, meaning that the greater part of the collection was probably purchased second-hand. Publication dates in the 1640s and earlier for these books

---

31   Astesano, *Summa Astensis. Clarissimi sacre theologie eximii professoris fratris Astesani de*
      Ast ... Summa de casibus amenissimam complectens disciplinarum divinarum & ecclesi-
      asticarum sanctionem ... (Lyon: Stephen Gueynard, 1519). Annotated copy in University
      of Leeds Brotherton Special Collections Library, shelfmark Ripon Cathedral Library
      XVII.G.18. Not listed in the USTC.

32   John Duns Scotus, *Sententiarum antea vitio impressorum depravatum: nunc vero a multi-*
      fariis erroribus purgatum: pristineque integritati restitutum (Lyon: Jacques Myt for Jacques
      Giunta and Francois Giunta, 1520). Annotated copy in University of Leeds Brotherton
      Special Collections Library, shelfmark Ripon Cathedral Library XVIII.F.20. USTC 145318;
      Astesano, *Summa Astensis.* Annotated copy in Brotherton Special Collections Library,
      shelfmark Ripon Cathedral Library XVII.G.18. Not listed in the USTC.

33   Guillaume Durand, *Rationale divinorum officiorum* (Basel: Nicolaus Kesler, 1488). Anno-
      tated copy in University of Leeds Brotherton Special Collections Library, shelfmark Ripon
      Cathedral Library XVIII.H.12. USTC 744526.

34   Pearson, 'The Libraries of English Bishops', p. 229; Matthew Yeo, *The Acquisition of Books*
      by Chetham's Library, 1655–1700 (Leiden: Brill, 2011), pp. 53–56.

also meant that the collection passed over some of the more divisive, polemical texts and tracts of the 1650s. In addition, the age of the books at the time of their purchase for the Gorton Chest parish library may account for their relative cheapness. As James Rigney has argued, printed books were associated with newness and age did not necessarily mean they were considered more valuable, as was the case for other objects.[35]

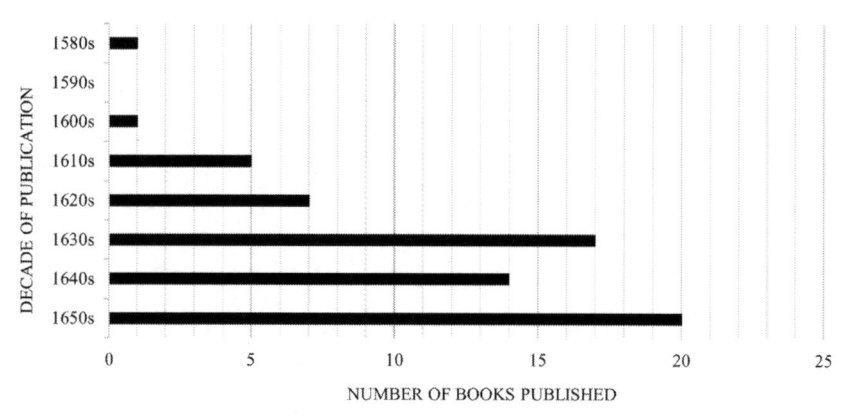

FIGURE 21   The publication dates of books in the Gorton Chest Library by decade

Chetham bequeathed £200 for the founding of five parish libraries. Whilst this was a significant sum of money, just £30 was allocated to the Gorton Chest parish library for the acquisition of books, and new books in particular could be expensive.[36] Certainly, John Tildsley lamented the sum as seemingly inadequate for its appointed task.[37] Robert Littlebury, the main bookseller from whom the vast majority of books for Chetham's libraries were purchased, was a principal practitioner in the second-hand book trade and acquired many

35   James Rigney, 'Sermons into Print' in Peter McCullough, Hugh Adlington and Emma Rhatigan (eds), *The Oxford Handbook of the Early Modern Sermon* (Oxford: Oxford University Press, 2011), p. 206.

36   Ian Mitchell, '"Old Books – New Bound"? Selling Second-Hand Books in England, c. 1680–1850' in Jon Stobart and Ilja Van Damme (eds), *Modernity and the second-hand trade: European consumption cultures and practices, 1700–1900* (Basingstoke: Palgrave Macmillan, 2010), p. 140.

37   Chetham's Library, Manchester, (CPP/2/141), Letter from John Tildsley to Rev. Hollinworth at Manchester.

second-hand books through *post mortem* valuations and sales of estates.[38] Therefore, by working with an expert in the second-hand book trade and by purchasing second-hand books that were often cheaper than new editions, the trustees were able to buy more volumes for the libraries.[39]

2.4   *Wimborne Minster Chained Library*

The dates of publication for Stone and Gillingham's books span a period of two hundred years, as shown in Figure 22 below, from the 1490s to the 1690s. A mixture of new and second-hand volumes were present in the collections of both Stone and Gillingham. Again, as is the case for the other parish libraries considered here, the age of the books at the time of their purchase and eventual donation has interesting implications for the surviving marginalia that they contain, which often provide an insight into the thoughts of their readers on the texts and likely influenced the experiences of later readers.

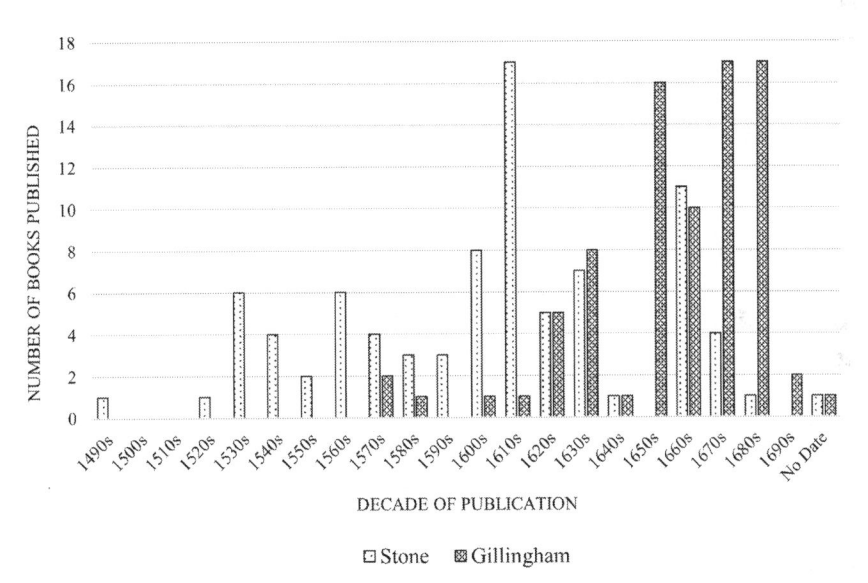

FIGURE 22   Publication dates by decade of the books donated to Wimborne Minster Chained Library by William Stone and Roger Gillingham

---

38   Yeo, *The Acquisition of Books by Chetham's Library*, p. 87.

39   Mitchell, 'Selling Second-Hand Books in England', pp. 139–140 and 153.

This visual representation of the publication dates of the books in Stone's collection makes clear that the vast majority of volumes Stone gifted to Wimborne Minster church were at least fifteen years old when they arrived in 1685. The age of the books at the time Stone purchased them for his own collection is unclear. M. N. E. Tiffany has suggested that Stone only started to collect the books that were eventually sent to Wimborne Minster church after his return to Oxford and his appointment as Principal of New Inn Hall in 1663.[40] Even if this was the case, the vast majority of books Stone purchased were still published a significant number of years, if not decades or even a century, before he acquired them. Most of the books in Stone's collection of Church Fathers were published in the 1630s or earlier, with a smaller number published in the latter half of the seventeenth century. Assuming that Stone did not begin collecting books until the early 1660s, and taking into consideration the time that books could spend unsold on booksellers' shelves and in warehouses, this could mean that Stone only purchased sixteen volumes new and that the remaining seventy-three books in his gift to Wimborne Minster were acquired second-hand. During his time at New Inn Hall, Oxford, Stone's access to the thriving book trade in Oxford and Cambridge would have been relatively easy. The trade was predicated on the needs of the students and faculty of the universities, which encouraged local booksellers to stock a wider range of Latin volumes printed primarily in Europe than perhaps would have been found in other areas where the book trade flourished.[41]

The sources of Gillingham's books are rather obscure. As has been shown, Gillingham's will stated that he had purchased thirty-four volumes with the explicit intention of donating them to the library in Wimborne Minster church and that the rest of his donated volumes came from his own collection. Gillingham's bookseller(s) remain unknown, but he probably took advantage of his residence near the Middle Temple to visit any number of the London booksellers who congregated in Little Britain, St Paul's Churchyard or elsewhere.[42] Much of Gillingham's collection was printed in the second half of the seventeenth century, though only a small number of volumes were printed in the 1690s, when Gillingham donated the volumes to Wimborne Minster church. The later publication dates of Gillingham's volumes reflect the secular

40   M. N. E. Tiffany, *The History of the Rev. Mr. William Stone and his Hospital together with that of other Almshouses in Oxford* (Headington: Tiffany Arts, 2000), p. 19.

41   John Barnard and Maureen Bell, 'The English Provinces' in John Barnard, D. F. McKenzie and Maureen Bell (eds), *The Cambridge History of the Book in Britain, Volume IV: 1557–1695* (Cambridge: Cambridge University Press, 2002), p. 669.

42   Simon Bradley and Nikolaus Pevsner, *London 1: The City of London* (London: Yale University Press, 2002), p. 534.

nature of many of the books. From the outset of printing, religious texts were the favoured genre across Europe: almost half of all the books printed in the fifteenth century were religious in their nature.[43] Even in the sixteenth and seventeenth centuries, religious texts were the mainstays of the printing industry: Bibles, catechisms, prayerbooks, homilies and more were frequently reprinted before secular literature began to grow in popularity at the end of the sixteenth century and the beginning of the seventeenth century.[44] Seventy-four percent of the books Gillingham donated, either those purchased directly for the library or those drawn from his personal collection, were published before 1680, meaning that around three quarters of the corpus was most likely second hand when Gillingham purchased them.

3   The Publication Locations of Parish Library Books and Links to the Continental Book Trade

The publication locations of the books in the parish libraries of Grantham, Ripon, Gorton and Wimborne Minster attest to the vibrancy and the reach of the continental book trade across England in the sixteenth and seventeenth centuries. Whilst the Gorton Chest contains only one book with a European imprint, the other three libraries are dominated by continental books printed in cities as wide ranging as Caen and Naples, Salamanca and Basel, Antwerp and Ingolstadt, Paris and Venice. Many of the European cities in which the volumes of these libraries were published are located in the countries that Andrew Pettegree has described as the 'steel spine' of printing in early modern Europe.[45] That should not, however, detract from the achievement of the English provincial book trade in enabling a book printed in Ingolstadt to find its way into a parish library collection in Yorkshire, nor a book published in Basel to be present in a collection in Lincolnshire.

3.1   *The Francis Trigge Chained Library*
The strong links between the continent and the book trade in London and its nearby market towns, including Cambridge, where the majority of the Trigge collection was purchased, are demonstrated by the range of cities and

43   Colin Clair, *A History of European Printing* (London: Academic Press, 1976), pp. 121–122.

44   Joad Raymond, 'The Development of the Book Trade in Britain' in Joad Raymond (ed.), *The Oxford History of Popular Print Culture: Volume One: Cheap Print in Britain and Ireland to 1660* (Oxford: Oxford University Press, 2011), p. 62.

45   Andrew Pettegree, 'Centre and Periphery in the European Book World', *Transactions of the Royal Historical Society*, 18 (2008), p. 104.

countries in which the volumes of this collection were published. Figures 23a and 23b below reflect the geographical spread of publication locations of works in this collection.

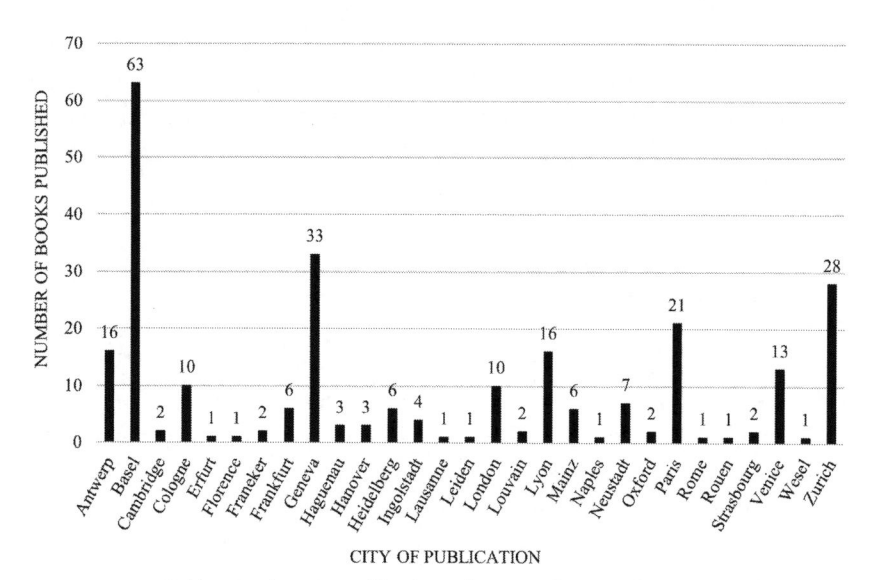

FIGURE 23A   Publication locations of books in the Francis Trigge Chained Library by city

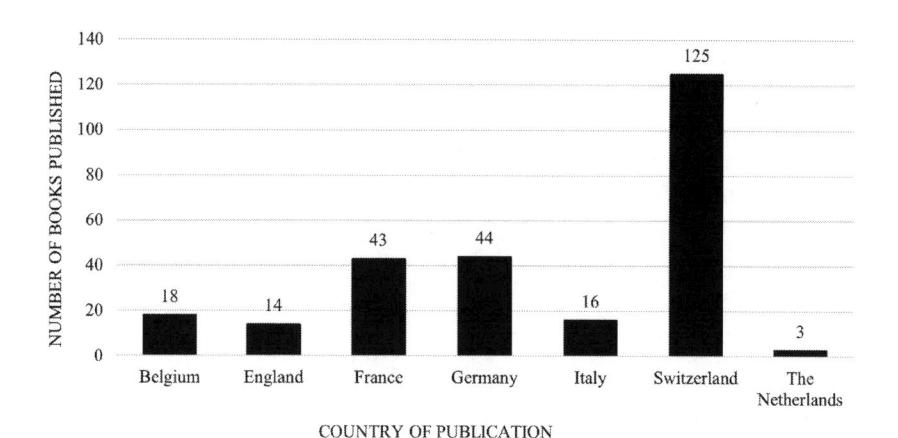

FIGURE 23B   Publication locations of books in the Francis Trigge Chained Library by country

As can be seen from the above figures, only a small minority of the books in the Francis Trigge Chained Library were originally printed in England. The number of continental imprints in the Trigge library collection reflect the strong Anglo-European book trade in the early modern period, reinforcing the argument put forward in chapter 3 that continental books were once more pervasive in England than surviving numbers in parish libraries now suggest. Before 1601, printed book production in Europe was concentrated in France, Italy, the German Empire, the Netherlands and the Swiss Confederation. These five territories were responsible for the production of over eighty percent of all books printed in Europe before the dawn of the seventeenth century.[46] This number rises even higher when focussing exclusively on Latin books. Within the Francis Trigge library, there is a correlation between the number of Latin books in the collection and the number of works printed in Europe. English book production in the sixteenth century largely centred on vernacular books and the books produced in England were not exported in any great numbers. The English book trade was thus heavily reliant on the international book trade for the scholarly Latin works it required.[47] The overwhelming majority of Latin books in the Francis Trigge library were produced on the continent, in one of the main centres of printing in either France, Germany, or Switzerland. These numbers reflected the printing prominence of these three countries and the large numbers of their books that were imported into England, which in turn limited the abilities of the English printing industry, particularly in the first half of the sixteenth century.[48]

Moreover, the high concentration of continental imprints in this collection is interesting considering the restrictive Henrician and Marian legislation that sought to constrain the activities of foreign merchants in England between the 1530s and 1550s. In the 1530s and 1540s, Henry VIII passed various legislation to prevent foreign printers setting up presses in England and to inhibit the importation of books from the continent, ostensibly with the intention of limiting the spread of continental heretical works in England. In 1534, for example, Henry VIII passed an Act of Parliament forbidding any but wholesale purchases of foreign books; he followed this in 1542 with a blanket ban on the importation of books from Europe.[49] Under Mary I, the charter of

---

46   *Ibid.*, pp. 105–106.

47   *Ibid.*, p. 106.

48   *Ibid.*, p. 106; Margaret Lane Ford, 'Importation of Printed Books into England and Scotland' in Lotte Hellinga and J. B. Trapp (eds), *The Cambridge History of the Book in Britain, III: 1400–1557* (Cambridge: Cambridge University Press, 1999), pp. 183–188.

49   Frank A. Mumby and Ian Norrie, *Publishing and Bookselling*, 5th edition (London: Cape, 1974), pp. 48–49, 53–54.

incorporation of the Company of Stationers in 1557 gave the company 'a police power over books, on behalf of the state', which allowed them to monopolise the London book trade.[50] These powers, in conjunction with other Marian legislation, significantly depleted the number of foreign books available on the English book market. Meanwhile, the fourteen books in the Francis Trigge collection that were printed in England hint at the growing prominence of domestic production in the second half of the sixteenth century, as demonstrated by Joad Raymond, though it had evidently not yet begun to challenge continental imports on a significant scale as it would later in the seventeenth century.[51]

3.2   *Ripon Minster Parish Library*

An examination of the publication places and dates of the theological works in Ripon Minster parish library evidence the continued strength and reach of the European and second-hand book trades in England into the first quarter of the seventeenth century. Higgin's collection of theological books has the largest range of publication cities of the four parish library collections considered in detail here. Basel, Paris, Antwerp and Cologne were – in addition to London – the four most common cities of publication for the surviving theological titles in Ripon Minster parish library. As will be seen, the same four European cities were the most prominent publication locations of the books in Wimborne Minster Chained Library in Dorset as well. The prevalence of these cities reflected their importance as part of the 'steel spine' of Europe's major trade routes that dominated the production of books in the scholarly languages in the sixteenth and seventeenth centuries.[52] Figure 24 below demonstrates the large number of cities in which Higgin's theological books were printed.

The religious nature of the books in the theology collection of Ripon Minster parish library that were printed in Basel, Paris and Antwerp are highly reflective of the respective religious position of each origin city. Basel was 'a relatively tolerant city where titles that would have been banned elsewhere could be published'.[53] This position led to Basel being the prominent printing centre in

---

50   John N. King and Mark Rankin, 'Print, Patronage and the Reception of Continental Reform: 1521–1603', *The Yearbook of English Studies*, 38 (2008), pp. 57–58; David Cressy, 'Book Burning in Tudor and Stuart England', *The Sixteenth Century Journal*, 36 (2005), pp. 363–364.

51   Raymond, 'The Development of the Book Trade in Britain', p. 61.

52   Pettegree, 'Centre and Periphery', p. 104.

53   Urs B. Leu, 'The Book and Reading Culture in Basel and Zurich during the Sixteenth Century' in Malcolm Walsby and Graeme Kemp (eds), *The Book Triumphant: Print in Transition in the Sixteenth and Seventeenth Centuries* (Leiden: Brill, 2011), p. 306.

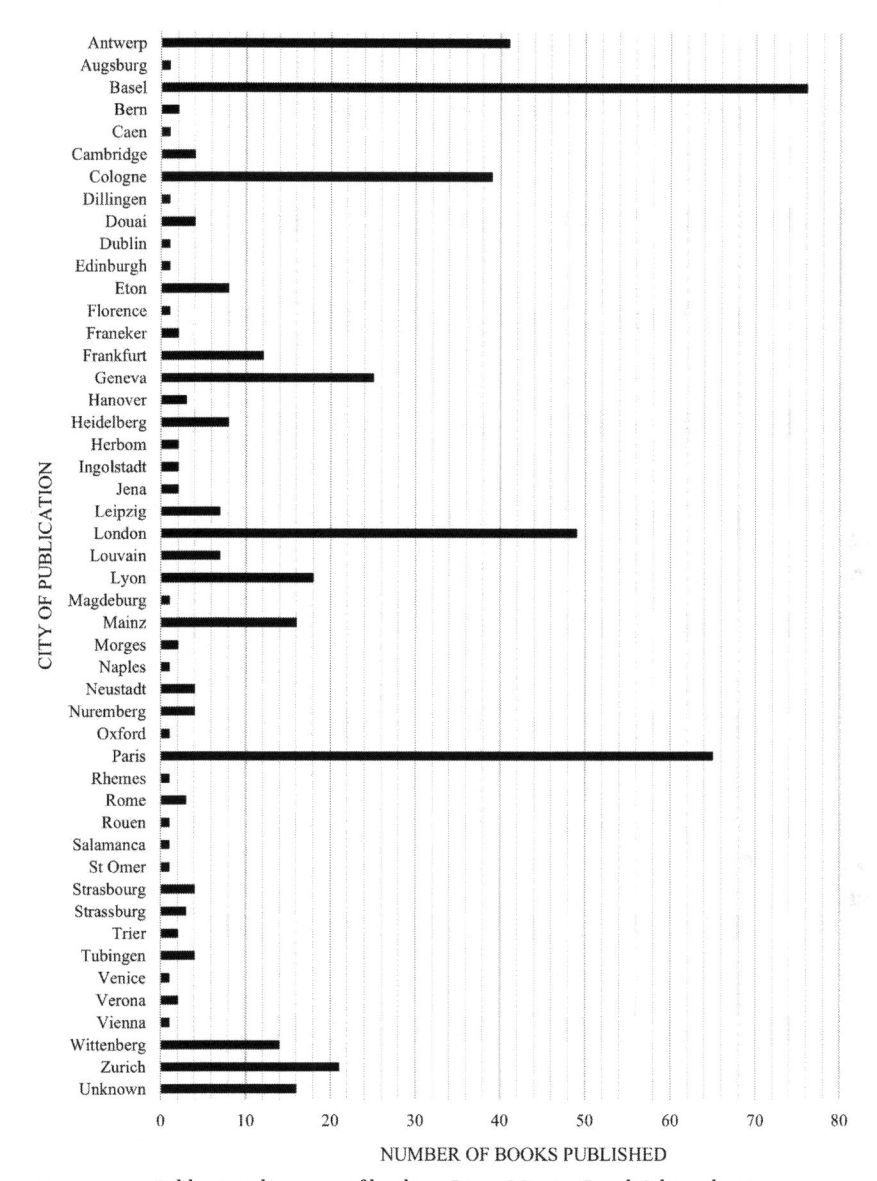

FIGURE 24 Publication locations of books in Ripon Minster Parish Library by city

Switzerland in the sixteenth century. It also explains why men of differing confessional identities, such as Saint Augustine, Desiderius Erasmus and Philipp Melanchthon, were the authors of several of the works with Basel imprints in the collection of Ripon Minster parish library. The city's printers produced 8,285 editions of works on various subjects, theology foremost amongst them, and dominated a significant portion of the European Latin book trade. Books printed in Basel were sold in numerous European countries, making it a relatively simple task for Higgin to purchase a Basel-published book from a bookseller in either London or York.[54]

Similarly, the books in the Minster's theology collection that were printed in Paris were predominantly written by medieval theologians and post-Reformation Catholic authors, reflecting the city's religious identity, which it maintained through various upheavals during the course of the sixteenth century.[55] Parisian books were widely distributed throughout Europe, accounting for the high number of Paris imprints in this collection.[56] Furthermore, Antwerp was a major Catholic printing centre and an international centre of book commerce that was responsible for fifty-five percent of all books published in the Netherlands between 1470 and 1600.[57] Antwerp's Catholic status explains why many of the books in Ripon Minster's collection with Antwerp imprints were by post-Reformation Catholic authors, including Robert Bellarmine, Nicholas Harpsfield and Thomas Harding.[58] The 'close and long-established' links between London and Antwerp engendered the availability of large numbers of Antwerp imprints on the English book market, enabling their easy purchase and accounting for their prominence in this collection.[59]

---

54 *Ibid.*, pp. 295–306.
55 Pettegree, 'Centre and Periphery', pp. 111–112.
56 Andrew Pettegree, *The Book in the Renaissance* (New Haven and London: Yale University Press, 2010), p. 87; James Raven, *The Business of Books: Booksellers and the English Book Trade, 1450–1850* (New Haven: Yale University Press, 2007), p. 14.
57 Andrew Pettegree, 'Printing in the Low Countries in the Early Sixteenth Century' in Malcolm Walsby and Graeme Kemp (eds), *The Book Triumphant: Print in Transition in the Sixteenth and Seventeenth Centuries* (Leiden: Brill, 2011), pp. 3, 9–10; Geert Vanpaemel, 'Science for Sale: the Metropolitan Stimulus for Scientific Achievements in Sixteenth-Century Antwerp' in Hugh Kennedy (ed.), *Urban Achievement in Early Modern Europe: Golden Ages in Antwerp, Amsterdam and London* (Cambridge: Cambridge University Press, 2009), p. 289.
58 Andrew Pettegree and Arthur der Weduwen, *The Bookshop of the World: Making and Trading Books in the Dutch Golden Age* (New Haven: Yale University Press, 2019), pp. 269–270.
59 Pettegree, 'Printing in the Low Countries', pp. 13–14.

The printing and publishing cities of Europe were connected through the complex business networks that linked together printers and booksellers across the continent. A series of annual trading events such as the Frankfurt Fair, at which 'most major printers were represented', facilitated the 'efficient supply' of books at a reasonable price to a widely dispersed readership'.[60] The presence of some of the top European publishing cities, whose printers were some of the most prominent participants in the Latin trade in early modern Europe, in the theology collection that Higgin gave to Ripon Minster reflected the efficacy of these events and networks in the distribution of books across Europe. Further, it also reinforces the argument that Higgin's collection was originally intended for his personal and professional use before he decided to give it to the Minster as a library. The high-quality scholarship of these works was necessary for two reasons. Firstly, the high scholarly value of such texts was a necessity in reducing the recusancy that has been shown to be rife in Yorkshire in the late sixteenth and early seventeenth centuries. Secondly, it was an important part of shaping pastoral and ministerial development for the clergy in Ripon and its surrounding areas, in a continuation of the minster church's objective, outlined in its Charter of Refoundation of 1604, to 'promote and so spread ... the true worship of God' through instruction and information.[61]

3.3   *The Gorton Chest Parish Library*

Sixty-one of the sixty-five titles in the Gorton Chest parish library were printed in London. Two titles were printed in Oxford, one in Edinburgh and one in Leiden in the Netherlands. The work printed at Leiden was Thomas Cartwright's *A Confutation of the Rhemists Translation, Glosses and Annotations on the New Testament,* published in 1618.[62] Cartwright was an English Presbyterian theologian and religious controversialist who, in the 1570s, was at the heart of the Admonitions Controversy, and was associated with John Field and Thomas Wilcox, the authors of *An Admonition to the Parliament.* The Admonition was a scathing attack on the English Church that was so extreme it was considered seditious libel. Cartwright had connections to both Antwerp and Leiden in the

---

60   Pettegree, *The Book in the Renaissance,* pp. 77, 80.

61   University of Leeds Brotherton Special Collections Library, Leeds, (MS Dep 1980/1/1.0), Letters Patent of James I (known as 1st Letters Patent), re-constituting the collegiate church of Ripon, 2nd August 1604; University of Leeds Brotherton Special Collections Library, Leeds, (MS Dep 1980/1/1.1), Copy of 1st Letters Patent. With Translation (1916) by J. T. Fowler.

62   Thomas Cartwright, *A Confutation of the Rhemists Translation, Glosses and Annotations on the New Testament* (Leiden: W. Brewster, 1618). USTC 3008255 and 1436816.

Netherlands and was offered the position of chair of the university at Leiden in 1580, which he declined. In 1582, Cartwright was encouraged by Francis Walsingham, who was motivated by a desire to see Cartwright converted to a more moderate and 'safe' puritan, to write a refutation of the Catholic New Testament published at Rheims. This was the basis of the *Confutation* published posthumously at Leiden in 1618.[63]

England's printing presses were centred in London and were famed for their concentration on vernacular religious books, in contrast to the European presses that focussed on the production of Latin texts.[64] The kinds of books desired by the trustees for the five parish libraries Chetham established made the London book market an ideal supplier of the required religious texts, thus rendering the need to look to the continental market largely unnecessary.

3.4   *Wimborne Minster Chained Library*

The publication locations of the books in Wimborne Minster Chained Library largely correspond to their genres. The scholarly Latin and religious works donated by William Stone to the church of Wimborne Minster – eighty-nine volumes of Fathers' and Commentators' works – were printed on presses in three English and fifteen European cities, including Basel, Antwerp, Paris and Cologne, which were part of the 'steel spine' of European printing in the sixteenth and seventeenth centuries. The dominance of these cities in the collection's imprints reflected the statuses of France and the German Empire as 'by far the most important' territories in early modern Europe 'both intellectually and in terms of book production'.[65] That such a large proportion of these volumes were imported and made available for sale speaks to the organisation and proliferation of the established continental book trade in England and demonstrates its continued prominence at the end of the seventeenth century.

The collection of primarily secular, English works that Roger Gillingham donated, on the other hand, were largely printed in England (with around eighty percent of them printed in London alone) and reflect the increasing strength of the domestic book trade in vernacular literature towards the end of the seventeenth century. Imprints from Cambridge and Oxford within the collection were printed on the learned presses at the universities, which by the 1690s were well established and run by professional

---

63   Patrick Collinson, 'Cartwright, Thomas (1534/5–1603)', *Oxford Dictionary of National Biography* (online, 2004).
64   Pettegree, 'Centre and Periphery', pp. 118–119.
65   *Ibid.*, p. 104.

printers.[66] Imprints from five different European cities also featured in Gillingham's bequeathed collection. The number of volumes printed in this vast array of English and European cities is demonstrated in Figure 25 below.

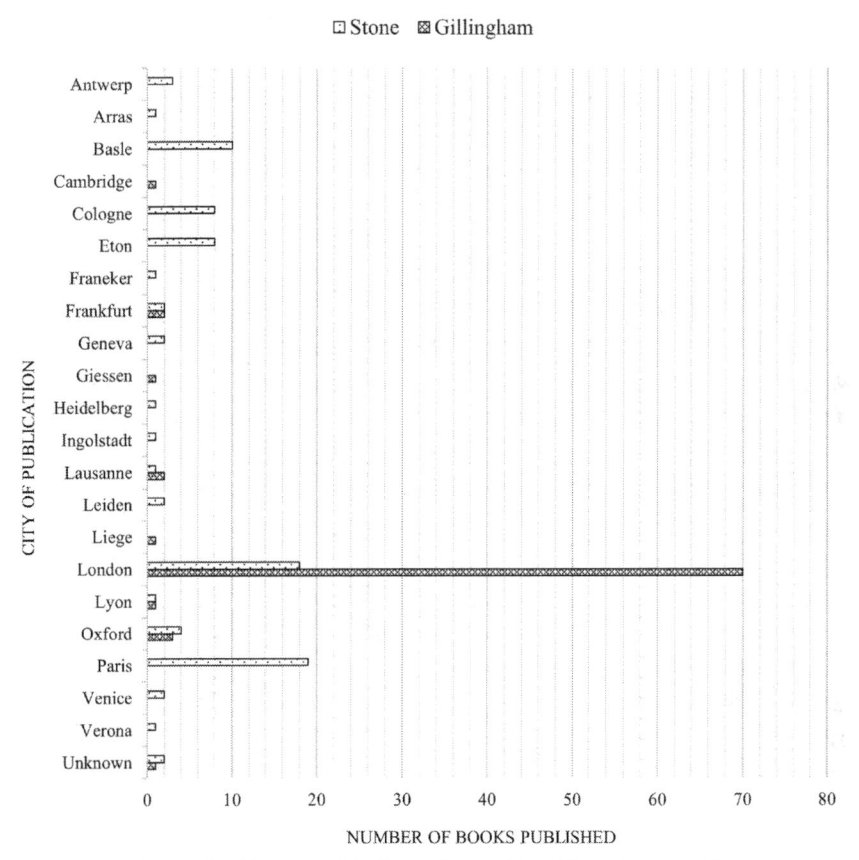

FIGURE 25   Cities of publication of the books donated by William Stone and Roger Gillingham to Wimborne Minster Chained Library

---

66   David McKitterick, 'University Printing at Oxford and Cambridge' in John Barnard, D. F. McKenzie and Maureen Bell (eds), *The Cambridge History of the Book in Britain, Volume IV: 1557–1695* (Cambridge: Cambridge University Press, 2002), p. 204.

The differences of topic and language in the books donated by Stone and Gillingham explain the variance in the number of European cities in which the books were produced. Latin religious texts dominated Stone's collection and were almost certainly imported into England as part of the Latin trade, 'a specialised trade' carried out by 'specialised personnel', who consisted of both Englishmen and Europeans, as opposed to solely Europeans as was once posited. The Latin trade itself was 'intended to facilitate intellectual exchange across Europe'.[67] In the sixteenth and early seventeenth centuries, Latin texts of Christian and humanist scholarship were imported into England in vast quantities, ostensibly owing to the simultaneous inability of English printers to produce editions of good quality and the ability of European printers to do exactly that, at a reasonable cost.[68] Considering the reputation for scholarship attached to the Latin trade, it is unsurprising that many of the great European printing houses were represented in Stone's collection. Some of the books he owned came from some of the most prominent publishers and booksellers in England and on the continent, including the Birckmanns of Cologne and the Frobens of Basel. This suggests that Stone, like other collectors, may have been keen to acquire the best possible versions of the texts he was interested in irrespective of when or where they were published, though this is difficult to determine with any certainty due to the obscure nature of Stone's collecting practices.

Conversely, most of the titles in Gillingham's donation were written in English and covered a wide variety of topics from religious literature to secular histories to health to agriculture, which continental printers had little economic incentive to print in a vernacular language. The predominance of books published in London in this primarily vernacular collection denotes the strength of the Stationers' Company in preventing the growth of the print industry outside that city – provincial printing in England was prohibited between 1557 and 1695. The growing consumer demand in early modern England for small volumes such as history books, almanacs, or manuals on 'gentility and politeness' is attested to by the prevalence of such works in Gillingham's donation.[69] London's dominance in Gillingham's collection also resulted from his proximity to the city's numerous booksellers during his forty

---

67   Julian Roberts, 'The Latin Trade' in John Barnard, D. F. McKenzie and Maureen Bell (eds), *The Cambridge History of the Book in Britain, Volume IV: 1557–1695* (Cambridge: Cambridge University Press, 2002), p. 141; Alan B. Farmer, 'Cosmopolitanism and Foreign Books in Early Modern England', *Shakespeare Studies*, 35 (2007), p. 60.

68   Farmer, 'Cosmopolitanism and Foreign Books', pp. 58–61.

69   John Hinks, 'The Book Trade in Early Modern Britain: Centres, Peripheries and Networks' in Benito Rial Costas (ed.), *Print Culture and Peripheries in Early Modern Europe: A*

years at the Middle Temple between 1654 and 1694. The Middle Temple was in close proximity to five prominent locales in London's book trade – including Little Britain, St Paul's Churchyard, Cheapside, Fleet Street and Paternoster Row – all of which housed large numbers of booksellers.[70] This would have made access to a wide range of books relatively easy for Gillingham and he may have purchased at least some of the books he later donated to Wimborne Minster church during his time at the Middle Temple.

4   The Language of Books in Parish Libraries

In three out of four of these parish library collections, Latin was the dominant language of print. Notable exceptions are the Gorton Chest parish library collection, which exclusively comprised works written in English, and Roger Gillingham's donation to Wimborne Minster library, whose primarily secular volumes were also largely written in English, with only a few texts in Latin and other academic languages. The decision to write in Latin was previously thought to preclude books from being used by any but the highly educated laity and the clergy. However, Jennifer Richards has recently demonstrated that Latin was taught to boys who attended and received a grammar school education.[71] The potential readership of these volumes was therefore much wider than has previously been conceived and this has important implications for the Latin volumes in the parish library collections of early modern England. They were not for the exclusive use of the clergy and the well-educated layman, and books being written in Latin did not necessarily negate a donor's wish for the repository to provide an education to all.

4.1   *The Francis Trigge Chained Library*
The Latin works in the Francis Trigge Chained Library provide an early example of a book collection that was accessible to a wider range of people than previously thought. Most literate people with a grammar school education were able to read Latin to a certain extent and thus the Latin nature of many of the books in the Trigge library did not necessarily prohibit

Contribution to the History of Printing and the Book Trade in Small European and Spanish Cities (Leiden: Brill, 2012), p. 117; Raven, *The Business of Books*, pp. 34–35.

70   Bradley and Pevsner, *London 1: The City of London*, p. 534; Raven, *The Business of Books*, pp. 26, 156.

71   Jennifer Richards, *Voices and Books in the English Renaissance: A New History of Reading* (Oxford: Oxford University Press, 2019), p. 76.

lay readership of the collection.[72] Only six of the 263 surviving volumes in the Trigge library were written in English, the remaining 257 were written in Latin. This may be a product of the library's early establishment and the age of the books, most of which were published before the English presses became a significant challenger to their European counterparts. Richards' work reveals that Latin volumes were not necessarily predisposed to the clergy and the well-educated, but could be read by the 'middling' sorts of people who were in receipt of a grammar school education. The number of these 'middling' sorts, as has been demonstrated by Ian Green, was rising throughout the late sixteenth and seventeenth centuries.[73] The central argument of this book, that post-Reformation parish libraries were significant parts of the religious and intellectual landscape of early modern England as means by which to educate and to distribute the religious messages of Protestantism to the widest possible range of lay and clerical readers, is therefore reinforced by Richards' work on Latin accessibility. The Latin books in the Trigge library collection would have been understandable by a broad range of people, thus enabling a deeper religious understanding for all of its readers and fulfilling Trigge's aim for the library to increase learning and knowledge.

4.2   *Ripon Minster Parish Library*

Like in the Francis Trigge Chained Library, the vast majority of the books in the theology collection of Ripon Minster parish library were written in Latin. This preponderance of Latin texts reflected the collection's original role as a working library for Anthony Higgin, which may also explain the presence of additional works in Greek and other academic and vernacular languages in the corpus.

Within the collection, there were 382 titles written in Latin (equating to seventy-nine percent of the total), limiting their use by all those without at least a grammar school education. Similar usage restrictions were implicit for the fifty-six titles written in other languages besides English. There were twenty-six titles written in Greek, suggesting Higgin, at least, had the ability to read the language. A further twenty-five titles were polyglots, including the eight volumes of the *Biblia Regia* (or Antwerp Polyglot) overseen by Benito Arias Montano and the collected works of Saint Basil of Caesarea in Greek and

72   *Ibid.*, p. 76.
73   Ian Green, *Print and Protestantism in Early Modern England* (Oxford: Oxford University Press, 2000), p. 34.

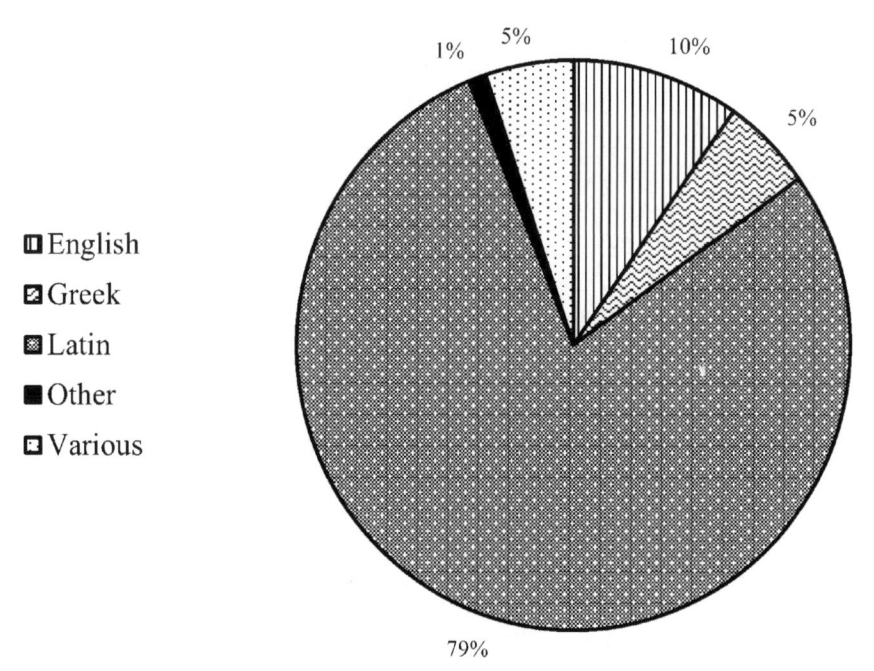

1% 5%   10%

5%

■ English
☒ Greek
▩ Latin
■ Other
▢ Various

79%

FIGURE 26   Languages of surviving books in Ripon Minster Parish Library

Latin.[74] In addition, there were two German titles, two Italian titles and one Hebrew work on the Pentateuch. Such titles were of no use to those without a grammar school education and probably of limited use even to those who had one: boys from middling and aristocratic households were taught Latin, but seemingly little Greek, whilst their female counterparts were more likely to be taught French.[75] Greek was unlikely to be encountered before university and the other languages featured in the polyglot volumes of this collection (Aramaic, Syriac, Hebrew and others) would likewise have required a high level of education to read.[76] The inclusion of works in these languages

---

74   Benito Arias Montano, *Biblia Sacra, Volumes I–VIII* (Antwerp: Christopher Plantin, 1569–1573). University of Leeds Brotherton Special Collections Library, shelfmarks Ripon Cathedral Library III.E.7/q–III.E.14/q. USTC 401394; Saint Basil of Caesarea, *Nunc primum Græcè et Latinè coniunctim edita, in duos tomos distributa …* (Paris: Michel Sonnius, 1618). University of Leeds Brotherton Special Collections Library, shelfmarks Ripon Cathedral Library XVI.C.9/q–XVI.C.11/q. USTC 6015104.

75   Richards, *Voices and Books in the English Renaissance*, pp. 76, 116.

76   John Roberts, Águeda M. Rodriguez Cruz and Jurgen Herbst, 'Exporting Models' in H. de Ridder-Symoens (ed.), *A History of the University in Europe, Volume II: Universities in Early Modern Europe, 1500–1800* (Cambridge: Cambridge University Press), p. 274.

unsurprisingly, considering its collector, suggests that the collection was of most use to members of the clergy and those of the laity with an elite education.

Just forty-seven of the surviving titles in Higgin's theology collection in Ripon Minster parish library were written in English. They largely comprised Biblical commentaries, attacks on the Catholic Church, sermons and works of theology. Such volumes would arguably have been more relevant and useful to a wider range of people, including the less educated laity as well as the clergy, hence their inclusion in the vernacular. Also in English were a number of the polemical writings of John Jewel and Thomas Harding who, from the 1560s onwards, were engaged in a bitter pamphlet war over Jewel's *Apology of the Church of England*. Jewel's numerous polemical works 'would remain significant throughout the early modern period', and Lucy Wooding has asserted that he did 'more than most to give the English Church credibility and a coherent Protestant identity'. Wooding demonstrated that Jewel's 'greatest achievement' was to 'create a clear-cut image of an English Protestant Church that was diametrically opposed to its Catholic critics'.[77] This was a particularly important sentiment in the context of the efforts of Higgin, Tobie Matthew and other clerics in northern England, who may have found Jewel's texts highly useful in their attempts to eradicate recusancy, further reinforcing the practical use of these works prior to their donation to Ripon Minster.

4.3   *Wimborne Minster Chained Library*

Similarly to the Ripon Minster parish library, the volumes in Stone's and Gillingham's collections in the Wimborne Minster Chained Library can be loosely linked to both their subject matter and their intended readers. The majority of books in William Stone's collection were written in Latin, a collection of works by the Church Fathers purchased for his own personal use. After their donation to Wimborne Minster church, the patristic texts were available to be read by any members of the clergy and laity with a grammar school education in Latin.[78] The majority of books in Gillingham's collection were written in English, making them more generally accessible to those without a grammar school education. Further, they were the types of books that would have been of most practical value to that demographic. The proportion of books in the combined collections of Stone and Gillingham, in their different languages, are demonstrated in Figure 27 below.

---

77   Lucy Wooding, 'Introduction: John Jewel and the Invention of the Church of England' in Angela Ranson, André A. Gazal and Sarah Bastow (eds), *Defending the Faith: John Jewel and the Elizabethan Church* (Philadelphia: University of Pennsylvania Press, 2018), pp. 1–2.

78   Richards, *Voices and Books in the English Renaissance*, p. 76.

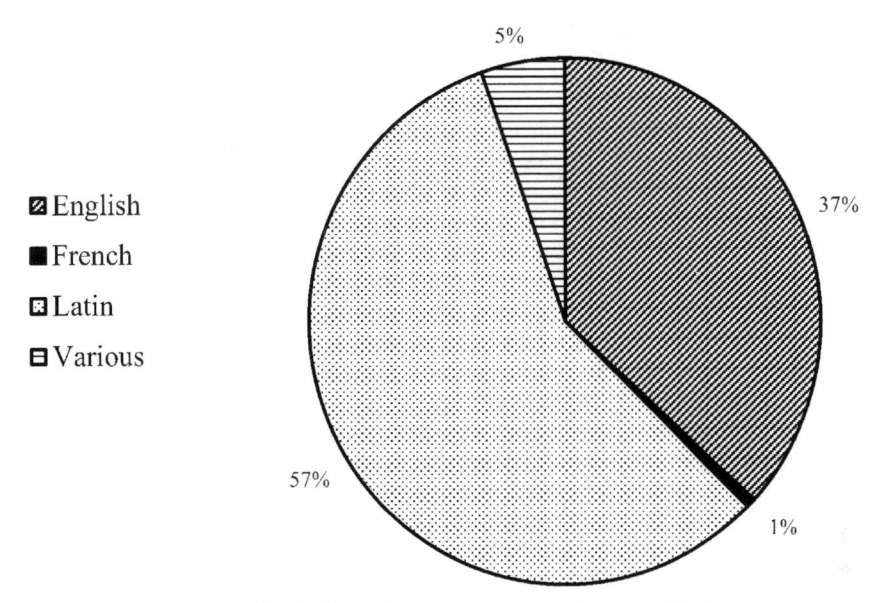

FIGURE 27   Languages of books donated by William Stone and Roger Gillingham to
Wimborne Minster Chained Library

Gillingham's collection also included a small number of volumes written in
other languages. Some of the multilingual books Gillingham donated included
the seven-volume Polyglot Bible by Walton *et al.* and the two volumes of
Castell's *Lexicon Heptaglotton*, both of which were written in various languages
including Arabic, Persian, Ethiopic, Hebrew and Samaritan. Gillingham also
donated a French work by François de la Mothe le Vayer, the controversial
French writer and tutor, under the pseudonym Orosius Tubero.[79] If Gillingham
could read any of these languages, it was a testament to the level of his education. Alternatively, his purchase of these volumes and their inclusion in
Wimborne Minster Chained Library may be a reflection of the perceived scholarly value and importance of these texts by Gillingham. Their usefulness to the
general readership of the town of Wimborne Minster, however, was likely to
have been limited.

---

79   Brian Walton, *Biblia Sacra, Polyglotta, Volumes I–V* (London: Thomas Roycroft, 1653–1657),
Wimborne Minster Chained Library, shelfmarks I11–I17. These editions not listed on the
USTC; Edmund Castell, *Lexicon Heptaglotton, Volumes I and II* (London: Thomas Roycroft,
1669). Wimborne Minster Chained Library, shelfmarks I9 and I10. These editions not
listed in the USTC; Ian Maclean, 'La Mothe le Vayer, François de (1588–1672)', *The New
Oxford Companion to Literature in French* (Oxford: Oxford University Press, 1995), p. 437.

5   Genres of Books in Early Modern Parish Libraries

Analysis of the collections of the Grantham, Ripon, Gorton and Wimborne
Minster parish libraries reveals that the genres of books chosen for inclusion
remained largely the same at the end of the seventeenth century as it was at
the end of the sixteenth century. Specifically, parish library collections continued to be dominated by religious and theological volumes written primarily in
Latin. They also included an increasing number of vernacular secular volumes
on subjects and genres as diverse as history, geography, philosophy, natural
history, medicine, civil law, encyclopaedias and dictionaries. The expanding
variety of genres available is evidence of Robert Darnton's 'communications
circuit' in practice: authors were readers; readers influenced authors. Darnton
argued that 'by reading and associating with other readers and writers, they
form notions of genre and style and a general sense of the literary enterprise,
which affects their texts' and which, in the context of this book, contributed to
a developing market in secular vernacular books.[80]

5.1   *The Francis Trigge Chained Library*

The 263 titles in the Francis Trigge Chained Library were predominantly theological in character. The breadth of religious literature – from homilies to
hagiographies, Biblical commentaries to religious or Church histories, general works of theology to doctrinal texts – suggests a comprehensive religious
library intended for practical application. The genres of books in the collection and the confessional identities of the authors who wrote them are demonstrated in Figure 28 below.[81]

Works by Protestants of varying confessional identities dominated the original collection of the Francis Trigge Chained Library. The presence of works
by medieval theological authors and post-Reformation Catholic writers is the
result of a conscious choice on the part of Trigge and his associates, as opposed
to the negligence that John Glenn previously asserted.[82] Protestant books
account for fifty-two percent of the total collection, whilst the works of medieval theological writers and post-Reformation Catholic authors account for
the more modest figures of fourteen percent and ten percent of the collection

---

80   Robert Darnton, 'What is the History of Books?', *Daedalus*, 111 (1982), pp. 67–68.
81   The 'Authors of Unknown/Other Religions' includes those authors whose names are
       unknown, those whose names are known but whose religions are not, and the classical
       and Romano-Jewish authors included in the Francis Trigge Chained Library collection.
82   Glenn, 'A Sixteenth-Century Library', p. 65.

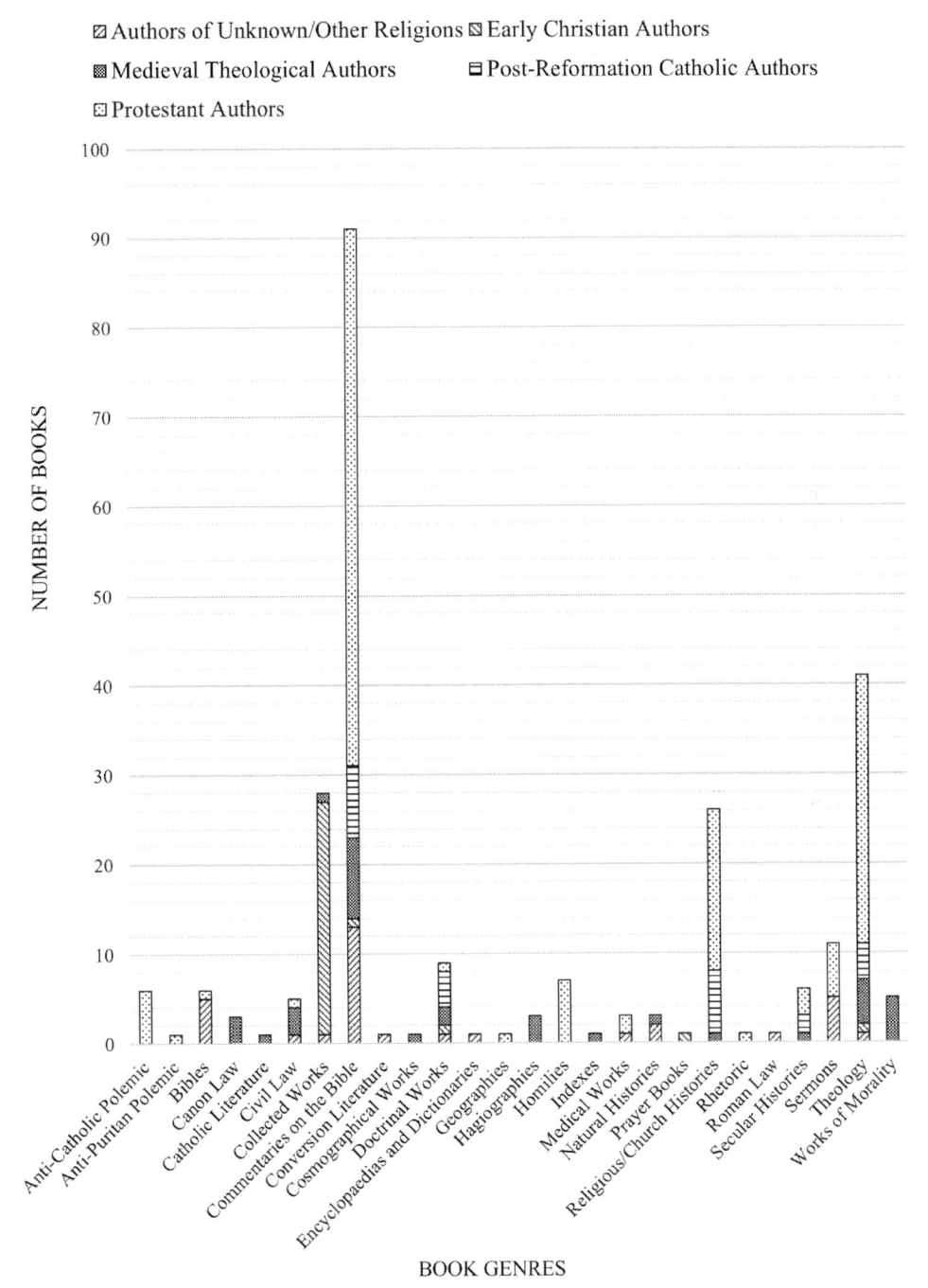

BOOK GENRES

FIGURE 28   The genres of books in the Francis Trigge Chained Library Collection

respectively. The disparity between these two figures can be attributed to two factors: firstly, Trigge and his colleagues were attempting to provide a library to increase learning and knowledge amongst the local clergy and laity. In keeping with Trigge's own moderate puritanism within the established Church, this meant promoting the Church of England and established religion, whilst also ensuring the clergy had access to Catholic texts to better understand and refute their arguments. The second reason for the larger number of Protestant texts than medieval or post-Reformation Catholic works was because of the better availability of Protestant books as the English state, in conjunction with the Company of Stationers, sought to suppress Catholicism through various means that included the confiscation and destruction of books.[83]

The combination of texts by Protestants and Catholics in scholarly and clerical libraries was not uncommon in the sixteenth and seventeenth centuries, as shown in the previous chapter. David Pearson has demonstrated that prominent Church of England bishops such as Arthur Lake, Samuel Harsnett and Lancelot Andrewes owned various works by Catholic writers in their collections, and that Catholic liturgy was an 'unfailing presence' within these clerical libraries because it enabled them to refute Catholic arguments regarding theology and doctrine.[84] The incentive to include a portion of medieval and post-Reformation Catholic works must have been strong in a theologically divided county such as Lincolnshire. Trigge and his colleagues' desire to provide a library to educate the local clergy and laity proved similarly motivational.

The Francis Trigge library included a number of Biblical commentaries written by Protestant authors of various denominations, in addition to several by medieval theological writers and post-Reformation Catholics. Christians had been writing Biblical commentaries since the end of the apostolic era and many Biblical commentators focussed on presenting to their readers the literal meaning of Scripture.[85] There are ninety-one Biblical commentaries in the Trigge library collection. Medieval theological writers wrote nine of these commentaries, with six being post-Reformation reprints of earlier

---

83   Cressy, 'Book Burning in Tudor and Stuart England', pp. 364–366.

84   Pearson, 'The Libraries of English Bishops', p. 229.

85   Marius Reiser, 'The History of Catholic Exegesis, 1600–1800' in Ulrich L. Lehner, Richard A. Muller and A. G. Roeber (eds), *The Oxford Handbook of Early Modern Theology, 1600–1800* (Oxford: Oxford University Press, 2016), p. 77; Ulrich G. Leinsle, 'Sources, Methods, and Forms of Early Modern Theology' in Ulrich L. Lehner, Richard A. Muller and A. G. Roeber (eds), *The Oxford Handbook of Early Modern Theology, 1600–1800* (Oxford: Oxford University Press, 2016), p. 32.

works, making them more readily available in the late fifteenth and sixteenth centuries.[86] Post-Reformation Catholics wrote eight of the Biblical commentaries in the collection. Their inclusion was not just about their ability to help Protestant divines refute Catholic arguments but was also a positive reflection of the quality of their scholarship, having been written by prominent Catholic theologians including Robert Bellarmine, Hector Pintus and Francis Ribera. The use of Catholic texts for Protestant purposes was relatively common. When the Catholic Robert Persons published his *The First Booke of the Christian Exercise* in 1582, for example, it became extremely popular, even amongst Protestants. So popular, in fact, that Edmund Bunny, rector of Bolton Percy in Yorkshire, felt compelled to 'deal with it' by producing a Protestant edition of the work. Bunny altered Persons' text by omitting and changing words and short passages, and adding his own interpretations, comments and additions in marginal notes to turn the work into a Protestant text.[87] Protestants of different denominations wrote sixty of the Biblical commentaries in the Francis Trigge collection. A breakdown of the works of theology by Protestant authors within the Trigge library collection evidences the preponderance of Protestant Calvinist theology, with eighteen of the thirty theological texts being written by Calvinist authors, though only one by John Calvin himself. These works include Theodore Beza's *Tractatus theologicarum*, a compilation of theological treatises on Calvinist theology, as well as works on more specific aspects of that theology, such as Hieronymus Zanchius's various works on predestination, *Miscellaneorum libri tres. Tertium nunc editi. De praedestinatione sanctorum.*[88]

In addition, the Trigge library also included seven titles concerned with Catholic theology, including Diego de Payva de Andrada's *Defensio Tridentinae fidei catholicae et integerrimae quinque libris comprehensa*, a defence of the Catholic doctrine as outlined at the Council of Trent (1563).[89] Alongside these were more reprints of medieval works of theology such as the *Summa theologica*

---

86   Carl R. Trueman, 'Scripture and Exegesis in Early Modern Reformed Theology' in Ulrich L. Lehner, Richard A. Muller and A. G. Roeber (eds), *The Oxford Handbook of Early Modern Theology, 1600–1800* (Oxford: Oxford University Press, 2016), p. 188.

87   Robert McNulty, 'The Protestant Version of Robert Parsons' "*The First Booke of the Christian Exercise*"', *Huntington Library Quarterly*, 22:4 (1959), pp. 271, 273–276.

88   Theodore Beza, *Tractatus Theologicarum*, 2nd edition ([Geneva]: Eustathius Vignon, 1582). Francis Trigge Chained Library, shelfmark D22. This edition not listed in the USTC; Hieronymus Zanchius, *Miscellaneorum libri tres. Tertium nunc editi. De praedestinatione sanctorum* (Neapoli Palatinorum: Matthaeus Harnisius, 1592). Francis Trigge Chained Library, shelfmark C15. This edition not listed in the USTC.

89   Diego de Payva de Andrada, *Defensio Tridentinae fidei catholicae et inegerrimae quinque libris comprehensa* (Ingolstadt: David Sartorius, 1580). Francis Trigge Chained Library, shelfmark B9. USTC 632166.

of Saint Antonio Forciglione and Peter Lombard's *Sacratissima sententiarum totius theologie quadripartita volumina.*[90]

These titles enabled the clergy to better their understanding of Catholicism as they attempted to convert the religiously conservative population of Grantham and the surrounding areas. This was a significant concern in Lincolnshire in the last decades of the sixteenth century and the early years of the seventeenth century. One of Francis Trigge's own published works, his *An apologie, or defence of our dayes, against the vaine murmurings & complaints of manie ...* (1589), acknowledged why many in the county retained their conservative views on religion. He recognised the upheavals brought about by the changes made to parish church interiors: 'the bare walles' that were 'lacking their golden images, their costly coapes their pleasant Orgaines, their sweet frankinsence, their gilded chalices ...' caused conservatives to 'bewayle this spoyling and laying waste of the Church'. Trigge also posited that a sense of disconnect with their ancestors confirmed people in their conservative opinions and in their unwillingness to accept Reform: 'they condemne all our forefathers, saye they, and therefore they will never be on our opinion'.[91]

5.2   *Ripon Minster Parish Library*

The composite genres of the theology section of Anthony Higgin's professional library that he donated to Ripon Minster reflect the types of books that he thought interesting and useful for his ministerial and pastoral duties and necessary for the defence of the Church of England. The genres of the books also demonstrate the types of works that were available to the clergy and laity to provide them with a religious education after the books' donation to the Minster. Providing readers with a secular and spiritual education was the primary purpose of a large number of parish libraries established in England in the sixteenth and seventeenth centuries and, more specifically in the case of this particular collection, the main aim of Ripon Minster as set down by James I in the Charter of Refoundation of 1604.

---

90 Antonio Forciglione, *Summa theologica* (Lyon: Johannes Cleyn, 1516). Francis Trigge Chained Library, shelfmark I15. This edition not listed in the USTC; Peter Lombard, *Sacratissima sententiarum totius theologie quadripartita volumina* (Venice: Gregorio De Gregori, 1514). Francis Trigge Chained Library, shelfmark G4. USTC 847956.

91 Francis Trigge, *An apologie, or defence of our dayes, against the vaine murmurings & complaints of manie wherein is plainly proved, that our dayes are more happie & blessed than the dayes of our forefathers* (London: John Wolfe, 1589), pp. 24, 28. USTC 511333.

Higgin compiled a manuscript catalogue of the theology portion of his library prior to his death, ostensibly in preparation for its donation to the Minster. In the manuscript catalogue, Higgin arranged the theology section of his library under eight different subject headings: *Biblia Sacra*, *Patres*, *Commentarii*, *Polemici*, *Conciones*, *Leiturgiae et Missalia*, *Scholastici* and *Loci Communes et Catecheses*, which were themselves separated into thirty classes. The proportion of volumes under each subject heading can be seen below in Figure 29, which, having been taken directly from Higgin's manuscript of c.1620, includes both surviving and missing titles. Within these classifications are multitudinous Biblical commentaries and interpretations, numerous volumes of the collected works of patristic writers, a large quantity of theological texts and several sermons, as well as works of other genres such as anti-Catholic polemics, catechisms and works on Christian life and practical divinity, making them not dissimilar to the collections of the other parish libraries considered in this work.

The genres of books included in the theology section of Anthony Higgin's library suggest a collection amassed for use by a clergyman in a functional and professional capacity prior to their donation to Ripon Minster as the basis of the church's parish library. Many of the volumes aided and improved Higgin's ministry. The corpus comprised numerous volumes that demonstrate Higgin's commitment to the Church of England, his belief in the importance of the Bible and the necessity of its being communicated and explained

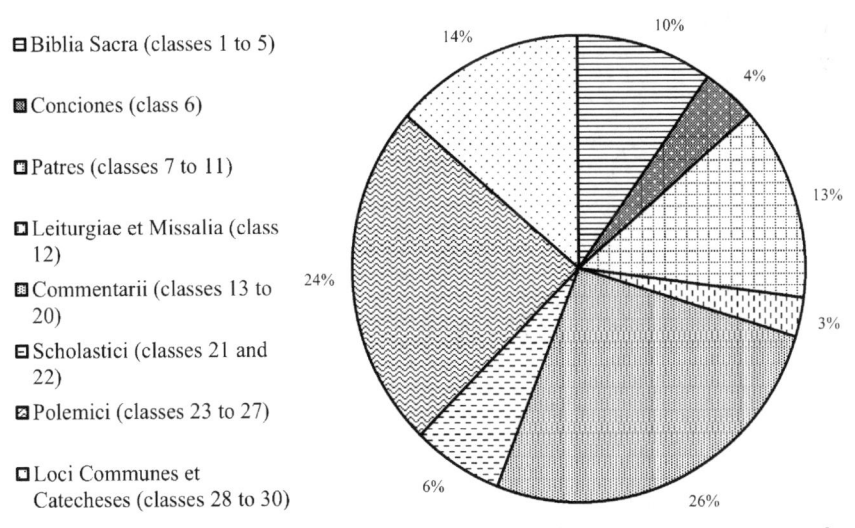

FIGURE 29   Anthony Higgin's classifications of his theological works in Ripon Minster Parish Library

to the laity through commentaries, interpretations and paraphrases. The prevalence of Biblical commentaries reflects their usefulness to both the clergy and the laity in summarising and simplifying complex passages of Scripture. Specialist commentaries in Latin and Greek aimed at academics, educated clergy and wealthy bibliophiles were often imported from the continent, whilst English commentaries were published for those whose knowledge of Latin was limited.[92] Of the surviving 122 Biblical commentaries in Ripon Minster parish library, just eight (approximately seven percent) were written in English. Works of theology, including various works on moral and pastoral theology, Christian life and education were the second largest genre in the surviving theology collection: eighty-three titles survive, accounting for seventeen percent of the total. The vast majority of both the Biblical commentaries and the works of theology in the collection were in Latin, limiting their usefulness to those without a grammar school education, in a similar manner to the Grantham and Wimborne Minster collections.

Sermons, official homilies, catechisms and books of practical divinity are numerous in this collection. The preponderance of these texts within the collection suggests their usefulness to Higgin and his clerical colleagues. Pastoral works were useful to early modern clerics as resources from which they could gather information for their own sermons to preach to their congregation. Higgin's manuscript notebooks demonstrate that he read catechetical works in preparation for 'expounding the staple items of Protestant catechetics [that] was deemed necessary in the Elizabethan and early Stuart Church' in his sermons to his congregation.[93] Furthermore, the pastoral works in Ripon Minster parish library had the potential to be beneficial to any lay readers using the collection: pastoral works increasingly encouraged the laity to 'pray fervently and frequently at home'.[94] This at-home, practical piety, which was closely monitored by the clergy, required ongoing self-examination on the part of the

---

92   Green, *Print and Protestantism*, pp. 103–104, 113–119.

93   Ian Green, 'Preaching in the Parishes' in Peter McCullough, Hugh Adlington and Emma Rhatigan (eds), *The Oxford Handbook of the Early Modern Sermon* (Oxford: Oxford University Press, 2011), p. 146. See also Higgin's manuscript notebooks: University of Leeds Brotherton Special Collections Library, Leeds, (Ripon Cathedral MSS 16–22, 24–27, 29–30, 32, 34–36, 38, 40).

94   Ian Green, 'Varieties of Domestic Devotion in Early Modern English Protestantism' in Jessica Martin and Alec Ryrie (eds), *Private and Domestic Devotion in Early Modern Britain* (Ashgate: Routledge, 2017), p. 9.

laity for signs of assurance of grace.[95] As the place to go for instruction on practical piety to be carried out at home, parish libraries like Ripon Minster were of significant importance to the laity and to the clerics who used them as repositories of religious knowledge.

5.3   *The Gorton Chest Parish Library*

Unlike the Trigge, Ripon and Wimborne Minster collections, all of which contained at least a small number of secular volumes, the Gorton Chest parish library contained none. The books in the Gorton Chest were all religious in nature and all were written in English. There was a strong and distinct pastoral leaning towards works of practical divinity in this collection. The character of the collection reflected the trustees' focus on providing a repository of Reformed Protestant religious knowledge to the 'common people' of Manchester through sermons, Biblical commentaries, catechisms and works of Christian life. The online catalogue held by Chetham's Library in Manchester, which now houses the Gorton Chest, has assigned Library of Congress subject headings to the Gorton Chest parish library's sixty-five remaining titles, which reveal that the range of subjects in this repository is considerably less varied than the Trigge, Ripon and Wimborne Minster libraries. This narrower concentration of subjects elucidates not only the close attention Chetham's trustees were paying to providing religious works, it also reflects Chetham's own desire, expressed in his will, for the parish libraries to edify and educate their readers in religion.[96] The proportion of titles in each category can be seen in Figure 30 below.

The general popularity of religious literature in the seventeenth century was growing as it became the chosen reading material of all serious and righteous readers.[97] Sermons – an important part of worship for Protestants who 'ascribed to the sermon a key role, with the help of the Holy Spirit, in bringing the faithful to salvation' – accounted for over a third of the titles in the Gorton Chest parish library.[98] This reflects the general pervasiveness of sermons in the seventeenth-century book market. Estimates suggest that over 1,000 sermons were printed between 1558 and 1603; 2,000 in the period from 1603 to 1640;

---

95   Alec Ryrie, *Being Protestant in Reformation Britain* (Oxford: Oxford University Press, 2015), pp. 39–48; C. Scott Dixon, *The Church in the Early Modern Age* (London: I. B. Tauris, 2016), p. 159.

96   Chetham's Library, Manchester, (Uncatalogued), Last Will and Testament of Humphrey Chetham.

97   David L. Gants, 'A Quantitative Analysis of the London Book Trade, 1614–1618', *Studies in Bibliography*, 55 (2002), p. 187; Rigney, 'Sermons into Print', pp. 204–205.

98   Green, *Print and Protestantism*, p. 194.

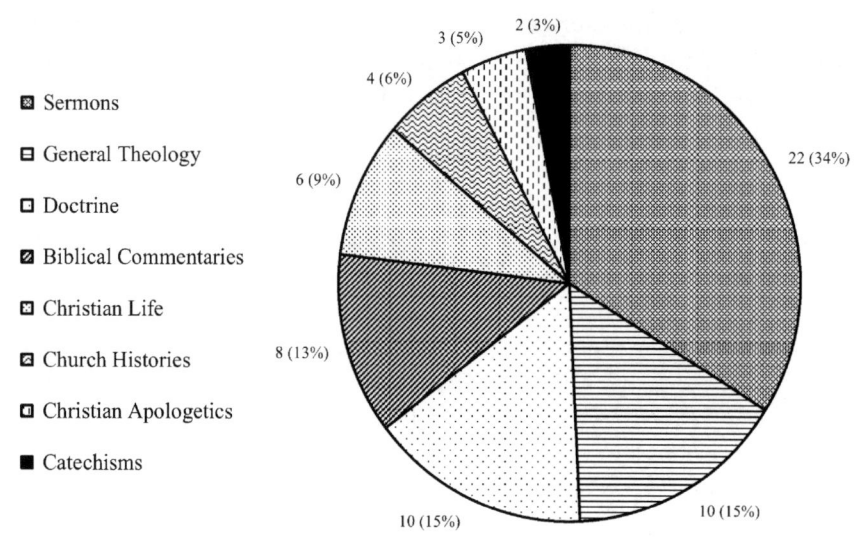

- ☒ Sermons
- ☱ General Theology
- ☐ Doctrine
- ☑ Biblical Commentaries
- ☒ Christian Life
- ☒ Church Histories
- ☐ Christian Apologetics
- ■ Catechisms

FIGURE 30   Subject classifications of books in the Gorton Chest Parish Library

and a staggering 24,000 between 1660 and 1783.[99] In his *A Christian Directory*, the seventeenth-century ejected minister and religious writer Richard Baxter provided four reasons for the popularity of the printed sermon. These included the ability of the sermon to convey the Spirit of God in the Holy Scriptures; the possibility for printed sermons to be written by a more able preacher than one's parish minister, meaning a better quality of sermon; the opportunity for printed sermons to be chosen by readers according to their individual needs, interests and concerns; and the fact that printed sermons were available at any time a person wished to read them.[100] James Rigney has argued, using Baxter's assertions as his evidence, that printed sermons were therefore popular because they provided the reader with a strong sense of autonomy and empowerment that released the reader from overreliance on a parish priest.[101] Furthermore, Ian Green has suggested that the printed sermons of Henry Smith, lecturer at St Clement Danes in London in the 1580s, were popular because they contained a straightforward explanation and application of a text, using simple vocabulary that made his messages easier to understand.[102]

---

99   *Ibid.*

100   Richard Baxter, *A Christian Directory* (London: Robert White 1673), pp. 60–61. This edition not listed on the USTC.

101   Rigney, 'Sermons into Print', p. 200.

102   Green, *Print and Protestantism*, pp. 197–198.

Many of these incentives for and benefits of reading printed sermons can be applied to those within the Gorton Chest parish library to explain the prominence of this genre within the collection.

The Gorton Chest also included numerous works of theology and practical divinity. For example, John Calvin's seminal text, *The Institution of Christian Religion*, a work of systematic theology that set out the paradigms of Reformed religion to all readers, was included in the Gorton Chest collection. Divided into four sections, *The Institution* simultaneously outlined the foundations of the Protestant religion to its readers and enabled the godly to better recognise God. Calvin himself stated his desire to 'prepare and furnish' his readers in 'reading of the Word of God, that they may both have an easy entry into it, and go forward without stumbling'.[103] Nine editions of this title, as translated by Thomas Norton, were published in England between 1561 and 1634.[104] In addition to this copy in the Gorton Chest, a further seventeen copies of the same edition of *The Institution* are recorded by the English Short Title Catalogue (ESTC) as surviving in England. Other theological works in the collection included volumes such as *Mr Bolton's Last and Learned Work of the Last Four Things*. In this volume, the Church of England clergyman Robert Bolton focussed on the ways in which people could identify the elect and enabled the godly to recognise themselves as such. In order to do this, Bolton asserted that the difference in the response of the godly to challenges and adversity, in comparison to 'the graceless', marked them out as those chosen by God for 'rescue' and relief. His readers were thereby able to undertake self-examination in order to discover whether they were members of the godly themselves.[105]

Apocalyptic literature was also a feature of the theological works in the Gorton Chest parish library: Thomas Brightman's *Works* on the Book of Revelation sat beside John Napier's *A Plain Discovery of the Whole Revelation of St John*, in which Napier concluded that the end of the world would come in either the 1650s or the 1690s.[106] Brightman sought to instil in Protestants a conviction of their being God's elect people by mapping contemporary events onto the apocalyptic narrative of the Book of Revelation to increase

---

103 John Calvin, *The Institution of Christian Religion*, trans. Thomas Norton (London: printed for Thomas Norton, 1611), sig. ¶3v. Annotated copy in the Gorton Chest, Chetham's Library, Manchester, shelfmark GC.2.11. USTC 3004572.

104 Green, *Print and Protestantism*, p. 607.

105 Robert Bolton, *Mr Bolton's Last and Learned Worke of the Foure Last Things* (London: George Miller, 1633), pp. 1–2. Gorton Chest, Chetham's Library, shelfmark 1.20(2). USTC 3016539.

106 Christopher Hill, 'God and the English Revolution', *History Workshop*, 17 (1984), p. 22.

their awareness of 'their own decisive role in the cosmic battle between Christ and Antichrist'. Apocalyptic tradition in Europe had been strengthened by the Protestant Reformation, as believers read apocalyptic texts that encouraged them to understand that 'the persecution and suffering of this world are part of God's plan yet unknown to man'. In England specifically, apocalyptic literature became an important source for explaining the break from the Roman Catholic Church. It gained even more popularity amongst Protestants, and Puritans particularly, in the late sixteenth century and early seventeenth century, as the English Reformation stalled and finally seemingly stopped and many began to question England's status as the Elect Nation. Brightman himself was instrumental in encouraging his readers to view themselves as God's elect people, who were responsible for continuing to advance the Reformation.[107]

Further, the Gorton Chest parish library also contained works of practical divinity by some of the genre's most notable authors, with the books of William Perkins, Richard Baxter and Richard Rogers sitting alongside those of Isaac Ambrose and Robert Bolton. The educational aims and intentions of the preachers who wrote these volumes directly aligned with Chetham's educational motivations for founding his five parish libraries. Richard Rogers advocated 'strict activities of piety and self-scrutiny' in order to obtain assurance of grace, whilst William Perkins' texts focussed 'not on identifying actions that satisfy a minimal standard of Christian behaviour, but on advancing, step-by-step, sometimes painfully and hesitatingly, towards the perfection that God intends for his people'.[108] Perkins' writings heavily influenced those of Richard Baxter, and the measured application of religion to everyday life by both men made their works popular with the reading public.[109] In the 'Premonition' to his *The Saints Everlasting Rest*, for example, Baxter pleaded:

> And now, Reader, whatever thou art, young or old, rich or poor, I intreat thee, and charge thee in the Name of thy Lord, (who will shortly call thee to a reckoning, and Judge thee to the everlasting unchangeable State,)

107   Avihu Zakai, 'Thomas Brightman and English Apocalyptic Tradition' in Yosef Kaplan, Henry Méchoulan and Richard H. Popkin (eds), *Menasseh ben Israel and his World* (Leiden: Brill, 1989), pp. 31–35.

108   Michael P. Winship, 'Weak Christians, Backsliders, and Carnal Gospelers: Assurance of Salvation and the Pastoral Origins of Puritan Practical Divinity in the 1580s', *Church History: Studies in Christianity and Culture*, 9 (2001), p. 462; W. B. Patterson, *William Perkins and the Making of a Protestant England* (Oxford: Oxford University Press, 2014), p. 103.

109   Louis B. Wright, 'William Perkins: Elizabethan Apostle of "Practical Divinity"', *Huntingdon Library Quarterly*, 3 (1940), pp. 181–182.

that thou give not these things the reading only, and so dismiss them with a bare approval: but that thou set upon this work, and Take God in Christ for thy only Rest, and set thy heart upon him above all. Jest not with God; do not only Talk of Heaven, but mind it, and seek it with all thy might; what greater business hast thou to do?[110]

Similarly, Richard Rogers stated his hopes for providing his readers with useful information in the preface of his *Seven Treatises*:

I desire in this treatise of mine to be some helpe and assistance, and to speake plainely, that such as would faine doe well, and yet cannot tell how, may hereby be eased and relieved.[111]

Finally, in the preface to the first volume of his *Workes*, William Perkins set out his desire to lift his readers out of their ignorance, for, he asserted, it was not enough simply to be able to recite the Creed, the Lord's Prayer and the Ten Commandments. People had to be able to understand them as well:

For an helpe in this your ignorance, to bring you to true knowledge, unfained faith, and sound repentance: here I have set downe the principall points of Christian religion in six plaine and easie rules: even such as the simplest may easily learne: and hereunto is adjoyned an exposition of them word by word. If ye doe want other good directions, then use this my labour for your instruction.[112]

Authors' intentions to educate their readers in matters of religion and provide them with manuals and templates by which to improve their spiritual lives underscored Humphrey Chetham's primary motivation for the establishment

---

110   Richard Baxter, *The Saints Everlasting Rest, or, A Treatise Of the blessed State of the Saints in their enjoyment of God in Glory* (London: Thomas Underhill and Francis Tyson, 1656), sig. C2v. Annotated copy in the Gorton Chest, Chetham's Library, Manchester, shelfmark GC.1.1. This edition not listed in the USTC.

111   Richard Rogers, *Seven Treatises* (London: Felix Kyngston, 1603), sig. A5v. Annotated copy in the Gorton Chest, Chetham's Library, Manchester, shelfmark GC.1.31. This edition not listed in the USTC.

112   William Perkins, *The Workes of that Famous and Worthy Minister of Christ in the University of Cambridge, Mr William Perkins: The First Volume* (London: John Legatt, 1626), sig. A2v. Annotated copy in the Gorton Chest, Chetham's Library, Manchester, shelfmark GC.2.13. USTC 3012639.

of his parish libraries, which was 'the edificac[i]on of the common people'.[113] This education could then be applied to material aspects of their everyday lives as guidance for living a life pleasing to God as a way to eternal salvation. As a complete collection, the volumes in the Gorton Chest parish library promoted a programme of religious reform that strongly reflected the Calvinist and Presbyterian confessional identities of Chetham, Johnson, Hollinworth and Tildsley. The library facilitated access to the most popular religious works of the time, many of which were concerned with godly living and the preparation for a godly death, but also included sermons and edifying annotations on all or parts of the Bible. It may have been Chetham's hope, implied by the stipulation of providing 'godly English Bookes' to the 'common people' in his will, that reading Reformed texts would lead to an increase of godliness in the lay population of Manchester, who used his parish libraries in search of a religious education.[114]

5.4 *Wimborne Minster Chained Library*

The collection of books donated by Roger Gillingham to the church of Wimborne Minster was much wider ranging than that given by William Stone a decade earlier. Where Stone's collection was exclusively religious and theological, Gillingham's included works in genres as disparate as history and household literature, philosophy and contemporary secular literature. The component parts of these collections can be seen in Figure 31 below.

Patristic texts, Bibles and Biblical commentaries were the most popular genres of books in the collection given to Wimborne Minster church by William Stone. The Church Fathers dominated the collection donated by Stone, despite being the subject of much criticism in the mid-seventeenth century. In the post-Restoration Church, however, the Church Fathers were in the vanguard of the Anglican defence of episcopacy.[115] Their writings were upheld as important evidence for a discontinuous church that was fractured by the corruption and adulteration of its original practices, in favour of the superstitions of the papal church, over the course of a millennium.[116] The works of the Church Fathers also provided Protestants with the means by which to demonstrate the corruption and innovations of the Roman Catholic Church

---

113 Chetham's Library, Manchester, (Uncatalogued), Last Will and Testament of Humphrey Chetham.

114 *Ibid.*

115 Robert D. Cornwall, 'The Search for the Primitive Church: The Use of Early Church Fathers in the High Church Anglican Tradition, 1680–1745', *Anglican and Episcopal History*, 59 (1990), pp. 305–306; Quantin, *The Church of England and Christian Antiquity*, pp. 203, 267.

116 *Ibid.*, pp. 68, 71.

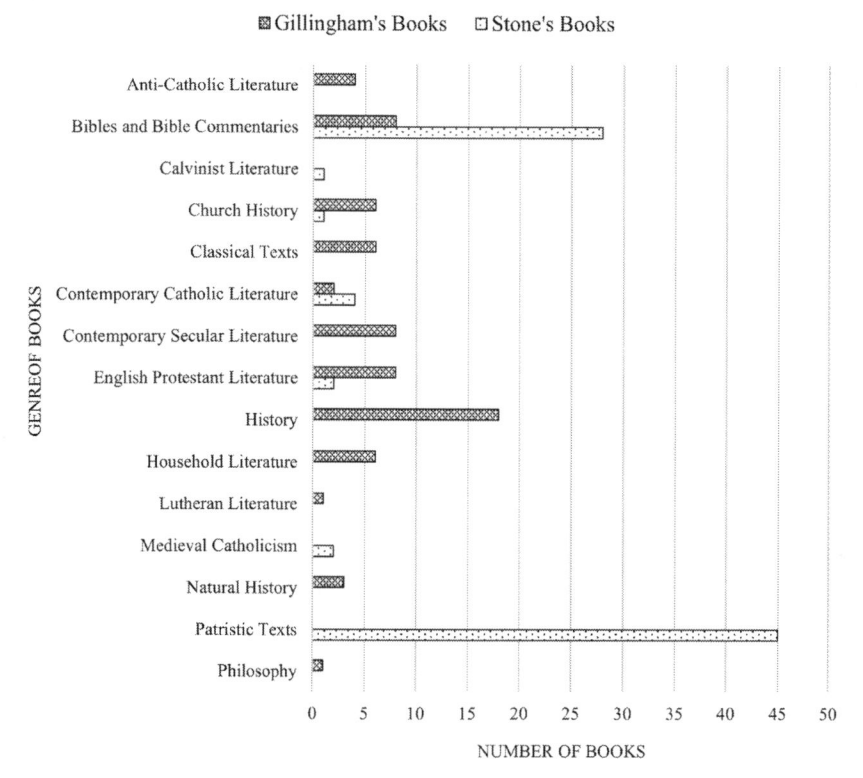

FIGURE 31   Genres of surviving books in the donations of William Stone and Roger
Gillingham to Wimborne Minster Chained Library

over the centuries. Further, Protestants used the Fathers' works to demonstrate
that they were restoring the original truth that had occasionally made itself
known in the past, through the Waldenses, the Wycliffites and the Hussites, for
example.[117] Many of the most commonly cited Church Fathers in the sixteenth
and seventeenth centuries (Saint Augustine, Saint Clement of Alexandria, Saint
Cyril, Saint Eusebius, Saint Hilary, Saint Jerome, Saint John Chrysostom and
Tertullian) appeared in Stone's donation, demonstrating his participation in
the collecting practices that saw learned men and dedicated scholars acquiring
a broad religious understanding in the seventeenth century.[118] Many of Stone's
patristic texts included in the library were published before 1630, meaning that
by the 1680s, when the collection was donated to Wimborne Minster church,

---

117   *Ibid.*, pp. 69–70.
118   *Ibid., passim.*

they provided library users with a somewhat dated view of Protestantism. The same is true of the small numbers of Protestant and post-Reformation Catholic literature by men such as John Prideaux and Jeronimo Osorio da Fonseca, which were included in the collection. These Protestant and Catholic works of the sixteenth and seventeenth centuries were all published in 1633 or earlier. They did not, therefore, engage with the religious disputes that arose within the English Church from the 1630s onwards, limiting the usefulness of this collection to the clergy in Wimborne Minster in the preparation of their sermons, and in their ministry to their parishioners.

Roger Gillingham's collection in Wimborne Minster Chained Library is demonstrably wider ranging than that of William Stone. This may have been a deliberate act on Gillingham's part, in order for it to be more useful to both the clergy and the lay inhabitants of the town. The collection was dominated by historical texts, contemporary religious works by Protestant and post-Reformation Catholic authors and contemporary secular literature, demonstrating the kinds of books that Gillingham thought 'fittest' to his intended readers.[119] The historical texts included the works of sixteenth- and seventeenth-century authors such as William Camden and William Howell, Edward Herbert and Sir Robert Cotton. Works of Church history by Thomas Fuller and Henry Isaacson were included in the collection, alongside Gilbert Burnet's *History of the Reformation of the Church of England* in two volumes.[120] A notable religious inclusion was Nathaniel Brent's English translation of Paolo Sarpi's *History of the Council of Trent*, in which Sarpi denounced the religious supremacy of the Roman Catholic Church and denied that it had returned to apostolic Christianity in the wake of the Council of Trent.[121] This was a different, later edition of the work than the one in the Gorton Chest parish library. Its sustained popularity was the result of its employment by later writers in increasing the popularity of the Church of England – and later, after the Restoration, the Anglican Church – through repeated denunciations of the pope and the papacy as the Antichrist.

---

119   The National Archives, Kew, (PROB 11/430/238), Will of Roger Gillingham of Middle Temple, Middlesex, 25 February 1696.

120   Gilbert Burnet, *History of the Reformation of the Church of England, Volume I* (London: T[homas] H[odgkin] for Richard Chiswell, 1679). Wimborne Minster Chained Library, shelfmark D10. This edition not listed on the USTC; Gilbert Burnet, *History of the Reformation of the Church of England, Volume II* (London: T[homas] H[odgkin] for Richard Chiswell, 1681). Wimborne Minster Chained Library, shelfmark D11. This edition not listed on the USTC.

121   Paolo Sarpi, *The History of the Council of Trent, translated by Nathaniel Brent* (London: J. Macock, 1676). Wimborne Minster Chained Library, shelfmark K2. This edition not listed on the USTC.

Sarpi's own Catholicism was seen as a strong indictment against the Catholic Church, which was here being criticised as a corrupt institution by one of its own.[122] In addition, the corpus also included English Protestant literature by authors including Arthur Lake, bishop of Bath and Wells, John Pearson, bishop of Chester, Robert Sanderson, bishop of Lincoln, and the theologian, William Chillingworth. In contrast to the dated texts of Stone's collection, several of the religious works in Gillingham's donation were published between 1629 and 1686 and thus engaged with the religious divisions and discussions of the mid-seventeenth century onwards. The inclusion of Sir William Dugdale's *Short View of the Late Troubles in England*, which recounted the dissensions that led the Three Kingdoms to war, is a particularly relevant example of this attempt to engage with contemporary religious disputes.[123]

6   Conclusion

The collections of the Francis Trigge, Ripon Minster and Wimborne Minster libraries all included numerous works by authors of diverse confessional identities. Such diversity was prevalent in the collections of scholarly books owned by English clerics and the educated laity in the seventeenth century, as David Pearson has shown.[124] These included works by authors as varied as Plato, Saint John Chrysostom, Tertullian, Desiderius Erasmus and John Calvin. All of these authors, and many others in these collections, were highly respected for the quality of their scholarship. Similarly, many of the authors of the volumes in the Gorton Chest parish library were highly respected English and European Protestant theologians, whose works were in high demand in the early modern period. By donating works by these various authors and others like them, Trigge, Higgin, Chetham, Stone and Gillingham were providing the users of their libraries with the best classical texts and religious works available at their respective times.

Latin texts dominate three of the four parish library collections considered here. This was not, however, the barrier to general use that it was once thought to be. By combining Ian Green's research on the increasing numbers of 'middling' sorts of people attending grammar school with Jennifer Richards'

---

122   Riverso, 'Paolo Sarpi', pp. 302–303.

123   William Dugdale, *Short View of the Late Troubles in England* (Oxford: printed at the Theatre for Moses Pitt, 1681). Wimborne Minster Chained Library, shelfmark D18. This edition not listed on the USTC.

124   Pearson, 'The Libraries of English Bishops', pp. 227–228; Pearson, 'Patterns of Book Ownership', p. 139.

work on the education of those grammar school students in Latin, and by applying their conclusions to these collections, it is probable that a wider range of people were able to read these volumes than previously thought.

These parish library collections are also significant because of what they tell historians about the success of the European book trade and the domestic second-hand book trade in England in the second half of the sixteenth century and throughout the seventeenth century. The presence of numerous prominent European printing cities in these collections reflects the efficacy of the complex business networks that linked together printers and booksellers across Europe, and serve as testament to European scholarship and printing capabilities.

The range of genres included in these repositories demonstrate their significance on the religious and intellectual landscape of early modern England. It reflects the role these books played in providing both the clergy and laity with a religious education that could be implemented either in their ministry or their everyday lives. Taken as a whole, the secular corpuses of the parish library collections of Grantham, Ripon and Wimborne Minster included works of geography alongside those of history, medical texts that sat on shelves next to books of natural history, philosophical treatises that complimented the works of morality, and more. Collectively, such texts represent the burgeoning market for non-religious volumes, as people increasingly began to read for pleasure, as well as for religious instruction and education. The exclusion of such works in the Gorton Chest parish library, founded during the Interregnum of the 1650s, is particularly interesting. Considering the saturation of the market with works of controversial literature and polemical pamphlets on the Civil War and the new government in England at that time, these works were deliberately excluded. Possibly this was to focus on bringing a sense of unity to the area through a Protestant-focussed religious collection.[125] As a whole, the four collections encompassed Biblical commentaries by both Protestant and post-Reformation Catholic authors, polemical texts and catechisms, sermons and theological works, as well as books of practical divinity. Depending upon the language in which they were written, many of these volumes contained messages and information that clerical and lay readers alike could understand, interpret and incorporate into their everyday lives, as Part 3 will examine.

---

125   Raymond, 'The Development of the Book Trade in Britain', pp. 60–61.

PART 3

Readership

∴

Introduction to Part 3

The final part of this volume comprises an in-depth study of the marginalia and other readers' marks extant in the library books of the Grantham (1598), Ripon (1624), Gorton (1653) and Wimborne Minster (1685, augmented 1695) parish libraries. This exploration of readership marks demonstrates that despite the social, religious and political upheavals that characterised the sixteenth and seventeenth centuries, the subjects, topics and themes that interested readers remained concentrated around the practical aspects of Protestant theology. In 1994, Elaine Whitaker argued that there were three main ways in which early modern readers engaged with their texts:

I. Editing
    a. Censorship
    b. Affirmation
II. Interaction
    d. Devotional Use
    e. Social Critique
III. Avoidance
    g. Doodling
    h. Daydreaming.[1]

The application of this framework to the marginalia and annotations in parish library books reveals that the readers of these texts primarily engaged in the practice of editing. Whitaker argued that this activity fell into two categories, which she described as editing through 'either (a) censoring with bisking or (b) emphasising with underlining, overlining, or nota bene sign', or as interacting with the text by '(a) accepting it and applying it to their own lives or by (b) appropriating it as a criticism or condemnation of someone else'.[2] The vast majority of annotations in the books of the four parish libraries considered in this volume comprise of either censorship, underlining, or otherwise marking a passage as important by use of a symbol noted in the margin. Where such practices are found in works of practical divinity or similar texts, it is reasonable to assume that marks were made by readers with the intention of applying the messages to their everyday lives, as Whitaker has suggested.

---

1 Elaine Whitaker, 'A Collaboration of Readers: Categorisation of the Annotations in Copies of Caxton's Royal Book', *Text*, 7 (1994), p. 235.

2 *Ibid.*, p. 236.

Sherman has argued that readers usually used symbols to denote a passage of importance, to signify that it was worthy of remembrance and to make it easier to find in the future. This theory has been adopted here and employed in conjunction with the application of those messages to everyday life.[3] Such practices also reflect elements of H. J. Jackson's 2001 definition of marginalia, which she described as 'a responsive kind of writing anchored to pre-existing written words'.[4] Early modern readers of the parish library books analysed in this work often paraphrased sections of the printed text in the adjacent margin or, occasionally, added headings to pages in order to summarise their main arguments. Such marks illustrate that early modern reading was an interactive and physical activity characterised by active engagement with the texts; it was not simply a passive exercise.

Most studies of early modern readers and readers' marks concentrate on individual well-known readers, who often produced large amounts of articulate marginalia or notes in commonplace books.[5] By focussing on particular readers, historians have been able to ascribe motivations such as political, social or career advancement to these readers and have been able to develop an understanding of how their readings were influenced by and impacted upon readers' lives and the events of their time. The reading practices and annotations of Sir William Drake, a seventeenth-century lawyer and politician who sat in the House of Commons, for example, demonstrate that Drake's reading experiences 'not only formed his general worldview, but also helped to script his specific responses to particular contemporary issues and events'.[6] Similarly, the professional reader Gabriel Harvey enacted comparable reading practices and reread his copy of Livy numerous times with different motivations, which depended upon the interests of the prominent and highly influential men, such as Philip Sidney, Sir Thomas Smith and Thomas Preston, who employed

---

3 William H. Sherman, *Used Books: Marking Readers in Renaissance England* (Philadelphia: University of Pennsylvania Press, 2009), pp. 25–29.

4 H. J. Jackson, *Marginalia: Readers Writing in Books* (New Haven; London: Yale University Press, 2001), p. 81.

5 Julie Crawford, 'Reconsidering Early Modern Women's Reading, or, How Margaret Hoby Read her de Mornay', *Huntington Library Quarterly*, 73:2 (2010); Elspeth Jajdelska, 'Pepys in the History of Reading', *The Historical Journal*, 50 (2007); Lisa Jardine and Anthony Grafton, '"Studied for Action": How Gabriel Harvey Read His Livy', *Past & Present*, 129 (1990); Fred Schurink, '"Like a Hand in the Margine of a Booke": William Blount's Marginalia and the Politics of Sidney's "Arcadia"', *The Review of English Studies*, 59:238 (2008); Kevin Sharpe, *Reading Revolutions: The Politics of Reading in Early Modern England* (London: Yale University Press, 2000); William H. Sherman, *John Dee: The Politics of Reading and Writing in the English Renaissance* (Amherst: University of Massachusetts Press, 1995).

6 Sharpe, *Reading Revolutions*, p. 74.

Harvey. With each rereading of his copy of Livy, Harvey's aims included, but were not limited to, understanding 'the forms of states' and the 'conditions of persons', understanding the various professions into which a man could enter, and understanding how the messages and lessons to be taken and learned from Livy could be applied in the real world.[7] On the other hand, Lady Margaret Hoby, the notable Puritan gentlewoman and diarist, had religion in mind when she chose both her books and her reading companions, selecting texts and fellow readers that would aid and improve her religious understanding and social influence.[8]

Microstudies such as these carried out by Julie Crawford on Hoby, Kevin Sharpe on Drake, and Lisa Jardine and Anthony Grafton on Harvey, as well as others like Elspeth Jajdelska, who examined the reading practices of seventeenth-century diarist, Samuel Pepys, enable historians to identify both the readers and approximately when they were reading.[9] As such, and because the surviving marginalia and annotations are often detailed and revealing, historians are able to understand how those readers' readings influenced their lives, enabled their political or social advancement and informed their responses to contemporary events. Whilst this approach provides an important contribution to the history of reading, the conclusions provided by microstudies on the reading practices of the wealthy and educated cannot be applied to a wider range of readers amongst the 'middling' and lower sorts of people. Such people could rarely, if ever, afford to possess vast libraries of their own and thus made use of the parish libraries that were being founded across England in the early modern period.

In his 2010 study of reading practices during the Scottish Enlightenment, Mark Towsey rightly pointed out that 'the possession of certain books or access to them ... can never illuminate fully the experience of the individual reader in the past'.[10] This book does not seek to understand who the readers of parish library books were. Nor does it seek to understand the experiences of an individual reader. Rather, by taking a generalised approach to the study of reading practices amongst the 'middling' sorts of people in early modern England, and by studying the largely anonymous marks of readership in the publicly accessible volumes housed in early modern parish libraries, this book seeks

---

7 Jardine and Grafton, 'Gabriel Harvey', pp. 35–44, *passim*.
8 Crawford, 'Reconsidering Early Modern Women's Reading', p. 194.
9 Jajdelska, 'Pepys in the History of Reading', *passim*.
10 Mark Towsey, *Reading the Scottish Enlightenment: Books and the Readers in Provincial Scotland, 1750–1820* (Leiden: Brill, 2010), p. 163.

to understand what types of books the middling sorts of people read and to analyse the topics and subjects in which such readers were most interested.

Identifying individual readers of parish library books is difficult and problematic: books in parish libraries were often purchased second-hand and the majority of parish libraries in early modern England did not keep user or reader records. Further, it is almost impossible to determine when the annotations were made in the books that now survive in early modern English parish libraries. It is often unclear whether a parish library user reading the book *in situ* made them, or whether the annotations were made by a previous owner of the book and therefore already in the book when it was donated to the parish library. In addition, most of the surviving marginalia and annotations in parish library books are inarticulate in nature and there is a general (though not complete) lack of ownership inscriptions in these volumes. Such factors further complicate the attempt to attribute motivations to these readers, to understand how contemporary events influenced their understanding of the texts they read, and to analyse how those texts impacted on their everyday lives. To do so risks stretching the evidence available to historians in a macrostudy such as this of numerous parish library collections. However, in reading inarticulate marginalia and annotations such as those found in parish library books, historians can gain valuable insight into the topics and concepts that were of interest to the 'middling' and lower sorts. Studying these readers' marks also reveals how such people engaged and interacted with their books and provides strong support for the kinds of actions demonstrated in research by Whitaker, Sherman and others.

The value of such a study, therefore, lies in its ability to enable historians to recognise and analyse patterns of reading that emerged over a long period of time, to reveal the topical foci of a large number of readers and to study their interactions with printed texts. Those subjects of interest to early modern readers, examined here in the third and final part of this book, included anti-Catholicism, the importance of Scripture, sin, repentance and salvation, and godly living and dying. These were all significant elements of popular religion and practical divinity in early modern England. Readers' interest in them is suggestive of a reduced focus on the theology of early modern Protestantism and an increased focus on its practical aspects.

Chapter 9 demonstrates that annotations on anti-Catholicism emphasised the errors, changes and corruptions of the Roman Catholic Church since the apostolic era. It highlights Protestant authors' belief that those corruptions stemmed from the corruption of the pope himself, who many Protestants believed to be the Antichrist. These corruptions were evident to Protestants in the doctrine of purgatory, the practice of selling indulgences, false worship and the veneration of images and idols.

In chapter 10, the perceived importance of Scripture and correct Scriptural understanding, as stressed in readers' annotations that focussed on Scripture as the Word of God, is examined. This chapter reveals that the main benefits of Scripture for early modern Protestants lay in its ability to teach and improve its readers and in the regulation of Christian life. Furthermore, Scripture was viewed as something that contained everything necessary for faith, which linked directly to Protestants' dislike of Roman Catholic inventions such as indulgences and the doctrine of purgatory expressed in the anti-Catholic marginalia.

The first half of chapter 11 examines the emphasis that readers frequently placed on the internal and external temptations that manifested in sinful actions committed by individuals on a daily basis. The second half of this chapter examines repentance, salvation and eternal life. Repentance was highlighted in early modern readers' marks as a complex process that functioned as the pathway back to God after sins had been committed. Other annotations emphasised that both salvation and eternal life could be achieved through justification and righteousness, through faith, and a life lived in service to fellow believers.

The final theme of readers' interest centred on godly living and preparation for death, which forms the basis of the final chapter of this book. Readers' annotations on this theme suggested that a godly life constituted regular prayer to God, goodness and good works – which for Protestants were the product of one's elect status and not the cause of one's salvation – and patience and trust in God. A good death, readers' marks highlight, could be made by seeking guidance and information from divines and by actively preparing for death during life to distract from worldly pleasures. Interestingly, marginalia in two parish library books concern the topic of suicide; these readers' marks adjoin printed debates on the contemporary acceptability of suicide and authors' expositions on situations in which the act might be justifiable, before they ultimately declared suicide unacceptable.

CHAPTER 9

Anti-Catholicism

Anti-Catholic ideology grew in prominence in England during the reigns of Elizabeth I and the early Stuarts. However, the books in the collections of the Grantham, Ripon, Gorton and Wimborne Minster parish libraries do not reflect the preoccupation with anti-Catholicism that historians such as Carol Wiener, Patrick Collinson, Anne McLaren and others have suggested nearly consumed English Protestants in the early modern period. Carol Wiener argued that what began as 'the private obsession of religious extremists developed into a part of the national ideology', an ideology that, as Patrick Collinson demonstrated, was the result of 'concern, mistrust and fear of Catholic powers, the pope and those rulers deemed to be his agents'.[1] Anne McLaren described anti-Catholic sentiments in England as something that increased in importance over the course of the second half of the sixteenth century, in response to the connected concerns surrounding the residence of the Catholic Mary Queen of Scots in England between 1568 and 1587 and Elizabeth I's refusal to marry and produce a Protestant heir to the English throne.[2] Christopher Haigh similarly argued that anti-Catholic sentiments were particularly prevalent during times of political crisis or uncertainty in England, such as around the time of the Spanish Armada in 1588 or in the months immediately following the Gunpowder Plot of 1605.[3] Certainly, anti-Catholic sentiment appears to have spiked considerably in the wake of the publication of the *Regnans in Excelsis* papal bull in 1570. These sentiments are reflected in the plethora of legislation passed against English Catholics with increasing frequency throughout the 1570s and 1580s. Some notable examples include the Act of Persuasions (1581), An Act against Jesuits, seminary priests, and such other like disobedient persons (1584), the Act against Priests (1585), and the Recusancy Act (1587). Alexandra Walsham has demonstrated that these anti-Catholic sentiments manifested themselves linguistically in the derogatory epithets of 'papist' or

---

1 Carol Z. Wiener, 'The Beleaguered Isle. A Study of Elizabethan and Early Jacobean Anti-Catholicism', *Past & Present*, 51 (1971), p. 27; Patrick Collinson, 'The Politics of Religion and the Religion of Politics in Elizabethan England', *Historical Research*, 82:215 (2009), p. 79.

2 Anne McLaren, 'Gender, Religion and Early Modern Nationalism: Elizabeth I, Mary Queen of Scots, and the Genesis of English Anti-Catholicism', *The American Historical Review*, 107:3 (2002), p. 740.

3 Christopher Haigh, *The Plain Man's Pathways to Heaven: Kinds of Christianity in Post-Reformation England, 1570–1640* (Oxford: Oxford University Press, 2007), p. 198.

'church papist'. Referring to the label of 'Puritan' specifically, Collinson argued that this gained 'meaning, substance and historical importance' in the 'context of confrontation'. Walsham reasoned that Collinson's argument applied equally to the label of 'papist'.[4]

Works of anti-Catholic polemic in the collections of the Grantham, Ripon, Gorton and Wimborne Minster parish libraries were not, however, as prominent as might be expected, considering the strong resentments that historians have argued Protestants harboured towards their Catholic countrymen. Without knowing when the surviving annotations were made, it is difficult to correlate crises or threats, such as the *Regnans in Excelsis* bull (1570), the influx of seminary priests into England beginning in the 1570s, the Spanish Armada (1588), the Gunpowder Plot (1605), or the Exclusion Crisis (1679–1681), with anti-Catholic annotations in parish library books. Less than seventy books across the entirety of the combined collections of the four parish libraries were anti-Catholic polemic, accounting for approximately thirteen percent of the overall corpus of texts in these repositories. Just six of the 263 volumes in the Francis Trigge collection in Grantham were anti-Catholic polemic, equivalent to less than three percent. Similarly, out of the 178 books in the combined donations of William Stone and Roger Gillingham to Wimborne Minster library, only four were anti-Catholic polemic, accounting for just over two percent of the collection. The slightly more significant number of fifty-five anti-Catholic polemical texts were included in the 758 books bequeathed to Ripon Minster by Anthony Higgin, equating to approximately seven percent of the collection. None of the books in the Gorton Chest parish library were explicitly anti-Catholic polemical texts.

Anti-Catholic annotations survive in very few of the books in any of the four parish libraries. When anti-Catholic annotations do survive, they were not necessarily in polemical texts against the Catholic Church. Of the more than one thousand volumes in the combined collections of the Grantham, Ripon, Gorton and Wimborne Minster libraries, just fourteen books by authors such as Thomas Brightman, Martin Luther, Francis White, Saint Athanasius and Saint Augustine contained annotations on the subject of anti-Catholicism. The most multitudinous annotations on the topic can be found in the Grantham copy of Martin Chemnitz's *Examinis Concilii Tridentini*. The *Examinis* constituted a four-part critique of the doctrines, decrees and canons of the Council of Trent

---

4 Alexandra Walsham, *Church Papists: Catholicism, Conformity and Confessional Polemic in Early Modern England* (Woodbridge: The Boydell Press, 1999), p. 111; Patrick Collinson, *The Birthpangs of Protestant England: Religious and Cultural Change in the Sixteenth and Seventeenth Centuries* (Basingstoke: Macmillan Press, 1988), p. 143.

(1545–1563) that was also a highly-charged piece of polemical and political literature.[5] Due to the infrequency of readers' marks on this topic, the annotations discussed in this chapter will be drawn from a relatively small range of authors and titles, few of which were primarily anti-Catholic polemical texts.

Readers' marks within these fourteen volumes reveal three patterns of focus for readers' interests that suggest a level of anti-Catholicism. One of most prominent concerns readers had pertained to the errors, changes and corruptions of the Catholic Church, as Protestants perceived them. The changes to the apostolic Church in the intervening centuries were the focus of numerous underlinings by readers, and several authors and readers particularly focussed on the willingness of the Catholic Church to devise and accept doctrines and practices that were not expounded in Scripture. Such actions went against the Protestant belief that Scripture contained everything necessary for faith, which will be explored more fully in the following chapter. Protestants' rejection of Catholic doctrines and practices that were not referred to in Scripture had a particular impact on the doctrine of purgatory and the practice of indulgences, both of which were the subject of several annotations that connoted their perceived importance. This dislike of Catholic practices of worship that were not explicitly referred to in the Bible fed into a more general Protestant dislike, evidenced by several readers' marks, of false worship, specifically the veneration of saints and images encouraged by the Catholic Church. Annotations concerned with attacking Catholic tendencies to venerate images reflected Protestants' fear that this practice had the potential to move people's focus away from God in favour of images and idols. Protestants were able to cite Scriptural precedent for their hatred of idols and idolatry, referring to passages in which Scripture asserted that God himself disliked idols. In a similar anti-Catholic vein, a small number of readers focussed on the guidance found in texts for the identification of a true and uncorrupted Church – ostensibly the Protestant Church – such as that found in the copy of William Chillingworth's *The Religion of the Protestants, A Safe Way to Salvation* in Wimborne Minster Chained Library.

1 The Errors, Changes and Corruptions of the Catholic Church

In the 1980s, Peter Lake suggested that the identification of the pope with the Antichrist 'served to bolster the Elizabethan church'. Both English and

---

5   R. Kolb, 'Chemnitz, Martin (1522–1586)', *The Oxford Encyclopedia of the Reformation* (online, 2005).

European Protestants were united in their conviction upon this point.[6] The root of Protestant belief in the corruption of the Catholic Church is shown to have stemmed from their belief in the corruption of the pope in annotations found within two parish library books. The marginal annotations in the copy of Thomas Brightman's *Workes* in the Gorton Chest parish library, for example, adjacent to a passage in which Brightman asserted that the Antichrist was indeed 'contrary to Christ' and argued that the name referred 'not [to] particular men, but a certain kingdom and succession,' suggest its perceived importance by a reader.[7] Francis White stated similar beliefs surrounding the corruption and fall of the pope in his *A Replie to Jesuit Fisher*. The page on which this discussion takes place has been marked by a reader of the copy of White's text now in the Gorton Chest parish library.[8] Christopher Hill has suggested that this belief was more widespread in the sixteenth and seventeenth centuries than these two annotations indicate, asserting that, for early modern Protestants, 'Antichrist ... was not merely the Pope as a person ..., but the papacy as an institution which subsumed within itself all evil'.[9]

Such corruption in the papacy as an institution manifested in the corruption of the apostolic Church. The Protestant belief in the invalidity of Catholic beliefs was reflected in annotations throughout the four parish library collections examined in this volume. The annotations of a reader of the Wimborne Minster copy of *The Religion of the Protestants, A Safe Way to Salvation* by William Chillingworth, for example, reflected the belief that Catholic doctrines and practices were invalid because they were additions to the apostolic Church. In a passage underlined by a reader, Chillingworth asserted that, 'neither will the Apostles depositing with the Church, all things belonging to truth, be any proof that the Church shall certainly keep this depositum, entire, and syncere, without adding to it'. The underlining of the statement suggests the significance of this passage to the reader.[10] Furthermore, in the copy of

---

6   Peter Lake, *Moderate Puritans and the Elizabethan Church* (Cambridge: Cambridge University Press, 1982), p. 56.

7   Thomas Brightman, *The Works of that Famous, Reverend, and Learned Divine, Mr. Thomas Brightman* (London: John Field, 1644), pp. 614–615. Annotated copy in the Gorton Chest, Chetham's Library, Manchester, shelfmark GC.1.22. USTC 3046550.

8   Francis White, *A Replie to Jesuit Fisher's Answer to Certain Questions Propounded by His Most Gracious Majesty, King James* (London: Adam Islip, 1624), p. 63. Annotated copy in the Gorton Chest, Chetham's Library, Manchester, shelfmark GC.1.27. USTC 3011511.

9   Christopher Hill, *Antichrist in Seventeenth-Century England*, revised edition (London, New York: Verso, 1990), p. 5.

10   William Chillingworth, *The Religion of the Protestants, A Safe Way to Salvation* (Oxford: Leonard Lichfield, 1638), p. 110. Annotated copy in Wimborne Minster Chained Library, shelfmark K19. USTC 3019801.

Martin Chemnitz's *Examinis Concilii Tridentini* now in the Francis Trigge Chained Library in Grantham, a reader underlined several parts of Chemnitz's discussion on the changes made to the doctrines and practices of the Church since the apostolic era specifically. By underlining Chemnitz's assertion that 'there is no doubt that the Church after the apostles added certain other rites for the purpose of edification, order and decorum', the reader emphasised their interest in the passage.[11] The underlining, like the rest of the inarticulate marginalia discussed in this book, gives no clear indication as to whether the reader agreed or disagreed with the sentiment, making it difficult to attribute the motive for reading or the reader's response. It might, however, reasonably be presumed that had they disagreed with the ideas and beliefs expressed, readers would have made this more explicit. More generally on the point of errors, changes and additions in the doctrines and practices of the Catholic Church, a reader of the copy of John White's *Workes* in the Gorton Chest parish library marked a page on which White noted 'particular corruptions that crept into particular writings and Churches, whereby our Adversaries have taken occasion to increase them'.[12] In addition, in a passage of his *A Replie to Jesuit Fisher* underlined by a reader of the Gorton Chest copy to signify its importance, Francis White proclaimed that the Roman Catholic Church had 'degenerate[d] and depart[ed] from the right Faith'.[13]

The annotations made by readers of parish library volumes demonstrate their interest in the Protestant rejection of Catholic practices and doctrines because they lacked a Scriptural basis. Protestants, and the godly specifically, believed that Scripture contained everything necessary for faith and instruction in living a good life, and so Protestants repudiated Catholic additions as departing from true faith and going beyond Scripture.[14] The polemicist John

---

11   Martin Chemnitz, *Examinis Concilii Tridentini, Part I* (Frankfurt: Peter Fabricius, 1585), p. 74. Annotated copy in the Francis Trigge Chained Library, shelfmark D2. Underlined Latin passage on p. 74 reads '... *Ecclesiam post Apostolos pro ratione aedificationis, ordinis & decori, alios quosdam ritus addidisse*'. This edition not listed in the USTC. English translation: Fred Kramer (trans.), *Examination of the Council of Trent, Part I* by Martin Chemnitz (London: Concordia Publishing House, 1971), p. 268.

12   John White, *The Workes of that Learned and Reverend Divine, John White, Doctor in Divinitie* (London: R. F., 1624), p. 246. Annotated copy in the Gorton Chest, Chetham's Library, Manchester, shelfmark GC.2.1. This edition not listed in the USTC.

13   White, *A Replie to Jesuit Fisher*, p. 4. Annotated copy in the Gorton Chest, Chetham's Library, Manchester, shelfmark GC.1.27. USTC 3011511.

14   For numerous examples of this, see the essays in Kevin Killeen, Helen Smith, and Rachel Willie (eds), *The Oxford Handbook of the Bible in Early Modern England, c. 1530–1700* (Oxford: Oxford University Press, 2018).

White asserted in his *Workes* that Roman Catholics 'know and confesse the most and greatest points of their religion, even welnigh all wherein they dissent from us, have no foundation on the Scriptures'. This page in the Gorton Chest copy of the text was marked by a reader to suggest its significance to them as justification for the rejection of Catholic beliefs.[15] Linking his attack on the corruptions of the Catholic Church to their impact on its adherents, Martin Chemnitz described 'how dangerous it is for the Church, and how destructive for the faith, to receive and venerate traditions concerning dogmas which cannot be proved with any testimony of Scripture', in a passage underlined by a reader of the Grantham copy of this work.[16] Similar anti-Catholic sentiments were reflected in several annotations in the Gorton Chest copy of Brightman's *Workes*, adjacent to his discussion of the Catholics' rejoicing at being delivered from the restrictions of Scripture. Brightman asked 'why might not the Papists hope, that the Pope their Lord ... will not suffer them from henceforth to receive any more grief and vexation from the Scriptures'.[17] Together, the various marked passages in these library volumes demonstrate both Protestants' rejection of the innovations and changes made to the apostolic Church by the Roman Catholic Church and the emphasis on the importance of Scripture in Reformed Protestantism. Historian Anthony Milton's justification for Protestants' rejection of Catholic practices is predicated on his argument that 'the points in controversy were thus mostly "additionals"' and that from a Protestant perspective, 'Rome did indeed err in the foundation of faith, and her errors were fundamental because they touched on the most basic tenets of salvation in Christ, the true Word of God, and the right administration of the sacraments'.[18]

Early modern Protestants rejected numerous innovations and changes of the Catholic Church, the doctrine of purgatory and the practice of selling indulgences perhaps foremost amongst them. The Catholic Church's innovation of prayers for the dead was condemned by the Cambridge-educated Church of England clergyman, John Dod in passage marked by one reader of his *A Plaine*

---

15   White, *Workes*, p. 10. Annotated copy in the Gorton Chest, Chetham's Library, Manchester, shelfmark GC.2.1. This edition not listed in the USTC.

16   Chemnitz, *Examinis Concilii Tridentini, Part I*, p. 76. Annotated copy in the Francis Trigge Chained Library, shelfmark D2. Underlined Latin passage on p. 76 reads '... *quam periculosum sit Ecclesiae, & quam perniciosum fidei, traditiones de dogmatibus, quae nullo Scripturae testimonio probari possunt*'. This edition not listed in the USTC. English translation: Kramer, *Examination of the Council of Trent, Part I*, p. 275.

17   Brightman, *Works*, p. 374. Annotated copy in the Gorton Chest, Chetham's Library, Manchester, shelfmark GC.1.22. USTC 3046550.

18   Anthony Milton, *Catholic and Reformed: The Roman and Protestant Churches in English Protestant Thought, 1600–1640* (Cambridge: Cambridge University Press, 1995), pp. 178–179.

and Familiar Exposition of the Ten Commandements now in the Gorton Chest parish library, suggesting its perceived importance to that reader. In the annotated passage, Dod stated that 'this serves to condemne the Papists, that are most guiltie in this point, and have defiled the whole worship of God with their owne inventions and superstitions [such] as by praying for the dead'.[19] The act of praying for the dead was intrinsically linked to purgatory, one of the most prominent Catholic doctrines repudiated by Protestants as having no basis in Scripture.

The lack of Scriptural foundation for purgatory was the main focus of a reader of part 3 of the Grantham copy of Chemnitz's *Examinis Concilii Tridentini*. As the reader underlined, 'the papalists carry their opinion about purgatory to Scripture, and do not get it from there'.[20] In the chapter of the *Examinis* concerning purgatory, Chemnitz provided a lengthy rebuttal of Catholic claims that the doctrine of purgatory had a Scriptural basis. A reader underlined several passages in this section, suggesting their interest in, and potentially their agreement with, Chemnitz's arguments. A reader of the *Examinis* wrote '*nota*' next to Chemnitz's explanation that he had discredited various passages from the Bible that Catholics used to argue in favour of purgatory, 'in order to show that the purgatory of the papalists cannot be proved'.[21]

Not being mentioned explicitly in the Bible led to the equivocal status of purgatory in English ecclesiastical legislation. While belief in purgatory was one of the first things to be removed from the Church of England after the break from Rome, prayers for the dead were still encouraged. The Act of Ten Articles (1536) issued under Henry VIII asserted that 'it is a very good and charitable deed to pray for souls departed', but prevaricated on the existence of purgatory, stating that the location of the souls prayed for was 'to us uncertain by

---

19   John Dod, *A Plaine and Familiar Exposition of the Ten Commandements* (London: Felix Kyngston, 1614), p. 74. Annotated copy in the Gorton Chest, Chetham's Library, Manchester, shelfmark GC.1.13(1). USTC 3005942.

20   Martin Chemnitz, *Examinis Concilii Tridentini, Part III* (Frankfurt: Peter Fabricius, 1585), p. 116. Annotated copy in the Francis Trigge Chained Library, shelfmark D2. Underlined Latin passage on p. 116 reads '*Antea aliquoties diximus, Pontificios opinionem purgatorii ad Scripturam adferre, non inde referre, sed cogere hoc videri in Scriptura dictum, quod ante lectionem praesumpserunt credendum*'. This edition not listed in the USTC. English translation: Fred Kramer (trans.), *Examination of the Council of Trent, Part III* by Martin Chemnitz (London: Concordia Publishing House, 1971), p. 330.

21   Chemnitz, *Examinis Concilii Tridentini, Part III*, p. 123. Annotated copy in the Francis Trigge Chained Library, shelfmark D2. Latin passage on p. 123 reads '... *ut ostendere pontificiorum purgatorium* ...'. This edition not listed in the USTC. English translation: Kramer, *Examination of the Council of Trent, Part III*, p. 351.

Scripture'.[22] The official stance on purgatory and prayers for the dead became more firmly opposed during the reign of Edward VI. The Act Dissolving the Chantries (1547) denounced 'vain opinions of purgatory and masses satisfactory, to be done for them which be departed' as superstition, before the English Communion service of 1552 eradicated all traces of intercessionary prayer from English services.[23] Prayers for the dead continued to be condemned by Elizabethan clergymen, most notably by John Jewel, bishop of Salisbury, in his *An Homily or Sermon Concerning Prayer* published in 1563.[24] However, by the seventeenth century, prayers for the dead had begun to find favour again, particularly amongst men such as James Ussher and Jeremy Taylor. Some of their works were included in the four parish libraries under close consideration here, but the copy of Taylor's *Antiquitates Christianae* in Wimborne Minster library no longer survives.[25] However, as Ralph Houlbrooke has shown, these clergymen and others who advocated for prayers for the dead did so on the basis that 'they were justified by the ancient practice of the Church'. They remained at pains to emphasise the fact that praying for the dead 'did not necessarily imply belief in purgatory'.[26]

Protestantism's repudiation of the doctrine of purgatory rendered the Catholic practice of selling indulgences obsolete. Indulgences were an intrinsic part of the penitential system of the medieval and Roman Catholic Church. They were declarations by the Catholic Church granting the recipient full or partial remission of the punishment for sins committed, thus reducing the time a person spent in purgatory. Alister McGrath has demonstrated that

---

22 Ralph Houlbrooke, *Death, Religion and the Family in England, 1480–1750* (Oxford: Clarendon Press, 2000), p. 38; Gerald Bray, *Documents of the English Reformation*, 3rd edition (Cambridge: James Clarke & Co., 2019), pp. 151–152.

23 Henry Gee and William John Hardy (eds), *Documents Illustrative of English Church History* (London: Macmillan and Co., 1896), p. 328; Houlbrooke, *Death, Religion and the Family in England*, p. 38.

24 Various Authors, *The Second Tome of Homilies* (London: Richard Jugge and John Cawood, 1563), ff. 128v–130r.

25 James Ussher, *A Body of Divinity, or the Sum and Substance of Christian Religion* (London: Thomas Downes and George Badger, 1653). The Gorton Chest, Chetham's Library, Manchester, shelfmark GC.2.7. This edition not listed in the USTC; James Ussher, *The Annals of the World* (London: E. Tyler, 1658). Wimborne Minster Chained Library, shelfmark K3. This edition not listed in the USTC; Jeremy Taylor, *Antiquitates Christianae or the History of the Life and Death of the Holy Jesus* (London: J. Macock and M Flesher, 1684). Wimborne Minster Chained Library, no long survives. This edition not listed in the USTC.

26 Houlbrooke, *Death, Religion and the Family in England*, p. 39.

the confused and vague theology of forgiveness of the late medieval period lent weight to the suggestion that it was possible to purchase the forgiveness of sins and procure the remission of "purgatorial penalties" through the purchase of indulgences.[27]

From the fifteenth century, indulgences applicable to the souls already in purgatory could be obtained, enabling the living to reduce the time the soul of a deceased relative spent in purgatory. An indulgence could be granted through various means, including financial contributions to the building or upkeep of churches, schools, hospitals and other important buildings or structures.[28] As McGrath summarised, 'in other words, the eternal penalties resulting from sinful actions could be reduced, if not eliminated, by payment of an appropriate sum of money to the appropriate ecclesiastical figure'.[29]

The seventeenth-century philosopher and diplomat, Edward Herbert expressed anti-Catholic sentiments in his attack against the practice of selling indulgences in his *The Life and Raigne of King Henry VIII*. His arguments on the subject were annotated by a reader of the copy of this work now in Wimborne Minster Chained Library. Herbert argued that the Catholic practice of selling indulgences, 'the conditions of which were, That, whosoever performed certaine Religious Rites, and paid certaine sums of Money, should have their sinnes forgiven', was something that was only allowed to continue for so long because when they first began to be used, 'no divine worship in the West parts of Europe, but what the Church of Rome prescrib'd, was publiquely knowne'.[30] In other words, Herbert believed that the practice was allowed by the public to continue for so long because there was no alternative religion. The manuscript marginalia surrounding this passage of Herbert's work suggests that one of his readers found this argument against a key Catholic practice particularly interesting. Once people were presented with a viable alternative to Catholicism indulgences began to lose significance. Diarmaid MacCulloch has noted that after the Reformation, the Protestant dismantling of indulgences

27   Alister E. McGrath, *Reformation Thought: An Introduction*, 4th edition (Oxford: Wiley-Blackwell, 2012), p. 123.

28   P. F. Palmer and G. A. Tavard, 'Indulgences' in Berard L. Marthaler (general ed.), *New Catholic Encyclopedia, Volume VII: Hol-Jub*, 2nd edition (Detroit: Thomson Gale, 2003), pp. 436–441.

29   McGrath, *Reformation Thought*, p. 123.

30   Edward Herbert, *The Life and Raigne of King Henry VIII* (London: Printed by E. G. for Thomas Whitaker, 1649), p. 70. Annotated copy in Wimborne Minster Chained Library, shelfmark D15. USTC 3047333.

was so thorough that the third session of the Council of Trent (1561–1563) eventually forbade the practice of selling them.[31]

The Catholic doctrine of purgatory contrasted starkly with the Protestant doctrine of justification by faith alone, which was first conceptualised by Martin Luther. Luther outlined his understanding of the concept of justification by faith alone in his preface to the first volume of the complete edition of his Latin writings. He wrote that,

> As I meditated day and night on the relation of the words "the righteousness of God is revealed in it, as it is written, the righteous person shall live by faith", I began to understand that "righteousness of God" as that by which the righteous person lives by the gift of God (faith); and this sentence, "the righteousness of God is revealed", to refer to a passive righteousness, by which the merciful God justifies us by faith, as it is written, "the righteous person lives by faith".[32]

Luther's understanding of justification by faith alone was predicated on the realisation that good works and penitence were not necessary for salvation. This theology was later developed and systematised by the Swiss Reformer John Calvin, who increasingly entwined justification and election, or predestination, the idea that God, by divine decree, predestined all humans to either heaven or hell at the time of their creation. Other, similar doctrines of justification, all based on Luther's conceptualisation, were also espoused by other branches of Reformed religion under men such as Huldrych Zwingli and Martin Bucer, and were promulgated amongst followers of Reformed religion.[33]

Annotations in several parish library volumes conveyed anti-Catholic sentiments in their apparent endorsement of justification by faith alone. Martin Luther propounded and outlined the notion of *sola fides* ('faith alone') in his *A Commentarie upon the Fiftene Psalmes*. In several sentences of Ripon Minster parish library's copy of this work that were underlined by a reader, Luther stated his conviction that the way to salvation was not via purgatory,

---

31 Diarmaid MacCulloch, *Reformation: Europe's House Divided, 1490–1700* (London: Penguin, 2004), p. 304.

32 The full Latin text and an English translation can be found in Alister E. McGrath, *Luther's Theology of the Cross: Martin Luther's Theological Breakthrough*, 2nd edition (Oxford: Wiley-Blackwell, 2011), pp. 128–131.

33 G. H. Tavard and P. De Letter, 'Justification' in Berard L. Marthaler (general ed.), *New Catholic Encyclopedia, Volume VIII: Jud-Lyo*, 2nd edition (Detroit: Thomson Gale, 2003), p. 84.

but through faith.[34] Moreover, in the Gorton Chest copy of White's *A Replie to Jesuit Fisher*, a reader marked the page on which the then dean of Carlisle was clear in his opinion that within Protestantism, salvation was achieved through Christ alone. White asserted that

> No Christian Church ever prised the oblation and merits of Christ more highly and religiously than wee ... and wee firmely beleeue the inestimable price and virtue thereof, for mans Redemption, Sanctification, Justification, and Glorification. And in particular wee beleeue expressely, and contrarie to our Adversaries accusation, That the same is all-sufficient to justifie a sinner in the sight of God.[35]

The Protestant abolition of the doctrine of purgatory in favour of the doctrine of justification by faith thus eliminated the need for indulgences in the Reformed faith. The marking of this passage by a reader suggests their belief in the importance of this change, which signalled a move away from believing that salvation was achievable through good works and other penitential acts and towards the understanding that good works were instead the product of faith and a sign of a person's elect status.[36] As such, a degree of anti-Catholicism can be perceived in the repudiation of the Catholic doctrines of salvation and purgatory in favour of the Protestant belief in justification by faith alone.

Other innovations by the Catholic Church that Protestants – and Protestant readers of parish library books – denounced and rejected were the acts required of people in order to achieve salvation: 'in most recent times the matter of the protection, merits, intercessions, help, aid, and benefits of the saints was forged into an article of faith'.[37] A reader of Arthur Hildersham's *CLII Lectures upon Psalm LI*, now in the Gorton Chest parish library, marked the page on which

---

34   Martin Luther, *A Commentarie upon the Fiftene Psalmes*, trans. Henry Bull (London: Thomas Vautroullier, 1577), p. 219. Annotated copy in University of Leeds Brotherton Special Collections Library, shelfmark Ripon Cathedral Library XVII.E.16. USTC 508422.

35   White, *A Replie to Jesuit Fisher*, p. 169. Annotated copy in the Gorton Chest, Chetham's Library, Manchester, shelfmark GC.1.27. USTC 3011511.

36   Jonathan Willis, *The Reformation of the Decalogue: Religious Identity and the Ten Commandments in England, c.1485–1625* (Cambridge: Cambridge University Press, 2020), p. 64.

37   Martin Chemnitz, *Examinis Concilii Tridentini, Part II* (Frankfurt: Peter Fabricius, 1585), p. 159. Annotated copy in the Francis Trigge Chained Library, shelfmark D2. Underlined Latin passage on p. 159 reads '*postremis vero temporibus, fabricatus est inde articulus fidei, de patrociniis, meritis, intercessionibus, auxilis, adjumentis & beneficiis sanctorum*'. This edition not listed in the USTC. English translation: Fred Kramer (trans.), *Examination of the Council of Trent, Part II* by Martin Chemnitz (London: Concordia Publishing House, 1971), p. 506.

the divine argued that in doctrines and practices such as these, the Catholic Church was not following God's example of mercy, but rather pursuing more vengeful policies.[38] William Perkins discussed such erroneous policies, doctrines and beliefs on a page marked by a reader of the Gorton Chest copy of the first volume of his *Workes*, suggesting the importance of these errors in the Catholic doctrine of salvation as perceived by the reader.[39] Similarly, a reader of the Grantham copy of Chemnitz's *Examinis* endorsed anti-Catholic sentiments on the subject of salvation by underlining the Lutheran divine's assertion that, in order to achieve salvation within the Catholic Church,

> people were directed now to the sanctity of required works, now to making their own satisfaction through works that are not required, now to works of supererogation, and again to the treasure of the merits of the religious orders, to various brotherhoods, to the pleading of the saints, to pilgrimages.[40]

Heaven was not an assured destination for even the most committed and conscientious Catholic. Another underlining by one of Chemnitz's readers highlighted the belief that Catholics were not guaranteed salvation, even if they performed all of the acts required by the Church: 'they left them in the saddest doubt, setting before them, alas, the consolation of the fire of purgatory'.[41] The undertaking of such acts as described by Chemnitz in order to achieve salvation stirred anti-Catholic sentiments because they were in direct contravention of the Protestant doctrine of justification by faith alone. Both Luther and

---

38   Arthur Hildersham, *CLII Lectures upon Psalm, LI* (London: J. Raworth, 1642), p. 115. Annotated copy in the Gorton Chest, Chetham's Library, Manchester, shelfmark GC.2.5(1). USTC 3052352.

39   William Perkins, *The Workes of that Famous and Worthy Minister of Christ in the University of Cambridge, Mr William Perkins: The First Volume* (London: John Legatt, 1626), p. 99. Annotated copy in the Gorton Chest, Chetham's Library, Manchester, shelfmark GC.2.13. USTC 3012639.

40   Chemnitz, *Examinis Concilii Tridentini, Part I*, p. 128. Annotated copy in the Francis Trigge Chained Library, shelfmark D2. Underlined Latin passage on p. 128 reads '... *jam ad proprias satisfactiones operum indebitorum, jam ad super erogationes, mox ad superflua merita ordinum, ad varias fraternitates, ad patrocinia sactorum, ad peregrinationes* ...'. This edition not listed in the USTC. English translation: Kramer, *Examination of the Council of Trent, Part I*, p. 461.

41   *Ibid.*, p. 128. Annotated copy in the Francis Trigge Chained Library, shelfmark D2. Underlined Latin passage on p. 128 reads '... *in tristissima dubitatione illas reliquerunt proposita (si dis placet) consolatione ignis purgatorii*'. English translation: Kramer, *Examination of the Council of Trent, Part I*, p. 461.

Calvin – and their adherents – subscribed to this doctrine, albeit with some differences, as outlined by Alister McGrath; both, however, emphasised the union between Christ and true believers that was linked to justification.[42]

2   False Worship, Images and Idolatry in the Catholic Church

Early modern Protestant readers of books in the four parish libraries of Grantham, Ripon, Gorton and Wimborne Minster were interested in written attacks against idolatry as a form of anti-Catholicism and proof of the corruption and errors of the Catholic Church. As Peter Lake has argued, 'crucial to the Protestant analysis of the falseness of these practices and doctrines was the concept of idolatry'. Early modern Protestants believed that 'the papists' reverence for the worship of idols and images and their use of the saints as intercessors' had 'supplanted and subverted' the worship of God.[43]

As the focus of annotations in parish library books reflects, many early modern Protestants argued that the veneration of images and other articles of faith was one of the most prominent innovations of the Catholic Church. As Chemnitz asserted in a passage underlined by a reader of the Grantham copy of the *Examinis Concilii Tridentini*, 'after the apostles, through 300 years, the veneration of relics about which the papalists now contend did not exist'.[44] Francis White, in his *A Replie to Jesuit Fisher*, expressed a similar anti-Catholic sentiment, refuting arguments that the worship of idols was present in the apostolic Church using a catechetical question-and-answer style. The marking of this page by a reader of the Gorton Chest copy of White's work suggests both the perceived importance of this subject and the anti-Catholic attitude of the reader.[45]

---

42   McGrath, *Reformation Thought*, pp. 117–127, 131–132.
43   Peter Lake, 'Anti-Popery: the Structure of a Prejudice' in Richard Cust and Ann Hughes (eds), *Conflict in Early Stuart England: Studies in Religion and Politics, 1603–1642* (London: Longman, 1989), p. 74.
44   Martin Chemnitz, *Examinis Concilii Tridentini, Part IV* (Frankfurt: Peter Fabricius, 1585), p. 12. Annotated copy in the Francis Trigge Chained Library, shelfmark D2. Underlined Latin passage on p. 12 reads '... *ostendimus in primitiva & antiquisma post Apostolos Ecclesia, per annos trecentos non fuisse illas venerationes reliquiarum, de quibus Pontificii nunc dimicant*'. This edition not listed in the USTC. English translation: Fred Kramer (trans.), *Examination of the Council of Trent, Part IV* by Martin Chemnitz (London: Concordia Publishing House, 1971), p. 47.
45   White, *A Replie to Jesuit Fisher*, p. 238. Annotated copy in the Gorton Chest, Chetham's Library, Manchester, shelfmark GC.1.27. USTC 3011511.

Protestants' denunciation of idolatry was rooted in Biblical precedent: as Anthony Milton has argued, 'the imputation of this error to Rome lay in the unequivocal denunciations of idolatry in the Old Testament'.[46] The idea of men creating their own gods was born in the book of Exodus, with Aaron's creation of a golden calf and the construction of an altar whilst Moses was in discussion with God on Mount Sinai.[47] The belief in Scriptural precedent for the condemnation of idolatry was likewise reflected in the annotations of several parish library books. The Church of Scotland minister and exegetist John Weemes, for example, discussed 'how base idols are in the sight of God' in his collected *Workes*, and a reader of the Gorton Chest's copy of this text marked the page on which Weemes expounded this belief.[48] The fourth-century Greek Church Father, Pope Athanasius I of Alexandria (referred to here as Saint Athanasius), was one of several Early Christian writers to reject idolatry based on the Bible. Saint Athanasius identified idolatry with non-Christians, and credited Christ as being ultimately responsible for the decline of idolatry both in his *Contra Gentes* and in his subsequent work, *De Incarnatione Verbi*.[49] Similar sentiments were expressed by Saint Augustine of Hippo, the early philosopher, theologian and bishop, in his *De Civitate Dei*. In the Ripon Minster copy of this work, a reader annotated passages that focussed on the theologian's warnings about the dangers of false gods. Two chapters in which Augustine discussed the 'calamities suffered before the religion of Christ began to compete with the worship of the gods' and how 'the worshippers of the gods never received from them any healthy moral precepts, and that in celebrating their worship all sorts of impurities were practiced', were annotated by a reader.[50] John Weemes echoed these warnings, telling his readers that to worship a false God contravened

---

46   Milton, *Catholic and Reformed*, p. 187.

47   Exodus 32:1–8.

48   John Weemes, *The Workes of Mr. John Weemes of Lathlocker in Scotland. The Second Volume* (London: Thomas Cotes, 1636), part 1, p. 82. Annotated copy in the Gorton Chest, Chetham's Library, Manchester, shelfmark GC.1.9. USTC 3018588.

49   Khaled Anatolios, *Athanasius: The Coherence of his Thought* (London: Routledge, 1998), p. 28.

50   Saint Augustine, *De Civitate Dei* in *Cuius praestantissima in omni genere monumenta, Volume V* (Basel: Ambrosius and Aurelius Froben, 1570), pp. 93–95. Annotated copy in University of Leeds Brotherton Special Collections Library, shelfmark Ripon Cathedral Library XIII.E.10/q. Latin passages on pp. 93 and 94 read '*De assumenda historia, qua ostenditur, quae mala acciderint Romanis, cum deos colerent, antequam religio Christiana creseeret*' and '*Quod cultores deorum nulla unquam a diis suis praecepta probitatis acceperint, & in sacris eorum turpia quae que celebraberint*'. USTC 626339. English translation: Marcus Dods (trans. and ed.), *The City of God, Volume I* (Edinburgh: T. & T. Clark, 1871), pp. 50–53.

the Commandments. The marking of this page by a reader of the Gorton Chest copy of Weemes' *Workes* suggests their anti-Catholic opinion and that Weemes' warnings were considered important and needed to be heeded.[51]

As Jonathan Sheehan has demonstrated, criticisms of idolatry were used 'as a stick to beat the Catholics', for whom imagery was an integral part of worship in the sixteenth and seventeenth centuries.[52] In England, attacks against the worship of saints, idols and images came in many forms: Thomas Cranmer spoke out against the worship of saints in a sermon at Paul's Cross in 1536; Edmund Grindal established a commission in 1571 to 'discover and demolish rood-lofts'; and there were instances of puritan gentry taking iconoclasm into their own hands in Cheshire in the 1580s.[53] All of these attacks reflected the strong sense of anti-Catholicism that historians have argued pervaded England in the sixteenth and seventeenth centuries, and reinforced Margaret Aston's argument that idolatry was a hot topic throughout the Elizabethan and early Stuart periods, when the godly were agitating for further reform.[54] Certainly, the sixteenth-century Calvinist theologian and reformer Peter Martyr Vermigli asserted the wrongness of idolatry in his work, *Common Places*. Vermigli condemned the altars Catholics built to images of the saints and argued that Catholics' assertions that such practices were pleasing to God were incorrect. The significance of this condemnation is suggested by a reader who marked this page in the copy of the *Common Places* now in the Gorton Chest parish library.[55] John Dod furthered the Protestant diatribe against the Catholic practice of idolatry by positing the idea that no true Christian would allow the worship of an idol: 'have you felt him [Christ], and received his body and blood in the Sacraments? If you have beheld his excellent beauty in these means, you will abhor an idol, as an ugly thing'. This was underlined by a reader of the Gorton Chest copy of Dod's work, suggesting the

51   Weemes, *Workes. The Second Volume*, part 1, p. 29. Annotated copy in the Gorton Chest, Chetham's Library, Manchester, shelfmark GC.1.9. USTC 3018588.

52   Jonathan Sheehan, 'Sacred and Profane: Idolatry, Antiquarianism and the Polemics of Distinction in the Seventeenth Century', *Past & Present*, 192 (2006), pp. 38–40; Margaret Aston, 'Puritans and Iconoclasm, 1560–1660' in Christopher Durston and Jacqueline Eales (eds), *The Culture of English Puritanism, 1560–1700* (Basingstoke: Palgrave Macmillan, 1996), p. 99.

53   Julie Spraggon, *Puritan Iconoclasm during the English Civil War* (Woodbridge: Boydell and Brewer, 2003), p. 4; Aston, 'Puritans and Iconoclasm, 1560–1660', pp. 97, 100–102.

54   Aston, 'Puritans and Iconoclasm, 1560–1660', p. 97.

55   Peter Martyr Vermigli, *The Common Places of the Most Famous and Renowmed Divine Doctor Peter Martyr* (London: Henry Denham and Henry Middleton, 1583), part 2, p. 308. Annotated copy in the Gorton Chest, Chetham's Library, Manchester, shelfmark GC.2.10. USTC 509866.

importance of the perceived link between the internal spiritual representation of Christ within a Christian during the Eucharist and the external worship of that same God.[56] If attacking the worship of images was an explicit expression of anti-Catholicism, the annotations in parish library books demonstrate that their readers agreed with such sentiments, or at the very least that they were aware of their significance.

Linked to the practice of idolatry and the worship of the images of saints was the controversial topic of the image of God himself. Annotations in several volumes demonstrated readers' interest in the routes through which one could see an image of God. A more implicit form of anti-Catholicism is detectable here than in Protestant attacks on idolatry, as Protestants disregarded Catholics' use of visual representations of God created by men. Saint Athanasius asserted that Christ himself was the image of God in his *Expositio Fidei*, an annotated copy of which survives in Ripon Minster parish library. Athanasius asserted that the 'absolutely perfect Son' was 'the true Image of the Father', next to which a Latin annotation reads '*et in filium ex patre perpetuo genitam*'. The marginal note is seemingly in two different hands and two different inks, suggesting the importance of this belief to multiple readers.[57] In a similar way, Luther asserted that those 'that pray unto God and fasten not their eyes and minds upon Christ, come not unto God, but worship the imaginations of their owne harts in steed of ye true God, & are plaine idolaters'. A reader annotated the margin adjacent to this passage in the Ripon Minster copy of Luther's *A Commentarie upon the Fiftene Psalmes*, suggesting its significance to that reader.[58] In order to provide an alternative to the highly discouraged practice of conjuring an image of God in one's own mind with no point of reference to Christ or Scripture, early modern Protestant readers of parish library books highlighted the belief that an image of God could be conjured in the minds of the faithful through reading His Word. This was propounded by the Lutheran theologian Martin Chemnitz, who, unsurprisingly considering Luther's own explicit link between mental

---

56 Dod, *A Plaine and Familiar Exposition*, p. 72. Annotated copy in the Gorton Chest, Chetham's Library, Manchester, shelfmark GC.1.13(1). USTC 3005942.

57 Saint Athanasius, *Expositio Fidei* in *Athanasii magni Alexandrini episcopy, graviss. scriptoris, et sanctiss. martyris, opera, in quatuor tomos distributa* (Basel, 1564), p. 80. Annotated copy in University of Leeds Brotherton Special Collections Library, shelfmark Ripon Cathedral Library XIII.C.17/q. Underlined Latin passage on p. 80 reads '... *sed Filium perfectum ... veram imaginem Patris*'. USTC 613803. English translation: Philip Schaff and Henry Wade (trans.), *Contra Gentes by Saint Athanasius* (New York: The Christian Literature Company, 1892), p. 84.

58 Luther, *A Commentarie upon the Fiftene Psalmes*, pp. 211–212. Annotated copy in the Brotherton Special Collections Library, shelfmark Ripon Cathedral Library XVII.E.16. USTC 508422.

images of God and idolatry, asserted that 'the best, surest, and most useful image of God and of Christ is the one which the understanding of our minds forms and conceives from the Word of God'. Apparently, this advice was significant to at least one reader of the Grantham copy of Chemnitz's *Examinis*, who underlined the passage.[59]

Expressions of hostility towards visual representations of God, Christ and other religious imagery in churches and sacred spaces, as objects that may have inspired devotion and worship in and of themselves, are pronounced within Protestantism. A dislike of religious imagery was particularly relevant to the experiences of Reformation in both Lincolnshire and Lancashire, where the Grantham and Gorton Chest parish libraries are located and in which many of these annotations can be seen. In the second half of the sixteenth century, Lincolnshire had been extremely slow to accept Protestantism after the Elizabethan Settlement, and it remained a conservative county in which many people still adhered to Catholicism even towards the end of Elizabeth I's reign. At least thirty-five Lincolnshire parishes did not destroy their rood screens until after 1560 and a 1566 enquiry into the diocese of Lincoln 'yielded a large harvest of [Catholic] objects for defacing and burning'.[60] Similarly, Lancashire was renowned for its high number of Catholics in the Elizabethan period, relative to other English counties: statues of saints were still present in numerous churches in 1564 and at least one parish church still retained their rood screen in 1574.[61]

3   Guidance for Identifying the True and Uncorrupted Church

Anthony Milton has argued that 'from the Reformation onwards, Protestant ecclesiology in England ... was preoccupied with the need to combat the claims of the visible Church of Rome to be the universal Catholic Church, the one true Church of God'.[62] This was certainly the case for several Protestant divines,

---

59   Chemnitz, *Examinis Concilii Tridentini, Part IV*, p. 22. Annotated copy in the Francis Trigge Chained Library, shelfmark D2. Underlined Latin passage on p. 22 reads '*Optimam vero, certissimas, & utilissimam Dei & Christi imaginem esse, quam mentis nostrae agnitio ex verbo Dei format & concipit*'. This edition not listed in the USTC. English translation: Kramer, *Examination of the Council of Trent, Part IV*, p. 80.

60   R. B. Walker, 'The Growth of Puritanism in the County of Lincoln in the Reign of Queen Elizabeth I', *Journal of Religious History*, 1:3 (1961), p. 150; Aston, 'Puritans and Iconoclasm, 1560–1660', p. 97.

61   Ronald Hutton, 'The Local Impact of the Tudor Reformations' in Christopher Haigh (ed.), *The English Reformation Revised* (Cambridge: Cambridge University Press, 1987), p. 135.

62   Milton, *Catholic and Reformed*, p. 128.

who were keen to assert the ways in which the true Church could be recognised. This was reflected in annotations and other readers' marks in parish library books. Francis White, for example, asserted in an underlined passage in the Gorton Chest copy of his *A Replie to Jesuit Fisher* that 'the Church wherein the Apostles taught and governed, was the ground and pillar of Truth, fully, entirely, and in all things'.[63] The English churchman William Chillingworth was another such divine who, in his *The Religion of the Protestants,* provided explicit guidance for his readers on how to recognise the true Church. A reader of the Wimborne Minster copy of Chillingworth's work annotated his assertion that 'the only note of a true and uncorrupted Church, is conformity with Antiquity; I mean the most ancient Church of all, that is the Primitive and Apostolique'.[64] As part of his guidance, Chillingworth exhorted his readers to 'by [their] own particular judgement, find out what was the doctrine of the Primitive Church, and what is the Doctrine of the present Church' and determine for themselves whether their religion was true.[65] The Protestant clergy of the Church of England appealed to the Early Church as the basis of their religion throughout the sixteenth and seventeenth centuries. As Anthony Milton has argued, many divines claimed that 'the Church of England essentially preserved entire the true doctrine of the Early Church'.[66]

4 Conclusion

Anti-Catholicism was a feature of annotations in only a limited number of books in the parish libraries of Grantham, Ripon, Gorton and Wimborne Minster, which does not reflect the prevalence of anti-Catholic sentiment that historians have argued abounded in England after the Reformation. This chapter has demonstrated that rather than focussing on general anti-Catholic sentiment, readers' marks in many of the fourteen volumes annotated on this topic focussed on three specific elements of anti-Catholicism. Readers were keen to emphasise the Catholic Church as corrupt, a state that readers' marks suggest was believed to be the result of the pope's true identity as the Antichrist, a label which was extended to the papacy in general. The corruption manifested

---

63 White, *A Replie to Jesuit Fisher,* p. 4. Annotated copy in the Gorton Chest, Chetham's Library, Manchester, shelfmark GC.1.27. USTC 3011511.
64 Chillingworth, *The Religion of the Protestants,* p. 95. Annotated copy in Wimborne Minster Chained Library, shelfmark K19. USTC 3019801.
65 *Ibid.* Annotated copy in Wimborne Minster Chained Library, shelfmark K19. USTC 3019801.
66 Milton, *Catholic and Reformed,* pp. 272–273.

in the addition of doctrines and practices not present in the apostolic Church. The doctrine of purgatory and the selling of indulgences were prominent complaints amongst the annotations in several volumes – both were condemned by Protestant readers as contradicting their belief in justification by faith alone. The need of the Catholic Church to institute additional doctrines and practices alongside those outlined in Scripture stemmed from their assertion that Scripture did not contain everything necessary for faith. This was a position rejected by many of the early modern Protestant authors and readers examined in this chapter, as can be seen from the surviving marginalia and annotations. The centrality of Scripture as the basis for faith, advocated by early modern Protestants, will be demonstrated in the next chapter. Moreover, the Catholic practice of revering images and idols was a prominent subject in surviving annotations, implying readers' belief in the wrongness of these acts. Surviving readers' marks reflect the early modern Protestant belief in the lack of Biblical precedent for idols and images, the absence of idolatry in the Early Church and in its association with non-Christians and men who raised other men up as gods. Annotations instead referred to the Protestant belief that images of God could be found through Christ and through the Word of God, again emphasising the importance of Scripture. Finally, a small number of annotations highlighted Protestant divines' attempts to assist their readers in recognising the true Church, which was identifiable through its similarity to and continuation of the doctrines of the apostolic Church.

CHAPTER 10

The Importance of Scripture

Protestantism was a bibliocentric religion that was grounded in reading, and in reading the Bible above all. In fact, as Alec Ryrie has argued, it would be difficult to over-emphasise the weight of importance placed upon the Bible by early modern Protestants.[1] The scope of religious reading undertaken by Protestants did extend beyond the Bible, but it was not particularly broad in range. Andrew Cambers has shown that the godly 'returned again and again to a relatively narrow strand of religious reading material' drawn from the wide range of religious texts that flew off the Protestant printing presses in the sixteenth and seventeenth centuries.[2] Reading these texts, Cambers has demonstrated, was not exclusively an individual activity, but also a social one that could be undertaken in many different rooms of the home and in other, more public spaces as well: in a town, public, or parish library, in the parish church or in a coffee house or bookshop.[3]

Bible reading was a practice believed to bring people closer to God. Ann Hughes, for example, has demonstrated that Bible reading was one of the activities through which early modern Protestant women developed a personal relationship with God.[4] Reading the Bible and listening to the Bible being read aloud, Charles Hambrick-Stowe has argued, were activities through which the faithful could expect to experience grace as they grew to understand God better.[5] Such activities needed to be undertaken frequently in order to be as efficacious as possible. Numerous Protestant and Puritan divines of the sixteenth and seventeenth centuries, including men like Edmund Grindal, archbishop of Canterbury, frequently encouraged at least daily Bible reading of one chapter from both the Old and New Testaments.[6] Most Protestants

---

1 Alec Ryrie, *Being Protestant in Reformation Britain* (Oxford: Oxford University Press, 2015), p. 270.
2 Andrew Cambers, *Godly Reading: Print, Manuscript and Puritanism in England, 1580–1720* (Cambridge: Cambridge University Press, 2011), p. 246; Ryrie, *Being Protestant*, p. 1.
3 Cambers, *Godly Reading, passim.*
4 Ann Hughes, 'Puritanism and Gender' in John Coffey and Paul C. H. Lim (eds), *The Cambridge Companion to Puritanism* (Cambridge: Cambridge University Press, 2008), p. 299.
5 Charles E. Hambrick-Stowe, 'Practical Divinity and Spirituality' in John Coffey and Paul C. H. Lim (eds), *The Cambridge Companion to Puritanism* (Cambridge: Cambridge University Press, 2008), p. 202.
6 William Nicholson (ed.), *The Remains of Edmund Grindal* (Cambridge: Cambridge University Press, 1843), pp. 129–130.

© KONINKLIJKE BRILL NV, LEIDEN, 2024 | DOI:10.1163/9789004363717_015

did read a chapter a day, but some went much further: as Ryrie has argued, 'Biblical-overeating was a recurring feature of heroic Protestant piety'.[7]

Considering the centrality of the Bible to early modern Protestantism, the prominence of marginalia and other marks of readership that focussed on the importance of Scripture and Scriptural understanding in numerous books from the four parish libraries of Grantham, Ripon, Gorton and Wimborne Minster, is unsurprising. Three broad patterns of interest emerge. Firstly, readers emphasised Scripture as the Word of God, which contained everything necessary for faith and could therefore be used as a practical tool for teaching, improvement and the regulation of Christian life and practice. Secondly, if Scripture was going to be used as the sole authority on Christian life, used to educate and guide people, it needed to be interpreted and understood correctly. This imperative was highlighted in numerous annotations by readers of various parish library volumes, emphasising the importance of entrusting the interpretation of the Bible to a council of learned men in conversation with one another, as opposed to the Catholic practice of relying solely on the pope for interpretation. Understanding the Bible was an important objective to early modern Protestants, but it was not enough merely to read the words. A Protestant reader had to engage their intellect and read the Bible critically, in order to internalise the text successfully. Numerous commentaries and paraphrases were produced from the second half of the sixteenth century onwards in order to support Bible readers of the 'middling' and lower sorts in this endeavour at understanding.[8] It comes as no surprise, then, that the accessibility of the Bible to all was a central tenet of Protestantism. A core endeavour of the Reformation was to make the Bible widely available and to encourage people to read it. The Henrician, Edwardian and Elizabethan injunctions contained numerous exhortations to that effect, as shown in chapter 3.[9] Thirdly, then, the readers of volumes in the libraries of Grantham, Ripon, Gorton and Wimborne Minster were keen to stress the importance of general accessibility to the Bible. However, it is worth mentioning that one reader of Edward Herbert's *The Life and Raigne of King Henry VIII*, now in Wimborne Minster Chained Library, did

---

7   Ryrie, *Being Protestant*, p. 271.

8   *Ibid.*, p. 276; Ian Green, *Print and Protestantism in Early Modern England* (Oxford: Oxford University Press, 2000), pp. 113–124.

9   Walter Howard Frere (ed.), *Visitation Articles and Injunctions of the Period of the Reformation, Volume II, 1536–1558* (London: Longmans, Green & Co., 1910), pp. 9, 117–118; Walter Howard Frere (ed.), *Visitation Articles and Injunctions of the Period of the Reformation, Volume III, 1559–1575* (London: Longmans, Green & Co., 1910), pp. 2, 10.

highlight Herbert's discussion of the controversies surrounding the provision of the Bible in English in the reign of Henry VIII.[10]

1 Scripture as the Word of God

Numerous Protestant divines rose to the challenge of providing their readers with guidance on how the faithful were able to recognise Scripture as the Word of God in the first place. Marginalia in several volumes from the four parish libraries demonstrate that this was a popular reading topic and suggests that readers may have put the advice they read into practice, in line with Whitaker's readership model of affirmation as an element of editing.[11] James Ussher's *A Body of Divinity*, for example, offered readers fifteen assurances as guidance on how they could be certain of the truth of Scripture, which included markers such as the godliness and holiness of the apostolic authors of Scripture.[12] The folded corners of the several pages on which Ussher outlined these criteria in the Gorton Chest copy of this work suggest the importance of this issue to readers. Likewise, they are also suggestive of the perceived applicability of these assurances to a life that centred on a desire for spiritual rightness. Moreover, the actions of a reader of the Gorton Chest copy of John White's *Workes* reinforce the importance of knowing that Scripture was the Word of God. A reader deliberately folded the corners of pages on which White eluci-dated 'the illumination of God's Spirit' and the 'vertue and power that sheweth itselfe in every line and leaf of the Bible' as methods by which to understand the truth of Scripture.[13] The inarticulate nature of readers' marks such as this make it difficult for historians to determine whether a reader agreed with the sentiments expressed on the marked page, but it does demonstrate the signif-icance of the passage to a reader and suggests its applicability to everyday life, whether in affirmation or rebuttal.

---

10 Edward Herbert, *The Life and Raigne of King Henry VIII* (London: Printed by E. G. for Thomas Whitaker, 1649). Annotated copy in Wimborne Minster Chained Library, shelf-mark D15. USTC 3047333.

11 Elaine Whitaker, 'A Collaboration of Readers: Categorisation of the Annotations in Copies of Caxton's Royal Book', *Text*, 7 (1994), pp. 235–236.

12 James Ussher, *A Body of Divinity, or the Sum and Substance of Christian Religion* (London: Thomas Downes and George Badger, 1653), pp. 8–11, 19–21. Annotated copy in the Gorton Chest, Chetham's Library, Manchester, shelfmark GC.2.7. This edition not listed in the USTC.

13 John White, *The Workes of that Learned and Reverend Divine, John White, Doctor in Divinitie* (London: R. F., 1624), p. 26. Annotated copy in the Gorton Chest, Chetham's Library, Manchester, shelfmark GC.2.1. This edition not listed in the USTC.

Similar examples of the means by which the faithful could recognise the Word of God are extant in annotated copies of Jean-François Salvard's *An Harmony of the Confessions of the Faith of the Christian and Reformed Churches* in the Gorton Chest parish library, and Martin Chemnitz's *Examinis Concilii Tridentini* and John Calvin's *Sermons upon the Booke of Job*, both in the Francis Trigge Chained Library in Grantham. In Salvard's text, a reader has deliberately folded a page on which Salvard elucidated that the Gospel could be recognised as having been written by the four Evangelists and the Apostles. A further instance of annotations suggesting how the faithful may recognise Scripture as God's Word can also be found in the Grantham copy of Martin Chemnitz's *Examinis Concilii Tridentini*.[14] The copy of John Calvin's *Sermons upon the Booke of Job* in Grantham is annotated on almost every page. Numerous ownership inscriptions survive within the book, two of which are those of William Higginbotham and his son, James.[15] The Higginbothams appear to have had a connection with St Wulfram's church in Grantham, as evidenced by James Higginbotham's donation of 10s. 6d. to the organ erected in the church in 1736.[16] The annotations more closely match the hand of William Higginbotham, who seems to have annotated the volume heavily before gifting it to his son James in 1704, who gave it to the library. The importance of this copy of Calvin's *Sermons* therefore lies in what it reveals about the reading practices of an otherwise unknown urban reader and how they responded to their texts.

In order for Protestants to interpret Scripture correctly, they 'needed to believe it in a saving sense for oneself'. This, Carl Trueman has argued, required a sense of true devotion and a commitment to prayer, as well as the full assistance of the Holy Spirit.[17] In order to receive this assistance, Andrew Cambers

---

14   John Calvin, *Sermons upon the Booke of Job*, trans. A. Golding (London: T. Dawson for G. Bishop and T. Woodcocke, 1579), p. 627. Annotated copy in the Francis Trigge Chained Library, shelfmark E10. USTC 508947; Jean-François Salvard, *An Harmony of the Confessions of the Faith of the Christian and Reformed Churches* (London: John Legatt, 1643), p. 108. Annotated copy in the Gorton Chest, Chetham's Library, Manchester, shelfmark GC.1.4. USTC 3049712; Martin Chemnitz, *Examinis Concilii Tridentini, Part II* (Frankfurt: Peter Fabricius, 1585), p. 89. Annotated copy in the Francis Trigge Chained Library, shelfmark D2. This edition not listed in the USTC. English translation: Fred Kramer (trans.), *Examination of the Council of Trent, Part II* by Martin Chemnitz (London: Concordia Publishing House, 1971), p. 296.

15   Calvin, *Sermons upon the Booke of Job*, blank folio leaf. Annotated copy in the Francis Trigge Chained Library, shelfmark E10. USTC 508947.

16   E. Turnor, *Collections for the History of the Town and Soke of Grantham*, (London: W. Bulmer and Co., 1806), p. 11.

17   Carl R. Trueman, 'Scripture and Exegesis in Early Modern Reformed Theology' in Ulrich L. Lehner, Richard A. Muller and A. G. Roeber (eds), *The Oxford Handbook of Early Modern Theology, 1600–1800* (Oxford: Oxford University Press, 2016), p. 187.

has shown that many Puritans in the early modern period used Bible reading as a means of channelling the Holy Spirit.[18] The role of the Holy Spirit as a facilitator for the interpretation of Scripture is clearly exemplified in an annotation in the Grantham copy of Chemnitz's *Examinis Concilii Tridentini*. In a passage underlined to highlight its significance, Chemnitz asserted that 'through the Word that is preached, heard, and pondered the Holy Spirit incites, begins, works, and effects in us'.[19]

For Protestants, Scripture contained everything that was necessary for faith. Many early modern readers demonstrated their keen interest in the topic by marking the passages of books in which this subject was discussed. In the late sixteenth century, Chemnitz outlined this belief in the sufficiency of Scripture in his *Examinis*. In a passage of the Grantham copy of his work, underlined to reflect its importance, Chemnitz stated that 'whatever is declared to be necessary in the church of Christ must be prescribed and commanded by the Word of God and have examples in Scripture'.[20] Furthermore, Chemnitz asserted in another underlined sentence that 'in these passages which are clearly and plainly in the Scripture all those things are found which define the faith and morals for living'. This certainly spoke to both the Lutheran and Calvinist preferences for vernacular religious literature that everyone would be able to read and understand.[21] In the early seventeenth century, the Puritan divine John Dod asserted in a passage of his *A Plaine and Familiar Exposition of the Ten Commandements*, now in the Gorton Chest parish library, that Scripture was important because 'the Word and Sacraments [were the place] wherein Christ

---

18 Cambers, *Godly Reading*, p. 16.

19 Chemnitz, *Examinis Concilii Tridentini, Part II*, p. 184. Annotated copy in the Francis Trigge Chained Library, shelfmark D2. Underlined Latin passage on p. 184 reads '... *sed Spiritus sanctus per verbum praedicatum, auditum & cogitatum, illam nobis excitat, inchoat, operatur & efficit*'. This edition not listed in the USTC. English translation: Kramer, *Examination of the Council of Trent, Part II*, p. 582.

20 Chemnitz, *Examinis Concilii Tridentini, Part II*, p. 89. Annotated copy in the Francis Trigge Chained Library, shelfmark D2. Underlined Latin passage on p. 89 reads '*Quicquid igitur in Ecclesia Christi necessarium esse statuitur, necesse est ut habeat praescriptum & mandatum verbi Dei, & Scripturae exempla*'. English translation: Kramer, *Examination of the Council of Trent, Part II*, p. 296.

21 Martin Chemnitz, *Examinis Concilii Tridentini, Part I* (Frankfurt: Peter Fabricius, 1585), p. 57. Annotated copy in the Francis Trigge Chained Library, shelfmark D2. Underlined Latin passage on p. 57 reads '*Scriptura posita sunt, inveniuntur illa omnia, quae continent fidem moresque vivendi*'. This edition not listed in the USTC. English translation: Fred Kramer (trans.), *Examination of the Council of Trent, Part I* by Martin Chemnitz (London: Concordia Publishing House, 1971), p. 207.

Jesus offereth himselfe' to the faithful.[22] The significance of this assertion is attested to by its having been underlined by one of Dod's readers. Twenty years after the publication of Dod's *Exposition*, the theologian William Chillingworth published his *The Religion of the Protestants, A Safe Way to Salvation*. In *The Religion of the Protestants*, Chillingworth asserted that Scripture was 'sufficiently perfect, sufficiently intelligible in things necessary, to all that have understanding, whether they be learned or unlearned ... because nothing is necessary to be believed, but what is plainly revealed'.[23] In the copy of Chillingworth's work now in Wimborne Minster Chained Library in Dorset, a reader drew three dots in the shape of a triangle in the margin of the page between these two quoted lines. According to Steve Leveen, the dots denote the word 'therefore'.[24] The drawing of this symbol connotes that that particular reader, at least, and perhaps later ones too, understood a clear connection between these two statements: Scripture contained everything necessary in religion, therefore only what was written in Scripture needed to be believed and adhered to. Trueman has argued that this belief had been a mainstay of Reformed Protestant thought since its earliest days. Trueman demonstrated that Reformed Protestantism was characterized by 'a basic commitment to the authority, sufficiency, and perspicuity of Scripture' and that it was 'moving toward a more formal development of a doctrine of Scripture' in the first half of the seventeenth century.[25]

The annotations on the sufficiency of Scripture for true faith in books published in the 1650s and in the second half of the seventeenth century suggest that this belief continued to be a popular concern over a century after the start of the English Reformation. A reader of the Gorton Chest copy of Ussher's *A Body of Divinity*, for example, marked several pages of the volume, on which Ussher used a catechetical style of writing to discuss how man could know that the Scriptures were sufficient and all that was necessary for instruction in achieving salvation. Ussher's assertions included the fact that God was the author of the Scriptures and so they were perfect, and that they taught all true

22   John Dod, *A Plaine and Familiar Exposition of the Ten Commandements* (London: Felix Kyngston, 1614), p. 35. Annotated copy in the Gorton Chest, Chetham's Library, Manchester, shelfmark GC.1.13(1). USTC 3005942.

23   William Chillingworth, *The Religion of the Protestants, A Safe Way to Salvation* (Oxford: Leonard Lichfield, 1638), p. 92. Annotated copy in Wimborne Minster Chained Library, shelfmark K19. USTC 3019801.

24   Steve Leveen and the Levenger Company, 'How to Leave Masterly Marginalia', cited in William H. Sherman, *Used Books: Marking Readers in Renaissance England* (Philadelphia: University of Pennsylvania Press, 2009), p. 26.

25   Trueman, 'Scripture and Exegesis in Early Modern Reformed Theology', pp. 179–180.

doctrine and rejected the false.[26] This was a particularly important consideration in the mid-seventeenth century, as a small number of sectaries called into question the act of Bible reading as a form of idolatry and challenged the very authority of the Bible itself.[27] Despite these challenges to its authority, belief in the sufficiency of Scripture continued in the second half of the seventeenth century. This belief is demonstrated by the annotations of William Stone, the Church of England clergyman who annotated a large number of his patristic texts before donating them to Wimborne Minster church in the 1680s. For example, in Stone's copy of Saint Augustine's *De Civitate Dei*, now in Wimborne Minster Chained Library in Dorset, Stone underlined Augustine's assertion that within 'Scripture are to be found all matters that concern faith and the manner of life, hope, to wit, and love'.[28] Marginalia on this topic can be seen in several books that were housed in libraries in different counties and were published over a period of approximately seventy years. Evidently the sense of the importance of this belief continued through doctrinal challenges and, perhaps, strengthened in the wake of the defeat of those challenges.

Given its status as the Word of God and Protestants' unshakeable conviction in its sufficiency for true faith, Scripture was an important tool for Protestants for teaching and improvement and for regulating Christian life and practice. Nowhere is this better elucidated than in the Gorton Chest's annotated copy of the third volume of the collected works of William Perkins, who was 'an excellent example of the moderate Puritan who helped transform the social and spiritual life of England in the late sixteenth and early seventeenth centuries'.[29] Perkins' assertion, taken from the Bible, that 'the Scripture is profitable to teach, improve, correct, instruct in righteousnesse' was underlined by a reader who, to further compound the point and assert its importance, also

---

26 Ussher, *A Body of Divinity*, pp. 19–21. Annotated copy in the Gorton Chest, Chetham's Library, Manchester, shelfmark GC.2.7. This edition not listed in the USTC.

27 Cambers, *Godly Reading*, pp. 16–21.

28 Saint Augustine, *D. Aurelii Augustini Hipponensis Episcopi, Complectens Ta Didaktika, hoc est, quae proprie ad docendum pertinent ..., Volume I, Book III* (Basel: ex officina Frobeniana, 1569), p. 25–26. Annotated copy in Wimborne Minster Chained Library, shelfmark A1. Underlined Latin passage on p. 25–26 reads '*In iis enim que aperte in Scriptura posita sunt, inveniunt illa omnia quae continent fidem moresque vivendi, spem scilicet atque charitatem ...*'. This edition not listed in the USTC. English translation: J. F. Shaw and S. D. Salmond (trans.) and Marcus Dods (ed.), *The Works of Aurelius Augustine, Bishop of Hippo, Volume IX: On Christian Doctrine; The Enchiridion; On Catechising; and On Faith and the Creed* (Edinburgh: T. & T. Clark, 1873), p. 43.

29 Louis B. Wright, 'William Perkins: Elizabethan Apostle of "Practical Divinity"', *Huntingdon Library Quarterly*, 3 (1940), p. 171.

drew two short diagonal 'slash' lines next to the statement.[30] Evidently, for this reader, the most important function of Scripture was for 'regulating Christian life and practice', as Trueman has argued it was for the vast majority of early modern Protestants.[31] Furthermore, in the Grantham copy of John Calvin's *Sermons upon the Booke of Job*, the book's annotating reader wrote a marginal note next to a passage of printed text that discussed the use of Scripture in the teaching of one's neighbours. The marginal note commented that this was 'a good lesson for the importance of the word of god', demonstrating its potential application in everyday life and providing further support for Whitaker's model of early modern reading.[32] Such an annotation further demonstrates that early modern Protestants believed that the Bible was not simply useful for one's own instruction, but in the instruction of others as well. The teaching of others linked to Protestant beliefs about a godly life being spent in the service of others and the importance of praying for the benefit and comfort of others, both of which will be discussed in more detail in chapter 12. Living a life in accordance with Scripture as God's Word was marked by a reader of Robert Harris's *A Treatise of the New Covenant*, included in the volume of his *Works* in the Gorton Chest, as the key to happiness. The marked page of Harris's *Treatise* described a man's happiness as being in direct correlation to his relationship with God: the better the relationship, the happier the man.[33]

2   Interpreting and Understanding Scripture

Before the Bible could be used to teach, it had to be correctly interpreted. The importance of correctly interpreting the Bible was underscored most prominently by a reader of the Grantham copy of Martin Chemnitz's *Examinis Concilii Tridentini*. Chemnitz, and seemingly his reader, rejected the monopoly of interpretation held by individuals in the Catholic ecclesiastical hierarchy. In this model, one person – the pope, an archbishop, bishop, a monk, or even

---

30   2 Timothy 3:16; William Perkins, *The Workes of that Famous and Worthy Minister of Christ in the Universitie of Cambridge, M. William Perkins: The Third and Last Volume* (London: John Haviland, 1631), p. 492. Annotated copy in Chetham's Library, Manchester, shelfmark GC.2.15. USTC 3015389 and 3015390.

31   Trueman, 'Scripture and Exegesis in Early Modern Reformed Theology', p. 186.

32   Calvin, *Sermons upon the Booke of Job*, p. 65. Annotated copy in the Francis Trigge Chained Library, shelfmark E10. USTC 508947; Whitaker, 'A Collaboration of Readers', pp. 235–236.

33   Robert Harris, *The Works of Robert Harris, Once of Hanwell* (London: Miles Flesher, 1654), p. 90. Annotated copy in the Gorton Chest, Chetham's Library, Manchester, shelfmark GC.1.28. This edition not listed in USTC.

a single parish clergyman – had responsibility for interpreting the Bible for those below him. Instead, Chemnitz demonstrated a clear preference for Scriptural interpretation undertaken by a small number of godly men in conference with one another, a sentiment that the annotations suggest his reader may have agreed with. The Scriptural foundation for this came from Saint Paul. Chemnitz stated that 'Paul describes how pious teachers ought in dark passages to seek the true interpretation by an exchange of opinions: "Let two or three prophets speak!"'. The annotating reader underlined the passage, suggesting its significance to them.[34] Though the *Examinis* was a Lutheran text, such sentiments evoke parallels with the Puritan prophesyings that occurred during the last quarter of the sixteenth century in England, in which individuals came together to discuss and interpret the Bible collectively.[35] Such practices were established in Lincolnshire (where the Trigge library is located in Grantham) in conjunction with Puritans after Thomas Cooper's election as bishop of Lincoln in 1571, and continued until Elizabeth I forced Bishop Cooper to suppress the prophesyings in the late 1570s.[36] There are references to 'exercises' taking place in Grantham in the episcopal records of Lincoln, as Bishop Cooper ordered 'Master Banester, vicar of Grantham ... not to speake at all in the Exercise until his moderacion shalbe better knowne'.[37] The highlighting of these ideas in the *Examinis* suggests that the reader may have had godly sympathies. This has interesting implications for the confessional landscape of Grantham in the early seventeenth century. Either there were Puritans or Puritan sympathisers living in the county, or else library users read this text complete with Puritan annotations that drew attention to thoughts, exercises and activities that were considered dangerous and subversive by the Crown. Without knowing who the annotating reader was, it is difficult to identify their confessional identity with any degree of certainty. Either way, the reader underlined arguments reminiscent of Puritanism that were the

---

34 Chemnitz, *Examinis Concilii Tridentini, Part I*, p. 58. Annotated copy in the Francis Trigge Chained Library, shelfmark D2. Underlined Latin passage on p. 58 reads '*Paulus describit, quomodo in obscuris locis, pii Doctores veram interpretationem communicates sententiis inquire re debeant: Prophetae duo aut tres dicant*'. This edition not listed in the USTC. English translation: Kramer, *Examination of the Council of Trent, Part I*, p. 210.

35 Roger E. Moore, 'Sir Philp Sidney's Defense of Prophesying', *Studies in English Literature, 1500–1900*, 5:1 (2000), p. 35.

36 R. B. Walker, 'The Growth of Puritanism in the County of Lincoln in the Reign of Queen Elizabeth I', *Journal of Religious History*, 1:3 (1961), pp. 150–151.

37 C. W. Foster (ed.), *Lincoln Episcopal Records in the Time of Thomas Cooper, S.T.P., Bishop of Lincoln, A.D. 1571 to A.D. 1584* (London: printed for the Canterbury and York Society, 1913), p. 114.

complete antithesis not only of Catholic Biblical interpretation practices but also those of the established Church of England, within a Lutheran text.

It was not enough, however, just to interpret the Bible correctly. Alec Ryrie has demonstrated the importance of Bible reading, suggesting that 'it did not mean merely eyes passing over print or lips murmuring words'. Rather it was both a spiritual and intellectual activity that required 'the right use of the critical faculties'.[38] Various annotations in the books of the Grantham, Ripon, Gorton and Wimborne Minster parish libraries demonstrate the importance of properly understanding the Bible. A reader of the Gorton Chest copy of the Church of England clergyman Francis Roberts' *Clavis Bibliorum. The Key of the Bible*, for example, marked a page that began Roberts' exposition of seven key pieces of information that people needed to know about the Old and New Testaments, in order to increase their understanding of the Bible as a whole. Roberts' guidance included advice such as being 'well acquainted with the 1 Order, 2 Titles, 3 Times, 4 Penmen, 5 Occasion, 6 Scope, and 7 Principal Parts of the books, both of the Old and N. Testament'.[39] Numerous marks of readership survive in several volumes on pages pertaining to how people were to properly understand Scripture. A reader of the second volume of William Perkins' collected works, now in the Gorton Chest parish library, folded the corner of a page on which Perkins detailed three ways in which to correctly consider God's Word. Firstly, the faithful were to observe the true sense and meaning of Scripture. Secondly, they were to note the truth of the Word that they had experienced in their own lives – temptation, for example, or repentance. Finally, they were to reflect on how obedient they had been to God and how far they had transgressed against Him.[40] An annotating reader of Chemnitz's *Examinis* in the Grantham library collection underlined the divine's assertion that 'you do not have the Scriptures by merely reading, but by understanding them'.[41] Moreover, William Stone's annotations in his copy of Saint Augustine's *On Christian Doctrine*, now in the library in Wimborne Minster church, focussed on the patristic writer's

---

38   Ryrie, *Being Protestant*, pp. 275–276.
39   Francis Roberts, *Clavis Bibliorum. The Key of the Bible, Unlocking the Richest Treasury of the Holy Scriptures* (London: T. R. and E. M., 1649), part 1, p. 43. Annotated copy in the Gorton Chest, Chetham's Library, Manchester, shelfmark GC.1.8. USTC 3052315.
40   William Perkins, *The Workes of that Famous and Worthy Minister of Christ in the University of Cambridge, M. William Perkins: The Second Volume* (London: John Legatt, 1631), p. 480. Annotated copy in the Gorton Chest, Chetham's Library, Manchester, shelfmark GC.2.14. USTC 3015392.
41   Chemnitz, *Examinis Concilii Tridentini, Part I*, p. 57. Annotated copy in the Francis Trigge Chained Library, shelfmark D2. Underlined Latin passage on p. 57 reads '*Scripturae non sunt in legendo, sed in intelligendo*'. This edition not listed in the USTC. English translation: Kramer, *Examination of the Council of Trent, Part I*, p. 207.

advice to explain Scriptural messages with other sections of Scripture, in order to aid understanding. Stone underlined Augustine's assertion that 'it is far safer to walk by the light of Holy Scripture'.[42] This was a characteristically Protestant interpretation of Augustine's message and the sufficiency of Scripture that reinforced its importance and practical application.[43]

The plethora of Bible reading-aids that flooded the book market in the sixteenth and seventeenth centuries reflected the importance of understanding the Bible correctly.[44] These aids came first in the form of commentaries on certain parts of the Bible, with a strong focus on the New Testament and its better-known books and passages, such as the Gospel of Matthew. Annotations that 'promised to focus on the harder or more significant words and passages' of the Bible and paraphrases that 'made the meaning clearer by rephrasing the whole or part of the text in question' soon followed. By the mid-seventeenth century, commentaries, annotations and paraphrases on the Bible had become so popular that commentators expanded their scope to the lesser-known books of the New Testament and to the Old Testament as well.[45] The collections of the Grantham, Ripon, Gorton and Wimborne Minster parish libraries reflected the general popularity of these Bible reading-aids. Bibles and Biblical commentaries and interpretations accounted for thirty-seven percent of Grantham's Francis Trigge Chained Library collection, thirty-six percent of Ripon Minster parish library collection, twelve percent of the Gorton Chest parish library collection, and twenty-three percent of the collection of Wimborne Minster Chained Library. Rather than devaluing the importance of understanding the Bible, these reading-aids were instead a manifestation of the commitment of the 'middling' sorts of people who used these parish libraries and read the volumes they contained, to reading the Bible critically and understanding it properly. The plethora of early modern marginalia pertaining to the topic demonstrates this importance and suggests that the lessons learned through this understanding may have been applicable in everyday life.

---

42 Saint Augustine, *Complectens Ta Didaktika, Volume I, Book III*, p. 57–58. Annotated copy in Wimborne Minster Chained Library, shelfmark A1. Underlined Latin passage on p. 57–58 reads *'Per Scripturas enim divinas multo tutius ambulatur ...'*. This edition not listed in the USTC. English translation: Shaw, Salmond and Dods, *The Works of Aurelius Augustine*, p. 104.

43 Kevin Killeen, Helen Smith, and Rachel Willie, 'Introduction to Part II', in Kevin Killeen, Helen Smith, and Rachel Willie (eds), *The Oxford Handbook of the Bible in Early Modern England, c. 1530–1700* (Oxford: Oxford University Press, 2018), p. 114; Alister E. McGrath, *Reformation Thought: An Introduction*, 4th edition (Oxford: Wiley-Blackwell, 2012), p. 98.

44 Ryrie, *Being Protestant*, p. 277.

45 Green, *Print and Protestantism*, pp. 113–124.

3   Accessibility of the Scriptures

The need for the Scriptures to be accessible to all was expressed in numerous instances of marginalia in several parish library volumes. William Stone, the clergyman who gave his collection of patristic texts to the church of Wimborne Minster before his death in 1685, annotated a large proportion of his books in his own hand. Stone's annotations in his copy of Saint Augustine's *Complectens illius Epistolas* ..., now in Wimborne Minster Chained Library, suggest his interest in the importance of universal accessibility to the Scriptures, which was a key principle of early modern Protestantism. Stone underlined one of Augustine's epistles to Volusianus in which Augustine extolled the simplicity of language used in Scripture. Augustine praised

> how accessible it is to all men, though its deeper mysteries are penetrable to very few. The plain truths which it contains it declares in the artless language of familiar friendship to the hearts both of the unlearned and of the learned.[46]

Stone underlined this statement and added two manuscript annotations in Latin in the margin. The first annotation Stone noted read '*Scriptura accessibilis omnibus, paucis penetrabilis*', whilst the second annotation adjacent to the passage read:

> *Quo consilio Scripturas in quibus*   *1. Facilis*
>   *2. Difficilis*

These annotations served to both reiterate and summarise the arguments made by Augustine, enabling Stone and any later readers to digest and understand them more easily.[47]

---

46   Saint Augustine, *D. Aurelii Augustini Hipponensis Episcopi, Complectens illius Epistolas* ..., *Volume I, Book II* (Basel: ex officina Frobeniana, 1569), p. 15–16. Annotated copy in Wimborne Minster Chained Library, shelfmark A1. Underlined Latin passage on p. 15–16 reads '... *que omnibus accessibilis, quamuis paucissimis penetrabilis, ea quae aperta continet quasi amicus familiaris sine fuco ad corloquitur indoctorum atque doctorum* ...'. This edition not listed in the USTC. English translation: Philip Schaff, *The Confessions and Letters of St. Augustin, with a Sketch of his Life and Work* (Edinburgh, T. & T. Clark, 1886), p. 687.

47   Saint Augustine, *Complectens illius Epistolas* ..., *Volume I, Book II*, p. 15–16. Annotated copy in Wimborne Minster Chained Library, shelfmark A1. This edition not listed in the USTC. English translation: Schaff, *The Confessions and Letters of St. Augustin*, p. 687; Mark

The accessibility of the Scriptures was not always encouraged and cele-
brated, however. It seems that a reader of Edward Herbert's *The Life and Raigne
of King Henry VIII*, now in Wimborne Minster Chained Library, paid close
attention to Herbert's thoughts on the topic, which were largely against providing the Bible to the general reading public. The discussion Herbert engaged
in on the vernacular Bible and its status as a source of religious confusion and
conflict is an interesting one. Both Protestant contemporaries and modern
sources usually couch the vernacular Bible positively in terms of increased
accessibility for the common laity.[48] However, unusually amongst the range
of texts studied in this book, Herbert presented a contrasting view of the vernacular Bible as a source of confusion and disruption. In 1539, the Great Bible
was published in the vernacular. By 1543, Henry VIII had passed the Act for
the Advancement of True Religion, which limited who could read the Bible.
Clerics, noblemen, the gentry and richer merchants were permitted to read
it whilst women below gentry rank, servants, apprentices and common people, were forbidden. Women of gentry rank and above were only permitted to
read the vernacular Bible in private. Herbert discussed the poor social behaviour engaged in by those who had not been permitted to read the Bible for
themselves before 1539, which Henry VIII perceived to be the consequence of
general lay access to Scripture in the vernacular after the publication of the
Great Bible. Herbert stated that 'they fell into many dangerous opinions: little caring how they liv'd, so they understood well, bringing Religion thus into
much irresolution and Controversie'.[49] The discussion in the printed text was
annotated with two manuscript manicules and a wavy line down the complete
length of the page (all drawn in the same hand) in order to draw attention
to the paragraph.[50] Due to the inarticulate nature of the marginalia and a
lack of knowledge about the annotator, it is unclear whether these passages
were marked to denote agreement or disagreement with Herbert's assertions.
However, it seems likely that had the annotator disagreed with Herbert's comments, the annotations would have reflected that disagreement in some way.

Towsey, *Reading the Scottish Enlightenment: Books and the Readers in Provincial Scotland,
1750–1820* (Leiden: Brill, 2010), p. 177.

48   Green, *Print and Protestantism*, pp. 46–47; Susan Wabuda, '"A Day After Doomsday":
Cranmer and the Bible Translations of the 1530s' in Kevin Killeen, Helen Smith, and
Rachel Willie (eds), *The Oxford Handbook of the Bible in Early Modern England, c. 1530–1700*
(Oxford: Oxford University Press, 2018), p. 26; Lucy E. C. Wooding, *Rethinking Catholicism
in Reformation England* (Oxford: Clarendon Press, 2000), p. 22.

49   Herbert, *The Life and Raigne of King Henry VIII*, mispaginated in manuscript as p. 361.
Annotated copy in Wimborne Minster Chained Library, shelfmark D15. USTC 3047333.

50   *Ibid.*, p. 323. Annotated copy in Wimborne Minster Chained Library, shelfmark D15. USTC
3047333.

Nevertheless, these tales of religious controversy would have been extremely familiar to a post-Civil War reader of Wimborne Minster's 1649 edition of *The Life and Raigne of Henry VIII*.

4   Conclusion

Scripture clearly held paramount importance in the lives of early modern Protestants. In numerous books from the parish libraries of Grantham, Ripon, Gorton and Wimborne Minster, annotating readers marked various passages in which authors outlined how Scripture could be recognised as the true Word of God and demonstrated their belief that, as the Word of God, Scripture contained everything necessary for faith. The Bible's practical use as a teaching tool was demonstrated by readers' marks in books that emphasised the importance of teaching one's neighbours as well as oneself. Before a person could use the Bible to teach, however, they had to be sure that they had interpreted and understood it correctly themselves, the importance of which was highlighted in several readers' annotations. Other readers' marks emphasised the importance of Scriptural interpretation being carried out by a group of learned men as opposed to one individual, so that the truth of Scripture could be better ascertained. Furthermore, the annotations in these volumes also demonstrate that understanding Scripture did not come merely from reading it, but from internalizing the messages of Scripture and incorporating both the text and its lessons into everyday life, as Whitaker, Sherman and others have suggested. This has important implications for Protestants' interest in sin, repentance and salvation, which are discussed in the next chapter. Finally, in order for as many people as possible to benefit from Scripture as the Word of God, the Bible needed to be widely accessible, both in terms of its language and in its physical availability. Whilst the use of the Bible by those unaccustomed to reading it was not without problems, many readers' marks on the topic of accessibility focussed on the more positive aspects of its use by both the learned and unlearned.

CHAPTER 11

Sin, Repentance and Salvation

The Protestant Reformation redefined the concepts of sin and salvation by obliterating the Catholic cycle of sin, repentance, absolution and penance.[1] Protestant repentance, however, remained a multi-step process and was something that did not come naturally, hence the wealth of instructive literature.[2] The ultimate goal of repentance was to receive assurance of grace in this life and salvation in the next, and only in true mourning for one's sins could assurance be felt.[3] Salvation was, however, only accomplished through faith and bestowed by God's mercy as a result of Christ's sacrifice. In Catholic theology, good works were a key component in increasing one's chances of salvation; in Reformed Protestant theology, good works were not the cause of salvation, but the result of one's elect status.[4] Protestant authors of all confessional identities set down such beliefs in their works, and the multiplicity of surviving annotations on the three interrelated topics of sin, repentance and salvation in parish library books suggest that they were taken to heart by their readers and assimilated into their everyday lives and practices. On the subject of sin, annotations reveal readers' preoccupation with the nature of sinful actions and the importance of avoiding such actions. These annotations specifically focussed on the need to resist both internal and external temptations that manifested themselves in lustfulness for either carnal or material things, and the need to avoid setting too much store by earthly pleasures and instead focus on the benefits accorded to the faithful in the afterlife. On repentance, readers' marks and annotations primarily focussed on the act of repentance as being the pathway back to God and salvation after having committed sin. Repentance was of intrinsic importance in attaining salvation and readers of parish library books were concerned with how salvation was to be achieved: through justification and righteousness, through faith and a life lived in service to fellow believers.

---

1 Jonathan Willis, *The Reformation of the Decalogue: Religious Identity and the Ten Commandments in England, c.1485–1625* (Cambridge: Cambridge University Press, 2020), pp. 177–178.

2 Alec Ryrie, *Being Protestant in Reformation Britain* (Oxford: Oxford University Press, 2015), pp. 49–55.

3 *Ibid.*, pp. 59, 62.

4 Carl R. Trueman, 'Scripture and Exegesis in Early Modern Reformed Theology' in Ulrich L. Lehner, Richard A. Muller and A. G. Roeber (eds), *The Oxford Handbook of Early Modern Theology, 1600–1800* (Oxford: Oxford University Press, 2016), p. 170.

Many annotated passages of these library volumes also discussed hard times and their role in leading the faithful to salvation whilst other marginalia suggest the significance of Christ's sacrifice and his role in the justification and sanctification of the faithful to early modern Protestants.

1   Sin

Multitudinous annotations in several parish library volumes attest that avoiding sin was of paramount importance to early modern Protestants. Various early modern Protestant authors exhorted their readers to strive against the internal corruptions of the flesh and against the external corruptions of the world and the devil.[5] These internal and external corruptions could take many forms. Most prominent amongst the external temptations were worldly possessions, earthly wealth and prosperity, whilst the internal temptations referred to included lust and the associated sins of the flesh. William Perkins identified two types of sins in the second volume of his *Workes*. First were sins of infirmity, caused by the passions of men that included grief, anger, sorrow and other, similar emotions. Second were sins of presumption, which arose from emotions like pride, arrogance and wilfulness.[6] The significance of these distinctions to an early modern audience is suggested by the annotations in this section of Perkins' works now in the Gorton Chest parish library.

The consequences of failing to resist either internal or external temptations were dire to early modern Protestants: it could lead to 'the dismal thoughts of an accusing, tormenting conscience' and the 'everlasting burnings' of hell. Early modern readers evidently took this advice in Isaac Ambrose's *Media* to heart: a reader of the copy now in the Gorton Chest marked the page on which Ambrose advocated relinquishing worldly possessions and fleshly lust in order to avoid such sufferings.[7] Similarly, a reader of the Gorton Chest copy of Joseph Mede's *Diatribæ* deliberately folded the corner of the page on which the biblical

---

5 Frank Luttmer, 'Persecutors, Tempters and Vassals of the Devil: The Unregenerate in Puritan Practical Divinity', *Journal of Ecclesiastical History*, 51 (2000), p. 60.

6 William Perkins, *The Workes of that Famous and Worthy Minister of Christ in the University of Cambridge, M. William Perkins: The Second Volume* (London: John Legatt, 1631), p. 6. Annotated copy in the Gorton Chest, Chetham's Library, Manchester, shelfmark GC.2.14. USTC 3015392.

7 Isaac Ambrose, *Prima, Media & Ultima: The First, Middle and Last Things* (London: T. R. and E. M., 1654), part 2, p. 112. Annotated copy in the Gorton Chest, Chetham's Library, Manchester, shelfmark GC.1.6(1). This edition not listed on the USTC.

scholar encouraged his readers to protect their souls from even the smallest of sins, lest they were taken incrementally further away from God.[8] William Higginbotham, whose annotated copy of John Calvin's *Sermons upon the Booke of Job* is now in the Francis Trigge Chained Library in Grantham, made numerous marginal annotations on the topic of sin. In one annotation, Higginbotham referred to sin as 'a disease that we have within us', which supports the argument made by Jonathan Willis that early modern Protestants defined sin as 'a breach of God's law'. Willis argued that early modern Protestants likened sin to a sickness: 'a corruption, a frightening malady which led inevitably to a terminal diagnosis'.[9]

The need to avoid external temptations and the consequences of not doing so looms large in the annotations of parish library books. The interlinked emotions of greed and envy were strongly connected to one's own and others' worldly possessions, and were seen as primary causes of sin. As one reader of the Gorton Chest copy of John Dod's *A Plaine and Familiar Exposition of the Ten Commandements* underlined, a man's greed could lead him to sin, 'for, give a covetous man wealth enough, and an ambitious man honour enough, and you may lead him whither you will'.[10] In this passage, Dod warned his readers against deviation from God in favour of other, temporal lords, which stemmed from covetousness and contravened God's First Commandment to obey none other than Himself. Similarly, envy, which Dod defined as 'a bitter affection, against the prosperity and pre-eminence of another' in a further passage underlined by a reader, was often inspired by the wealth and honour perceived in others.[11] Envy was a sin that undermined the love shown by God to His elect, which He expected His true believers to exemplify in their dealings with others and which potentially jeopardised a person's salvation. In this context, Higginbotham's marginal note in Grantham's copy of Calvin's *Sermons* that reminded himself and any later readers that 'we most not lik to well of our prosperity' seems

8   Joseph Mede, *Diatribæ Pars IV. Discourses on Sundry Texts of Scripture* (London: J. F., 1652), p. 225. Annotated copy in the Gorton Chest, Chetham's Library, Manchester, shelfmark GC.1.12. This edition not listed in the USTC.

9   John Calvin, *Sermons upon the Booke of Job*, trans. A. Golding (London: T. Dawson for G. Bishop and T. Woodcocke, 1579), p. 19. Annotated copy in the Francis Trigge Chained Library, shelfmark E10. USTC 508947; Willis, *The Reformation of the Decalogue*, pp. 139, 148.

10   John Dod, *A Plaine and Familiar Exposition of the Ten Commandements* (London: Felix Kyngston, 1614), pp. 52–53. Annotated copy in the Gorton Chest, Chetham's Library, Manchester, shelfmark GC.1.13(1). USTC 3005942.

11   *Ibid.*, pp. 261–263. Annotated copy in the Gorton Chest, Chetham's Library, Manchester, shelfmark GC.1.13(1). USTC 3005942.

particularly pertinent.[12] Higginbotham also wrote a note in the margin of Calvin's *Sermons* next to a passage in which the author instructed his readers 'not to set our mindes to much upon the world'. Higginbotham summarised this passage in the note, which read: 'we most sett our mindes uppon hevenly thinges for this world is ... full of evell'.[13] There was Biblical precedent for the corruptive nature of worldly possessions and goods. William Perkins, for example, used the New Testament to argue that those who neglected their faith and obedience to God in favour of material possessions were fools.[14]

However, early modern readers did note that men were not necessarily expected to relinquish their worldly goods; rather, they were simply expected not to become so attached to them that they became more enamoured with their prosperity than with God. A reader of John Dod's *Ten Sermons Tending Chiefly to the Fitting of Men for the Worthy Receiving of the Lord's Supper*, now in the Gorton Chest parish library, annotated the margin adjacent to a passage in which Dod asserted that the desire of the faithful for the kingdom of Heaven should render earthly possessions and valuables meaningless. For Dod and the faithful, Christ and salvation were worth far more than worldly goods: 'he should withdraw his confidence from these, and his immoderate love of these, being content to forsake them quite, rather than to forgoe Christ, and to forfeit his owne salvation'.[15] Similarly, a page on which Isaac Ambrose encouraged his readers to deny themselves worldly pleasures in order to remain close to Christ was marked by a reader of the copy of Ambrose's *Prima, Media & Ultima* now in the Gorton Chest library.[16] Such sentiments were likewise expressed on a marked page of the Gorton Chest copy of Richard Baxter's *The Saints Everlasting Rest*.[17] Furthermore, these views were reinforced by Higginbotham's

---

12   Calvin, *Sermons upon the Booke of Job*, p. 287. Annotated copy in the Francis Trigge Chained Library, shelfmark E10. USTC 508947.

13   *Ibid.*, p. 247. Annotated copy in the Francis Trigge Chained Library, shelfmark E10. USTC 508947.

14   W. B. Patterson, *William Perkins and the Making of a Protestant England* (Oxford: Oxford University Press, 2014), p. 110.

15   John Dod, *Ten Sermons Tending Chiefly to the Fitting of Men for the Worthy Receiving of the Lord's Supper* (London: T. P., 1621), p. 149. Annotated copy in the Gorton Chest, Chetham's Library, Manchester, shelfmark GC.1.13(2). USTC 3009792.

16   Ambrose, *Prima, Media & Ultima*, part 2, p. 156. Annotated copy in the Gorton Chest, Chetham's Library, Manchester, shelfmark GC.1.6(1). This edition not listed on the USTC.

17   Richard Baxter, *The Saints Everlasting Rest, or, A Treatise Of the blessed State of the Saints in their enjoyment of God in Glory* (London: Thomas Underhill and Francis Tyson, 1656), sig. C2v. Annotated copy in the Gorton Chest, Chetham's Library, Manchester, shelfmark GC.1.1. This edition not listed in the USTC.

underlining of passages of the Grantham copy of Calvin's *Sermons*, in which Calvin reminded his readers, 'so then if our Lorde give us any goodes, let us learne not too intangle oure selves in them'.[18] These marked pages and annotations suggest their readers' interest in these topics and highlighted them for later readers. They also denote a highly practical focus on the part of the readers, demonstrating their search for guidance that they could assimilate into their lives in order to make themselves more pleasing to God. Such actions serve to reinforce Whitaker's model of reading in the early modern period.[19]

For the early modern readers of books in the Grantham, Ripon, Gorton and Wimborne Minster parish libraries, sin could not be relieved by further sinful actions, nor could a person be saved from sin by any other means than by God himself. This belief is reflected in the annotations of William Stone in the Wimborne Minster copies of Saint Augustine's *Confessions* and *De Civitate Dei*. Augustine was one of the first to perpetuate the idea that sin could not relieve sin, and in *De Civitate Dei*, Stone underlined Augustine's musings on forgiveness, asking 'is it not better to commit a wickedness which penitence may heal, than a crime which leaves no place for healing contrition?'.[20] Further, in Augustine's *Confessions*, Stone also highlighted Augustine's thanks to God for His remission of Augustine's sins: 'unto thy grace and mercy do I ascribe, that thou has dissolved my sins as it were ice'. Stone wrote a marginal note asking that 'God bless us and keep us from sin' adjacent to the passage.[21] Stone's annotations on these topics suggest some degree of agreement with Augustine's sentiments and intimate Stone's belief in Protestant theologies relating to sinful behaviour and God's forgiveness. Annotations suggesting readers' belief that

---

18 Calvin, *Sermons upon the Booke of Job*, p. 358. Annotated copy in the Francis Trigge Chained Library, shelfmark E10. USTC 508947.

19 Elaine Whitaker, 'A Collaboration of Readers: Categorisation of the Annotations in Copies of Caxton's Royal Book', *Text*, 7 (1994), pp. 235–236.

20 Saint Augustine, *D. Aurelii Augustini Hipponensis Episcopi, De Civitate Dei Libros XXII, Volume II, Book V* (Basel: ex officina Frobeniana, 1569), p. 73–74. Underlined Latin passage on p. 73–74 reads '*Nonne satius est, flagitium committere, quod poenitendo sanetur, quam tale facinus ubi locus talis poenitentiae non relinquitur?*'. Annotated copy in Wimborne Minster Chained Library, shelfmark A2. USTC 698766. English translation: Marcus Dods (trans. and ed.), *The City of God, Volume I* (Edinburgh: T. & T. Clark, 1871), p. 36.

21 Saint Augustine, *Primus Tomus eximii Patris, inter summa Latinae Ecclesiae ornamenta ac lumina principis, D. Aurelii Augustini Hipponensis Episcopi, Cuius praestantissima in omni genere monimenta ..., Volume I, Book I* (Basel: Ambrosius and Aurelius Froben, 1569), p. 79–80. Annotated copy in Wimborne Minster Chained Library, shelfmark A1. Underlined Latin passage on p. 75–76 reads '*Gratiae tuae deputo & misericordie tue, quod peccata mea tamquam glaciem solvisti ...*'. USTC 686573. English translation: William Watts (trans.), T. E. Page and W. H. D. Rouse (eds), *Saint Augustine's Confessions* (London: William Heinemann, 1912), p. 89.

only God, albeit in different guises, could alleviate sin can also be found in the Gorton Chest copy of John Weemes' *Workes*.[22] Moreover, readers marked the pages of the Gorton Chest copies of Anthony Burgess's *Spiritual Refining or A Treatise of Grace and Assurance* and Richard Rogers' *Seven Treatises*, on which the divines commented on people's inability to be saved without the will of God. Such a multiplicity of annotations together suggest the significance of these arguments to the early modern Protestant readers of these volumes.[23]

2   Repentance and Salvation

Repentance and trust in God were the only ways to regain the hope of salvation after committing sinful acts. The cruciality of this belief for early modern Protestant readers is clear in the plethora of annotated passages. Many readers focussed on the ways in which salvation was to be achieved and discussions on repentance were foremost amongst these annotations. For early modern Protestants, repentance was the pathway back to God and assurance of salvation. Assurance was an important feeling for early modern Protestants. As Higginbotham noted in a margin of the Grantham copy of Calvin's *Sermons upon the Booke of Job*, the happiness that resulted from this assurance was 'something God's children may rejoice in'.[24] Several of the surviving annotations on the topic of repentance link to the doctrine of predestination and the scope of the atonement. As noted by Calvin and underlined by Higginbotham in the twelfth sermon on the third chapter of the Book of Job, for example, 'in death there is not rest for all men'.[25] This links to the concept sometimes referred to as double predestination, which was put forward by Calvin and in which God selected some for eternal life and the rest for eternal torment and damnation.[26]

---

22   John Weemes, *The Workes of John Weemse of Lathocker in Scotland, in four Volumes* (London: T. Cotes, 1637), part 1, p. 308. Annotated copy in the Gorton Chest, Chetham's Library, Manchester, shelfmark GC.1.23. USTC 3019107.

23   Anthony Burgess, *Spiritual Refining: or, A Treatise of Grace and Assurance* (London: A. Miller, 1652), p. 200. Annotated copy in the Gorton Chest, Chetham's Library, Manchester, shelfmark GC.1.30. This edition not listed in the USTC; Richard Rogers, *Seven Treatises* (London: Felix Kyngston, 1603), p. 7. Annotated copy in the Gorton Chest, Chetham's Library, Manchester, shelfmark GC.1.31. This edition not listed in the USTC.

24   Calvin, *Sermons upon the Booke of Job*, p. 18. Annotated copy in the Francis Trigge Chained Library, shelfmark E10. USTC 508947.

25   *Ibid.*, p. 55. Annotated copy in the Francis Trigge Chained Library, shelfmark E10. USTC 508947.

26   Paul Helm, *Calvin at the Centre* (Oxford: Oxford University Press, 2010), pp. 145–146.

More generally, on the topic of salvation, readers of early modern parish library books highlighted passages on justification and righteousness as ways to salvation, alongside the maintenance of faith in God through the hardships people faced in their lifetime. Other readers were particularly keen to emphasise in their marginalia the importance of Christ's sacrifice and the role he played in the sanctification and justification of the faithful that led them to salvation – in other words, whether he suffered and died for the benefit of all, or only for the elect. This debate gained prominence during the predestinarian controversy in the ninth century and remained a subject of contention between Reformers in the sixteenth and seventeenth centuries.[27] Alec Ryrie has argued that many early modern Protestants were highly concerned with their spiritual wellbeing and their elect status. He has also demonstrated that these preoccupations gave rise to a significant number of published works that outlined the signs or the symptoms that denoted one's election to salvation.[28] This concern with recognising oneself as saved was reflected in several annotations on sections of advice from various divines regarding the ways in which salvation could be attained and assured. Much of the advice pertained to the process of sanctification that was, for most early modern Protestants, lifelong. William Perkins, for example, was one of many early modern Protestant authors who sought to provide his readers with assurances of grace that, as Charles Hambrick-Stowe has argued, took into account 'the human penchant to swing between self-confidence ... and remorse for ongoing doubt and sin'.[29]

Repentance was such a complex practice that the practical advice of divines on how to undertake it was, unsurprisingly, an important feature of the annotations in these parish library books. Protestant divines encouraged readers firstly to examine themselves in order to determine whether they were ready to repent. On two marked pages of the Gorton Chest copy of his *Diatribæ*, the Biblical scholar and Hebraist, Joseph Mede outlined a three-step self-examination process for readers to follow in order to decide whether they were a true penitent that was ready to repent of their sins.[30]

Once a person was ready to repent, they needed to know how to do so. In the first volume of his *Workes*, William Perkins discussed the forms of repentance

---

27 Alister E. McGrath, *Reformation Thought: An Introduction*, 4th edition (Oxford: Wiley-Blackwell, 2012), pp. 192–204.
28 Ryrie, *Being Protestant*, p. 39.
29 Charles E. Hambrick-Stowe, 'Practical Divinity and Spirituality' in John Coffey and Paul C. H. Lim (eds), *The Cambridge Companion to Puritanism* (Cambridge: Cambridge University Press, 2008), pp. 193–194.
30 Mede, *Diatribæ Pars IV*, pp. 100–101. Annotated copy in the Gorton Chest, Chetham's Library, Manchester, shelfmark GC.1.12. This edition not listed in the USTC.

and the sorts of people who should repent. He also outlined the four-step process of repentance, which involved examining one's conscience, acknowledging their sins, praying for God's pardon, and finally, praying for God's grace.[31] The marking of this page by a reader of the Gorton Chest copy of Perkins' *Workes* suggests the practical value of Perkins' advice to that reader. Moreover, a reader of the first part of Chemnitz's *Examinis Concilii Tridentini* in the Grantham library collection underlined the Lutheran divine's discussion of the purging of sins 'first through remission, through the removal of the guilt, or by non-imputation. Thereafter it occurs through mortification and renewal'.[32] In the Grantham copy of Calvin's *Sermons upon the Booke of Job*, William Higginbotham wrote 'hear we may learn how we shall be clensed from our sinnes' next to a paragraph in which Calvin outlined the process of repentance, suggesting its significance and practical applicability.[33] Alec Ryrie has demonstrated that repentance was a complicated process in which early modern Protestants engaged, involving earnestness, regularity and thoroughness. Ryrie argued that readiness to undertake this process was a stark demarcation between the regenerate and the reprobate, stating that the point of repentance was 'to attain assurance in this life and Heaven in the next'.[34] These annotations appear to reflect the significance and importance to early modern Protestant readers of correctly performing this process of repentance in order to obtain the assurance of grace and salvation that they so desperately desired.

Other early modern Protestant writers and readers placed a different emphasis on the practice of repentance. Arthur Hildersham, for example, provided his readers with reassurances on the topic of repentance on two marked pages of the copy of his *CVIII Lectures upon the Fourth of John* now in the Gorton Chest parish library. On these pages, Hildersham related proofs of the doctrine that the sins of the elect could not separate men from God once they had truly

31   William Perkins, *The Workes of that Famous and Worthy Minister of Christ in the University of Cambridge, Mr William Perkins: The First Volume* (London: John Legatt, 1626), p. 458. Annotated copy in the Gorton Chest, Chetham's Library, Manchester, shelfmark GC.2.13. USTC 3012639.

32   Martin Chemnitz, *Examinis Concilii Tridentini, Part I* (Frankfurt: Peter Fabricius, 1585), p. 101. Annotated copy in the Francis Trigge Chained Library, shelfmark D2. Underlined Latin passage on p. 101 reads '*Dicimus autem eam fieri, primo remissione, solutione reatus, seu non imputatione*'. This edition not listed in the USTC. English translation: Fred Kramer (trans.), *Examination of the Council of Trent, Part I* by Martin Chemnitz (London: Concordia Publishing House, 1971), p. 362.

33   Calvin, *Sermons upon the Booke of Job*, p. 10. Annotated copy in the Francis Trigge Chained Library, shelfmark E10. USTC 508947; Mark Towsey, *Reading the Scottish Enlightenment: Books and the Readers in Provincial Scotland, 1750–1820* (Leiden: Brill, 2010), p. 177.

34   Ryrie, *Being Protestant*, pp. 55–59.

repented of those sins, before going on to list his evidence, which included 'foure principall points':

1. He is never a whit the more unwilling to offer his grace unto them, and to seeke their conversion, for any hanious sinne they lived in before their calling

2. He thinkes never a whit the worse of them for that they have beene, or for any sins they have lived in before their conversion, after once they have repented of them

3. He likes never the worse of the good workes, done by them after their conversion, because of the corruption that is mingled with them

4. He makes their very sinnes turne to their good, and to the furtherance of their salvation.[35]

Hildersham explicitly stated that 'yet can no sinne of Gods Elect, how hanious soever, cause God to hate or reject them'.[36] Frank Luttmer has demonstrated that the daily need for repentance reflected the unavoidably sinful nature of everyday life for even the most devout of God's true believers, who would occasionally find themselves backsliding before recovering themselves and returning once more to God.[37] Numerous readers' preoccupation with the need for repentance demonstrates its significance and suggests that they sought to apply the advice of the Protestant divines to their everyday lives.

Irrespective of how repentance manifested in the godly, true repentance had to be meant in order to lead successfully to salvation. One reader of the Gorton Chest copy of Francis White's *A Replie to Jesuit Fisher* folded the corner of a page and underlined several passages of a paragraph that stated that 'the promise of remission of sinnes is conditionall ... and the same becommeth not absolute, until the condition be fulfilled'. A reader also underlined White's assertion that 'the full assurance of remission of sinnes succeedeth Repentance, Faith, Obedience, and Mortification'.[38] The importance of true repentance to early modern Protestants is further reinforced by an underlined passage of the Grantham copy of Chemnitz's *Examinis*, in which the Lutheran Chemnitz asserted that 'contrition is altogether necessary in those who truly

---

35   Arthur Hildersham, *CVIII Lectures upon the Fourth of John* (London: Moses Bell, 1647), pp. 87–89. Annotated copy in the Gorton Chest, Chetham's Library, Manchester, shelfmark GC.2.5(2). USTC 3043316.

36   *Ibid.*, p. 88. Annotated copy in the Gorton Chest, Chetham's Library, Manchester, shelfmark GC.2.5(2). USTC 3043316.

37   Luttmer, 'Persecutors, Tempters and Vassals of the Devil', p. 61.

38   Francis White, *A Replie to Jesuit Fisher's Answer to Certain Questions Propounded by His Most Gracious Majesty, King James* (London: Adam Islip, 1624), p 162. Annotated copy in the Gorton Chest, Chetham's Library, Manchester, shelfmark GC.1.27. USTC 3011511.

and earnestly repent'.[39] These annotations support the arguments made by
Ryrie about the importance of repentance to early modern Protestants and the
belief 'that repentance meant action, not words ... that true repentance was
marked by a sincere and earnest intent to moral reform'.[40] The annotations
made by early modern readers also suggest an element of the 'identification
of faith with assurance' of salvation.[41] It may be that the desire to truly repent,
combined with the difficulties in recognising the truth of assurance, prompted
these and other readers to engage in the sort of self-examination favoured by
Puritans of the late sixteenth and early seventeenth centuries. This was a process in which the faithful scrutinised themselves for signs of election. Those
who were convinced of their elect status allowed their conviction to manifest
in their behaviour. Signal characteristics of the elect included 'heightened
internal spiritual temperance and compulsion to spread the fever ...' through
the writing of spiritual diaries, pious autobiographies, religious verse and other
works of that ilk.[42]

The centrality of faith in God to salvation is widely reflected in annotations
on the topic of salvation more generally, which also touched on the scope of
Christ's atonement, his sacrifice and his role in the justification of the faithful.
Martin Luther was engaged in discussions on the scope of Christ's atonement
in the sixteenth century. He was effusive on the topic of achieving salvation and
rigorously promoted his doctrine of justification by faith, which asserted that
God gave 'justifying righteousness to people without the need for any merit
on their part'.[43] A reader of Luther's *A Commentarie upon the Fiftene Psalmes*
annotated certain psalms in the copy of this text that is now in Ripon Minster
parish library. One of the most heavily annotated psalms in this volume was
Luther's commentary on Psalm 130, which Luther himself declared 'emongst
the most excellent & principall psalms: for it setteth forth the chiefest point of

---

39   Martin Chemnitz, *Examinis Concilii Tridentini, Part II* (Frankfurt: Peter Fabricius, 1585),
      p. 184. Annotated copy in the Francis Trigge Chained Library, shelfmark D2. Underlined
      Latin passage on p. 184 reads '*Omnino in iis, qui veram & seriam agunt poenitentiam,
      necessaria est contritio*'. This edition not listed in the USTC. English translation: Fred
      Kramer (trans.), *Examination of the Council of Trent, Part II* by Martin Chemnitz (London:
      Concordia Publishing House, 1971), p. 581.

40   Ryrie, *Being Protestant*, p. 58.

41   Michael P. Winship, 'Weak Christians, Backsliders, and Carnal Gospelers: Assurance
      of Salvation and the Pastoral Origins of Puritan Practical Divinity in the 1580s', *Church
      History: Studies in Christianity and Culture*, 9 (2001), p. 470.

42   Margo Todd, 'The Problem of Scotland's Puritans' in John Coffey and Paul C. H. Lim (eds),
      The Cambridge Companion to Puritanism (Cambridge: Cambridge University Press, 2008),
      pp. 181–183.

43   McGrath, *Reformation Thought*, p. 193.

our salvation'.[44] It is therefore unsurprising to find it so thoroughly annotated in pencil by a reader. Similar pencil annotations – presumably by the same reader – can also be found in Luther's commentary on Psalm 124. The annotations on the commentary on Psalm 130 are in the introduction and in Luther's commentary on the first four verses of the psalm. In these four annotated verses, the orator called to God and asked that He be attentive to the pleas He heard, before continuing to a discussion on the immorality of sin and the need for God's forgiveness, expounding this need as a reason to fear God.[45] As Andrew Pettegree has pointed out, for Luther, free will and men's deeds were irrelevant to salvation, which depended on God's will alone.[46] This argument is supported by an annotated passage of Luther's commentary on the third verse of Psalm 130, in which he declared:

> For what teach we else at this day, but that we are saved by fayth alone in the death and blood of Christ? that by the merite of Christ onely, our sinnes are covered and taken away, according to that saying: *Blessed are they whose sinnes are forgiven*. Forgivenes of sinnes then is that heaven under the which we dwell through our trust and confidence in the merite of Christ.[47]

The annotations on this passage suggest the significance to the reader of Luther's thoughts on the doctrine of justification by faith alone, which Peter Marshall has demonstrated was 'a bold reinterpretation of the doctrine of salvation' and that was 'for many encountering it ... a life-changing insight'. Certainly, this moment of epiphany seems to be reflected in the annotations of this reader of Luther's *Commentarie*. Salvation was the result of God's generosity in bestowing the faithful with righteousness.[48] Many of the annotations in Luther's *Commentarie* are suggestive of a reader who was interested not only

---

44   Martin Luther, *A Commentarie upon the Fiftene Psalmes*, trans. Henry Bull (London: Thomas Vautroullier, 1577), p. 210. Annotated copy in University of Leeds Brotherton Special Collections Library, shelfmark Ripon Cathedral Library XVII.E.16. USTC 508422.

45   Laurence Kriegshauser, *Praying the Psalms in Christ* (Notre Dame, Indiana: University of Notre Dame Press, 2019), pp. 276–277.

46   Andrew Pettegree, *Brand Luther: How an Unheralded Monk Turned His Small Town into a Center of Publishing, Made Himself the Most Famous Man in Europe – and Started the Protestant Reformation* (New York: Penguin Books, 2015), pp. 233–234.

47   Luther, *A Commentarie upon the Fiftene Psalmes*, pp. 219–220. Annotated copy in the Brotherton Special Collections Library, shelfmark Ripon Cathedral Library XVII.E.16. USTC 508422.

48   Peter Marshall, *Heretics and Believers: A History of the English Reformation* (London: Yale University Press, 2018), p. 144.

in the concept of salvation, but specifically in Luther's profession of the importance of faith in God's Word, the belief that righteousness was a gift from God
and that His mercy was the only way to salvation.[49]

Furthermore, the importance of faith to achieving salvation was also under-
lined and highlighted by a reader of Saint Athanasius's *Contra Gentes* and *De
Incarnatione Verbi*, now in the Ripon Minster parish library. Athanasius was
a leader of the Alexandrian school of theological thought, which centred on
Christ as the saviour of humanity.[50] As Aza Goudriaan has demonstrated,
Athanasius's writings were used as an authority on numerous theological
topics during the Reformation, 'and especially in the polemics with Roman
Catholic theology'.[51] As such, his work was utilised by several early modern
European Reformers including John Calvin, Abraham Scultetus, a German professor of theology and court preacher for Elector Frederick v of the Palatinate,
and Amandus Polanus, a German theologian and early Reformer.[52] A reader's
underlining of the final sentences of the Ripon Minster copy of the *Contra
Gentes*, which summarised Athanasius's arguments in favour of faith in Christ
as a constituent part of salvation, suggests the importance of this belief to the
reader. Athanasius asserted that

> having faith and piety towards Whom [i.e. God], my Christ-loving friend,
> be of good cheer and of good hope, because immortality and the king-
> dom of heaven is the fruit of faith and devotion towards Him ... for just as
> for them who walk after his example, the prize is everlasting life.[53]

---

49   McGrath, *Reformation Thought*, p. 120.

50   Alister E. McGrath, *Christian Theology: An Introduction*, 6th edition (Chichester: Wiley-
     Blackwell, 2017), pp. 219–220.

51   Aza Goudriaan, 'Athansius in Reformed Protestantism: Some Aspects of Reception
     History (1527–1607)', *Church History and Religious Culture*, 90:2/3 (2010), p. 275.

52   James I. Good, *History of the Reformed Church of Germany, 1620–1890* (Reading, PA: Daniel
     Miller, 1894), p. 18; Robert Letham, 'Amandus Polanus: A Neglected Theologian?', *The
     Sixteenth Century Journal*, 21:3 (1990), pp. 463–476.

53   Saint Athanasius, *Contra Gentes* in *Athanasii magni Alexandrini episcopi, graviss. scripto-
     ris, et sanctiss. martyris, opera, in quatuor tomos distributa* (Basel, 1564), p. 35. Annotated
     copy in University of Leeds Brotherton Special Collections Library, shelfmark Ripon
     Cathedral Library XIII.C.17/q. Underlined Latin passage on p. 35 reads '... *in quem quum tu
     fidem habeas & amorem, o Christi studiose, gratulare tibi, et certo persuadeas, in mercedem
     emolumentum que istius in ipsum fidei et religionis, immortalitatem et regnum coelorum
     tibi destina tum esse ... aeterna vita pro praemio est ...*'. USTC 613803. English translation:
     Philip Schaff and Henry Wade (trans.), *Contra Gentes by Saint Athanasius* (New York: The
     Christian Literature Company, 1892), p. 30.

This was the crux of Protestantism, the combination of the principle of *sola fides* and the pious act of imitating Christ, the idea that faith alone would lead to salvation but that a holy life was additionally beneficial.

Several annotations in the books of the Grantham, Ripon, Gorton and Wimborne Minster parish libraries concerned Christ's sacrifice and his role in the justification of the faithful. Others highlighted Christ's dual nature as both human and divine, which was a key doctrine of early modern Protestantism discussed by many of the leading theologians of the period. Paul Helm has demonstrated that Calvin, for example, outlined to the readers of his *Institutes of Christian Religion* that 'there is need of human salvation' that only a saviour who was both God and man could provide.[54] Several annotations in Saint Athanasius's *De Incarnatione Verbi* suggest that at least one reader of the Ripon Minster copy was interested in Christ's dual nature: His divinity manifested in the miracles He worked, His humanity manifested in His corporeal body. At the top of a page on which Athanasius outlined some of Christ's miracles, a reader noted that 'Christ's divinity is evidenced by his miracles', suggesting the importance of Athanasius's arguments on this topic to the reader. Such an annotation also infers that the reader may have simplified or summarised Athanasius's message in this way in order to aid their own comprehension and understanding, as Mark Towsey has suggested.[55] Other, similar annotations demonstrate the same practice. On the topic of Christ's humanity, probably the same reader interpreted and summarised in a marginal annotation Athanasius's assertion that Christ was 'conjoined with all by a like nature' as the source of man's dignity.[56] Belief in the two natures of Christ was a principal creed of the ancient Church, so it is unsurprising that this belief was retained within Protestantism, a religion whose constant refrain was a desire to return to the primitive Church.[57]

---

54 Helm, *Calvin at the Centre*, pp. 163–167.

55 Saint Athanasius, *De Incarnatione Verbi* in *Athanasii magni Alexandrini episcopi, graviss. scriptoris, et sanctiss. martyris, opera, in quatuor tomos distributa* (Basel, 1564), p. 47. Annotated copy in University of Leeds Brotherton Special Collections Library, shelfmark Ripon Cathedral Library XIII.C.17/q. Latin MSS note at the top of p. 47 reads '... *Christi divinitas ex miraculis quae Christus fecit constat* ...'. USTC 613803. English translation: Philip Schaff and Henry Wade (trans.), *De Incarnatione Verbi by Saint Athanasius* (New York: The Christian Literature Company, 1892), p. 46; Towsey, *Reading the Scottish Enlightenment*, p. 177.

56 Saint Athanasius, *De Incarnatione Verbi*, p. 41. Annotated copy in the Brotherton Special Collections Library, shelfmark Ripon Cathedral Library XIII.C.17/q. Latin MSS note at the top of p. 41 reads '... *hominis dignitas per christum factum hominem* ...'. USTC 613803. English translation: Schaff and Wade, *De Incarnatione Verbi by Saint Athanasius*, p. 41.

57 Dewey D. Wallace, Jr, 'Puritan Polemical Divinity and Doctrinal Controversy' in John Coffey and Paul C. H. Lim (eds), *The Cambridge Companion to Puritanism* (Cambridge:

Some of the annotations on the scope of Christ's sacrifice focussed specifically on the limited atonement controversy of the sixteenth and seventeenth centuries, which debated just who Christ died for. For instance, a reader of the Grantham copy of John Calvin's *In Omnes Pauli Apostoli epistolas et in omnes epistolas canonicas* underlined Calvin's discussion on the scope of the atonement. *In Omnes Pauli Apostoli epistolas* reflected Calvin's belief in the universality of Christ's death, but also the variable degree to which the atonement applied to individuals. Calvin asserted that 'Christ suffered sufficiently for the whole world, but efficiently only for the elect'.[58] The annotations on this passage, and on the redeeming nature of Christ's sacrifice more generally, not only fed into contemporary theological controversies surrounding atonement and salvation, they also suggest the importance of the topic to early modern Protestant readers. For example, a reader of the copy of William Chillingworth's *The Religion of the Protestants, A Safe Way to Salvation*, now in Wimborne Minster Chained Library, annotated Chillingworth's discussion on the redeeming nature of Christ, in which he noted that

> whosoever dies with Faith in Christ, and Contrition for all sinnes known and unknown (in which heal all his sinfull errours must be compriz'd), can no more be hurt by any the most malignant and pestilent errour.[59]

Chillingworth was a highly controversial figure in his day. Initially an adherent of the Church of England, in 1629 Chillingworth, under the influence of the Jesuit John Fisher, announced his conversion to Roman Catholicism. The seventeenth-century politician and historian, Edward Hyde, who knew William Chillingworth personally, described Chillingworth as having, in the 1620s,

> contracted such an irresolution and habit of doubting, that by degrees he grew confident of nothing, and a sceptic, at least in the greatest mysteries of faith. This made him, from first wavering in religion, and indulging to

---

Cambridge University Press, 2008), p. 206.

58   John Calvin, *In Omnes Pauli Apostoli epistolas et in omnes epistolas canonicas* (Geneva: Eustathium Vignon, 1580), p. 173. Annotated copy in the Francis Trigge Chained Library, shelfmark E4. This edition not listed in the USTC.

59   William Chillingworth, *The Religion of the Protestants, A Safe Way to Salvation* (Oxford: Leonard Lichfield, 1638), p. 159. Annotated copy in Wimborne Minster Chained Library, shelfmark K19. USTC 3019801.

scruples, to reconcile himself too soon and too easily to the church of Rome.[60]

Chillingworth's irresolution persisted and by the mid-1630s he had returned to the Church of England and was being recommended to prominent positions by Archbishop Laud. Chillingworth refused those positions on grounds of conscience as he was unable to subscribe to two of the Thirty-Nine Articles (1571).[61] Chillingworth's comments on right and true faith were particularly significant in light of his conversion and reconversion, and his reader seemingly perceived a sense of importance and authority in Chillingworth's guidance that caused them to annotate these passages.[62]

Similar themes can be seen in the annotations of both Jean-François Salvard's *An Harmony of the Confessions of the Faith of the Christian and Reformed Churches*, now in the Gorton Chest parish library, and Thomas Bilson's *The Effect of Certain Sermons Touching the Full Redemption of Mankind by the Death and Bloud of Christ Jesus*, now in the Ripon Minster parish library. A reader demonstrated their interest in Salvard's discussion of Christ's voluntary sacrifice on the Cross and his argument that Christ's resurrection was a symbol of man's justification by marking the page on which these ideas were discussed, suggesting the significance of Salvard's arguments to that reader and drawing the passages to the attention of later readers. On the marked page, Salvard asserted that 'our Lord Jesus offered himselfe a voluntary sacrifice unto his Father for us ... that we should be absolved before the tribunall seat of our God' and that 'our Lord Jesus crucified, dead and buried ... did rise againe for our justification'.[63] Further to this, in the copy of Thomas Bilson's *The Effect of Certain Sermons Touching the Full Redemption of Mankind*, a reader highlighted the importance of Christ's sacrifice to salvation. Bilson's statement that 'the ground of our salvation then is the obedience, humility and charitie of the sonne of God, yielding himselfe not onelie to serve in our steed, but to die for our sinnes' was underlined in pencil, suggesting the significance of this belief to an early modern Protestant

---

60 Edward Hyde, *The Life of Edward Earl of Clarendon, Lord High Chancellor of England, and Chancellor of the University of Oxford*, Volume I (Oxford: Clarendon Press, 1827), p. 63.
61 Warren Chernaik, 'Chillingworth, William, (1602–1644)', *Oxford Dictionary of National Biography* (online, 2010).
62 Chernaik, 'Chillingworth, William', *ODNB*.
63 Jean-François Salvard, *An Harmony of the Confessions of the Faith of the Christian and Reformed Churches* (London: John Legatt, 1643), part 2, p. 10. Annotated copy in the Gorton Chest, Chetham's Library, Manchester, shelfmark GC.1.4. USTC 3049712.

reader.[64] The centrality of Christ's sacrifice seems to have pervaded every aspect of believers' lives. It reflected the contemporary belief that no work or act of any man was pleasing to God on its own merit, without the effect of Christ's sacrifice upon it. Protestants needed to understand and accept this in order to maintain faith and act in a way that was agreeable to God.[65]

Annotations on the importance of keeping faith even through hard times as a way to salvation were more numerous in the books of the Gorton Chest parish library than in any of the other three examined in this work. Why is unclear, though it may be because the Gorton Chest parish library tended more clearly towards books of practical divinity than the other repositories. In Richard Baxter's *The Saints Everlasting Rest*, for example, a reader marked a page on which Baxter asserted that 'Labour and Trouble are the common way to Rest' and that 'through many tribulations we must enter into the Kingdom of Heaven'.[66] A reader of Anthony Burgess's *CXLV Expository Sermons upon the Whole 17th Chapter of the Gospel According to St John* folded the corners of two consecutive pages on which Burgess outlined the reasons why Protestants were afflicted with troubles on earth – namely, so that they did not become too attached to their earthly existence.[67] This suggests a desire to understand why God would allow the faithful to suffer, which also seems to have interested one of William Perkins' readers. They underlined a passage in which the divine advised the godly on what they may learn from bearing their afflictions in good faith: 'the first, that God is well pleased with us, and that wee are reconciled to God in Christ: the second, that al our miseries shal in the end turne to our good and everlasting salvation'.[68] Luther's theology of the Cross provided an explanation for the value of the hard times, struggles and afflictions that early modern Protestants suffered, asserting that persecution and difficulty was a sign of God's favour.[69] So important were hard times to faith and salvation that

---

64   Thomas Bilson, *The Effect of Certain Sermons Touching the Full Redemption of Mankind by the Death and Bloud of Christ Jesus* (London: Peter Short for Walter Burre, 1599), p. 44. Annotated copy in University of Leeds Brotherton Special Collections Library, shelfmark Ripon Cathedral Library XVII.E.14. USTC 513859.

65   Willis, *The Reformation of the Decalogue*, p. 191.

66   Baxter, *The Saints Everlasting Rest*, part 3, p. 252. Annotated copy in the Gorton Chest, Chetham's Library, Manchester, shelfmark GC.1.1. This edition not listed in the USTC.

67   Anthony Burgess, *CXLV Expository Sermons upon the Whole 17th Chapter of the Gospel According to St John* (London: Abraham Miller, 1656), pp. 287–288. Annotated copy in the Gorton Chest, Chetham's Library, Manchester, shelfmark GC.1.24. This edition not listed on the USTC.

68   Perkins, *Workes: The First Volume*, p. 481. Annotated copy in the Gorton Chest, Chetham's Library, Manchester, shelfmark GC.2.13. USTC 3012639.

69   Ryrie, *Being Protestant*, p. 417.

Alec Ryrie was able to demonstrate that Protestants exploited and exaggerated real and plausible dangers in order to maintain a sense of the threat they felt necessary to maintain faithfulness.[70]

3 Conclusion

The interlinked subjects of sin, repentance and salvation were of high importance to early modern Protestant readers. They maintained a longstanding significance, as evidenced by annotations on the subject in numerous volumes from the Grantham, Ripon, Gorton and Wimborne Minster parish libraries, which were founded at various points over a period of a hundred years. Readers tended to focus on practical advice that they could assimilate into their everyday lives: the best ways to avoid sin and temptation; the process of repentance; and how to achieve salvation. Annotations on the topic of sin and temptation suggest that many early modern Protestant readers believed that sin could be avoided by placing more emphasis on faith in God than on material possessions, whilst readers' marks on the topic of repentance demonstrate the importance of the process to early modern Protestants as the pathway back to God and salvation after sin had been committed. Salvation was achieved through a complex process of true repentance that involved several steps. The number of annotations in books by various divines who outlined the method suggests the importance of completing these steps successfully. Salvation was the ultimate goal for early modern Protestants. Their belief in the doctrine of justification by faith alone and that salvation was achieved through faith in God and the sacrifice of Christ on the Cross, which redeemed the faithful, was of paramount importance, as was the necessity of living a godly life and making a good death, which will be discussed in the next chapter.

---

70   *Ibid.*, pp. 419–420.

CHAPTER 12

Godly Living and Death

Godly living and preparation for death were two central aspects of practical pastoral theology for early modern Protestants. The frequency of annotations on the topics of godly living and preparation for death suggests a widespread interest in these practices amongst readers of parish library books. Ian Green has argued that a godly life required both inward faith, in the form of self-examination and repentance, and outward expressions of faith, such as good works in the home and the wider community. Authors of sixteenth- and seventeenth-century handbooks on godly living often focussed on either one aspect of piety or the other.[1] Previous chapters in this book have considered some of the internal signs of faith in God, such as acknowledging the importance of Scripture as the Word of God and the need to avoid sin and repent for any transgressions. This chapter, therefore, will focus primarily on those outward expressions of faith that were important to early modern Protestants, as demonstrated by the plethora of surviving annotations. Such outward manifestations of belief comprised the acts of praying to God, listening to learned, godly preachers, and the acts of good works that fostered a sense of community amongst the godly.

The pervasive importance of godly living and preparation for death, and the resultant compelling need felt by early modern Protestants to live a good life and make a good death, is demonstrated by annotations in numerous books from all four parish library collections considered here. Annotations on a godly life included three main components that each reflected a strand of godly living. Firstly, early modern readers focussed on preaching and prayer, the importance and significance of which is reflected in the willingness of the early modern godly to travel several miles, sometimes across parish boundaries, in order to hear sermons preached.[2] Secondly, readers highlighted the importance of goodness and of carrying out good works, such as the religious education of one's household, which were the product of one's trust in God

---

1 Ian Green, *Print and Protestantism in Early Modern England* (Oxford: Oxford University Press, 2000), p. 305.
2 Alexandra Walsham, 'The Godly and Popular Culture' in John Coffey and Paul C. H. Lim (eds), *The Cambridge Companion to Puritanism* (Cambridge: Cambridge University Press, 2008), p. 287.

© KONINKLIJKE BRILL NV, LEIDEN, 2024 | DOI:10.1163/9789004363717_017

and one's elect status.[3] Many early modern Protestants, including prominent authors such as William Perkins and Anthony Burgess, were keen to emphasise that the good works they considered a prerequisite of a godly life were mani-festations of one's elect status and not the cause of their salvation, as readers frequently highlighted. Paul Lim and Eamon Duffy have also argued that early modern Protestants viewed the conversion of the ungodly as an important good work.[4] Finally, readers' annotations emphasised that patience was an important element of a good life: authors exhorted their readers to be thankful to God when He corrected the faithful and to bear with fortitude the advan-tages and disadvantages that He sent to both the regenerate and the unregen-erate. Several of the works containing annotations on these topics were books of Puritan practical divinity; such handbooks of advice on godly living and dying were popular in sixteenth- and seventeenth-century England and their usefulness to early modern Protestants is evidenced by the plethora of reader-ship marks in these books from several parish libraries.[5]

The second part of a godly life on which early modern Protestants rumi-nated in their annotations was the necessity of making a good death. On that subject, readers of several volumes now in the parish libraries of Grantham, Ripon, Gorton and Wimborne Minster highlighted the necessity of preparing for death throughout one's lifetime and the belief that death was not the end, but merely the start of eternal life. Ralph Houlbrooke has argued that the need to prepare for death as the most important part of life was a longstanding prac-tice. He asserted that it was a view shared 'by most preachers and writers of Christian advice literature between the Middle Ages and the early eighteenth century'.[6] The handbooks on godly living and dying that were so popular in the sixteenth and seventeenth centuries were aimed at those who did not know when to expect the point of their death and so should always be prepared. Calvinism brought with it to many of its adherents a sense of despair, as Alec

---

3 Christopher Hill, *Society and Puritanism in Pre-Revolutionary England* (London: Secker and Warburg, 1964), pp. 445–446; Keith V. Thomas, 'Women and the Civil War Sects', *Past & Present*, 13 (1958), p. 42.

4 Paul C. H. Lim, 'Puritans and the Church of England: Historiography and Ecclesiology' in John Coffey and Paul C. H. Lim (eds), *The Cambridge Companion to Puritanism* (Cambridge: Cambridge University Press, 2008), p. 232; Eamon Duffy, 'The Long Reformation: Catholicism, Protestantism and the Multitude' in Nicholas Tyacke (ed.), *England's Long Reformation, 1500–1800* (London: UCL Press, 2003), p. 42.

5 Green, *Print and Protestantism*, pp. 346–368.

6 Ralph Houlbrooke, *Death, Religion and the Family in England, 1480–1750* (Oxford: Clarendon Press, 2000), p. 57.

Ryrie has demonstrated.[7] At its most extreme, this sense of despair caused some people to attempt, or to actually commit, suicide. Michael MacDonald and Terence Murphy have argued that contemporaries viewed suicide as a 'heinous, even diabolical act'.[8] Nevertheless, early modern Protestants also grappled with whether suicide was ever acceptable. John Calvin, for example, echoed the assertions of Saint Augustine that suicide was never an acceptable act in the eyes of God, no matter how desperate a person may have felt. These discussions were the subject of several readers' marks on the topic of suicide.

1   Godly Living in Early Modern Protestantism

Early modern Protestant readers' preoccupation with instructions on living a godly life, as demonstrated by numerous annotations in various parish library books, suggests an intrinsic link between faith and the doctrine of assurance.[9] In order to determine whether they were among the elect, Ian Green has argued that Protestants focussed on both the inner, spiritual elements and the outer signs of faith.[10] In order to maintain their faith and live a godly life, the readers of parish library books highlighted the importance of listening to godly preachers, praying to God, practicing patience and trust in God through difficult times, and seeking solace in the doing of good works that they believed signified their election to eternal life.

The hearing of sermons given by learned, godly preachers was an important part of godly living for early modern Protestants and an experience for which many people were prepared to travel considerable distances.[11] Alexandra Walsham has demonstrated that sermons played a central role in early modern Protestantism because they were an 'addictive and enthralling experience' in which 'talented preachers did not simply instruct their hearers in the lessons embedded in Scripture', but also 'roused them to a pitch of emotional fervour'.[12]

---

7   Alec Ryrie, *Being Protestant in Reformation Britain* (Oxford: Oxford University Press, 2015), p. 27.

8   Michael MacDonald and Terence R. Murphy, *Sleepless Souls: Suicide in Early Modern England* (Oxford: Clarendon Press, 1990), p. 74.

9   Michael P. Winship, 'Weak Christians, Backsliders, and Carnal Gospelers: Assurance of Salvation and the Pastoral Origins of Puritan Practical Divinity in the 1580s', *Church History: Studies in Christianity and Culture*, 9 (2001), p. 465.

10   Green, *Print and Protestantism*, p. 305.

11   John Craig, 'The Growth of English Puritanism' in John Coffey and Paul C. H. Lim (eds), *The Cambridge Companion to Puritanism* (Cambridge: Cambridge University Press, 2008), p. 44.

12   Walsham, 'The Godly and Popular Culture', p. 286.

Similarly, church services were also held in high estimation by early modern authors and readers. The importance of godly church services was emphasised by Arthur Hildersham in his *CVIII Lectures upon the Fourth of John*. In the copy of this work now in the Gorton Chest parish library, a reader marked a page on which the divine asserted that church services were to be greatly esteemed and always attended by the godly.[13] In addition, a reader of Hildersham's *CLII Lectures upon Psalm, LI*, also in the Gorton Chest, underlined the author's assertion that a good Christian, whilst listening to the Word of God in a sermon, should be wholly present in His presence and pay attention to the preacher. This was because, as the annotated passage reads, 'it is God's Word, and not man's that you hear [during the sermon]'.[14] This sentiment also found support from a reader of the Grantham copy of Martin Chemnitz's *Examinis Concilii Tridentini*, who underlined the Lutheran divine's assertion that 'the assumed outward appearance of worship, without the inner spiritual impulses, does not please God'.[15]

The official Elizabethan homily on prayer used Saint Augustine's definition of prayer as 'a lifting up of the mind to God; that is to say, an humble and lowly pouring out of the heart to God'. The definition continued to be used throughout the early modern period.[16] Thus, prayer was a central tenet of the Protestant faith, its significance to early modern Protestants rooted in its capacity to allow them to communicate with God, whom many Protestants believed commanded prayer.[17] Protestant prayer was undertaken both in church and in private, in various forms, for numerous different reasons. Divines who discussed the correct form of and reasons for prayer had their arguments annotated by several readers of copies of their works now housed in parish library

13 Arthur Hildersham, *CVIII Lectures upon the Fourth of John* (London: Moses Bell, 1647), p. 336. Annotated copy in the Gorton Chest, Chetham's Library, Manchester, shelfmark GC.2.5(2). USTC 3043316.

14 Arthur Hildersham, *CLII Lectures upon Psalm, LI* (London: J. Raworth, 1642), p. 33. Annotated copy in the Gorton Chest, Chetham's Library, Manchester, shelfmark GC.2.5(1). USTC 3052352.

15 Martin Chemnitz, *Examinis Concilii Tridentini, Part II* (Frankfurt: Peter Fabricius, 1585), p. 84. Annotated copy in the Francis Trigge Chained Library, shelfmark D2. Underlined Latin passage on p. 84 reads '... *externam simulatione cultus, sine interioribus spiritualibus motibus, Deo non placere* ...'. This edition not listed in the USTC. English translation: Fred Kramer (trans.), *Examination of the Council of Trent, Part II* by Martin Chemnitz (London: Concordia Publishing House, 1971), p. 281.

16 Unknown Author, *Certain Sermons or Homilies Appointed to be Read in Churches in the Time of the Late Queen Elizabeth* (Oxford: Oxford University Press, 1844), p. 289; Ryrie, *Being Protestant*, p. 99.

17 Green, *Print and Protestantism*, p. 239.

collections. Prayer was an important act on the part of ministers. In the copy
of John Dod's *A Plaine and Familiar Exposition of the Ten Commandements*
now in the Gorton Chest parish library, a reader highlighted the belief that it
was 'a great sin against God in the minister, if he be not frequent in prayer for
his people'.[18] Prayers by ministers given during church services were, Charles
Hambrick-Stowe has argued, to be '"conceived" in the heart of the pastor,
pre-meditated in preparation for the service and offered extemporaneously
rather than merely read aloud from a printed page'. Ministers' prayers served
several purposes, including 'invoking God's presence, petitioning, interceding
and giving thanks for his blessings'.[19] This was certainly the view of John Dod,
whose lengthy assertion that the faithful must show 'reverence' to their minister, whose role it was to look after his congregation and intercede with God
on their behalf through his prayers, was underlined by one of his readers, suggesting its significance.[20] This was not the same sort of intercessory role played
by the Catholic priest, however. A large part of the appeal of private prayer for
early modern Protestants was the opportunity to converse with God directly.[21]
Numerous underlined passages of the Grantham copy of Saint Cyprian's
Epistles, particularly Epistle II in the second book and Epistle IV in the fourth
book, demonstrate the importance of private prayer to God.[22] One of the main
reasons as to why Cyprian's comments on this topic were so important to their
reader was because they implied reciprocity, the idea that through prayer an
individual could speak directly to God and expect a response without the inter-
jections of a mediatory priest, as was necessary in Catholicism. Private prayer
was the sustenance of the relationship between God and the faithful, as one of

---

18   John Dod, *A Plaine and Familiar Exposition of the Ten Commandements* (London:
      Felix Kyngston, 1614), p. 232. Annotated copy in the Gorton Chest, Chetham's Library,
      Manchester, shelfmark GC.1.13(1). USTC 3005942.

19   Charles E. Hambrick-Stowe, 'Practical Divinity and Spirituality' in John Coffey and
      Paul C. H. Lim (eds), *The Cambridge Companion to Puritanism* (Cambridge: Cambridge
      University Press, 2008), pp. 200–201.

20   Dod, *A Plaine and Familiar Exposition*, pp. 234–235. Annotated copy in the Gorton Chest,
      Chetham's Library, Manchester, shelfmark GC.1.13(1). USTC 3005942.

21   Ryrie, *Being Protestant*, p. 200.

22   Saint Cyprian, *Opera* (Basel: the Office of Johann Froben, 1521), pp. 44–50, 121–124.
      Annotated copy in the Francis Trigge Chained Library, shelfmark F27. USTC 679668.
      English translation: Robert Ernest Wallis (trans.), Alexander Roberts and James
      Donaldson (eds), *The Writings of Cyprian, Bishop of Carthage, Volume I* (Edinburgh: T. & T.
      Clark, 1868), pp. 1–13, 27–32.

Cyprian's readers underlined the patristic author's exhortation to 'be constant as well in prayer ... now speak with God, now let God speak with you'.[23]

Annotations on the topic of prayer in several parish library texts reveal the range of reasons an early modern Protestant could have for praying. One reason for prayer highlighted in readers' annotations was for the benefit of others. The merit of praying for others was discussed by Anthony Burgess, for example, in his *CXLV Expository Sermons upon the Whole 17th Chapter of the Gospel According to St John*. Burgess asserted that as Christ had prayed for others, so too should the faithful, and argued that prayers for the benefit of others were the most likely to be heard by God. A reader of the Gorton Chest copy of this work marked this page, suggesting its importance to that reader and bringing it to the attention of later readers.[24] Further, a reader of the Grantham copy of Saint Cyprian's *Opera* underlined the Church Father's emphasis on the importance of diligent prayer not only for the benefit of oneself, but also for the advancement of those around you. In the underlined appeal to his readers, Cyprian requested they

> lift up our eyes to heaven, lest the earth with its delights and enticements deceive us. Let each one of us pray God not for himself only, but for all the brethren, even as the Lord has taught us to pray, when He bids to each one, not private prayer, but enjoined them, when they prayed, to pray for all in common prayer and concordant supplication.[25]

Christ and the apostles themselves served as models for this kind of prayer. As Cyprian's reader underlined: 'the apostles also ceased not to pray day and night; and the Lord also Himself, the teacher of our discipline, and the way

---

23 Saint Cyprian, *Opera*, p. 50. Annotated copy in the Francis Trigge Chained Library, shelfmark F27. Underlined Latin passage on p. 50 reads '*Sit tibi uel oratio assidua, uel lectio: nunc cum deo loquere, nunc deus tecum ...*'. USTC 679668. English translation: Wallis, *The Writings of Cyprian, Volume I*, pp. 12–13.

24 Anthony Burgess, *CXLV Expository Sermons upon the Whole 17th Chapter of the Gospel According to St John* (London: Abraham Miller, 1656), p. 230. Annotated copy in the Gorton Chest, Chetham's Library, Manchester, shelfmark GC.1.24. This edition not listed on the USTC.

25 Saint Cyprian, *Opera*, p. 124. Annotated copy in the Francis Trigge Chained Library, shelfmark F27. Underlined Latin passage on p. 124 reads '*Oculos erigamus ad coelum, ne oblectamentis & illecebris nos suis terra decipiat. Unusquisque oret dominum non pro se tantum, sed & pro omnibus fratribus, sicut dominus Jesus orare non docuit, ubi non singulis privatam precem mandavit, sed communi & concordi prece orare pro omnibus iussit*'. USTC 679668. English translation: Wallis, *The Writings of Cyprian, Volume I*, p. 32.

of our example, frequently and watchfully prayed'.[26] Annotations like these support the arguments made by Ryrie that the frequency of prayer to God exhorted by the Bible – Psalm 119 makes reference to prayers said seven times a day, for example – was largely impractical in the everyday lives of most people and so many practiced daily prayer.[27]

Prayer could also be made to God for protection from worldly temptations and the devil. For example, Calvin's sixth sermon on the first chapter of the Book of Job touched on praying to God for protection, 'forasmuch as while we be in this world, we are as it were in a wild wood full of robbers'. William Higginbotham, who annotated this volume before it was added to the library in Grantham, added a marginal note adjacent to this passage stating this was 'a lesson worth noting' and emphasising its importance and practical application.[28] This lesson also evidences a connection between prayer to God and trust in Him: by praying to God for protection from worldly temptations, sin and the devil, Protestants implicitly trusted not only that God would heed their prayers but also that He would grant them the protection they desired. Such trust manifested in prayer is similarly demonstrated by Calvin's appeal to God that He not allow the faithful to fall into the hands of Satan, and a repetition of this request by Higginbotham in an adjacent marginal annotation that read, 'we must pray God that he will not let us fall into Satan's snare'.[29] Ultimately, as another of Higginbotham's marginal notes on Calvin's eighth sermon on the first chapter of the Book of Job stated, Protestants 'need not be afraid of the devil if we be strong in faith'.[30] Faith needed to be strong if Protestants were to protect themselves from the despair and distraction that were the primary weapons of the devil.

There was some debate amongst sixteenth- and seventeenth-century divines as to whether set forms of prayer or extempore prayer was most beneficial. Set forms of prayer were laid down in authorised texts, most prominently in the Book of Common Prayer. Extempore prayers were improvised, 'conceived

---

26   Saint Cyprian, *Opera*, p. 123. Annotated copy in the Francis Trigge Chained Library, shelf-mark F27. Underlined Latin passage on p. 123 reads '*Nam & apostoli oratore diebus ac noctibus non destiterunt, & dominus quoque ipse disciplinae magister & exempli nostri via frequenter & vigilanter oravit ...*'. USTC 679668. English translation: Wallis, *The Writings of Cyprian, Volume I*, p. 30.

27   Psalm 119:164; Ryrie, *Being Protestant*, p. 148.

28   John Calvin, *Sermons upon the Booke of Job*, trans. A. Golding (London: T. Dawson for G. Bishop and T. Woodcocke, 1579), p. 20. Annotated copy in the Francis Trigge Chained Library, shelfmark E10. USTC 508947.

29   *Ibid.*, p. 16. Annotated copy in the Francis Trigge Chained Library, shelfmark E10. USTC 508947.

30   Ryrie, *Being Protestant*, p. 246.

by the person speaking them', as Ryrie has observed.[31] In 1646, the Church of England clergyman John Geree described extempore prayers as 'by the gift of God, expressions [that] were varied according to present wants and occasions' in his pamphlet, *The Character of an Old English Puritane or Nonconformist.*[32] Many sixteenth- and early seventeenth-century Protestant divines advised their followers to pray at set times each day, but left specific times up to individuals.[33] As Alec Ryrie has argued, the establishment had advocated set forms of prayer since the Reformation and this practice continued to be favoured until the mid-seventeenth century. At that point, Ryrie observed, Puritans began to voice their opposition and instead promote extempore prayer.[34] However, Ian Green has demonstrated that there was a significant degree of overlap between the forms of prayers published by English divines for at least a century after the Reformation. This reflects Ryrie's argument that, despite the public dispute over the most effective form of prayer, in private, most people 'accepted that both [set and extempore prayer] were legitimate'.[35] A reader of Saint Cyprian's *Epistles*, now in the library at Grantham, underlined Cyprian's emphasis on the need for regularity in prayer in Epistle IV of the fourth book, suggesting a level of agreement from the reader themselves.[36] Moreover, a reader of the copy of Joseph Mede's *Diatribæ* now in the Gorton Chest marked a page on which Mede expounded the virtues of set forms of worship over extempore prayer. Mede argued that only through set prayer could the common believer become more closely associated with God.[37] The large number of prayer books that continued to be printed throughout the period best evidences the sustained popular preference for set prayers, but not everyone found them beneficial. As Judith Maltby has argued, 'to some of the godly, the use of set forms [of prayer] was a shallow

---

31   Ryrie, *Being Protestant*, p. 214; Christopher Durston and Jacqueline Eales, 'Introduction: The Puritan Ethos, 1560–1700' in Christopher Durston and Jacqueline Eales (eds), *The Culture of English Puritanism, 1560–1700* (Basingstoke: Palgrave Macmillan, 1996), pp. 15, 17.

32   John Geree, *The Character of an Old English Puritane or Nonconformist* (London: Printed by A. Miller for Christopher Meredith, 1646), pp. 1–2.

33   Ryrie, *Being Protestant*, p. 148.

34   *Ibid.*, p. 215.

35   Green, *Print and Protestantism*, p. 243; *Ibid.*, p. 215.

36   Saint Cyprian, *Opera*, p. 123. Annotated copy in the Francis Trigge Chained Library, shelfmark F27. USTC 679668. English translation: Wallis, *The Writings of Cyprian, Volume I*, p. 30.

37   Joseph Mede, *Diatribæ. Discourses on Diverse Texts of Scripture* (London: M. F., 1642), p. 10. Annotated copy in the Gorton Chest, Chetham's Library, Manchester, shelfmark GC.1.11. USTC 3046642.

exercise'.[38] The debate around the efficacy of set forms of prayer versus extempore prayer was one that began in the 1570s and would continue intermittently until at least the 1640s.[39]

Good works were another element of living a godly life. In Calvinist thought, the act of doing good works stemmed from an internal notion of one's goodness and election. These good works took the forms of helping one's neighbours, teaching and instructing in right faith, and converting one's neighbours to godliness, amongst others. The importance of a sense of community amongst the godly was emphasised by William Higginbotham several times in his marginal notes on John Calvin's *Sermons upon the Booke of Job*. One exemplar note observed that 'we most imbrace one another in a godly manner', which supports Whitaker's reading model and demonstrates the implementation of the text's message in everyday life.[40] On a marked page of the Gorton Chest copy of the Church of England clergyman Richard Rogers' *Seven Treatises*, the divine asserted his desire to help those who did not yet find godly living an easy task.[41] Similarly, John Dod exhorted husbands to edify their wives in an underlined passage of his *A Plaine and Familiar Exposition of the Ten Commandements* in the Gorton Chest: 'he must dwell with her, as a man of knowledge and edifie her, both by his good example, and also by good instructions'.[42] This corresponds with Christopher Hill's argument that as the importance of the priest diminished within Protestantism, so the role of the family and the authority of the head of the household increased.[43] Hill's arguments supported those of Keith Thomas, who asserted that the head of the household was expected, 'particularly by Puritans, to conduct daily worship at home and to see to the

---

38   Susan M. Felch (ed.), *Elizabeth Tywhit's Morning and Evening Prayers* (Aldershot: Ashgate, 2008), pp. 29–34; Judith Maltby, *Prayer Book and People in Elizabethan and Early Stuart England* (Cambridge: Cambridge University Press, 2009), p. 30.

39   Christopher Durston, 'By the Book or with the Spirit: the Debate over Liturgical Prayer during the English Revolution', *Historical Research*, 79:203 (2006), pp. 52–54; Judith Maltby, '"Extravagancies and Impertinencies": Set Forms, Conceived and Extempore Prayer in Revolutionary England' in Natalie Mears and Alec Ryrie (eds), *Worship and the Parish church in Early Modern Britain* (Farnham: Ashgate, 2013), pp. 221–224.

40   Calvin, *Sermons upon the Booke of Job*, p. 7. Annotated copy in the Francis Trigge Chained Library, shelfmark E10. USTC 508947; Elaine Whitaker, 'A Collaboration of Readers: Categorisation of the Annotations in Copies of Caxton's Royal Book', *Text*, 7 (1994), pp. 235–236.

41   Richard Rogers, *Seven Treatises* (London: Felix Kyngston, 1603), p. 412. Annotated copy in the Gorton Chest, Chetham's Library, Manchester, shelfmark GC.1.31. This edition not listed in the USTC.

42   Dod, *A Plaine and Familiar Exposition*, p. 228. Annotated copy in the Gorton Chest, Chetham's Library, Manchester, shelfmark GC.1.13(1). USTC 3005942.

43   Hill, *Society and Puritanism*, pp. 445–446.

general spiritual welfare of all in his household'.[44] Both John Calvin and John Dod also encouraged their readers to help in converting their ungodly neighbours. In a passage underlined by Higginbotham in the Grantham copy of Calvin's *Sermons upon the Booke of Job*, Calvin asserted that

> here you see that god's instructing of us first, is to the end that when we see our neighbours ignorant, we should endeavour to lead them with us into the same way whereinto we ourselves are entered already.[45]

Moreover, in an underlined passage of his *Exposition on the Ten Commandements*, John Dod stated that 'he that can thus convert his brother from going astray, hath done the part of a good man, and loving friend'.[46] Similarly, John Calvin discussed the need to liberate Catholics from the superstition of popery in his *Praelectiones in librum prophetiarum Danielis*. In the copy of the *Praelectiones* now in the Francis Trigge Chained Library in Grantham, Calvin exhorted his readers to take action thus: 'it is your duty, dearest brethren, as far as lies in your power, and your calling demands it, to use your hearty endeavours, that true religion may recover its perfect state'.[47] The annotation of this passage by a reader of this volume indicated the significance of Calvin's exhortations to uphold true religion and may suggest the reader's belief in his duty to convert the ungodly. These conversions often took many forms. Paul Lim has demonstrated that conversion could come through 'catechising and personal instruction, eventually leading to an intimate knowledge of the soul's state', for example. Eamon Duffy has argued that 'conversion ... meant not merely bringing the heathen to knowledge of the gospel, but bringing the tepid to the boil'.[48]

In their annotations in parish library books, early modern Protestant readers stressed their belief that good works were the product of one's elect status

---

44   Thomas, 'Women and the Civil War Sects', p. 42.

45   Calvin, *Sermons upon the Booke of Job*, p. 276. Annotated copy in the Francis Trigge Chained Library, shelfmark E10. USTC 508947.

46   Dod, *A Plaine and Familiar Exposition*, p. 360. Annotated copy in the Gorton Chest, Chetham's Library, Manchester, shelfmark GC.1.13(1). USTC 3005942.

47   John Calvin, *Praelectiones in librum prophetiarum Danielis* (Geneva: Jean de Laon, 1561), sig. *v r. Annotated copy in the Francis Trigge Chained Library, shelfmark E7. Annotated Latin passage on sig. *v r reads '*Porrò vstrum est, optimi fratres, quantum ferret cuiusque facultas, & vacation postulabit, cordate satagere ut vera religio integrum statum recuperet*'. USTC 450107. English translation: Thomas Meyers, *Commentaries on the Book of the Prophet Daniel by John Calvin* (Grand Rapids, MI: Christian Classics Ethereal Library, 1999), p. 39.

48   Lim, 'Puritans and the Church of England', p. 232; Duffy, 'The Long Reformation', p. 42.

as opposed to the cause of one's election. As John Knox asserted in his *The Historie of the Reformation of the Church of Scotland*, 'it is proved that works neither make us righteous nor unrighteous. Ergo, No works neither make us good nor evil … a good man maketh good works, and an evil man evil works'. In the copy of Knox's *Historie* now in the Gorton Chest parish library, a reader has marked the page on which Knox stated this distinction, suggesting its significance to that reader and possibly to other, later readers as well.[49] Similar sentiments were expressed in Anthony Burgess's *Spiritual Refining or A Treatise of Grace and Assurance*. In the Gorton Chest copy of this text, a reader annotated the page on which Burgess reflected on the importance placed on good works and charitable acts towards neighbours by Protestants in general, and Puritans in particular. Good works were perceived by Protestants and Puritans alike as a sign of elect status, as a consequence of assurance of salvation and as evidence of having received God's grace.[50] Furthermore, a marked page of the Gorton Chest copy of Peter Martyr Vermigli's *Common Places* highlighted the contrast between the Protestant belief that good works were the product of assurance of salvation and the Catholic belief that good works were the cause of salvation. The marking of this page by a reader suggests their agreement with and the significance of the statement, and serves to draw the attention of later readers of this volume to this important distinction.[51]

For Luther as well, good works were not the way to salvation but the product thereof. In his *A Commentarie upon the Fiftene Psalmes*, Luther affirmed that 'we must acknowledge & confesse that we know nothing but the righteousnes of Christ: not that we should not now worke and bring forth the fruites of a holy life'. His assertion was annotated with brackets in pencil by a reader of the Ripon Minster copy of this work.[52] Dewey Wallace has suggested that sixteenth- and seventeenth-century Puritans were keen to stress 'the importance of good

---

49   John Knox, *The Historie of the Reformation of the Church of Scotland* (London: John Raworth, 1644), p. 12. Annotated copy in the Gorton Chest, Chetham's Library, Manchester, shelfmark GC.2.6. USTC 3052353.

50   Anthony Burgess, *Spiritual Refining: or, A Treatise of Grace and Assurance* (London: A. Miller, 1652), p. 307. Annotated copy in the Gorton Chest, Chetham's Library, Manchester, shelfmark GC.1.30. This edition not listed in the USTC.

51   Peter Martyr Vermigli, *The Common Places of the Most Famous and Renowmed Divine Doctor Peter Martyr* (London: Henry Denham and Henry Middleton, 1583), part 3, p. 56 mispaginated as p. 58. Annotated copy in the Gorton Chest, Chetham's Library, Manchester, shelfmark GC.2.10. USTC 509866.

52   Martin Luther, *A Commentarie upon the Fiftene Psalmes*, trans. Henry Bull (London: Thomas Vautroullier, 1577), p. 220. Annotated copy in University of Leeds Brotherton Special Collections Library, shelfmark Ripon Cathedral Library XVII.E.16. USTC 508422.

works in the Christian life as evidence of justification', lest their opponents use the theology of predestination to 'undercut moral striving'.[53] Thus, whilst acknowledging that 'the good works that flow from Christian charity will never win salvation', for many Protestants their faith in God gave rise to a desire to do good works. Andrew Pettegree has argued that this desire was, in early modern Protestants' view, 'the fruits of God's grace in those whom God has called to lives of service'.[54] The Lutheran divine Martin Chemnitz's view that 'good works are called fruits of the Spirit' is unsurprisingly reminiscent of Luther's own view of this subject. The underlining of Chemnitz's statement by a reader of the Grantham copy of his *Examinis Concilii Tridentini* suggests its wider significance.[55] Still other marks of readership in the second volume of Perkins' *Workes* in the Gorton Chest library asserted that good works and acts of charity were best performed in consideration of God's providence and patience. Such advice reinforced the belief that Protestantism was the true faith and that Protestants were true Christians and the best representations of God, by carrying out good works through His will.[56] As Dewey Wallace has demonstrated, 'the commonplace of Reformed theology [was] that the predestined were elected to holiness ... that they should be a holy and sanctified people on earth, known by their good works'.[57] These annotations and readers' marks reflect how important the debate over the nature and benefits of good works was not just to the Protestant readers of these parish library books, but to early modern Protestants in general.

---

53 Dewey D. Wallace, Jr, 'Puritan Polemical Divinity and Doctrinal Controversy' in John Coffey and Paul C. H. Lim (eds), *The Cambridge Companion to Puritanism* (Cambridge: Cambridge University Press, 2008), p. 218.

54 Andrew Pettegree, *Brand Luther: How an Unheralded Monk Turned His Small Town into a Center of Publishing, Made Himself the Most Famous Man in Europe – and Started the Protestant Reformation* (New York: Penguin Books, 2015), pp. 128–129; W. B. Patterson, *William Perkins and the Making of a Protestant England* (Oxford: Oxford University Press, 2014), p. 102.

55 Martin Chemnitz, *Examinis Concilii Tridentini, Part I* (Frankfurt: Peter Fabricius, 1585), p. 134. Annotated copy in the Francis Trigge Chained Library, shelfmark D2. Underlined Latin passage on p. 134 reads '... *sed est donum & operatio Spiritus Santi, unde bona opera vocantur fructus Spiritus* ...'. This edition not listed in the USTC. English translation: Fred Kramer (trans.), *Examination of the Council of Trent, Part I* by Martin Chemnitz (London: Concordia Publishing House, 1971), p. 482.

56 William Perkins, *The Workes of that Famous and Worthy Minister of Christ in the University of Cambridge, M. William Perkins: The Second Volume* (London: John Legatt, 1631), p. 480. Annotated copy in the Gorton Chest, Chetham's Library, Manchester, shelfmark GC.2.14. USTC 3015392.

57 Wallace, 'Puritan Polemical Divinity and Doctrinal Controversy', p. 218.

In his sixty-ninth sermon on the nineteenth chapter of the Book of Job, John Calvin discussed the care that God showed for the faithful in revealing to them their errors and offering correction. This implicit request for patience was seemingly of significant personal importance to William Higginbotham, the annotator of the copy of this work now in the Grantham library collection. In addition to drawing brackets around the passage, Higginbotham also added a marginal note that read: 'let us be thankful for the care that god has for us'.[58] Moreover, Higginbotham also demonstrated his belief that God's guidance must be accepted by the faithful, as he underlined Calvin's exhortation to 'refuse not the correction of the almighty' in Calvin's twenty-first sermon on the fifth chapter of the Book of Job.[59] Such patience and acceptance of God's admonishments was linked to an implicit trust in God and a belief in His care for the spiritual wellbeing of the faithful. This may be why there are a number of annotations on the subject of the afflictions of the godly, and the need to bear those trials with good grace, in the parish library books of Grantham, Ripon, Gorton and Wimborne Minster. Higginbotham seemingly agreed with Calvin's appeals for people to endure in good faith the trials sent by God. He added the marginal note, 'mark this', next to a passage in the thirty-sixth sermon on the ninth chapter of the Book of Job, in which Calvin advised people to think about the good things that God had done for them when He also afflicted them.[60]

In his *De Civitate Dei*, Saint Augustine suggested that God sent advantages and disadvantages to both good and evil men in order that He might encourage the wicked to reform and repent. As a reader of the copy of *De Civitate Dei* now in Ripon Minster parish library underlined, 'the patience of God still invite[s] the wicked to repentance, even as the scourge of God educates the good to patience'.[61] The faithful would be marked out by how they bore these challenges differently from the wicked:

---

58 Calvin, *Sermons upon the Booke of Job*, p. 324. Annotated copy in the Francis Trigge Chained Library, shelfmark E10. USTC 508947.

59 *Ibid.*, p. 97. Annotated copy in the Francis Trigge Chained Library, shelfmark E10. USTC 508947.

60 *Ibid.*, p. 169. Annotated copy in the Francis Trigge Chained Library, shelfmark E10. USTC 508947.

61 Saint Augustine, *De Civitate Dei* in *Cuius praestantissima in omni genere monumenta, Volume v* (Basel: Ambrosius and Aurelius Froben, 1570), pp. 45–46. Annotated copy in University of Leeds Brotherton Special Collections Library, shelfmark Ripon Cathedral Library XIII.E.10/q. Underlined Latin passage on pp. 45–46 reads '... *tamen patientia Dei ad poenitentiam invitat malus, sicut flagellum Dei ad patientiam erudit bonos* ...'. USTC 626339. English translation: Marcus Dods (trans. and ed.), *The City of God, Volume I* (Edinburgh: T. & T. Clark, 1871), p. 10.

> For even in the likeness of the sufferings, there remains an unlikeness in the sufferers; and though exposed to the same anguish, virtue and vice are not the same thing ... and thus it is that in the same affliction the wicked detest God and blaspheme, while the good pray and praise.[62]

Similar sentiments were echoed in various works of puritan practical divinity by authors such as William Perkins, who, in the third volume of his *Workes*, asserted that the godly 'man cares not what God laieth on him in this life, who is perswaded that after this life God will give him heaven'.[63] The significance of such beliefs, as indicated by the marginalia, supports Alec Ryrie's observation that divines such as Perkins and Henry Scudder, a seventeenth-century Presbyterian minister, thought that faith in God could lead to an indifference to worldly misfortune and a trust that enabled Protestants to 'accept either triumph or disaster with equanimity'.[64] The mid-seventeenth century was a time of religious and political upheaval, as first 'elaborate forms of Laudian worship and decoration' began to take root in the established Church before the country devolved into civil war during the 1640s. A brief resolution came in the form of the short-lived period of Puritan triumph during the Interregnum of the 1650s before the return of the king and the restoration of the Church of England alongside the monarchy.[65] As such, these and other assurances found in similar works may have been particularly pertinent to seventeenth-century readers of these texts, as they attempted to weather the religious storms that buffeted England after 1630.

The ability to accept hard times during life with fortitude was often perceived as a sign of one's elect status, helping the godly to bear these troubles in the knowledge that they were guaranteed salvation. In a passage underlined by a reader of the first volume of his *Workes* now in the Gorton Chest library, Perkins stated that the ability to abide these trials with patience stemmed from Protestants' faith in God and His promise that their sufferings would end in

---

62 Saint Augustine, *De Civitate Dei, Volume V*, pp. 45–46. Annotated copy in the Brotherton Special Collections Library, shelfmark Ripon Cathedral Library XIII.E.10/q. Underlined Latin passage on pp. 45–46 reads '... *Manet enim dissimilitudo passorum etiam in similitudine passionum* ...'. USTC 626339. English translation: Dods, *The City of God, Volume I*, p. 11.

63 William Perkins, *The Workes of that Famous and Worthy Minister of Christ in the Universitie of Cambridge, M. William Perkins: The Third and Last Volume* (London: John Haviland, 1631), part 2, p. 78. Annotated copy in Chetham's Library, Manchester, shelfmark GC.2.15. USTC 3015389 and 3015390.

64 Ryrie, *Being Protestant*, p. 81.

65 Anthony Milton, 'Unsettled Reformations, 1603–1662' in Anthony Milton (ed.), *The Oxford History of Anglicanism, Volume I: Reformation and Identity, c.1520–1662* (Oxford: Oxford University Press, 2019), p. 73.

'good and everlasting salvation'. This, Perkins argued in an annotated passage, should have brought 'contentation in any estate' to the faithful.[66] John Calvin, on a page marked by a reader of the Gorton Chest copy of his *The Institution of Christian Religion*, warned his godly readers to prepare themselves for a difficult life in order to prove themselves to God. The marking of this page again suggests that this statement of necessity held a sense of importance.[67] Similar sentiments were expressed on two pages of Anthony Burgess's *CXLV Expository Sermons upon the Whole 17th Chapter of the Gospel According to St John*, both of which were marked by a reader of the Gorton Chest copy. On those pages, Burgess outlined 'the Grounds and Reasons Why the world is thus made by God a disquieting and troublesome place to the Godly'.[68] A reader of the Gorton Chest copy of *The Works of Robert Harris* marked a page on which Harris set out the ways in which the godly could know that their troubles would end in the comfort of salvation. Harris asserted that godly sorrows that indicated eventual salvation were concerned with godly matters; he argued that such sorrows flowed from godly sources, such as zeal for His name or indignation against sin. Harris also stated that the effects of those sorrows could signify that the godly would be taken away from sin and brought to God's love.[69] Recognising the legitimacy of these hardships, but cognisant of the toll they could potentially take on the faithful who suffered them, Richard Rogers attempted to provide his readers with some comfort in his *Seven Treatises*. He encouraged them to don their Christian armour and persevere, for the godly should have known that even during difficult times in their lives, they had not been forsaken by God. This page was also marked by a reader, which again suggests its significance and draws attention to these reassuring words in amongst a plethora of warnings.[70] These struggles, which early modern readers sought to understand the reasons for and how to bear them, invoked elements of the

66   William Perkins, *The Workes of that Famous and Worthy Minister of Christ in the University of Cambridge, Mr William Perkins: The First Volume* (London: John Legatt, 1626), p. 481. Annotated copy in the Gorton Chest, Chetham's Library, Manchester, shelfmark G C.2.13. USTC 3012639.

67   John Calvin, *The Institution of Christian Religion*, trans. Thomas Norton (London: printed for Thomas Norton, 1611), part 3, p. 335. Annotated copy in the Gorton Chest, Chetham's Library, Manchester, shelfmark GC.2.11. USTC 3004572.

68   Burgess, *CXLV Expository Sermons*, pp. 287–288. Annotated copy in the Gorton Chest, Chetham's Library, Manchester, shelfmark GC.1.24. This edition not listed on the USTC.

69   Robert Harris, *The Works of Robert Harris, Once of Hanwell* (London: Miles Flesher, 1654), p. 128. Annotated copy in the Gorton Chest, Chetham's Library, Manchester, shelfmark GC.1.28. This edition not listed in USTC.

70   Rogers, *Seven Treatises*, p. 263. Annotated copy in the Gorton Chest, Chetham's Library, Manchester, shelfmark GC.1.31. This edition not listed in the USTC.

Protestant doctrine of predestination, which 'gave greater depth and meaning to the perplexing divisions of England'. The doctrine of predestination, Peter Marshall suggested, taught that 'the struggles, travails and contradictions experienced by the godly in this life were but echoes of another, elemental and invisible contest between the forces of light and darkness, elect and non-elect, Christ and Antichrist'.[71] As such, to have experienced hard times during one's lifetime could be understood as a sign of one's election.

2　Godly Dying and Suicide in Early Modern Protestantism

A godly life was, in itself, a lifelong preparation for a good death. The removal of the doctrine of purgatory had changed early modern perceptions of death: 'there was no painful waiting, no uncomfortable holding in purgatory, and of course, no purpose at all in prayers for the dead'.[72] As Michael MacDonald and Terence Murphy have argued, 'during the seventeenth and eighteenth centuries, less and less emphasis was placed on the hour of death. The art of dying became more dependent on the art of living, living as a good Christian'.[73] Early modern Protestants placed a high level of importance on preparing for death in order to achieve salvation. This was an intrinsic element of Protestant beliefs about eternal life after death, as is reflected in the numerous examples of marginalia on the topic. Another interesting aspect of the early modern Protestant culture of death was suicide, which was also considered in several readers' annotations.

The desire for everlasting life is evident in annotations found in the Grantham copy of John Calvin's *Sermons upon the Booke of Job*. In one annotation on Calvin's fifty-third sermon on the fourteenth chapter of the Book of Job, Higginbotham, the annotating reader, underlined Calvin's assertion that 'god wil bring us to a good end by receiving us intoo his everlasting rest'. In a second annotation, in the fifty-sixth sermon on the same chapter of Job, Higginbotham underlined Calvin's assertion that death was a good thing, 'bicause that by that meanes God taketh us out of the miseries of this worlde, to make us partakers of his riches and glorious immortalitie'.[74] Eternal life also

---

71　Peter Marshall, *Heretics and Believers: A History of the English Reformation* (London: Yale University Press, 2018), p. 353.

72　David Cressy, *Birth, Marriage, and Death: Ritual, Religion, and the Life-Cycle in Tudor and Stuart England* (Oxford: Oxford University Press, 1997), p. 386.

73　MacDonald and Murphy, *Sleepless Souls*, p. 1.

74　Calvin, *Sermons upon the Booke of Job*, pp. 250, 265. Annotated copy in the Francis Trigge Chained Library, shelfmark E10. USTC 508947.

had another benefit for the early modern godly: their separation after death from the ungodly, as a marked page of John Weemes' *Workes* in the Gorton Chest parish library demonstrates.[75] This belief was linked to predestination, the doctrine in which 'God chose certain humans for eternal life, irrespective of their merits and achievements'.[76]

In order to achieve the everlasting life of which Protestants were so desirous, it was necessary to appropriately prepare for death. This imperative led to books, tracts and sermons providing guidance on how to do so being printed in droves between the late fifteenth and early eighteenth centuries.[77] Many examples of these books survive in the parish libraries of Grantham, Ripon, Gorton and Wimborne Minster, and were annotated by their readers to highlight the importance of the information they contained. On the topic of the necessity of making a good death, a reader of the Gorton Chest copy of Hildersham's *CLII Lectures upon Psalm, LI*, for example, twice folded the corner of a page on which Hildersham outlined the benefits of consciously thinking about death during life. On the marked page, Hildersham explained that by thinking about one's own death, it would distract the mind from focussing on the worldly pleasures that had been sacrificed for God, lest they should draw a person in to sin. It was intended that thinking about their own death would enable Reformed Protestants to view their trials and troubles less bitterly, and even render death itself less terrible.[78] Due to the inarticulate nature of this reader's marks, their thoughts on this can only be assumed. That it held significance for the reader, however, is clear from their interaction with the text.

William Perkins was one of Protestantism's most vocal advocates of the need to prepare for death throughout one's lifetime. The large number of annotations on the subject in the three volumes of his *Workes* now in the Gorton Chest parish library suggests that readers may have targeted these books specifically in search of information on this topic. Those readers marked many of the passages in Perkins' *Workes* that outlined how to physically ingratiate preparations for death into daily life, emphasising their applicability to everyday life and suggesting the reader's motivation for reading these texts. Perkins

---

75   John Weemes, *The Workes of M. John Weemes of Lathocker in Scotland. The Third Volume* (London: M. Dawson, 1636), part 2, p. 206. Gorton Chest, Chetham's Library, shelfmark GC.1.2. This edition not listed in the USTC.

76   Marshall, *Heretics and Believers*, p. 292; Wallace, 'Puritan Polemical Divinity and Doctrinal Controversy', p. 214.

77   Houlbrooke, *Death, Religion and the Family in England*, p. 59.

78   Hildersham, *CLII Lectures*, p. 241. Annotated copy in the Gorton Chest, Chetham's Library, Manchester, shelfmark GC.2.5(1). USTC 3052352.

encouraged his readers to live their lives in the manner in which they wished to continue after death. In an annotated passage from the third volume of his *Workes*, Perkins stated that 'whatsoever wee would doe when we die, that we must now begin'.[79] A reader of the second volume of Perkins' *Workes* annotated the margin next to a passage explaining three different things to do in preparation for death. Perkins recommended his readers live each day as if it were their last, disarm death by avoiding sin and attempt to find some semblance of eternal life in the earthly one.[80] Preparing for death throughout one's lifetime was sensible advice because, as Ralph Houlbrooke has observed, early modern life was not guaranteed to be long, and preparations for death should therefore be begun as soon as possible – 'indeed, it was the most important business of earthly existence'.[81]

Suicide was an important element of the early modern culture of death, on which there are several noteworthy studies.[82] Whilst early modern readers' marks on this topic are not numerous in the parish library books of Grantham, Ripon, Gorton and Wimborne Minster, they do indicate broader preoccupations with death in this period. The prospect of eternal life after death prompted many Protestants to prepare actively for their deaths because 'that moment had enduring consequences'. Indeed, some may have considered hastening their arrival at that moment in order to avoid as many worldly temptations as possible.[83] For many, suicide may now seem an extreme technique for evading the sin of temptation, but both Saint Augustine and John Calvin, amongst others, wrestled with the topic. Their thoughts on whether suicide was a justifiable act were annotated by readers of the Ripon Minster copy of Saint Augustine's *De Civitate Dei* and the Grantham copy of Calvin's *Sermons upon the Booke of Job*, with the extant marginalia suggesting readers' interest in their arguments and conclusions.[84] Augustine's views on suicide heavily influenced the thinking of John Calvin, whose ideas in turn were highly influential

---

79 Perkins, *Workes: The Third and Last Volume*, part 1, p. 149. Annotated copy in Chetham's Library, Manchester, shelfmark GC.2.15. USTC 3015389 and 3015390.

80 Perkins, *Workes: The Second Volume*, p. 34. Annotated copy in the Gorton Chest, Chetham's Library, Manchester, shelfmark GC.2.14. USTC 3015392.

81 Houlbrooke, *Death, Religion and the Family in England*, p. 57.

82 For examples of important studies into early modern suicide, see, Jeffrey R. Watt, 'Calvin on Suicide', *Church History*, 66:3 (1997), pp. 463–476; MacDonald and Murphy, *Sleepless Souls*; R. A. Houston, *Punishing the Dead?: Suicide, Lordship, and Community in Britain, 1500–1830* (Oxford: Oxford University Press, 2010); Ryrie, *Being Protestant*, especially pp. 27–31.

83 Ryrie, *Being Protestant*, pp. 28, 461.

84 Saint Augustine, *De Civitate Dei, Volume V*. Annotated copy in the Brotherton Special Collections Library, shelfmark Ripon Cathedral Library XIII.E.10/q. USTC 626339; Calvin,

in the Church of England and the Church of Scotland.[85] The parallels between the two sets of annotations are clear: both authors arrived at the conclusion that suicide was ultimately unlawful and unjustifiable in the eyes of God.

After grappling with the topic for some time in his *De Civitate Dei*, Saint Augustine concluded that 'in no passage of the holy canonical books there can be found either divine precept or permission to take away our own life'.[86] Augustine asserted that whilst someone who took their own life might initially seem admirable for their 'greatness of soul', he questioned, 'is it not rather proof of a feeble mind, to be unable to bear either the pains of bodily servitude or the foolish opinion of the vulgar?'. A reader of the Ripon Minster copy of this work underlined this question, which highlights its importance.[87] It may also suggest that the annotating reader had, in some capacity, personal experience of suicide or suicidal thoughts. Despite the perceived unlawfulness of committing suicide in the early modern period, Alec Ryrie has demonstrated that the godly were often so afflicted by despair that they did, indeed, consider – and sometimes even attempt – suicide. Nehemiah Wallington is one of the best-known examples of an early modern individual so plagued by his own conscience that he attempted suicide on numerous occasions throughout his life.[88] One of Augustine's readers underlined sections of the patristic author's scathing remarks on the subject of whether suicide ought to be committed in order to avoid further sin. The underlined suggestion that sin could be justifiably committed 'to prevent one's falling into sin either through the blandishments of pleasure or the violence of pain' was almost immediately afterwards dismissed by Augustine: 'it is wicked to say this; it is therefore wicked to kill oneself'.[89]

       Sermons upon the Booke of Job. Annotated copy in the Francis Trigge Chained Library, shelfmark E10. USTC 508947.

85   Watt, 'Calvin on Suicide', pp. 463–476; Jean-Louis Quantin, *The Church of England and Christian Antiquity: The Construction of a Confessional Identity in the 17th Century* (Oxford: Oxford University Press, 2009), pp. 85–86.

86   Saint Augustine, *De Civitate Dei, Volume V*, pp. 67–68. Annotated copy in the Brotherton Special Collections Library, shelfmark Ripon Cathedral Library XIII.E.10/q. USTC 626339. English translation: Dods, *The City of God, Volume I*, p. 30.

87   Saint Augustine, *De Civitate Dei, Volume V*, pp. 69–70. Annotated copy in the Brotherton Special Collections Library, shelfmark Ripon Cathedral Library XIII.E.10/q. Underlined Latin passage on pp. 69–70 reads '... *Magis enim mens infirma deprehenditur, quae ferre non potest, uel duram sui corporis servitutem, uel stultam vulgi opinionem* ...'. USTC 626339. English translation: Dods, *The City of God, Volume I*, p. 33.

88   Ryrie, *Being Protestant*, pp. 27–28.

89   Saint Augustine, *De Civitate Dei, Volume V*, pp. 75–76. Annotated copy in the Brotherton Special Collections Library, shelfmark Ripon Cathedral Library XIII.E.10/q. Underlined Latin passage on pp. 75–76 reads '... *scilicet ne in peccatum irruat, uel blandiente voluptate,*

The inability to justify sin as an acceptable rationalisation for suicide in the early modern period can be seen in Calvin's work as well. Calvin's fundamental objection to the act of committing suicide, Jeffrey Watt argued, was that 'in taking one's life, one is being disobedient by refusing to submit to the will of God'.[90] In his *Sermons upon the Booke of Job*, Calvin asserted that 'it is not lawfull for the faithfull to mislike their owne life, and too wishe so for death'. The passage was underlined by William Higginbotham, in the annotated copy of this text now in the Grantham library collection.[91] Calvin made clear the distinction between the lawfulness of wishing for death – as stated in the underlined proposal that 'we may wish for death in one respect: which is, in consideration that we be hild here in such bondage of sinne, as we can not serve God so freely as were to be wished' – and the unlawfulness of acting upon that wish oneself. Next to this passage, Higginbotham added the marginal note: 'how we may lawfully wish for death'.[92] Alec Ryrie, Michael MacDonald and Terence Murphy have all commented on the links between sin and worldly temptations and early modern suicide. Ryrie described Calvinism as a 'theology of despair' for many early modern Protestants and this despair was often linked to suicide, or attempted suicide. He noted that 'the longer you live in sin, the worse the condemnation you earn. A quick suicide might at least cut your losses'.[93] Michael MacDonald and Terence Murphy together demonstrated the role that the temptations of the devil played in instigating suicide and highlighted the perils of everyday life, honour and shame, and the afflictions of the heart as motivating factors in suicide.[94] The clear distinction between the acceptability of the thought of suicide and the acceptability of actually committing the act, irrespective of the impetus, is reflected in R. A. Houston's work. He argued that whilst 'Scots Calvinists saw a clear place for suicidal thoughts in their soteriology ... the idea that suicide itself was defensible remained marginal'.[95]

---

uel dolore saeviente. USTC 626339. English translation: Dods, *The City of God, Volume I*, pp. 38–39.

90 Watt, 'Calvin on Suicide', p. 465.

91 Calvin, *Sermons upon the Booke of Job*, p. 58. Annotated copy in the Francis Trigge Chained Library, shelfmark E10. USTC 508947.

92 *Ibid.*, p. 58. Annotated copy in the Francis Trigge Chained Library, shelfmark E10. USTC 508947.

93 Ryrie, *Being Protestant*, pp. 27–28.

94 MacDonald and Murphy, *Sleepless Souls*, pp. 42–76, 259–300.

95 Houston, *Punishing the Dead?*, p. 228.

3   Conclusion

The sheer volume of readers' marks on the topics of godly living and a good death demonstrates their importance to early modern Protestants and reveals the complex interconnectivity between the concepts of living a godly life and making a good death that would eventually lead one to eternal salvation. The pattern of readers' focus on these topics in the books of the Grantham, Ripon, Gorton and Wimborne Minster parish libraries tended towards the practical advice proffered by authors who instructed their readers in how a godly life manifested itself in actuality, and the nature of a godly life as one long preparation for death. On the subject of godly living, readers' annotations evidenced a clear interest in the importance of private prayer as a form of direct communication with God and preaching as an indirect connection with God through the minister, who spoke God's words. Goodness and good works were crucial to a godly life, though authors and readers alike were at pains to stipulate that good works were a manifestation of one's faith and elect status, as opposed to the cause of one's salvation. These good works centred on the idea of community, of comforting fellow members of the godly and of attempting to convert the ungodly. Elements of a godly life also included trusting in God and bearing the hard times He sent the godly with patience and forbearance; they were linked to the elect status of the godly and reflected an invisible struggle between good and evil. On the subject of death and the correct way to prepare for it, readers' marks demonstrated that Protestants believed the moment of death had enduring consequences and so thorough preparation was necessary. Suicide, which it was eventually decided was unjustifiable under any circumstances, was also the topic of annotations by at least two readers. This suggests the personal significance of the subject to those readers, but also provides an insight into the darker side of Protestantism and the somewhat negative effect it could have on its adherents.

Conclusion

This book offers an overview of parish libraries in early modern England, highlighting their importance as repositories for the 'middling' and lower sorts of people in the sixteenth and seventeenth centuries. It has presented four geographically and chronologically distinct parish libraries, and their books, as case studies that have been used to reconstruct the interests of, and provide insight into, the responses of largely unknown urban readers to the books. These responses typically fall into four thematic groupings: anti-Catholic sentiments, the importance of Scripture, the interconnected beliefs around sin, repentance and salvation, and godly living and dying. All four of these themes speak to the contemporary Protestant preoccupation with practical divinity and indicate a reduced focus on Protestant theology.

Many studies of marginalia and readers' marks in early modern books focus on well known, elite individual readers and ask questions of the how, when and why variety. How readers read their books; when they read them and how contemporary events might have influenced or impacted their reading; and why readers read, the impetus behind the act of reading. Some examples can be seen in the reading practices of Gabriel Harvey, Sir William Drake and Samuel Pepys, which demonstrated the ways in which contemporary events and personal circumstances affected how and why these men read. These studies showed how their reading either enhanced or reflected their lives and careers, in terms of professional or social advancements, or in receiving similar benefits.[1]

By concentrating primarily on the inarticulate marginalia and annotations of unknown readers, such as underlinings, marginal symbols and folded corners of pages, this book has conceptualised these markings as intrinsically important to a holistic history of early modern reading practices and created a framework for analysing them as an insight into what people read. Because the readers of books in parish libraries are typically anonymous, questions around when they were reading are difficult to answer with any degree of certainty, and why they were reading can often only be inferred, based on what they annotated. By thinking about what people read, and more specifically what passages and parts of their texts they annotated, historians are able to develop

---

1 Lisa Jardine and Anthony Grafton, '"Studied for Action": How Gabriel Harvey Read His Livy', *Past & Present*, 129 (1990); Kevin Sharpe, *Reading Revolutions: The Politics of Reading in Early Modern England* (London: Yale University Press, 2000); Elspeth Jajdelska, 'Pepys in the History of Reading', *The Historical Journal*, 50 (2007).

their understanding of the themes and topics with which the general early modern Protestant reading public were concerned.

Examination and analysis of these inarticulate markings serve to enhance existing models of and current thinking about early modern books and reading practices. Mark Towsey's argument that readers 'created marginalia as intellectual aids, simplifying or summarising the text to more easily digest its key themes', in relation to the anonymous but dateable annotations in the Newhailes copy of David Hume's *History of Great Britain*, is also reflected in several parish library books.[2] Such findings demonstrate both the longevity and the ubiquity of this practice. Non-verbal annotations in the books of the four case study parish libraries also extend the model of readership put forward by Elaine Whitaker in 1994. Whitaker examined the annotations of various named readers of the twenty-two extant manuscript and printed copies of William Caxton's *Royal Book*. She sorted these annotations into three categories, each of which had two subcategories.[3] The evidence presented in this book extends and supports that model by demonstrating the application of several of Whitaker's categories – particularly that of 'Editing' – and subcategories – those of 'Censorship' and 'Affirmation', for example – to a much wider range of books and readers across a considerable time period and a variety of spatial locations. They can be used to analyse and categorise what people thought of, and the ways in which they responded to and interacted with, what they read.

Post-Reformation parish libraries as repositories of religious and spiritual education evolved out of the collections of service books, liturgical works and other religious texts kept in the parish churches of the pre-Reformation period. Pre-Reformation book collections were established by a mixture of clerics and laymen, though they were primarily intended for use by the parish clergy in preparing their services and carrying out their pastoral duties. Post-Reformation parish libraries were likewise established by both clergymen and the laity, though these mixed benefactors were reflected in a mixed intended audience for the repositories established after the mid-sixteenth century. This book has shown that there was a significant degree of continuity between the two types of repositories which, in line with Arnold Hunt's argument, manifested in an enduring pattern of religious book ownership.[4] The small collections of

---

2   Mark Towsey, *Reading the Scottish Enlightenment: Books and the Readers in Provincial Scotland, 1750–1820* (Leiden: Brill, 2010), p. 177.

3   Elaine Whitaker, 'A Collaboration of Readers: Categorisation of the Annotations in Copies of Caxton's Royal Book', *Text*, 7 (1994), pp. 233–240.

4   Arnold Hunt, 'Clerical and Parish Libraries' in Elisabeth Leedham-Green and Teresa Webber (eds), *The Cambridge History of Libraries, Volume I, to 1640* (Cambridge: Cambridge University Press, 2008), p. 401.

religious and liturgical works and service books in the pre-Reformation parish churches expanded in their post-Reformation counterparts to include a
wider range of theological and other religious works, including Church histories, commentaries and paraphrases on the Bible, patristic texts, and works
of pastoral theology and practical divinity. Foundation rates for these institutions increased at a reasonably steady pace between the mid-sixteenth and
the mid-seventeenth centuries. In the second half of the seventeenth century,
there was a proliferation of parish libraries in both the urban and rural areas
of England. In the 1690s, Thomas Bray and the Society for Promoting Christian
Knowledge began to establish them on an institutional scale, with the aim of
providing every parish in England with a repository of religious knowledge and
education.

Post-Reformation parish libraries founded from the mid-sixteenth century onwards were usually established for educational purposes, as demonstrated by various foundation documents.[5] Some founders, such as Humphrey
Chetham, who founded the Gorton Chest parish library and four others in
Lancashire in the 1650s, focussed explicitly on providing his readers with a
religious education in the Protestant religion. Other founders, such as Francis
Trigge in Grantham, sought to provide a Protestant religious education when
he established his library in 1598, but included a number of texts by medieval
and post-Reformation Catholic authors as well. Trigge was not alone in this
practice, and this book has argued that these inclusions were most likely the
result of the exemplary scholarship of these authors. Further, as David Pearson
has suggested, books by medieval and post-Reformation Catholics may also
have been included in these collections in order to equip readers with a thorough knowledge of Catholicism, so that they might better refute its arguments
and claims to legitimacy.[6] This widening of both intended audience and genre
availability had several consequences. Because they were intended to be used
by both the clergy and the laity, the range of genres included in these book
collections broadened to encompass a more extensive collection of secular
books, such as medical texts, works of natural history, and encyclopaedias
and dictionaries. A larger number of works in English, as well as Latin, a language that Jennifer Richards has shown was perhaps more accessible than
previously thought, were also included.[7] This intended audience also resulted

---

5   See, for example, Lincolnshire Archives, Lincolnshire, (Grantham St Wulfram Par/23/1),
    Documents relating to the Trigge Library: Agreement; and Chetham's Library, Manchester,
    (Uncatalogued), Last Will and Testament of Humphrey Chetham.

6   David Pearson, 'The Libraries of English Bishops, 1600–1640', *The Library*, 14 (1992), p. 229.

7   Jennifer Richards, *Voices and Books in the English Renaissance: A New History of Reading*
    (Oxford: Oxford University Press, 2019), pp. 76–79.

in the removal of these repositories from the holier, more sacred parts of the church, in which the books of pre-Reformation parish churches were housed, to areas of the parish church that were ostensibly more easily accessible, such as a converted room on the upper floor of the church.

The educational intentions of these parish libraries appear to have been fulfilled, though it has been noted that it is difficult to determine whether the surviving marginalia and annotations were made in the books before or after they were included in the libraries' collections. Nevertheless, filling a gap in knowledge that has previously focussed on the practices, interests and motivations of individual elite readers, this book has demonstrated that reading interests amongst early modern Protestants remained much the same for over a century, and that readers were primarily interested in the practical aspects of Protestant theology. Specifically, this book has shown that the unknown urban readers of the 'middling sorts' for whom these repositories were intended were interested firstly in the errors and corruptions of the Catholic Church, and the changes that Church had made to various doctrines since the apostolic era. Secondly, readers were interested in the importance of Scripture as the Word of God and as containing everything necessary for faith, and thus that it should be widely accessible. Thirdly, they were concerned with the need to avoid sin, the process of repentance as the way back to God, and the idea that faith in God alone was enough to achieve salvation. Finally, readers demonstrated a keen interest in the necessity of living a godly life that was grounded in goodness and the act of carrying out good works, patience in the face of hardship, and an acknowledgement of the importance of preaching and prayer.

This book is only a partial study of the history of parish libraries in early modern England and the readership of the texts they contained. It nevertheless has some important implications. Further analyses of other parish libraries and the surviving anonymous marginalia in their books can only add to historians' knowledge of early modern reading practices and textual interpretations and implementations. It is to be hoped that in the fullness of time more attention will be paid to these regional repositories of religious and secular information. They were often the only point of access to this sort of knowledge for many people in the localities, and the history of libraries and of reading will be enhanced by other studies using this book as a framework to examine the annotations of unknown urban readers and analyse the themes and topics in which these readers were interested. In doing so, it will open up another avenue into the popular experience of the Reformation and the religious, social and political changes that swept through England in the sixteenth and seventeenth centuries.

List of Books in the Gorton Chest Parish Library

Author	Title	Printer	Place	Date	Edition	Extant?	Shelfmark
Ambrose, Isaac	*Media: The Middle Things*	T. R. and E. M.	London	1652	Second	Y	GC.1.6(2)
Ambrose, Isaac	*Prima, Media & Ultima: The First, Middle and Last Things*	T. R. and E. M.	London	1654		Y	GC.1.6(1)
Augustine, Saint	*The Confessions of the Incomparable Doctor S. Augustine*	[Unknown]	[Unknown]	[Unknown]		N	–
Baxter, Richard	*The Saints' Everlasting Wrest*	–	London	1656	Sixth	Y	GC.1.1
Baxter, Richard	*Plain Scripture Proof of Infants' Church-Membership and Baptism*	T. V. F. T	London	1656	Fourth	Y	GC.1.32
Beard, Thomas	*The Theatre of God's Judgement*	S. I. [Susan Islip] and M. H. [Mary Hearne]	London	1648	Fourth	Y	GC.1.26
Bolton, Robert	*Mr. Bolton's Last and Learned Work of the Four Last Things*	George Miller	London	1633		Y	GC.1.20(2)
Bolton, Robert	*Some General Directions for a Comfortable Walking with God*	John Legatt	London	1638	Fifth	Y	GC.1.20(1)

Author	Title	Printer	Place	Date	Edition	Extant?	Shelfmark
Bolton, Robert	*Two Sermons Preached at Northampton at Two Several Assizes There*	George Miller	London	1639		Y	GC.1.20(3)
Brightman, Thomas	*The Works of that Famous, Reverend, and Learned Divine, Mr Tho. Brightman*	John Field	London	1644		Y	GC.1.22
Burgess, Anthony	*Spiritual Refining: or a Treatise of Grace and Assurance*	A. Miller	London	1652		Y	GC.1.30
Burgess, Anthony	*The True Doctrine of Justification, in Two Parts*	A. M.	London	1655		Y	GC.1.16
Burgess, Anthony	*CXLV Expository Sermons upon the Whole 17th Chapter of the Gospel According to St John*	Abraham Miller	London	1656		Y	GC.1.24
Calvin, John	*The Institution of Christian Religion*	Eliot's Court Press	London	1611		Y	GC.2.11
Cartwright, Thomas	*A Confutation of the Rhemists Translation, Glosses and Annotations on the New Testament*	W. Brewster	Leiden	1618		Y	GC.2.8
Author	Title	Printer	Place	Date	Edition	Extant?	Shelfmark

Author	Title	Printer	Place	Date	Edition	Extant?	Shelfmark
Chillingworth, William	*The Religion of the Protestants, a Safe Way to Salvation*	Leonard Lichfield	Oxford	1638		Y	GC.1.29
Clarke, Samuel	*A General Martyrology Containing a Collection of all the Greatest Persecutions which have Befallen the Church of Christ*	[Unknown]	[Unknown]	[Unknown]		N	–
Clarke, Samuel	*The Marrow of Ecclesiastical History: Contained in the Lives of the Fathers*	[Unknown]	[Unknown]	[Unknown]		N	–
Crooke, Samuel	*The True Guide unto Blessedness*	[Unknown]	[Unknown]	[Unknown]		N	–
Dod, John	*A Plain and Familiar Exposition of the Ten Commandments*	Felix Kyngston	London	1614		Y	GC.1.13(1)
Dod, John	*Ten Sermons Tending Chiefly to the Fitting of Men for the Worthy Receiving of the Lord's Supper*	Thomas Purfoot	London	1621		Y	GC.1.13(2)
Dod, John	*Ten Sermons Tending Chiefly to the Fitting of Men for the Worthy Receiving of the Lord's Supper*	Thomas Harper	London	1634		Y	GC1.14(2)
Dod, John	*A Plain and Familiar Exposition on the Lord's Prayer*	M. Dawson	London	1635	Second	Y	GC.1.14(1)

(*cont.*)

Author	Title	Printer	Place	Date	Edition	Extant?	Shelfmark
Drake, Roger	*Sacred Chronology*	James and Joseph Moxon	London	1648		Y	GC.1.10
Du Moulin, Pierre	*The Anatomy of Arminianism*	Humphrey Lowndes	London	1626		Y	GC.1.19
Estwick, Nicholas	*A Learned and Godly Sermon Preached on the XIX Day of December*	George Miller	London	1639		Y	GC.1.20(4)
Foxe, John	*Acts and Monuments*	[Unknown]	[Unknown]	[Unknown]		N	–
Fulke, William	*Confutation of the Rhemish Testament*	[Unknown]	[Unknown]	[Unknown]		N	–
Gee, Edward	*A Treatise of Prayer: and of Divine Providence as Relating to it*	J. M.	London	1653		Y	GC.1.18
Author	Title	Printer	Place	Date	Edition	Extant?	Shelfmark
Hakewill, George	*An Apology or Declaration of the Power and Providence of God in the Government of the World*	William Turner	Oxford	1635	Third	Y	GC.2.2
Harris, Robert	*The Works of Robert Harris once of Hanwell*	James Flesher	London	1654		Y	GC.1.28

Author	Title	Printer	Place	Date	Edition	Extant?	Shelfmark
Hildersham, Arthur	*CLII Lectures upon Psalm, LI*	John Raworth	London	1642		Y	GC.2.5(1)
Hildersham, Arthur	*CVIII Lectures upon the Fourth of John*	Moses Bell	London	1647	Third	Y	GC.2.5(2)
Josephus, Flavius	*Antiquities of the Jews*	[Unknown]	[Unknown]	[Unknown]		N	–
Knox, John	*The History of the Reformation of the Church of Scotland*	John Raworth	London	1644		Y	GC.2.6
Love, Christopher	*Grace: the Truth and Growth and Different Degrees thereof*	–	London	1654		Y	GC.1.17(1)
Love, Christopher	*The Combat Between the Flesh and Spirit*	T. R. and E. M.	London	1654		Y	GC.1.17(5)
Love, Christopher	*A Treatise of Effectual Calling and Election*	–	London	1655		Y	GC.1.17(4)
Love, Christopher	*Heaven's Glory, Hell's Terror, or Two Treatises*	–	London	1655		Y	GC.1.17(3)
Love, Christopher	*The Zealous Christian Taking Heaven by Holy Violence in Several Sermons*	John Rothwell	London	1654		Y	GC.1.17(2)
Mayer, John	*A Treasury of Ecclesiastical Expositions, upon the Difficult and Doubtful Places of the Scriptures*	[Unknown]	[Unknown]	[Unknown]		N	–

(*cont.*)

Author	Title	Printer	Place	Date	Edition	Extant?	Shelfmark
Mayer, John	*Ecclesiastica Interpretatio*	John Haviland	London	1627		Y	GC.1.5
Mede, Joseph	*Diatribæ. Discourses on Diverse Texts of Scripture*	Miles Flesher	London	1648		Y	GC.1.11
Mede, Joseph	*Diatribæ. Part Four.*	J. F.	London	1652		Y	GC.1.12
Morton, Thomas	*A Catholic Appeal for Protestants, Out of the Confessions of the Roman Doctors*	Richard Field	London	1610		Y	GC.2.16
Morton, Thomas	*The Grand Imposture of the (Now) Church of Rome*	George Miller	London	1628	Second	Y	GC.1.33
Napier, John	*A Plain Discovery of the Whole Revelation of St. John*	–	Edinburgh	1645	Fifth	Y	GC.1.7
Author	Title	Printer	Place	Date	Edition	Extant?	Shelfmark
Pemble, William	*The Works of that Late Learned Minister of God's Holy Word, Mr William Pemble*	[Unknown]	[Unknown]	[Unknown]		N	–
Perkins, William	*The Works of that Famous and Worthy Minister of Christ in the University of Cambridge, Mr. William Perkins, Volume I*	John Legatt	London	1626		Y	GC.2.13

(cont.)

Author	Title	Printer	Place	Date	Edition	Extant?	Shelfmark
Perkins, William	The Works of that Famous and Worthy Minister of Christ in the University of Cambridge, M. William Perkins, Volume II	John Legatt	London	1631		Y	GC.2.14
Perkins, William	The Works of that Famous and Worthy Minister of Christ in the University of Cambridge, M. W. Perkins, Volume III	John Haviland	London	1631		Y	GC.2.15
Raleigh, Sir Walter	The History of the World	[Unknown]	[Unknown]	[Unknown]		N	–
Reynolds, Edward	The Shields of the Earth	Felix Kyngston	London	1636	Second	Y	GC.1.15(4)
Reynolds, Edward	A Sermon Touching the Peace & Edification of the Church	Felix Kyngston	London	1638		Y	GC.1.15(3)
Reynolds, Edward	Meditations on the Holy Sacrament of the Lord's Last Supper	John Norton	London	1639	Second	Y	GC.1.15(2)
Reynolds, Edward	A Treatise of the Passions and Faculties of the Soul of Man	R. H.	London	1640		Y	GC.1.15(1)
Reynolds, Edward	An Explication of the Hundred and Tenth Psalm	T. B.	London	1642	Third	Y	GC.1.21(1)

(*cont.*)

Author	Title	Printer	Place	Date	Edition	Extant?	Shelfmark
Reynolds, Edward	*Three Treatises of the Vanity of the Creature, the Sinfulness of Sin, the Life of Christ*	W. Hunt	London	1651	Fifth	Y	GC.1.21(2)
Richardson, John	*Choice Observations and Explanations upon the Old Testament*	T. R. and E. M.	London	1655		Y	GC.1.25
Roberts, Francis	*Clavis Bibliorum. The Key of the Bible*	T. R. and E. M.	London	1649	Second	Y	GC.1.8
Rogers, Richard	*Seven Treatises*	Felix Kyngston	London	1603		Y	GC.1.31
Rogers, Richard	*Seven Treatises*	Felix Kyngston	London	1610	Third	Y	GC.2.12
Salvard, Jean Francois	*An Harmony of the Confessions of the Faith of the Christian and Reformed Churches*	John Legatt	London	1643		Y	GC.1.4
Sarpi, Paolo	*The History of the Council of Trent*	Robert Young and John Raworth	London	1640	Third	Y	GC.2.9
Trapp, John	*A Commentary or Exposition upon all the Books of the New Testament*	R. W.	London	1656	Second	Y	GC.2.17

(cont.)

Author	Title	Printer	Place	Date	Edition	Extant?	Shelfmark
[Unknown]	Annotations upon all the Books of the Old and New Testament	John Legatt	London	1651	Second	Y	GC.2.3–4
Ursinus, Zacharius	The Sum of Christian Religion	James Young	London	1645		Y	GC.2.18
Ussher, James	A Body of Divinity, or the Sum and Substance of Christian Religion	Tho. Downes and Geo. Badger	London	1653		Y	GC.2.7
Vermigli, Peter Martyr	The Common Places of the Most Famous and Renowned Divine Doctor Peter Martyr	Henry Denham and Henry Middleton	London	1583		Y	GC.2.10
Weemes, John	A Treatise of the Four Degenerate Sons	Thomas Cotes	London	1636		Y	GC.1.3
Weemes, John	The Works of John Weemes of Lathlocker in Scotland. The Second Volume	Tho. Cotes	London	1636		Y	GC.1.9
Weemes, John	The Works of John Weemes of Lathlocker in Scotland. The Third Volume	M. Dawson	London	1636		Y	GC.1.2
Weemes, John	The Works of John Weemes of Lathlocker in Scotland, in Four Volumes	T. Cotes	London	1637		Y	GC.1.23

(*cont.*)

Author	Title	Printer	Place	Date	Edition	Extant?	Shelfmark
White, Francis	*A Reply to Jesuit Fisher's Answer to Certain Questions Propounded by His Most Gracious Majesty: King James*	Adam Islip	London	1624		Y	GC.1.27
White, John	*The Works of that Learned and Reverend Divine, John White Doctor in Divinity*	-	London	1624		Y	GC.2.1
Wolleb, Johannes	[*Unknown*]	[Unknown]	[Unknown]	[Unknown]		N	-

List of Books in the Turton and Walmsley Parish Libraries

Turton*

Author	Title	£	s.	d.
-	A great bible	01	10	00
Barlow, Thomas	On Tim:	00	07	00
Baxter, Richard	Works in 2 vol:	01	02	00
Baynes, Paul	On Col:	00	04	06
Baynes, Paul	On the Ephes:	00	10	06
Beard, Thomas	Theatr: of gods Judgmts:	00	06	00
Blake, Thomas	Covt: of grace	00	04	06
Bolton, Robert	Works 2 vol:	00	10	00
Bolton, Samuel	Arraigmt: of error	00	02	06
Burroughs, Jeremiah	Irenicu:	00	02	08
Byfield, Nicholas	On Col: & on Peetr:	00	15	00
Calvin, John	Institutions	00	07	06
Calvin, John	On Job	00	08	00
Caryl, Joseph	On Job 5 vol:	01	16	06
Clarke, Samuel	Marrow of Eccl: history	00	10	00
Clarke, Samuel	Martyrologie	00	15	00
Culverwell, Nathaniel	Light of nature	00	02	09
Elton, Edward	On the romans	00	12	00
Elton, Edward	On the Col:	00	06	00
Foxe, John	Acts and Monumts:	02	00	00
Gillespie, George	Arons rod	00	05	00

---

* This list of books from the Turton and Walmsley libraries has been taken from the original invoices in Chetham's Library, Manchester, (Chet/4/5/2), Invoices of Books, 1655–1685, f.58r and from David Roderick Evans, 'The Five Parochial Libraries Founded by Humphrey Chetham', (Unpublished MA thesis, Manchester Metropolitan University, 1993), pp. 41–42. It has been alphabetised according to authors' surnames and thus is not in the original order.

© KONINKLIJKE BRILL NV, LEIDEN, 2024 | DOI:10.1163/9789004363717_020

(cont.)

Author	Title	£	s.	d.
Goodwin, Thomas	Select cases	00	06	06
Goodwin, Thomas	Christ. armr:	00	08	00
Gouge, William	On the heb. 2 vol.	01	00	00
Greenham, Richard	Works	00	13	00
Greenhill, William	On Ezek: 3 vol	00	10	00
Heylyn, Peter	Cosmography	01	00	00
Hildersham, Arthur	On Psal. 51	00	15	06
Jenkyn, William	On Jude	00	10	06
Jermin, Michael	On ye Pvrbs:	00	06	00
Jermin, Michael	On the Ecclesiast:	00	06	00
Jewel, John	Apolog:	01	00	00
Love, Christopher	Works	00	08	00
Mayer, John	On the bible 5 vol.	03	00	00
Mornay, Philippe Du Plessis	Mistery of Iniquitie And on the Mass 2 vol.	00	10	00
Morton, Thomas	Cathol: appeal	00	07	00
Perkins, William	Works 3 vol:	01	17	00
Slater, [Unknown]	On Thess:	00	05	00
Ursinus, Zacharias	Cattachisme	00	08	00
Ussher, James	Answer to ye Jesuites	00	04	06
Ussher, James	Body of divinity	00	06	06
White, Francis	Answr: to fisher	00	05	00
White, John	Works	00	05	06
Willet, Andrew	Works in 7 vol:	03	15	00

Walmsley

Author	Title	£	s.	d.
–	Book of homilies	00	04	00
Attersoll, William	On ye Sacramt:	00	03	06
Foxe, John	Book Martyres	02	00	00
Jewel, John	Apol:	01	00	00

(*cont.*)

Author	Title	£	s.	d.
Leigh, Edward	Body of divinitie	oo	12	oo
Martyr, Peter	Como: places	oo	12	oo
Mornay, Philippe Du Plessis	Mystery of Iniquitie and on the mass	oo	10	oo
Perkins, William	[Works] 3 vol:	o1	17	oo
Rutherford, Samuel	4 vol:	oo	13	oo
Stoughton, [Unknown]	–	oo	o7	o6
Taylor, [Unknown]	6 vol:	o1	o9	oo
Taylor, [Unknown]	Works	oo	10	oo
Topsell, Edward	On Joell	oo	o5	oo
Ursinus, Zacharias	Cattachisme	oo	o8	oo
Ussher, James	Som: Christ religio:	oo	o6	o6

© KONINKLIJKE BRILL NV, LEIDEN, 2024 | DOI:10.1163/9789004363717_021

List of Books in the Stone and Gillingham Donations to Wimborne Minster Chained Library

William Stone's Donation

Author	Title	Printer	Place	Date	Extant?	Shelfmark
Arethas of Caesarea	*Commentarii D Joannis apocalypsim compendiaria ...*	[Unknown]	[Unknown]	1618	N	–
Aretius, Benedictus	*Comment in Apocalypsin D. Joannis Apostoli facili ...*	Jean le Preux	Paris	1581	Y	J8
Aretius, Benedictus	*Commentarii in Evang. D.N. Jesu Christ, secundam Lucam ...*	Franciscus le Preux	Lausanne	1579	Y	M18
Athenagora	*Opuscula*	[Unknown]	[Unknown]	[Unknown]	N	-
Beza, Theodore	*Jesu Christi D.N. Novum Testamentum*	Thomas Vautrollier	London	1585	Y	J34
Binius, Severin	*Concilia Generalia, et Provincialia, quotquot reperiri. Item Epistolae Decretales ...*	Antony Hierat	Cologne	1606	Y	F17

Author	Title	Printer	Place	Date	Extant?	Shelfmark
Calvin, John	*Institutio Christianae Religionis ...*	Adam and Jean Rivery	Geneva	1554	Y	J18
Cassian, John	*Opera omnia / cum Commentariis D. Alard Gazaei*	Joannem Baptistam	Arras	1628	Y	G3
Clement of Alexandria	*Opera Graece et Latine quae extant ...*	Johannes Patius	Leiden	1616	Y	B15
Colladon, Nicolas	*Methodus Facilima ad Explicationem sacrosanctae Apocalypseos Joannis theology ...*	Jean le Preux	Paris	1581	Y	[Unknown]
Cologne Cathedral Chapter	*Antididagma, seu Christianae et Catholicae religionis ...*	Jacques Kerver	Paris	1549	Y	[Unknown]
Erasmus, Desiderius	*Chiliades adagiorum, opus integrum et perfectum ...*	Joannis Gymnici	Cologne	1540	Y	G4
Eusebius of Emesa	*Homilies in Evangelia ...*	Jérôme de Marnef	Paris	1554	Y	J10
Facundus of Hermiana	*Pro Defensione Trium Capitulorum Concilii Calchedonensis ...*	Sébastien Cramoisy	Paris	1629	Y	J26
Fonseca, Jeronimo Osorio da	*De Justitia caelesti, libri decem. Ad Reginaldum cardinalem Polum ...*	Arnold Birckmann	Cologne	1572	Y	J24

(*cont.*)

Author	Title	Printer	Place	Date	Extant?	Shelfmark
Fumi, Bartolomeo	*Summa; quæ Aurea Armilla inscribitur, continens breviter ... quæcunque in jure canonico et apud Theologos circa animarum curam ...*	Aldus Manutius	Venice	1554	N	–
Gorus, Johannes	*Summa de exemplis ac similitudinibus rerum ...*	Damiano Zenaro	Venice	1576	N	–
Gregory of Nazianzus	*Cognomento theologi, orationes trigintaocto*	Claude Chevallon	Paris	1532	Y	B7
Gregory of Nazianzus	*Opera, nunc primum Graece et Latine conjunctim ... Volume I*	[Unknown]	Paris	1630	Y	B5
Gregory of Nazianzus	*Opera, nunc primum Graece et Latine conjunctim ... Volume II*	[Unknown]	Paris	1630	Y	B6
Lactantius, Lucius	*Divina opera ... Apologeticus adversus getes ...*	Joannem Paruum	Paris	1525	Y	[Unknown]
Ley, John	*Annotations upon all the Books of the Old and New Testaments ...*	John Legatt and John Raworth	London	1645	Y	G2
Oecumenius	*Expositiones antiquae ... ex diuersis sanctorum patrum ... ed. by Donato*	Stephanum & fratres Sabios	Verona	1532	Y	B14

(cont.)

Author	Title	Printer	Place	Date	Extant?	Shelfmark
Pearson, John	*Critici Sacri. Volume I*	James Flesher	London	1660	Y	F1
Pearson, John	*Critici Sacri. Volume II*	James Flesher	London	1660	Y	F2
Pearson, John	*Critici Sacri. Volume III*	James Flesher	London	1660	Y	F3
Pearson, John	*Critici Sacri. Volume IV*	James Flesher	London	1660	Y	F4
Pearson, John	*Critici Sacri. Volume V*	James Flesher	London	1660	Y	F5
Pearson, John	*Critici Sacri. Volume VI*	James Flesher	London	1660	Y	F6
Pearson, John	*Critici Sacri. Volume VII*	James Flesher	London	1660	Y	F7
Pearson, John	*Critici Sacri. Volume VIII*	James Flesher	London	1660	Y	F8
Pearson, John	*Critici Sacri. Volume IX*	James Flesher	London	1660	Y	F9
Pearson, John	*Critici Sacri. Volume X*	James Flesher	London	1660	Y	F10
Poole, Matthew	*Synopsis Criticorum aliorumque S. Scripturae interpretum. Volume I*	James Flesher and Thomas Roycroft	London	1669	Y	F11
Poole, Matthew	*Synopsis Criticorum aliorumque S. Scripturae interpretum. Volume II*	James Flesher and Thomas Roycroft	London	1672	Y	F12
Poole, Matthew	*Synopsis Criticorum aliorumque S. Scripturae interpretum. Volume III*	James Flesher and Thomas Roycroft	London	1673	Y	F13

(*cont.*)

Author	Title	Printer	Place	Date	Extant?	Shelfmark
Poole, Matthew	*Synopsis Criticorum aliorumque S. Scripturae interpretum. Volume IV*	James Flesher and Thomas Roycroft	London	1674/1676	Y	F14
Pope Gregory I	*Opera D. Gregorii Papae, huius nominis primi ... Volumes I and II*	Hieronymus Froben	Basel	1564	Y	A11
Pope Saint Clement	*Clementis ad Corinthios epistola prior ... interpret. Patricius Junius*	John Lichfield	Oxford	1633	Y	L19
Pope Saint Leo I the Great	*Heptas Praesulum Christiana ... ed. by Raynaudus et al.*	Claude Du-Four	Lyon	1633	Y	F16
Prideaux, John	*Orationes novem inaugurals de totidem theologiae apicibus ...*	John Lichfield	Oxford	1626	Y	L13
Prideaux, John	*Lectiones decem. De totidem Religionis capitibus ...*	John Lichfield	Oxford	1626	Y	L13
Saint Ambrose	*Opera omnia quae extant, ex editione Romana: sacrae ... Volumes I to III*	Antonio Hierat	Cologne	1616	Y	A6
Saint Ambrose	*Opera omnia quae extant, ex editione Romana: sacrae ... Volumes IV and V*	Antonio Hierat	Cologne	1616	Y	A7

(cont.)

Author	Title	Printer	Place	Date	Extant?	Shelfmark
Saint Anselm	Opuscula beati Anselmi archiepiscopi Cantuariensis ordinis Sancti Benedicti	Johann Amerbach	Basel	1495	Y	[On Display]
Saint Augustine	Cuius praestantissima in omni genere monimenta ... Volumes I to III	Ambrosius Froben	Basel	1569	Y	A1
Saint Augustine	Cuius praestantissima in omni genere monimenta ... Volumes IV and V	Ambrosius Froben	Basel	1569	Y	A2
Saint Augustine	Cuius praestantissima in omni genere monimenta ... Volumes VI and VII	Ambrosius Froben	Basel	1569	Y	A3
Saint Augustine	Cuius praestantissima in omni genere monimenta ... Volumes VIII and IX	Ambrosius Froben	Basel	1569	Y	A4
Saint Augustine	Cuius praestantissima in omni genere monimenta ... Volume X	Ambrosius Froben	Basel	1569	Y	A5
Saint Augustine	Contra secundum Juliani responsionem, operis imperfect ... ed. by Menard	Sebastian Chappelet	Paris	1617	Y	J25

(*cont.*)

Author	Title	Printer	Place	Date	Extant?	Shelfmark
Saint Augustine	*Liber de Gestis Pelagii … ed. by Menard*	Sebastian Chappelet	Paris	1617	Y	J25
Saint Bernard of Clairvaux	*Opera omnia: tam quae vere Germana illius esse nemo inficias …*	John Keerberg	Antwerp	1609	Y	F15
Saint Cyprian	*Opera, iam quartum accuratioro uigilantia a mendis … per. Des. Erasmum Roterod.*	Hieronymus Froben	Basel	1530	Y	B9
Saint Cyprian	*Opera, recognita & illustrata per Joannem Oxoniensem episcopum …*	Printed at the Theatre	Oxford	1682	Y	B8
Saint Cyril of Alexandria	*Scita & elegantia commentaria in quinque priores Moysis libros … ed. by Andreae Schotti*	Martin Nutius and John Verdussen	Antwerp	1618	Y	B11
Saint Cyril of Alexandria	*Sermones paschales triginta: ex interpretatione Antonij Salmatiae …*	Martin Nutius and John Verdussen	Antwerp	1618	Y	B11
Saint Cyril of Alexandria	*S. Cyrillus Patriarcha Alexandrinus, in XII Prophetas: ex biblioth. Vatic. et Bauar …*	Adami Sartorii	Ingolstadt	1607	Y	B12

(cont.)

Author	Title	Printer	Place	Date	Extant?	Shelfmark
Saint Cyril of Alexandria	*Adversus anthropomorphitas, liber unus graece et latine, Ejusdem, de incarnatione ...*	Joannis Patii	Leiden	1605	Y	K18
Saint Cyril of Jerusalem	*Cyrilli Hierosolymorum archie-piscopi opera, quae reperiuntur: ex variis Bibliothecis praecipue Vaticana ...*	Charles Morel	Paris	1631	Y	E20
Saint Hilary of Poitiers	*D. Hilarii Pictauorum episcopi Lucubrationes quotquot extant ...*	Per Eusebium Episcopium, et Nicolai fratris haeredes	Basel	1570	Y	G10
Saint Ignatius of Antioch	*S. Ignatii episcopi Antiocheni & martyris quae exstant omnia: in duos libros distincta ...*	Widow of Peter de la Roviere	Geneva	1623	Y	K15
Saint Irenaeus	*Divi Irenae, adversus Valentini, et similium Gnosticorum haereses, libri quinque ...*	Birckmann	Cologne	1596	Y	B10
Saint Isadore of Pelusium	*S. Isidori Pelusiotae de inter-pretatione diuinae scripturae epistolarum libri IV ...*	Hieronymus Commelinus	Heidelberg	1605	Y	F18

Author	Title	Printer	Place	Date	Extant?	Shelfmark
Saint Isadore of Pelusium	*Sanct. Isidori Pelusiotae presbyteri Epistolarum, quae in Billii & Rittershusii editionibus desiderantur, volumen reliquum ...*	Matthaei Kempfferi	Frankfurt	1629	Y	G1
Saint Isadore of Seville	*D. Isidori Hispalensis Episcopi de summo bono lib. III ... Quibus aditus est eiusdem ...*	Petri Regnault	Paris	1538	Y	[On Display]
Saint Jerome	*Opera, ed. by Mariani. Volume I, Tomes I to IV*	Sebastian Nivellium	Paris	1602	Y	A8
Saint Jerome	*Opera, ed. by Mariani. Volume II, Tomes V to VII*	Sebastian Nivellium	Paris	1602	Y	A9
Saint Jerome	*Opera, ed. by Mariani. Volume III, Tomes VIII and IX*	Sebastian Nivellium	Paris	1602	Y	A10
Saint Jerome	*Sancti Hieronymi Stridoniensis Indiculus de hæresibus Judæorum: Nunc primum in lucem ...*	Sebastian Chappelet	Paris	1617	Y	[Unknown]
Saint John Chrysostom	*Opera. Volume I, ed. by Sir H Savile*	John Norton	Eton	1612	Y	A12

Author	Title	Printer	Place	Date	Extant?	Shelfmark
Saint John Chrysostom	*Opera. Volume II, ed. by Sir H Savile*	John Norton	Eton	1612	Y	A13
Saint John Chrysostom	*Opera. Volume III, ed. by Sir H Savile*	John Norton	Eton	1612	Y	A14
Saint John Chrysostom	*Opera. Volume IV, ed. by Sir H Savile*	John Norton	Eton	1612	Y	A15
Saint John Chrysostom	*Opera. Volume V, ed. by Sir H Savile*	John Norton	Eton	1612	Y	A16
Saint John Chrysostom	*Opera. Volume VI, ed. by Sir H Savile*	John Norton	Eton	1612	Y	A17
Saint John Chrysostom	*Opera. Volume VII, ed. by Sir H Savile*	John Norton	Eton	1612	Y	A18
Saint John Chrysostom	*Opera. Volume VIII, ed. by Sir H Savile*	John Norton	Eton	1612	Y	B1
Saint John Chrysostom	*Commentaria in sacrosancta quatuor Christi Evangelia …*	Charlotte Guillard	Paris	1544	Y	M13

(*cont.*)

Author	Title	Printer	Place	Date	Extant?	Shelfmark
Saint John Chrysostom	*In Sanctum Iesv Christi Evangelium secundu[m] Matthæum co[m]mentarii luculentissimi …*	Joannis Steelsii	Antwerp	1542	Y	J7
Saint Justin	*Opera Graecus textus multis in locis correctus & Latine*	Sébastien Cramoisy	Paris	1615	Y	B13
Saint Macarius the Elder of Egypt	*Homiliae Spirituales quin- quaginta, de integritate quae decet …*	Widow of Johann Wechel	Frankfurt	1594	Y	J28
Saint Optatus of Mela	*Optati Afri Mileuitani Episcopi De schismate Donatistarum con- tra Parmenianum Donatistam libri septem …*	John Legatt	London	1631	Y	J27
Saint Vincent of Lerins	*Aduersus prophanas haereseōn nouationes libellus verè aureus …*	Birckmann	Cologne	1613	Y	[Unknown]

(cont.)

Author	Title	Printer	Place	Date	Extant?	Shelfmark
Salvianus	*De vero iudicio et providentia dei: ad S. Salonium episcopum Vienensem libri VIII ...*	Hieronymus Froben	Basel	1530	Y	G7
Tertullianus, Quintus Septimius Florens	*Opera quae adhuc reperiri potuerunt omnia ex editione Iacobi Pamelii Brugensis ...*	Gillis van den Rade	Franeker	1597	Y	H13
Theophylactus of Ochrida	*In D. Pauli Epistolas commentarii ...*	Robert Barker	London	1636	N	–
Theophylactus of Ochrida	*In quatuor Evangelia enarrationes ...*	Gottfried Hittorp	Cologne	1532	Y	[On Display]
Walker, Obadiah	*A Paraphrase and Annotations upon the Epistles of St Paul ...*	Printed at the Theatre	Oxford	1675	N	-

Author	Title	Printer	Place	Date	Extant?	Shelfmark
Allestree, Richard	*A Discourse concerning the Period of Humane Life ...*	Printed for Enoch Wyer	London	1677	N	–
Baker, Richard	*Chronicle of the Kings of England from the Time of the Romans ...*	Ellen Cotes	London	1665	Y	D19
Barnes, Joshua	*Edward III. History of that Most Victorious Monarch, King of England and France ...*	John Haynes	Cambridge	1688	Y	K1
Browne, Thomas	*Pseudodoxia Epidemica ... together with the Religio Medici ...*	J. R.	London	1672	Y	K17
Burnet, Gilbert	*History of the Reformation of the Church of England, Volume I*	T. H.	London	1679	Y	D10
Burnet, Gilbert	*History of the Reformation of the Church of England, Volume II*	T. H.	London	1681	Y	D11
Burton, Robert	*Anatomy of Melancholy*	Printed for Henry Cripps	Oxford	1638	Y	K11

(cont.)

Author	Title	Printer	Place	Date	Extant?	Shelfmark
Camden, William	History of the Most Renowned and Victorious Princess Elizabeth late Queen of England	Thomas Harper	London	1635	Y	E9
Castell, Edmund	Lexicon Heptaglotton ... Volume I	Thomas Roycroft	London	1669	Y	I9
Castell, Edmund	Lexicon Heptaglotton ... Volume II	Thomas Roycroft	London	1669	Y	I10
Chamber-layne, Edward	Anglia Notitia or The Present State of England	T. N.	London	1670	Y	J20
Charleton, Walter	Two Discourses: I. Concerning the Different Wits of Men: II. Of the Mysteries of Vinters	F. L.	London	1675	Y	J11
Chillingworth, William	Religion of the Protestants, A Safe Way to Salvation	Leonard Lichfield	Oxford	1638	Y	K19
Cicero, Marcus Tullius	Opera quae extant omnia ... Volume I, ed. by Littleton	John Dunmore	London	1681	Y	I5
Cicero, Marcus Tullius	Opera quae extant omnia ... Volume II, ed. by Littleton	John Dunmore	London	1681	Y	I6

(*cont.*)

Author	Title	Printer	Place	Date	Extant?	Shelfmark
Comines, Philippe de	*History of Philippe Comines ... trans. by T. Danett*	Printed for Samuel Mearne	London	1674	Y	K7
Cotton, Robert	*Cottoni Posthuma: Divers Choice Pieces of that Renowned Antiquary ... by J. Howell*	Printed for Richard Lowndes	London	1672	Y	L11
Cudworth, Ralph	*The True Intellectual System of the Universe ...*	Printed for Richard Royston	London	1678	Y	D17
Daniel, Samuel	*The Collection of the History of England ...*	Edward Griffin	London	1650	Y	L22
Dugdale, William	*History of St Paul's Cathedral in London from its Foundations until these times ...*	Thomas Warren	London	1658	Y	D7
Dugdale, William	*Short View of the Late Troubles in England*	Printed at the Threatre	Oxford	1681	Y	D18
E., D.	*A Vindication of Historiographer of the University of Oxford*	Randal Taylor	London	1693	N	–

(cont.)

Author	Title	Printer	Place	Date	Extant?	Shelfmark
Eusebius of Caesarea	*Ancient Ecclesiastical histories of the First Six Hundred Years after Christ ... trans. M. Hanmer*	Abraham Miller	London	1663	Y	G11
Evelyn, John	*French Gardiner ...*	S. S.	London	1672	Y	J19
Fuller, Thomas	*Church-History of Britain from the Birth of Jesus Christ until the Year 1648*	Printed for John Williams	London	1655	Y	I7
Graunt, John	*Reflections on weekly Bills of Mortality for the Cities of London and Westminster ...*	Printed for Samuel Speed	London	1665	N	–
Grew, Nehemiah	*Musaeum Regalis Societatis, or a Catalogue and Description of the Natural and Artificial Rarities belonging to the Royal Society ...*	William Rawlins	London	1681	Y	D13
Grimeston, Edward	*General History of the Netherlands...*	Adam Islip	London	1608	Y	[Unknown]
Hammond, Henry	*Paraphrase & Annotations upon all the Books of the N.T.*	John Macock and Miles Flesher	London	1681	Y	D6

(*cont.*)

Author	Title	Printer	Place	Date	Extant?	Shelfmark
Hammond, Henry	*The Works of Henry Hammond, ed. by William Fulman, Volumes I and II*	Thomas Newcomb and Miles Flesher	London	1684	Y	D4
Hammond, Henry	*The Works of Henry Hammond, ed. by William Fulman, Volumes III and IV*	Thomas Newcomb and Miles Flesher	London	1684	Y	D5
Hartlib, Samuel	*Enlargement of the Discourse of Husbandry used in Brabant and Flanders*	Robert and William Leybourn	London	1652	Y	J6
Herbert, Edward	*The Life and Reign of King Henry the Eighth*	E. G.	London	1649	Y	D15
Hooker, Richard	*Of the Laws Ecclesiastical Politie*	Printed for Robert Scot, Thomas Basset, John Wright and Richard Chiswell	London	1682	Y	K10
Howell, William	*An Institution of General History; or the History of the Ecclesiastical Affairs of the World ... Volume I*	Printed for Henry Herringham and Thomas Bassett	London	1680	Y	D1

Author	Title	Printer	Place	Date	Extant?	Shelfmark
Howell, William	*An Institution of General History; or the History of the Ecclesiastical Affairs of the World … Volume II*	Printed for Henry Herringham and Thomas Bassett	London	1680	Y	D2
Howell, William	*An Institution of General History; or the History of the Ecclesiastical Affairs of the World … Volume III*	Miles Flesher	London	1685	Y	D3
Hughes, William	*The Complete Vineyard …*	John Crooke	London	1670	Y	J15
Isaacson, Henry	*Saturni Ephemerides, sive Tabula Historico-chronologica. Containing a chronological series …*	Bernard Alsop and Thomas Fawcet	London	1633	Y	I8
Lake, Arthur	*Sermons with some religious and divine meditations …*	William Stansby	London	1629	Y	D14
Laud, William	*Relation of the Conference between W. Laud … and Mr Fisher, the Jesuite …*	Richard Badger	London	1639	Y	D16

Author	Title	Printer	Place	Date	Extant?	Shelfmark
Machiavelli, Nicolo	*The Works of the Famous Nicolas Machiavel ... trans. by H. Neville*	Printed for John Starkey	London	1675	Y	K6
Markham, Gervase	*Way to Get Wealth by the Approved Rules of Practice ...*	Roger Jackson	London	1625	N	–
Micanzio, Fulgenzio	*Life of the most learned Father Paul: of the order of the Servie. Councillor of State ...*	Printed for Humphrey Moseley	London	1651	Y	M9
More, Henry	*A Collection of Several Philosophical Writings ...*	James Flesher	London	1662	Y	K20
More, Henry	*An Explanation of the Grand Mystery of Godliness ...*	James Flesher	London	1660	Y	K21
More, Henry	*A Modest Enquiry into the Mystery of Iniquity ...*	James Flesher	London	1664	Y	K22
Pearson, John	*Exposition of the Creed*	John Macock	London	1683	Y	D12
Phillippes, Henry	*The Purchasers Pattern*	Robert and William Leybourn	London	1653	N	–
Plato	*Opera quae extant omnia ... Volumes I and II*	Henri Estienne	Lausanne	1578	Y	I1

(*cont.*)

Author	Title	Printer	Place	Date	Extant?	Shelfmark
Plato	*Opera quae extant omnia ... Volumes III and IV*	Henri Estienne	Lausanne	1578	Y	I2
Plutarch	*Quae extant omnia, Volume I*	Daniel and David Aubriorum, and Clement Schleichii	Frankfurt	1620	Y	I3
Plutarch	*Quae extant omnia*	Daniel and David Aubriorum, and Clement Schleichii	Frankfurt	1620	Y	I4
Primatt, Stephen	*The City and Country Purchaser and Builder*	Printed for S. Speed	London	1667	Y	J12
Raleigh, Walter	*The History of the World*	Robert Young	London	1634	Y	K4
Ramesey, William	*The Gentleman's Companion: or, a Character of True Nobility and Gentility...*	Edward Okes	London	1672	Y	J23
Rogers, Thomas	*Treatise upon Sundry Matters contained in the Thirty-Nine Articles*	William Hunt	London	1658	Y	[Unknown]
Ross, Alexander	*The History of the World: the second part, being a continuation of the Famous History of Sir Walter Raleigh*	Printed for John Saywell	London	1652	Y	K5

(*cont.*)

Author	Title	Printer	Place	Date	Extant?	Shelfmark
Saint-Amour, Louis de Gorin	*Journal of Monsr. De St. Amour ... Containing a Full Account of all the Transactions both in France and at Rome ...*	Thomas Ratcliff	London	1664	Y	D20
Sanctorius, Santorio	*Medicina Statica: or Rules of Health, English'd by J. Davies*	Printed for John Starkey	London	1676	N	–
Sanderson, Robert	*De obligatione conscientiae prælectiones decem ...*	Robert Littlebury	London	1686	Y	M7
Sarpi, Paolo	*The History of the Council of Trent ... trans. by N. Brent*	John Macock	London	1676	Y	K2
Scheibler, Christoph	*Metaphysica specialis sive Metaphysicorum liber II ...*	Nikolaus Hampel	Giessen	1622	Y	J35
Secundus, Pliny	*Historiae mundi libri XXXVII*	Patrus Santandreanus	Lyon	1582	Y	D8
Serres, Jean de	*A General History of France ... much augmented ...*	George Eld	London	1611	Y	D9
Tallents, Francis	*A View of Universal History, from the Creation, to the Destruction of Jerusalem ...*	[Unknown]	[Unknown]	[Unknown]	N	-

(cont.)

Author	Title	Printer	Place	Date	Extant?	Shelfmark
Taylor, Jeremy	*Antiquitates Christianae or the History of the Life and Death of the Holy Jesus ...*	John Macock and Miles Flesher	London	1684	N	–
Temple, William	*Miscellanae by a Person of Honour*	A. M. and R. R.	London	1680	Y	L10
Temple, William	*Miscellanae. The Second Part ...*	T. M.	London	1690	Y	J5
Temple, William	*Observations upon the United Provinces of the Netherlands*	Anne Maxwell	London	1673	Y	L12
Trussell, John	*Continuation of the ... History of England ...*	Mary Dawson	London	1636	Y	K3
Tryon, Thomas	*The Way to Health, Long Life and Happiness ...*	Andrew Sowle	London	1683	N	–
Tubero, Oratius	*Cinq Dialogues faits a l'imitation des anciens ...*	G. Rousselin	Liege	1673	N	–
Ussher, James	*The Annals of the World deduced from the Origin of Time ...*	Evan Tyler	London	1658	Y	K3

(*cont.*)

Author	Title	Printer	Place	Date	Extant?	Shelfmark
Venner, Tobias	*Via recta ad vitam longam, or, A treatise wherein the right way and best manner of living for attaining to a long and healthfull life ...*	James Flesher	London	1650	N	–
Walton, Brian	*Biblia Sacra, Polyglotta. Prolegomena from Volume I*	Thomas Roycroft	London	1653	Y	I17
Walton, Brian	*Biblia Sacra, Polyglotta. Volume I*	Thomas Roycroft	London	1653	Y	I11
Walton, Brian	*Biblia Sacra, Polyglotta. Volume II*	Thomas Roycroft	London	1655	Y	I12
Walton, Brian	*Biblia Sacra, Polyglotta. Volume III*	Thomas Roycroft	London	1657	Y	I13
Walton, Brian	*Biblia Sacra, Polyglotta. Volume IV*	Thomas Roycroft	London	1657	Y	I14
Walton, Brian	*Biblia Sacra, Polyglotta. Volume V*	Thomas Roycroft	London	1657	Y	I15
Walton, Brian	*Biblia Sacra, Polyglotta. Volume VI*	Thomas Roycroft	London	1657	Y	I16

Bibliography

Primary Sources

Biblioteca del Seminario Vescovile, Padua
*Registro in cui dal 1614 fino all'anno 1765 moltissimi inglesi, scozzesi e irlandesi scrissero i
loro nomi e cognomi* (ms. 634).

Bodleian Library, Oxford
1 May 1695: Walker, Obadiah, 1616–1699 to Halton, Timothy, 1633–1704 (MS Ballard 21,
fol. 103).
New Testament (early Wycliffite version) (MSS. Rawl. C. 258).

Borthwick Institute of Archives (BIA), University of York
Will of Anthony Higgin, 12 November 1624 (Archbishop Register 31, f. 238v–239r).
Will of Richard Russell, York, 10 December 1435 (Probate Register 3, f. 439r–441r).

Chetham's Library, Manchester
Accession Register, 1655–1880 (Chet/4/11/1).
Account: Note of Debts Owing (CPP/3/18).
Account: Payments for Fustians at Bolton (CPP/3/19).
Draft of the Last Will and Testament of Humphrey Chetham of Turton, Lancashire, Esq
(ChetDeeds/5/12).
Invoices of Books, 1655–1685 (Chet/4/5/2).
Last Will and Testament of Humphrey Chetham (Uncatalogued).
Last Will and Testament of Humphrey Chetham, 1631 (ChetDeeds/5/4).
Letter from John Tildsley to Rev. Hollinworth at Manchester (CPP/2/141).
Letter from Richard Johnson to Humphrey Chetham (CPP/3/72).
Letter from Richard Johnson to Humphrey Chetham (CPP/3/73).
Letter from Richard Johnson to Humphrey Chetham (CPP/3/88).
Letter from Richard Johnson to Humphrey Chetham (CPP/3/95).
Letter from Richard Johnson to Humphrey Chetham (CPP/3/96).
Letter from Richard Johnson to Humphrey Chetham (CPP/3/97).
Letter from Richard Johnson to Humphrey Chetham (CPP/3/98).
Letter from Richard Johnson to Humphrey Chetham (CPP/3/99).
Minute Book, 6 Dec 1653–16 Apr 1752 (Chet/1/2/1).

City of Westminster Archives, Westminster
Marriages 16 October 1653–29 May 1669 (SML/PR/3/2).

Dorset History Centre, Dorset
Christenings 1656–1659, 1662–1808. Marriages 1656–1754. Burials 1656–1657/8, 1661–1808 (PE-LMA/RE/1/1).
Appointments of Schoolmasters with recommendations of suitable candidates, 1600–1760 (PE-WM/GN/2/2/4).
Account Book, 1640–1696 (PE-WM/CW/1/42).
Appointments of Ministers, 1633–1665 (PE-WM/GN/2/2/7).

John Rylands Library, Manchester
Summa que vocatur sinistra pars oculi sacerdotum (Latin MS 339).

Lancashire Records Office, Lancashire
Archdeaconry of Chester Probate Records, Will of George Gee, dated 21 April 1636 (WCW/Supra/C116C/8).

Lincolnshire Archives, Lincolnshire
Documents relating to the Trigge Library: Agreement (Grantham St Wulfram Par/23/1).
Documents relating to the Trigge Library: Catalogue of Books Given by Francis Trigge (Grantham St Wulfram Par/23/4).
Documents relating to the Trigge Library: Consent of the Bishop of Lincoln (Grantham St Wulfram Par/23/2).
Documents relating to the Trigge Library: Schedule of Orders and Constitutions (Grantham St Wulfram Par/23/3).
Wills proved in the Lincoln Consistory Court, number 252 (LCC Wills/1606).

London Metropolitan Archives, London
Register of Marriages October 1653–August 1656 (P93/DUN/267).

National Library of Scotland, Edinburgh
A Proposal for Erecting Parochial Libraries in the Meanly endow'd Cures throughout England (Crawford.MB.962) <https://digital.nls.uk/188068616>.

Oxfordshire Record Office, Oxford
Subscription to the 39 Articles by William Stone (Oxf dioc, pp. e 13, p. 441).

Shropshire Archives, Shropshire
More Church Library Trust Deeds with Rules (P193/S/1/1).

The National Archives, Kew

Attorney General v Fry, 1695 (C8/446/3).

Will of Barnabas Oley, Vicar of Great Gransden, Huntingdonshire, 15 March 1686 (PROB 11/383/4).

Will of Henry Bury, Clerk of Bury, Lancashire, 24 May 1636 (PROB 11/171/190).

Will of John Clungeon, Haberdasher of London, 9 November 1646 (PROB 11/198/73).

Will of Reverend John Newcome, Doctor of Divinity, Master of Saint John's College University of Cambridge, 12 March 1765 (PROB 11/907/118).

Will of Reverend Thomas White, Bishop of Peterburgh, Doctor of Divinity, 19 July 1698 (PROB 11/446/372).

Will of Richard Gillingham of Wimborne Minster, Dorset, 19 February 1681 (PROB 11/365/283).

Will of Richard Lloyd, Clerk of Wimborne Minster, Dorset, 12 December 1738 (PROB 11/693/256).

Will of Roger Gillingham of Middle Temple, Middlesex, 25 February 1696 (PROB 11/430/238).

Will of Sir John Kidderminster of Langley Marish, Buckinghamshire, 7 May 1631 (PROB 11/159/567).

Will of Stephen Camborne, Rector of Lawshall, Suffolk, 29 March 1706 (PROB 11/487/325).

Will of Thomas Alston, Clerk of Assington, Suffolk, 31 January 1691 (PROB 11/403/170).

Will of Thomas Anstye, Clerk of Wimborne Minster, Dorset, 2 November 1669 (PROB 11/331/257).

Will of Thomas Holway, Joiner of Wimborne Minster, Dorset, 11 August 1742 (PROB 11/720/99).

Will of William Smarte of Ipswich, Suffolk, 2 November 1599 (PROB 11/94/340).

Will of William Stone, Clerk of Oxford, Oxfordshire, 27 July 1685 (PROB 11/380/483).

Will of William White, Clerk of Pusey, Berkshire, 1 July 1678 (PROB 11/357/182).

University of Leeds Brotherton Special Collections Library, Leeds

Account Book of Work Done on the Church Fabric, 1661–1676 (MS Dep 1980/1/80).

Catalogus librorum, compiled by Anthony Higgin, followed by Latin exercises and commentaries on Ovid's *Heroides and Tristia*, written by Roger Phillips (Ripon Cathedral MS 35).

Copy of 1st Letters Patent. With Translation (1916) by J. T. Fowler (MS Dep 1980/1/1.1).

Draft of Memorial from the parishioners of Ripon complaining of the neglected state of the church and parish (MS Dep 1980/1/0.7).

Letters Patent of James I (known as 1st Letters Patent), re-constituting the collegiate church of Ripon, 2nd August 1604 (MS Dep 1980/1/1.0).

Miscellaneous notebooks on theological subjects by Anthony Higgin (Ripon Cathedral MSS 16–22, 24–27, 29–30, 32, 34–36, 38, 40).

Petition to the Earl of Northampton from the clergy of Ripon, requesting him to use his influence in promoting the re-establishment of the Collegiate Church. Signed by Moses Fowler (MS Dep 1980/1/0.8).

Parish Library Books Referenced

Francis Trigge Chained Library

Andrada, Diego de Payva de, *Defensio Tridentinae fidei catholicae et inegerrimae quinque libris comprehensa* (Ingolstadt: David Sartorius, 1580). Shelfmark 7. USTC 632166.

Balbus, Johannes, *Summa que Catholicon appellatur* (Lyon: Nicolaus Wolff, 1503). Shelfmark 27. USTC 142905.

Baronius, Caesar, *Annales ecclesiastici*, in six volumes (Mainz: Balthasar Lippi, 1601–1603). Shelfmarks 29.1–29.6. These editions not listed in the USTC.

Beza, Theodore, *Tractatus Theologicarum*, 2nd edition ([Geneva]: Eustathius Vignon, 1582). Shelfmark 38. This edition not listed in the USTC.

Calvin, John, *In Omnes Pauli Apostoli epistolas et in omnes epistolas canonicas* (Geneva: Eustathium Vignon, 1580). Annotated. Shelfmark E4. This edition not listed in the USTC.

Calvin, John, *Praelectiones in librum prophetiarum Danielis* (Geneva: Jean de Laon, 1561). Annotated. Shelfmark E7. USTC 450107.

Calvin, John, *Sermons Upon the Booke of Job* (*Trans. A. Golding*) (London: T. Dawson for G. Bishop and T. Woodcocke, 1579). Annotated. Shelfmark E10. USTC 508947.

Chemnitz, Martin, *Examinis Concilii Tridentini* (Frankfurt: Peter Fabricius, 1585). Annotated. Shelfmark D2. This edition not listed in the USTC.

Diez, Phillipus, *Concionum quadruplicium libri* (*altera editio*)*: Tomus quartus concionium dominicarum aestivalium* (Lyon: Petrum Landry, 1589). Annotated. Shelfmark A15. USTC 203452.

Diez, Phillipus, *Concionum quadruplicium libri* (*altera editio*)*: Tomus quintus concinionum quadruplicium super evangelia* (Lyon: Petrum Landy, 1589). Annotated. Shelfmark A16. USTC 138037.

Forciglione, Antoninus, *Historia Venerabilis Antonini, Volumes I–III* (Basel: Nicolaus Kasler, 1502). Shelfmarks 13.1–13.3. These editions not listed in the USTC.

Forciglione, Antonio, *Summa theologica* (Lyons: Johannes Cleyn, 1516). Shelfmark 14. This edition not listed in the USTC.

Foxe, John, *Eicasmi seu meditationes in sacram Apocalypsin* (London: T. Dawson for George Bishop, 1587). Shelfmark 149. USTC 510753.

Lombard, Peter, *Sacratissima sententiarum totius theologie quadripartita volumina* (Venice: Gregorio De Gregori, 1514). Shelfmark 266. USTC 847956.

Lycosthenes, Conrad, *Similium loci communes* (Basel: ex officina Episcopiorum, 1575). Annotated. Shelfmark A6. USTC 624811.

More, Henry, *An explanation of the grand mystery of godliness* (London: J. Flesher, 1660). Shelfmark 246. This edition not listed in the USTC.

More, Henry, *Enchiridion ethicum praecipua moralis philosophiae rudimenta complectens* (London: J. Flesher, 1669). Shelfmark 244. This edition not listed in the USTC.

More, Henry, *Enchiridion metaphysicum. Pars prima* (London: E. Flesher, 1671). Shelfmark 245. This edition not listed in the USTC.

More, Henry, *Opera philosophica tum quae Latine tum quae Anglice primitus scripta sunt ... Volumes I and II* (London: printed by J. Macock for J. Martyn and Gualt. Kettilby, 1679). Shelfmarks 248.1 and 248.2. These editions not listed in the USTC.

Musculus, Wolfgang, *Loci Communes Sacrae Theologie* (Basel: ex officina Heruagiana per Eusebium Eposcopium, 1567). Annotated. Shelfmark B12. USTC 673364.

Saint Bonventure, *In secundum Lucam evangelium commentarii* (Antwerp: excudebat Joannes Crinitus apud Gregorius de Bonte, 1539). Annotated. Shelfmark A8. USTC 437999.

Saint Cyprian, *Opera* (Basel: the Office of Johann Froben, 1521). Annotated. Shelfmark F27. USTC 679668.

Tertullianus, Quintus Septimus, *Opera* (Basel: ex officina Frobeniana, 1528). Annotated. Shelfmark J9. USTC 679657.

Wesenbecius, Matthaeus, *Paratitla in pandectas juris civilis ab authore recognita & aucta. Accesserunt prolegomena de finibus studiorum juriprudentiae* (Basel: Eusebium Eposcopium et Nicolai fratris haeredes, 1568). Annotated. Shelfmark F21. USTC 675407.

Whitaker, William, *Disputatio de sacra scriptura contra huius temporis papistas imprimis Robertum Bellarminum Jesuitam ... & Thoma Stapletonum ...* (Cambridge: Thomas Thomas, 1588). Annotated. Shelfmark H28. USTC 511100.

Willett, Andrew, *Synopsis Papismi, that is a general view of Papistry* (London: Felix Kingston for Thomas Man, 1600). Shelfmark 338. USTC 515024.

Zanchius, Hieronymus, *Miscellaneorum libri tres. Tertium nunc editi. De praedestinatione sanctorum* (Neapoli Palatinorum: Matthaeus Harnisius, 1592). Shelfmark 354. This edition not listed in the USTC.

Zwinger, Theodor, *Theatrum humanae vitae*, in four volumes (Basel: ex officina Episcopiorum, 1586–1587) Shelfmarks 365.1–365.4. USTC 606252.

Ripon Minster Parish Library

Astesano, *Summa Astensis. Clarissimi sacre theologie eximii professoris fratris Astesani de Ast ... Summa de casibus amenissimam complectens disciplinarum divinarum & ecclesiasticarum sanctionem ...* (Lyon: Stephen Gueynard, 1519). Annotated. Shelfmark Ripon Cathedral Library XVII.G.18. This edition not listed in the USTC.

Beckenhub, Johann, *Index alphabeticus sive Reptorium domini Johannis Beckenhaub Moguntini in scripta divi Bonaventure super quattuor libris sententiarum* (Paris: n.

p., 1510?). Shelfmark Ripon Cathedral Library XVIII.E.21. This edition not listed in the USTC.

Bell, Thomas, *The Survey of Popish Religion* (London: Valentine Sims, 1596). Annotated. Shelfmark Ripon Cathedral Library XVII.F.13. USTC 513050.

Beza, Theodora, *Jesu Christi D.N. Novum Testamentum, Volumes I and II* (London: Thomas Vautrollier, 1574). Annotated. Shelfmarks Ripon Cathedral Library XVII.A13 and XVII.A.14. USTC 507733.

Beza, Theodore, *Ad acta Colloquii Montisbelgardensis Tubingae edita* (Geneva: Joannes Le Preux, 1588). Annotated. Shelfmark Ripon Cathedral Library II.C.10. USTC 451142.

Bilson, Thomas, *The Effect of Certain Sermons Touching the Full Redemption of Mankind by the Death and Bloud of Christ Jesus* (London: Peter Short for Walter Burre, 1599). Annotated. Shelfmark Ripon Cathedral Library XVII.E.14. USTC 513859.

Cruciger, Caspar, *Enarratio Symboli Niceni, complectens ordine doctrinam ecclesiae Dei fideliter recitatem* (Wittenberg: ex officina Hans Lufft, 1550). Annotated. Shelfmark Ripon Cathedral Library X.B.12. USTC 650060.

Drusius, Joannes the Elder, *Joh. Drusii ad loca difficiliora Josuæ, Judicum, & Samuelem commentaries liber ...* (Franeker: Fredericus Heynsius, 1618). Annotated. Shelfmark Ripon Cathedral Library I.B.8. USTC 1018085.

Duns Scotus, John, *Sententiarum antea vitio impressorum depravatum: nunc vero a multifariis erroribus purgatum: pristineque integritati restitutum* (Lyon: Jacques Myt for Jacques Giunta and Francois Giunta, 1520). Annotated. Shelfmark Ripon Cathedral Library XVIII.F.20. USTC 145318.

Durand, Guillaume, *Rationale divinorum officiorum* (Basel: Nicolaus Kesler, 1488). Annotated. Shelfmark Ripon Cathedral Library XVIII.H.12. USTC 744526.

Est, Willem Hesselszoon van, *Annotationes aureæ in præcipua ac difficiliora Sacræ Scripturæ loca* (Cologne: widow of Johann Crith, 1622). Annotated. Shelfmark Ripon Cathedral Library I.B.15. USTC 2019159.

Giovio, Paolo, *Pauli Jovii Novocomensis, episcopi Nucerini, Historiarum sui temporis, Primus Tomus* (Strasbourg: apud Augustin Fries, 1556). Annotated. Shelfmark Ripon Cathedral Library XII.B.1. USTC 683314.

Gorran, Nicolaus de, *In Acta Apostolorum ...* (Antwerp: n. p., 1620). Annotated. Shelfmark Ripon Cathedral Library XVI.C.12/q. USTC 112708.

Haddon, Walter, *Contra Hieron. Osorium, eiusq[ue] odiosas infectationes pro Evangelicae veritatis necessaria Defensione, Responsio Apologetica* (London: John Day, 1577). Shelfmark Ripon Cathedral Library XVII.A.17. USTC 508369.

Kling, Conrad, *Loci communes theologici* (Paris: Nicolas Chesneau, 1563). Annotated. Shelfmark Ripon Cathedral Library XII.G.1. USTC 198658.

Kling, Conrad, *Loci communes theologici reverend D. Conradi Klingii Franciscani ...* (Paris: apud Claude Fremy, 1563). Annotated. Shelfmark Ripon Cathedral Library XII.G.1. USTC 153443.

Lindt, Willem Van der, *Panoplia evangelica: sive De verbo Dei evangelico libri quin-que* ... (Paris: Jean Le Blanc, Guillaume Julian and Michel Julian, 1564). Annotated. Shelfmark Ripon Cathedral Library XII.G.10. USTC 153579.

Luther, Martin, *A Commentarie upon the Fiftene Psalmes*, trans. Henry Bull (London: Thomas Vautroullier, 1577). Annotated. Shelfmark Ripon Cathedral Library XVII. E.16. USTC 508422.

Montano, Benito Arias, *Biblia Sacra, Volumes I–VIII* (Antwerp: Christopher Plantin, 1569–1573). Shelfmarks Ripon Cathedral Library III.E.7/q–III.E.14/q. USTC 401394.

Pigge, Albert, *De libero hominis arbitrio & divina gratia* (Cologne: ex officina Melchior von Neuß, 1542). Annotated. Shelfmark Ripon Cathedral Library XI.D.3/q. USTC 630363.

Saint Athanasius, *Athanasii magni Alexandrini episcopi, graviss. scriptoris, et sanctiss. martyris, opera, in quatuor tomos distributa* (Basel, 1564). Annotated. Shelfmark Ripon Cathedral Library XIII.C.17/q. USTC 613803.

Saint Augustine, *Cuius praestantissima in omni genere monumenta, Volume V* (Basel: Ambrosius and Aurelius Froben, 1570). Annotated. Shelfmark Ripon Cathedral Library XIII.E.10/q. USTC 626339.

Saint Augustine, *D. Aurelii Augustini Hipponensis Episcopi Confessionum libri XIII. Opera theologorum Lovaniensium ex manuscriptis codicibus multum emendati. Eiusdem Confessio theologica tripartite* (Louvain: Hieronymus Welleus, 1573). Annotated. Shelfmark Ripon Cathedral Library XIII.A.33. USTC 406004.

Saint Basil of Caesarea, *Nunc primum Græcè et Latinè coniunctim edita, in duos tomos distributa* ... (Paris: Michel Sonnius, 1618). Shelfmarks Ripon Cathedral Library XVI.C.9/q–XVI.C.11/q. USTC 6015104.

Saint Clement, *Divi Clementis Recognitionum libri X* (Basel: n. p., 1526). Annotated. Shelfmark Ripon Cathedral Library XVII.J.8/q. This edition not listed in the USTC.

Saint John Chrysostom, *Accipe candidissime lector opera Divi Joannis Chrisostomi archi-episcopi constantinopolitani* (Venice: cura & solerti studio Bernardino I Stagnino & Gregorio De Gregori, 1503). Annotated. Shelfmark Ripon Cathedral Library XVII.H.4. USTC 762277.

Theodoret, Bishop of Cyrus, *De selectis scripturae divinae quaestionibus ambiguis* (Paris: Jacques du Puys, 1558). Shelfmark Ripon Cathedral Library XII.D.1. USTC 152441.

Theodoret, Bishop of Cyrus, *Theodoreti Episcopi Cyri De providential sermones X. Nunc primum in lucem editi* (Rome: Antonio Blado, 1545). Annotated. Shelfmark Ripon Cathedral Library XVIII.E.3. USTC 858943.

Toledo, Francisco de, *In sacrosanctum Ioannis Evangelium commentarii* ... (Cologne: in officina Birckmannica, 1599). Annotated. Shelfmark Ripon Cathedral Library XVI.B.16/q. USTC 626093.

Unknown Author, [*Novum Testamentum*] (s. l.: 1550). Annotated. Shelfmark Ripon Cathedral Library X.B.7. This edition not listed in the USTC.

Gorton Chest Parish Library

Ambrose, Isaac, *Prima, Media & Ultima: The First, Middle and Last Things* (London: T. R. and E. M., 1654). Annotated. Shelfmark GC.1.6(1). This edition not listed on the USTC.

Baxter, Richard, *The Saints Everlasting Rest, or, A Treatise Of the blessed State of the Saints in their enjoyment of God in Glory* (London: Thomas Underhill and Francis Tyson, 1656). Annotated. Shelfmark GC.1.1. This edition not listed in the USTC.

Bolton, Robert, *Mr Bolton's Last and Learned Worke of the Foure Last Things* (London: George Miller, 1633). Shelfmark 1.20(2). USTC 3016539.

Brightman, Thomas, *The Works of that Famous, Reverend, and Learned Divine, Mr. Thomas Brightman* (London: John Field, 1644). Annotated. Shelfmark GC.1.22. USTC 3046550.

Burgess, Anthony, *CXLV Expository Sermons upon the Whole 17th Chapter of the Gospel According to St John* (London: Abraham Miller, 1656). Annotated. Shelfmark GC.1.24. This edition not listed in the USTC.

Burgess, Anthony, *Spiritual Refining: or, A Treatise of Grace and Assurance* (London: A. Miller, 1652). Annotated. Shelfmark GC.1.30. This edition not listed in the USTC.

Calvin, John and Thomas Norton (trans.), *The Institution of Christian Religion* (London: printed for Thomas Norton, 1611). Annotated. Shelfmark GC.2.11. USTC 3004572.

Dod, John, *A Plaine and Familiar Exposition of the Ten Commandements* (London: Felix Kyngston, 1614). Annotated. Shelfmark GC.1.13(1). USTC 3005942.

Dod, John, *Ten Sermons Tending Chiefly to the Fitting of Men for the Worthy Receiving of the Lord's Supper* (London: T. P., 1621). Annotated. Shelfmark GC.1.13(2). USTC 3009792.

Harris, Robert, *The Works of Robert Harris, Once of Hanwell* (London: Miles Flesher, 1654). Annotated. Shelfmark GC.1.28. This edition not listed in USTC.

Hildersham, Arthur, *CLII Lectures upon Psalm, LI* (London: J. Raworth, 1642). Annotated. Shelfmark GC.2.5(1). USTC 3052352.

Hildersham, Arthur, *CVIII Lectures upon the Fourth of John* (London: Moses Bell, 1647). Annotated. Shelfmark GC.2.5(2). USTC 3043316.

Knox, John, *The Historie of the Reformation of the Church of Scotland* (London: John Raworth, 1644). Annotated. Shelfmark GC.2.6. USTC 3052353.

Mede, Joseph, *Diatribæ Pars IV. Discourses on Sundry Texts of Scripture* (London: J. F., 1652). Annotated. Shelfmark GC.1.12. This edition not listed in the USTC.

Mede, Joseph, *Diatribæ. Discourses on Diverse Texts of Scripture* (London: M. F., 1642). Annotated. Shelfmark GC.1.11. USTC 3046642.

Perkins, William, *The Workes of that Famous and Worthy Minister of Christ in the University of Cambridge, Mr William Perkins: The First Volume* (London: John Legatt, 1626). Annotated. Shelfmark GC.2.13. USTC 3012639.

Perkins, William, *The Workes of that Famous and Worthy Minister of Christ in the Universitie of Cambridge, M. William Perkins: The Third and Last Volume* (London: John Haviland, 1631). Annotated. Shelfmark GC.2.15. USTC 3015389 and 3015390.

Perkins, William, *The Workes of that Famous and Worthy Minister of Christ in the University of Cambridge, M. William Perkins: The Second Volume* (London: John Legatt, 1631). Annotated. Shelfmark GC.2.14. USTC 3015392.

Roberts, Francis, *Clavis Bibliorum. The Key of the Bible, Unlocking the Richest Treasury of the Holy Scriptures* (London: T. R. and E. M., 1649). Annotated. Shelfmark GC.1.8. USTC 3052315.

Rogers, Richard, *Seven Treatises* (London: Felix Kyngston, 1603). Annotated. Shelfmark GC.1.31. This edition not listed in the USTC.

Salvard, Jean-François, *An Harmony of the Confessions of the Faith of the Christian and Reformed Churches* (London: John Legatt, 1643). Annotated. Shelfmark GC.1.4. USTC 3049712.

Ussher, James, *A Body of Divinity, or the Sum and Substance of Christian Religion* (London: Thomas Downes and George Badger, 1653). Annotated. Shelfmark GC.2.7. This edition not listed in the USTC.

Vermigli, Peter Martyr, *The Common Places of the Most Famous and Renowmed Divine Doctor Peter Martyr* (London: Henry Denham and Henry Middleton, 1583). Annotated. Shelfmark GC.2.10. USTC 509866.

Weemes, John, *The Workes of John Weemse of Lathocker in Scotland, in four Volumes* (London: T. Cotes, 1637). Annotated. Shelfmark GC.1.23. USTC 3019107.

Weemes, John, *The Workes of M. John Weemes of Lathocker in Scotland. The Third Volume* (London: M. Dawson, 1636). Annotated. Shelfmark GC.1.2. This edition not listed in the USTC.

Weemes, John, *The Workes of Mr. John Weemes of Lathlocker in Scotland. The Second Volume* (London: Thomas Cotes, 1636). Annotated. Shelfmark GC.1.9. USTC 3018588.

White, Francis, *A Replie to Jesuit Fisher's Answer to Certain Questions Propounded by His Most Gracious Majesty, King James* (London: Adam Islip, 1624). Annotated. Shelfmark GC.1.27. USTC 3011511.

White, John, *The Workes of that Learned and Reverend Divine, John White, Doctor in Divinitie* (London: R. F., 1624). Annotated. Shelfmark GC.2.1. This edition not listed in the USTC.

Wimborne Minster Chained Library

Burnet, Gilbert, *History of the Reformation of the Church of England, Volume I* (London: T[homas] H[odgkin] for Richard Chiswell, 1679). Shelfmark D10. This edition not listed on the USTC.

Burnet, Gilbert, *History of the Reformation of the Church of England, Volume II* (London: T[homas] H[odgkin] for Richard Chiswell, 1681). Shelfmark D11. This edition not listed on the USTC.

Calvin, John, *Institutio Christianae Religionis* (Geneva: Adam Rivery and Jean Rivery, 1554). Annotated. Shelfmark J18. USTC 450061.

Castell, Edmund, *Lexicon Heptaglotton, Volumes I and II* (London: Thomas Roycroft, 1669). Shelfmarks I9 and I10. These editions not listed in the USTC.

Chillingworth, William, *The Religion of the Protestants, A Safe Way to Salvation* (Oxford: Leonard Lichfield, 1638). Annotated. Shelfmark K19. USTC 3019801.

Cicero, Marcus Tullius, *Opera quae extant omnia, Volumes I–IV* (London: J. Dunmore, 1681). Shelfmarks I5 and I6. These editions not listed in the USTC.

Dugdale, William, *Short View of the Late Troubles in England* (Oxford: printed at the Theatre for Moses Pitt, 1681). Shelfmark D18. This edition not listed on the USTC.

Fuller, Thomas, *The Church-History of Britain* (London: Printed for John Williams, 1655). Shelfmark I7. This edition not listed in the USTC.

Hammond, Henry, *The Works of the Reverend and Learned Henry Hammond, Volumes I–IV* (London: Printed for R. Royston, 1684). Shelfmarks D4 and D5. These editions not listed in the USTC.

Herbert, Edward, *The Life and Raigne of King Henry VIII* (London: Printed by E. G. for Thomas Whitaker, 1649). Annotated. Shelfmark D15. USTC 3047333.

Howell, William, *An Institution of General History, Volume I* (London: Printed for Henry Herringman et al., 1680). Shelfmark D1. This edition not listed in the USTC.

Howell, William, *An Institution of General History, Volume II* (London: Printed for Thomas Bassett et al., 1680). Shelfmark D2. This edition not listed in the USTC.

Howell, William, *An Institution of General History, Volume III* (London: Miles Flesher, 1685). Shelfmark D3. This edition not listed in the USTC.

Lake, Arthur, *Sermons with some religious and divine meditations* (London: William Stansby for Nathaniel Butter, 1629). Shelfmark D14. USTC 3014201.

Laud, William, *A Relation of the Conference between William Laud and Mr Fisher, the Jesuit* (London: Richard Badger, 1639). Shelfmark D16. USTC 3020501 and 3020493.

Nazianzus, Gregory, *Orationes ...* (Paris: Claude Chevallon, 1532). Annotated. Shelfmark B7. USTC 181373.

Plato, *Opera quae extant omnia* (Lausanne: Henr. Stephanus, 1578). Shelfmarks I1 and I2. These editions not listed in the USTC.

Plutarch, *Quae extant omnia* (Frankfurt: Daniel and David Aubry and Clemens Schleich, 1620). Shelfmarks I3 and I4. These editions not listed in the USTC.

Raleigh, Walter, *The History of the World* (London: George Lathum and Robert Young, 1634). Shelfmark K4. USTC 3017553.

Ramesey, William, *The Gentleman's Companion: or, a Character of True Nobility, and Gentility* (London: E. Okes, for Rowland Reynolds, 1672). Shelfmark J23. This edition is not listed in the USTC.

Rogers, Thomas, *Treatise upon Sundry Matters Contained in the 39 Articles* (London: William Hunt, 1658). Shelfmark unknown. This edition not listed in the USTC.

Saint Ambrose, *Opera omnia quae extant ...* (Cologne: Anton Hierat the Elder, 1616). Annotated. Shelfmarks A6 and A7. USTC 2130280.

Saint Augustine, *D. Aurelii Augustini Hipponensis Episcopi, Complectens Ta Didaktika, hoc est, quae proprie ad docendum pertinent ..., Volume I, Book III* (Basel: ex officina Frobeniana, 1569). Annotated. Shelfmark A1. This edition not listed in the USTC.

Saint Augustine, *D. Aurelii Augustini Hipponensis Episcopi, Complectens illius Epistolas ..., Volume I, Book II* (Basel: ex officina Frobeniana, 1569). Annotated. Shelfmark A1. This edition not listed in the USTC.

Saint Augustine, *D. Aurelii Augustini Hipponensis Episcopi, De Civitate Dei Libros XXII, Volume II, Book V* (Basel: ex officina Frobeniana, 1569). Annotated. Shelfmark A2. USTC 698766.

Saint Augustine, *Primus Tomus eximii Patris, inter summa Latinae Ecclesiae ornamenta ac lumina principis, D. Aurelii Augustini Hipponensis Episcopi, Cuius praestantissima in omni genere monimenta ..., Volume I, Book I* (Basel: Ambrosius and Aurelius Froben, 1569). Annotated. Shelfmark A1. USTC 686573.

Saint Cyprian, *Opera, iam quartum accuratioro uigilantia a mendis ...* (Basel: ex officina Johann Froben, 1530). Annotated. Shelfmark B9. USTC 640566.

Saint Irenaeus, *Divi Irenae, adversus Valentini, et similium Gnosticorum haereses ...* (Cologne: in officina Birckmannica, 1596). Annotated. Shelfmark B10. USTC 640415.

Sanderson, Robert, *The Obligation of Conscience to Attend the School of Theology at Oxford* (London: Robert Littlebury, 1686). Shelfmark M7. This edition not listed on the USTC.

Sarpi, Paolo, *The History of the Council of Trent, translated by Nathaniel Brent* (London: J. Macock, 1676). Shelfmark K2. This edition not listed on the USTC.

Ussher, James, *The Annals of the World* (London: E. Tyler, 1658). Shelfmark K3. This edition not listed in the USTC.

Walton, Brian, *Biblia Sacra, Polyglotta, Volumes I–V* (London: Thomas Roycroft, 1653–1657). Shelfmarks I11–I17. These editions not listed in the USTC.

Pre-1800 Books and Newspapers

Barwick, John, *Hieronikēs, or The Fight, Victory, and Triumph of S. Paul. Accommodated to the Right Reverend Father in God Thomas Late L. Bishop of Duresme ... Together with the Life of the Said Bishop* (London: Printed for R. Royston, 1660). This edition not listed in the USTC.

Baxter, Richard, *A Christian Directory* (London: Robert White, 1673). This edition not listed on the USTC.

Birch, Thomas, 'The Life of John Thurloe, Esq.' in *A Collection of the State Papers of John Thurloe, Esq., Volume I* (London, 1742).

Calamy, Edmund, *An account of the ministers, lecturers, masters and fellows of colleges and schoolmasters: who were ejected or silenced after the Restoration in 1660, by or before, the Act of Uniformity*, Volume II, 2nd edition (London: printed for J. Lawrence, 1713).

Geree, John, *The Character of an Old English Puritane or Nonconformist* (London: Printed by A. Miller for Christopher Meredith).

Mercurius Academicus, 2 March 1645, pp. 109–110.

Taylor, John, *The Carriers Cosmographie* (London: Printed by A. G. [Anne Griffin], 1637). USTC 3019285.

Tickell, John, *The History of the Town and County of Kingston Upon Hull* (Hull: Thomas Lee & Co., 1798).

Tildsley, John, *The True Relation of the Taking of the Town of Preston, by Colonell Seatons Forces from Manchester* (London: J. R. for Luke Fawn, 1642). USTC 3052212.

Trigge, Francis, *A Godly and Fruitfull Sermon Preached at Grantham 1592* (Oxford: Joseph Barnes, 1594). USTC 512686.

Trigge, Francis, *A touchstone, whereby may easilie be discerned, which is the true Catholike faith, of all them that professe the name of Catholiques in the Church of Englande, that they bee not deceived taken out of the Catholike Epistle of S. Jude* (London: Peter Short, 1599). USTC 514096.

Trigge, Francis, *A touchstone, whereby may easilie be discerned, which is the true Catholike faith, of all them that professe the name of Catholiques in the Church of Englande, that they bee not deceived taken out of the Catholike Epistle of S. Jude*, 2nd edition (London: Peter Short, 1600). USTC 514973.

Trigge, Francis, *An apologie, or defence of our dayes, against the vaine murmurings & complaints of manie wherein is plainly proved, that our dayes are more happie & blessed than the dayes of our forefathers* (London: John Wolfe, 1589). USTC 511333.

Trigge, Francis, *The svmme of true Catholike doctrine: plainly laid downe and prooued by scriptures and auncient fathers, and also by the testimonies of some of the best (even) of the Romish Catholikes themselues. Where also the true Catholike is rightly desciphered and taught what doctrine he ought to embrace, and what to auoid: so that hereby are handled, most of the weightiest matters of controversie, betwixt the pseudocatholickes and vs* (London: Humphrey Lownes for John Royston, 1613). USTC 3005561.

Trigge, Francis, *The true Catholique, formed according to the truth of the Scriptures, and the shape of the ancient fathers, and best sort of the latter Catholiques, which seeme to fauour the Church of Rome ...* (London: Peter Short, 1602). USTC 3000846.

Trigge, Francis, *To the Kings most excellent Maiestie. The humble petition of two sisters the Church and Common-wealth: for the restoring of their ancient commons and liberties, which late inclosure with depopulation, vncharitably hath taken away: containing seuen reasons as euidences for the same* (London: Felix Kingston for George Bishop, 1604). USTC 3001647 and 3001646.

Unknown author, *The Harmonious Consent of the Ministers of the Province within the County Palatine of Lancaster* (London: printed for Luke Fawne, 1648). USTC 3046480.

Wright, James, *The History and Antiquities of the County of Rutland* (London: Printed for Bennet Griffin, 1684). This edition not listed on the USTC.

Secondary Sources

Ammannati, Francesco and Angela Nuovo, 'Investigating Book Prices in Early Modern Europe: Questions and Sources', *JLIS.it: Italian Journal of Library and Information Science*, 8:3 (2017), pp. 1–25.

Anatolios, Khaled, *Athanasius: The Coherence of his Thought* (London: Routledge, 1998).

Andersen, Jennifer and Elizabeth Sauer, 'Current Trends in the History of Reading' in Jennifer Andersen and Elizabeth Sauer (eds), *Books and Readers in Early Modern England: Material Studies* (Philadelphia: University of Pennsylvania Press, 2002), pp. 1–20.

Aston, Margaret, 'Puritans and Iconoclasm, 1560–1660' in Christopher Durston and Jacqueline Eales (eds), *The Culture of English Puritanism, 1560–1700* (Basingstoke: Palgrave Macmillan, 1996), pp. 92–121.

Aston, Margaret, 'Segregation in Church' in W. J. Sheils and D. Wood (eds), *Women in the Church* (Oxford: Blackwell, 1990), pp. 237–294.

Aveling, Dom Hugh, *Post Reformation Catholicism in East Yorkshire, 1558–1790* (s. l.: East Yorkshire Local History Society, 1960).

Backus, Irena, *Historical Method and Confessional Identity in the Era of the Reformation (1378–1615)* (Leiden: Brill, 2003).

Baines, Edward, *History of the County Palatine and Duchy of Lancaster, Volume III* (London: Fisher, Son & Co., 1836).

Barnard, John and Maureen Bell, 'The English Provinces' in John Barnard, D. F. McKenzie and Maureen Bell (eds), *The Cambridge History of the Book in Britain, Volume IV: 1557–1695* (Cambridge: Cambridge University Press, 2002), pp. 665–686.

Barnard, John and Maureen Bell, *The Early Seventeenth-Century York Book Trade and John Foster's Inventory of 1616* (Leeds: The Leeds Philosophical and Literary Society Ltd, 1994).

Barr, C. B. L., 'Parish Libraries in a Region: the Case of Yorkshire', *Proceedings of the Library Association Study School and National Conference*, Nottingham, 1979, pp. 32–41.

Bayman, Anna, 'Printing, Learning, and the Unlearned' in Joad Raymond (ed.), *The Oxford History of Popular Print Culture: Volume One: Cheap Print in Britain and Ireland to 1660* (Oxford: Oxford University Press, 2011), pp. 76–87.

Beddard, R. A. P. J., 'Walker, Obadiah (1616–1699)', *Oxford Dictionary of National Biography*, (online, 2008).

Bellingradt, Daniel and Jeroen Salman, 'Books and Book History in Motion: Materiality, Sociality and Spatiality' in Daniel Bellingradt, Paul Nelles and Jeroen Salman (eds), *Books in Motion in Early Modern Europe: Beyond Production, Circulations and Consumption* (Cham: Palgrave Macmillan, 2017), pp. 1–11.

Bendall, Sarah, 'Speed, John (1551/2–1629)', *Oxford Dictionary of National Biography*, (online, 2008).

Best, Graham, 'Books and Readers in Certain Eighteenth-Century Parish Libraries', (Unpublished PhD Thesis, Loughborough University, 1985).

Blackwood, B. G., 'Parties and Issues in the Civil War in Lancashire', *Transactions of the Historic Society of Lancashire and Cheshire*, 132 (1982), pp. 99–125.

Blackwood, B. G., 'The Catholic and Protestant Gentry of Lancashire during the Civil War Period', *Transactions of the Historic Society of Lancashire and Cheshire*, 126 (1977), pp. 1–29.

Blades, William, *Bibliographical Miscellanies. No. 2. Books in Chains* (London: Blades, East & Blades, 1890).

Blades, William, *Books in Chains and Other Bibliographical Papers* (London: Elliot Stock, 1892).

Blair, Ann, 'An Early Modernist's Perspective', *Isis*, 95 (2004), pp. 420–430.

Blatchly, J. M., 'Ipswich Town Library', *The Book Collector*, 35:2 (1986), pp. 191–198.

Bliss, Philip, *Reliquiae Hearnianae: The Remains of Thomas Hearne, M.A., of Edmund Hall* (London: John Russell Smith, 1869).

Bossy, John, *Peace in the Post-Reformation* (Cambridge: Cambridge University Press, 1998).

Bradley, Simon and Nikolaus Pevsner, *London 1: The City of London* (London: Yale University Press, 2002).

Bradstock, Andrew, *Radical Religion in Cromwell's England: A Concise History from the English Civil War to the End of the Commonwealth* (London; New York: I. B. Tauris, 2011).

Bray, Gerald, *Documents of the English Reformation*, 3rd edition (Cambridge: James Clarke & Co., 2019).

Broadway, Jan, 'Harington, John, first Baron Harington of Exton, (1539/40–1613)', *Oxford Dictionary of National Biography*, (online, 2005).

Broadway, Jan, 'Hutton, Matthew (1638/9–1711)', *Oxford Dictionary of National Biography*, (online, 2008).

Brown, K. Brinkmann, 'Sarpi, Paolo (1552–1623)', *The Oxford Encyclopedia of the Reformation*, (online, 2005).

Bullett, Maggie, 'The Reception of the Elizabethan Religious Settlement in Three Yorkshire Parishes, 1559–72', *Northern History*, 48:2 (2011), pp. 225–252.

Calabresi, Bianca F. C., '"Red Incke": Reading the Bleeding on the Early Modern Page' in Douglas A. Brooks (ed.), *Printing and Parenting in Early Modern England* (Abingdon: Routledge, 2016), pp. 237–264.

Cambers, Andrew and Michelle Wolfe, 'Reading, Family Religion and Evangelical Identity in Late Stuart England', *The Historical Journal*, 47:4 (2004), pp. 875–896.

Cambers, Andrew, 'Pastoral Laudianism? Religious Politics in the 1630s: A Leicestershire Rector's Annotations', *Midland History*, 27:1 (2002), pp. 38–51.

Cambers, Andrew, *Godly Reading: Print, Manuscript and Puritanism in England, 1580–1720* (Cambridge: Cambridge University Press, 2011).

Carlyle, E. I. and Andrew McRae, 'Trigge, Francis (1547?–1606)', *Oxford Dictionary of National Biography*, (online, 2004).

Carr, William and Stuart Handley, 'Spelman, Clement (bap. 1598, d. 1679)', *Oxford Dictionary of National Biography*, (online, 2004).

Carron, Helen, 'William Sancroft (1617–93): A Seventeenth-Century Collector and his Library', *The Library*, 1:3 (2000), pp. 290–306.

Carter, Edmund, *The History of the County of Cambridge from the Earliest Account to the Present Time* (London, 1819).

Central Council for the Care of Churches, *The Parochial Libraries of the Church of England* (London: Faith Press, 1959).

Certain Sermons or Homilies, Appointed to be Read in Churches, in the Time of the Late Queen Elizabeth of Famous Memory (London: Printed for the Prayer-Book and Homily Society, 1852).

Chartier, Roger, *The Order of Books* (Cambridge: Polity Press, 1994).

Cheney, C. R., 'The so-called Statues of John Pecham and Robert Winchelsey for the Province of Canterbury', *The Journal of Ecclesiastical History*, 12:1 (1961), pp. 14–34.

Chernaik, Warren, 'Chillingworth, William, (1602–1644)', *Oxford Dictionary of National Biography*, (online, 2010).

Christie, Richard Copley, *The Old Church and School Libraries of Lancashire* (Manchester: Charles E. Simms for the Chetham Society, New Series, 7, 1885).

Clair, Colin, *A History of European Printing* (London: Academic Press, 1976).

Clark, Andrew (ed.), *The Life and Times of Anthony Wood, antiquary, of Oxford, 1632–1695, described by Himself, Volume I: 1632–1663* (Oxford: Clarendon Press, 1891).

Clark, Andrew (ed.), *The Life and Times of Anthony Wood, antiquary, of Oxford, 1632–1695, described by Himself, Volume III: 1664–1681* (Oxford: Clarendon Press, 1892).

Clark, John Willis, *The Care of Books: An Essay on the Development of Libraries and their Fittings, from the Earliest Times to the end of the Eighteenth Century* (Cambridge: Cambridge University Press, 1901).

Clarke, Elizabeth R., 'Oley, Barnabas (bap. 1602, d. 1686)', *Oxford Dictionary of National Biography*, (online, 2008).

Clay, C. G. A., *Economic Expansion and Social Change: England, 1500–1700. Volume I: People, Land and Towns* (Cambridge: Cambridge University Press, 1984).

Coffey, John and Paul C. H. Lim, 'Introduction' in John Coffey and Paul C. H. Lim (eds), *The Cambridge Companion to Puritanism* (Cambridge: Cambridge University Press, 2008), pp. 1–15.

Coffey, John, 'Puritanism and Liberty Revisited: The Case for Toleration in the English Revolution', *The Historical Journal*, 41:4 (1998), pp. 961–985.

Colby, Andrew M., 'Dolben, John (1625–1686)', *Oxford Dictionary of National Biography*, (online, 2006).

Collier, Jay T., *Debating Perseverance: The Augustinian Heritage in Post-Reformation England* (New York: Oxford University Press, 2018).

Collins, Jeffrey R., 'The Church Settlement of Oliver Cromwell', *History*, 87:285 (2002), pp. 18–40.

Collinson, Patrick and John Craig, 'Introduction' in Patrick Collinson and John Craig (eds), *The Reformation in English Towns, 1500–1640* (Basingstoke: Macmillan, 1998), pp. 1–19.

Collinson, Patrick, 'The Politics of Religion and the Religion of Politics in Elizabethan England', *Historical Research*, 82:215 (2009), pp. 74–92.

Collinson, Patrick, Arnold Hunt and Alexandra Walsham, 'Religious Publishing in England, 1557–1640' in John Barnard, D. F. McKenzie and Maureen Bell (eds), *The Cambridge History of the Book in Britain, Volume IV: 1557–1695* (Cambridge: Cambridge University Press, 2002), pp. 29–66.

Collinson, Patrick, *The Birthpangs of Protestant England: Religious and Cultural Change in the Sixteenth and Seventeenth Centuries* (Basingstoke: Macmillan Press, 1988).

Condren, Conal, 'More Parish Library, Salop', *Library History*, 7:5 (1987), pp. 141–162.

Cooper, David and Ian N. Gregory, 'Mapping the English Lake District: a Literary GIS', *Transactions of the Institute of British Geographers*, New Series, 36:1 (2011), pp. 89–108.

Cornwall, Robert D., 'The Search for the Primitive Church: The Use of Early Church Fathers in the High Church Anglican Tradition, 1680–1745', *Anglican and Episcopal History*, 59 (1990), pp. 303–329.

Coulton, Barbara, 'The Establishment of Protestantism in a Provincial Town: A Study of Shrewsbury in the Sixteenth Century', *The Sixteenth Century Journal*, 27:2 (1996), pp. 307–335.

Couth, Bill, *Grantham During the Interregnum: The Hallbook of Grantham, 1641–1649* (Woodbridge: The Boydell Press for Lincoln Record Society, 1995).

Cowie, Leonard W., 'Bray, Thomas (bap. 1658, d. 1730)', *Oxford Dictionary of National Biography*, (online, 2012).

Craig, John, 'The Growth of English Puritanism' in John Coffey and Paul C. H. Lim (eds), *The Cambridge Companion to Puritanism* (Cambridge: Cambridge University Press, 2008), pp. 34–47.

Crawford, Julie, 'Reconsidering Early Modern Women's Reading, or, How Margaret Hoby Read her de Mornay', *Huntington Library Quarterly*, 73:2 (2010), pp. 193–223.

Cressy, David, 'Book Burning in Tudor and Stuart England', *The Sixteenth Century Journal*, 36 (2005), pp. 359–374.

Cressy, David, 'Educational Opportunity in Tudor and Stuart England', *History of Education Quarterly*, 16 (1976), pp. 301–320.

Cressy, David, *Birth, Marriage, and Death: Ritual, Religion, and the Life-Cycle in Tudor and Stuart England* (Oxford: Oxford University Press, 1997).

Cressy, David, *Literacy and the Social Order: Reading and Writing in Tudor and Stuart England* (Cambridge: Cambridge University Press, 1980).

Crome, Andrew, 'Constructing the Political Prophet in 1640s England', *The Seventeenth Century*, 26 (2011), pp. 279–298.

Crosby, Alan G., 'Chetham, Humphrey (bap. 1580, d. 1653)', *Oxford Dictionary of National Biography*, (online, 2008).

Cross, Clare, 'The Church in England, 1646–1660' in G. E. Aylmer (ed.), *The Interregnum: the Quest for Settlement, 1646–1660* (London: Macmillan, 1972), pp. 99–120.

Crossley, James (ed.), *The Diary and Correspondence of Dr. John Worthington, Volume II, Part I* (Manchester: Charles Simms and Co. for the Chetham Society, 1855).

Darnton, Robert, 'First Steps toward a History of Reading', *Australian Journal of French Studies*, 23 (1986), pp. 5–30.

Darnton, Robert, 'What is the History of Books?', *Daedalus*, 111 (1982), pp. 65–83.

Daybell, James, 'Interpreting letters and reading script: evidence for female education and literacy in Tudor England', *History of Education*, 34 (2005), pp. 695–715.

Deanesly, Margaret, *The Lollard Bible: And Other Medieval Biblical Versions* (Cambridge: Cambridge University Press, 1920).

Dibdin, Thomas Frognall, *A Bibliographical Antiquarian and Picturesque Tour in the Northern Counties of England and in Scotland, Volume I* (London: C. Richards, 1838).

Ditchfield, Simon and Helen Smith, 'Introduction' in Simon Ditchfield and Helen Smith (eds), *Conversions: Gender and Religious Change in Early Modern Europe* (Manchester: Manchester University Press, 2017), pp. 1–20.

Dixon, C. Scott, *The Church in the Early Modern Age* (London: I. B. Tauris, 2016).

Dods, Marcus (trans. and ed.), *The City of God, Volume I* (Edinburgh: T. & T. Clark, 1871).

Duff, E. Gordon, *A Century of the English Book Trade* (London: Blades, East & Blades, 1905).

Duffy, Eamon, 'The Long Reformation: Catholicism, Protestantism and the Multitude' in Nicholas Tyacke (ed.), *England's Long Reformation, 1500–1800* (London: UCL Press, 2003), pp. 33–70.

Duffy, Eamon, *The Stripping of the Altars: Traditional Religion in England 1400–1580*, 2nd edition (New Haven and London: Yale University Press, 2005).

Dugmore, C. W., *The Mass and the English Reformers* (London: Macmillan, 1958).

Durston, Christopher and Jacqueline Eales, 'Introduction: The Puritan Ethos, 1560–1700' in Christopher Durston and Jacqueline Eales (eds), *The Culture of English Puritanism, 1560–1700* (London: Macmillan Press, 1996), pp. 1–31.

Durston, Christopher, 'By the Book or with the Spirit: the Debate over Liturgical Prayer during the English Revolution', *Historical Research*, 79:203 (2006), pp. 50–73.

Dyer, Alan, 'Small Market Towns, 1540–1700' in Peter Clark (ed.), *The Cambridge Urban History of Britain, Volume II: 1540–1840* (Cambridge: Cambridge University Press, 2000), pp. 425–450.

Farmer, Alan B. and Zachary Lesser, 'Structures of Popularity in the Early Modern Book Trade', *Shakespeare Quarterly*, 56:2 (2005), pp. 206–213.

Farmer, Alan B., 'Cosmopolitanism and Foreign Books in Early Modern England', *Shakespeare Studies*, 35 (2007), pp. 58–65.

Farrer, William and J. Brownbill (eds), *The Victoria History of the County of Lancaster, Volume IV* (London: Constable and Company, 1911).

Feingold, Mordechai, 'The Humanities' in Nicholas Tyacke (ed.), *The History of the University of Oxford, Volume IV: Seventeenth-Century Oxford* (Oxford: Oxford University Press, 1997), pp. 211–358.

Felch, Susan M. (ed.), *Elizabeth Tywhit's Morning and Evening Prayers* (Aldershot: Ashgate, 2008).

Fisher, R. M., 'William Crashawe and the Middle Temple Globes, 1605–15', *The Geographical Journal*, 140:1 (1974), pp. 105–112.

Fitch, J. A., 'Some Ancient Suffolk Parochial Libraries', *Proceedings of the Suffolk Institute for Archaeology and History*, 30:3 (1964), pp. 44–87.

Fitch, John, 'Historical Introduction' in *Suffolk Parish Libraries: A Catalogue* (London: Mansell, 1977).

Flanders, Judith, *A Place for Everything: The Curious History of Alphabet Order* (Basingstoke: Picador, 2020).

Fletcher, J. M J., *A Dorset Worthy, William Stone, Royalist and Divine (1615–1685)* (Dorchester: Dorset County Chronicle Printing Works, 1915).

Ford, Margaret Lane, 'Importation of Printed Books into England and Scotland' in Lotte Hellinga and J. B. Trapp (eds), *The Cambridge History of the Book in Britain, III: 1400–1557* (Cambridge: Cambridge University Press, 1999), pp. 179–201.

Foster, C. W. (ed.), *Lincoln Episcopal Records in the Time of Thomas Cooper, S.T.P., Bishop of Lincoln, A.D. 1571 to A.D. 1584* (London: printed for the Canterbury and York Society, 1913).

Foster, C. W. (ed.), *The State of the Church in the Reigns of Elizabeth and James I as Illustrated by Documents relating to the Diocese of Lincoln, Volume I* (s. l.: Alpha Editions, 2020).

Foster, Joseph (ed.), *Alumni Oxonienses: The Members of the University of Oxford, 1500–1714, Volume I – Early Series* (Oxford: Parker & Co., 1891).

Foster, Joseph (ed.), *Alumni Oxonienses: The Members of the University of Oxford, 1500–1714, Volume II – Early Series* (Oxford: Parker & Co., 1891).

Foster, Joseph (ed.), *Alumni Oxoniensis: the Members of the University of Oxford, 1500–1714: Volume IV – Early Series* (Oxford: James Parker & Co., 1891).

Foster, Joseph, *The Register of Admissions to Gray's Inn, 1521–1889* (London: the Hansard Publishing Union, Limited, 1889).

Fowler, J. T., 'Ripon Minster and its Founder', *The Yorkshire Archaeological and Topographical Journal*, 2 (1873), pp. 371–402.

Fox, Adam, 'Religion and Popular Literature Culture in England', *Archiv für Reformationsgeschichte-Archive for Reformation History*, 95 (2004), pp. 266–282.

French, Anna, 'Raising Christian Children in Early Modern England: Salvation, Education and the Family', *Theology*, 116:2 (2013), pp. 93–102.

French, Gilbert J. (ed.), *Bibliographical Notices of the Church Libraries at Turton and Gorton, bequeathed by Humphrey Chetham*, printed for the Chetham Society (Manchester: Charles Simms and Co., 1855).

French, H. R., 'The Search for the "Middle Sort of People" in England, 1600–1800', *The Historical Journal*, 43:1 (2000), pp. 277–293.

Frere, Walter Howard (ed.), *Visitation Articles and Injunctions of the Period of the Reformation, Volume II, 1536–1558* (London: Longmans, Green & Co., 1910).

Frere, Walter Howard (ed.), *Visitation Articles and Injunctions of the Period of the Reformation, Volume III, 1559–1575* (London: Longmans, Green & Co., 1910).

Frost, Carolyn O., 'The Bodleian Catalogs of 1674 and 1738: An Examination in the Light of Modern Cataloging Theory', *The Library Quarterly: Information, Community, Policy*, 46:3 (1976), pp. 248–270.

Gants, David L., 'A Quantitative Analysis of the London Book Trade, 1614–1618', *Studies in Bibliography*, 55 (2002), pp. 185–213.

Gee, Henry and William John Hardy (eds), *Documents Illustrative of English Church History* (London: Macmillan and Co., 1896).

Gee, Stacey, 'Parochial Libraries in Pre-Reformation England' in Sarah Rees Jones (ed.), *Learning and Literacy in Medieval England and Abroad* (Turnhout: Brepols, 2003), pp. 199–222.

Gibbons, Alfred, *Early Lincoln Wills: An Abstract of all the Wills and Administrations Recorded by the Episcopal Registers of the Old Diocese of Lincoln … 1280–1547* (Lincoln: James Williamson, 1888).

Gilbert, C. D., 'Hall, Thomas (1610–1665)', *Oxford Dictionary of National Biography*, (online, 2015).

Girouard, Mark, *Life in the English Country House* (London: Yale University Press, 1978).

Glenn, John and David Walsh, *Catalogue of the Francis Trigge Chained Library, St Wulfram's Church, Grantham* (Cambridge: D. S. Brewer, 1988).

Glenn, John, 'A Sixteenth-Century Library: the Francis Trigge Chained Library of St Wulfram's Church, Grantham' in Daniel Williams (ed.), *Early Tudor England:*

Proceedings of the 1987 Harlaxton Symposium (Woodbridge: The Boydell Press, 1989), pp. 61–71.

Good, James I., *History of the Reformed Church of Germany, 1620–1890* (Reading, PA: Daniel Miller, 1894).

Goose, Nigel, 'English Pre-Industrial Urban Economies' in Jonathan Barry (ed.), *The Tudor and Stuart Town: A Reader in English Urban History, 1530–1688* (London: Longman, 1990), pp. 63–73.

Goudriaan, Aza, 'Athansius in Reformed Protestantism: Some Aspects of Reception History (1527–1607)', *Church History and Religious Culture*, 90:2/3 (2010), pp. 257–276.

Gratton, Malcolm, 'Mosley, Nicholas', *Oxford History of National Biography*, (online, 2004).

Graves, C. Pamela, 'Social space in the English medieval parish church', *Economy and Society*, 18:3 (1989), pp. 297–322.

Gray, Sarah and Chris Baggs, 'The English Parish Library: a Celebration of Diversity', *Libraries & Culture*, 35 (2000), pp. 414–433.

Green, Ian and Kate Peters, 'Religious Publishing in England, 1640–1695' in John Barnard, D. F. McKenzie and Maureen Bell (eds), *The Cambridge History of the Book in Britain, Volume IV: 1557–1695* (Cambridge: Cambridge University Press, 2002), pp. 67–94.

Green, Ian, 'Career Prospects and Clerical Conformity in the Early Stuart Church', *Past & Present*, 90 (1981), pp. 71–115.

Green, Ian, 'Libraries for School Education and Personal Devotion' in Giles Mandelbrote and K. A. Manley (eds), *The Cambridge History of Libraries in Britain and Ireland, Volume II: 1640–1850* (Cambridge: Cambridge University Press, 2006), pp. 47–64.

Green, Ian, 'Preaching in the Parishes' in Peter McCullough, Hugh Adlington and Emma Rhatigan (eds), *The Oxford Handbook of the Early Modern Sermon* (Oxford: Oxford University Press, 2011), pp. 137–154.

Green, Ian, 'Varieties of Domestic Devotion in Early Modern English Protestantism' in Jessica Martin and Alec Ryrie (eds), *Private and Domestic Devotion in Early Modern Britain* (Ashgate: Routledge, 2017), pp. 9–32.

Green, Ian, *Print and Protestantism in Early Modern England* (Oxford: Oxford University Press, 2000).

Green, Ian, *The Christian's ABC: Catechisms and Catechizing in England, c. 1530–1740* (Oxford: Oxford University Press, 2004).

Gregory, Ian N. and Paul S. Ell, *Historical GIS: Technologies, Methodologies and Scholarship* (Cambridge: Cambridge University Press, 2007).

Gregory, Ian N., *A Place in History: A Guide to using GIS in Historical Research* (Oxford: Oxbow Books, 2003).

Guscott, S. J., *Humphrey Chetham, 1580–1653: Fortune, Politics and Mercantile Culture in Seventeenth-century England* (Manchester: The Chetham Society, 2003).

Hackel, Heidi Brayman, "'Boasting of Silence": Women Readers in a Patriarchal State' in Kevin Sharpe and Steven N. Zwicker (eds), *Reading, Society and Politics in Early Modern England* (Cambridge: Cambridge University Press, 2009), pp. 101–121.

Haigh, Christopher, 'The Continuity of Catholicism in the English Reformation', *Past & Present*, 93 (1981), pp. 37–69.

Hill, Christopher, *Antichrist in Seventeenth-Century England*, revised edition (London, New York: Verso, 1990).

Haigh, Christopher, *Reformation and Resistance in Tudor Lancashire* (Cambridge: Cambridge University Press, 1975).

Haigh, Christopher, *The Plain Man's Pathways to Heaven: Kinds of Christianity in Post-Reformation England, 1570–1640* (Oxford: Oxford University Press, 2007).

Hallett, Cecil, *The Cathedral Church of Ripon: A Short History of the Church and a Description of its Fabric* (London: George Bell and Sons, 1901).

Halley, Robert, *Lancashire: its Puritanism and Nonconformity*, 2nd edition (Manchester: Tubbs and Brook; London: Hodder and Stoughton, 1872).

Hambrick-Stowe, Charles E., 'Practical Divinity and Spirituality' in John Coffey and Paul C. H. Lim (eds), *The Cambridge Companion to Puritanism* (Cambridge: Cambridge University Press, 2008), pp. 191–205.

Handley, Stuart, 'Spelman, Sir Henry (1563/4–1641)', *Oxford Dictionary of National Biography*, (online, 2005).

Hardy, Nicholas, 'The Septuagint and the Transformation of Biblical Scholarship in England, from the King James Bible (1611) to the London Polyglot (1657)' in Kevin Killeen, Helen Smith and Rachel Willie (eds.), *The Oxford Handbook of the Bible in Early Modern England, c. 1530–1700* (Oxford: Oxford University Press, 2018), pp. 117–130.

Harris, Kate, 'The Patronage and Dating of Longleat House MS 24, a Prestige Copy of the *Pupilla Oculi* Illuminated by the Master of the *Troilus* Frontispiece' in Felicity Riddy (ed.), *Prestige, Authority and Power in Late-Medieval Manuscripts and Texts* (Woodbridge: York Medieval Press, 2000).

Heath, Peter, *The English Parish Clergy on the Eve of the Reformation* (Abingdon: Routledge, 2007).

Hegarty, A. J., 'Prideaux, John (1578–1650)', *Oxford Dictionary of National Biography*, (online, 2008).

Helm, Paul, *Calvin at the Centre* (Oxford: Oxford University Press, 2010).

Herbert, Anne L., 'Oakham Parish Library', *Library History*, 6:1 (1982), pp. 1–11.

Hill, Christopher, 'God and the English Revolution', *History Workshop*, 17 (1984), pp. 19–31.

Hill, Christopher, *Economic Problems of the Church from Archbishop Whitgift to the Long Parliament* (New York: Oxford University Press, 1956).

Hill, Christopher, *Society and Puritanism in Pre-Revolutionary England* (London: Secker and Warburg, 1964).

Hillebrand, Hans J. (ed.), *The Oxford Encyclopedia of the Reformation*, (online, 2005).

Hingeston-Randolph, F. C. (ed.), *The Register of Edmund Stafford, (A.D. 1396–1419)* (London: George Bell and Sons, 1886).

Hinks, John, 'The Book Trade in Early Modern Britain: Centres, Peripheries and Networks' in Benito Rial Costas (ed.), *Print Culture and Peripheries in Early Modern Europe: A Contribution to the History of Printing and the Book Trade in Small European and Spanish Cities* (Leiden: Brill, 2012), pp. 101–126.

Hoare, Peter, 'Some Parochial Libraries in the East Midlands', *Library & Information History*, 27:4 (2011), pp. 223–228.

Houlbrooke, Ralph, *Death, Religion and the Family in England, 1480–1750* (Oxford: Clarendon Press, 2000).

Houston, R. A., *Literacy in Early Modern Europe: Culture and Education, 1500–1800*, 2nd edition (Harlow: Longman, 2002).

Houston, R. A., *Punishing the Dead?: Suicide, Lordship, and Community in Britain, 1500–1830* (Oxford: Oxford University Press, 2010).

Hughes, Ann, 'Puritanism and Gender' in John Coffey and Paul C. H. Lim (eds), *The Cambridge Companion to Puritanism* (Cambridge: Cambridge University Press, 2008), pp. 294–308.

Hunt, Arnold, 'Clerical and Parish Libraries' in Elisabeth Leedham-Green and Teresa Webber (eds), *The Cambridge History of Libraries, Volume 1, to 1640* (Cambridge: Cambridge University Press, 2008), pp. 400–419.

Hutton, Ronald, 'The Local Impact of the Tudor Reformations' in Christopher Haigh (ed.), *The English Reformation Revised* (Cambridge: Cambridge University Press, 1987), pp. 114–138.

Hutton, Sarah, 'More, Henry (1614–1687)', *Oxford Dictionary of National Biography*, (online, 2008).

Irwin, Raymond, *The Heritage of the English Library* (London: George Allen & Unwin Ltd, 1964).

Jack, Sybil M., *Towns in Tudor and Stuart Britain* (Basingstoke: Macmillan, 1996).

Jackson, H. J., *Marginalia: Readers Writing in Books* (New Haven; London: Yale University Press, 2001).

Jacob, W. M., 'Libraries and Philanthropy, 1690–1740', *Bulletin of the Association of British Theological and Philosophical Libraries*, 4:2 (1997), pp. 6–12.

Jacob, W. M., 'Libraries for the Parish: Individual Donors and Charitable Societies' in Giles Mandelbrote and K. A. Manley (eds), *The Cambridge History of Libraries in Britain and Ireland, Volume II: 1640–1850* (Cambridge: Cambridge University Press, 2006), pp. 65–82.

Jacob, W. M., 'Parochial Libraries and their Users', *Library and Information History*, 27:4 (2011), pp. 211–216.

Jajdelska, Elspeth, 'Pepys in the History of Reading', *The Historical Journal*, 50 (2007), pp. 549–569.

Jardine, Lisa and Anthony Grafton, '"Studied for Action": How Gabriel Harvey Read His Livy', *Past & Present*, 129 (1990), pp. 30–78.

Jenkins, Gary W., *John Jewel and the English National Church: The Dilemmas of an Erastian Reformer* (Ashgate: Routledge, 2006).

Jewell, Helen M., *Education in Early Modern England* (Basingstoke: Macmillan Press, 1998).

Johns, Adrian, *The Nature of the Book: Print and Knowledge in the Making* (London: University of Chicago Press, 1998).

Kainulainen, Jaska, *Paolo Sarpi: A Servant of God and State* (Leiden: Brill, 2014).

Keitt, Andrew W., *Inventing the Sacred: Imposture, Inquisition, and the Boundaries of the Supernatural in Golden Age Spain* (Boston: Brill, 2005).

Kelly, Thomas, 'Historical Introduction' in Shropshire County Library (eds), *Catalogue of Books from Parochial Libraries in Shropshire* (London: Mansell, 1971), pp. vii–xii.

Kelly, Thomas, *Early Public Libraries: a History of the Public Libraries in Great Britain before 1850* (London: Library Association, 1966).

Ker, N. R. (ed.), *Medieval Libraries of Great Britain: A List of Surviving Books*, 2nd edition (London: Royal Historical Society, 1964).

Killeen, Kevin, Helen Smith, and Rachel Willie (eds), *The Oxford Handbook of the Bible in Early Modern England, c. 1530–1700* (Oxford: Oxford University Press, 2018).

Killeen, Kevin, Helen Smith, and Rachel Willie, 'Introduction to Part II', in Kevin Killeen, Helen Smith, and Rachel Willie (eds), *The Oxford Handbook of the Bible in Early Modern England, c. 1530–1700* (Oxford: Oxford University Press, 2018), pp. 113–115.

King, John N. and Mark Rankin, 'Print, Patronage and the Reception of Continental Reform: 1521–1603', *The Yearbook of English Studies*, 38 (2008), pp. 49–67.

Kishlansky, Mark, *A Monarchy Transformed: Britain, 1603–1714* (London: Penguin Books, 1997).

Knighton, C. S., 'Busby, Richard (1606–1695)', *Oxford Dictionary of National Biography*, (online, 2004).

Kolb, R., 'Chemnitz, Martin (1522–1586)', *The Oxford Encyclopedia of the Reformation*, (online, 2005).

Kramer, Fred (trans.), *Examination of the Council of Trent, Part I* by Martin Chemnitz (London: Concordia Publishing House, 1971).

Kramer, Fred (trans.), *Examination of the Council of Trent, Part II* by Martin Chemnitz (London: Concordia Publishing House, 1971).

Kramer, Fred (trans.), *Examination of the Council of Trent, Part III* by Martin Chemnitz (London: Concordia Publishing House, 1971).

Kramer, Fred (trans.), *Examination of the Council of Trent, Part IV* by Martin Chemnitz (London: Concordia Publishing House, 1971).

Kriegshauser, Laurence, *Praying the Psalms in Christ* (Notre Dame, Indiana: University of Notre Dame Press, 2019).

Kunze, Johannes, 'Chemnitz (Kemnitz), Martin' in Philip Schaff (ed.), *The New Schaff-Herzog Encyclopedia of Religious Knowledge, Volume III: Chamier-Draendorf* (Grand Rapids, Michigan: Baker Book House, 1950), pp. 24–25.

Lake, Peter, 'Anti-Popery: the Structure of a Prejudice' in Richard Cust and Ann Hughes (eds), *Conflict in Early Stuart England: Studies in Religion and Politics, 1603–1642* (London: Longman, 1989), pp. 72–106.

Lake, Peter, 'Puritanism, Arminianism and a Shropshire Axe-Murder', *Midland History*, 40 (1990), pp. 37–64.

Lake, Peter, *Moderate Puritans and the Elizabethan Church* (Cambridge: Cambridge University Press, 1982).

Lamont, William M., *Godly Rule: Politics and Religion, 1603–60* (London: Macmillan and Co. Ltd, 1969).

Leinsle, Ulrich G., 'Sources, Methods, and Forms of Early Modern Theology' in Ulrich L. Lehner, Richard A. Muller and A. G. Roeber (eds), *The Oxford Handbook of Early Modern Theology, 1600–1800* (Oxford: Oxford University Press, 2016), pp. 25–42.

Leland, John, *The Laboryouse Journey & Serche of John Leylande, for Englandes Antiquitees* (London: John Bale, 1549, reprinted Manchester: Priory Press, 1895).

Letham, Robert, 'Amandus Polanus: A Neglected Theologian?', *The Sixteenth Century Journal*, 21:3 (1990), pp. 463–476.

Leu, Urs B., 'The Book and Reading Culture in Basel and Zurich during the Sixteenth Century' in Malcolm Walsby and Graeme Kemp (eds), *The Book Triumphant: Print in Transition in the Sixteenth and Seventeenth Centuries* (Leiden: Brill, 2011), pp. 295–319.

Levy, F. J., 'Savile, Henry, of Banke (1568–1617)', *Oxford Dictionary of National Biography*, (online, 2004).

Lim, Paul C. H., 'Puritans and the Church of England: Historiography and Ecclesiology' in John Coffey and Paul C. H. Lim (eds), *The Cambridge Companion to Puritanism* (Cambridge: Cambridge University Press, 2008), pp. 223–240.

Luttmer, Frank, 'Persecutors, Tempters and Vassals of the Devil: The Unregenerate in Puritan Practical Divinity', *Journal of Ecclesiastical History*, 51 (2000), pp. 37–68.

MacCulloch, Diarmaid, *Reformation: Europe's House Divided, 1490–1700* (London: Penguin, 2004).

MacDonald, Michael and Terence R. Murphy, *Sleepless Souls: Suicide in Early Modern England* (Oxford: Clarendon Press, 1990).

MacGeagh, Henry F. and H. A. C. Sturgess (eds), *Register of Admissions to the Honourable Society of the Middle Temple: From the Fifteenth Century to the Year 1944, Volume 1: Fifteenth Century to 1781* (London: Butterworth & Co. Ltd., 1949).

Maclean, Ian, 'La Mothe le Vayer, François de (1588–1672)', *The New Oxford Companion to Literature in French* (Oxford: Oxford University Press, 1995), p. 437.

Maltby, Judith, '"Extravagancies and Impertinencies": Set Forms, Conceived and Extempore Prayer in Revolutionary England' in Natalie Mears and Alec Ryrie (eds), *Worship and the Parish church in Early Modern Britain* (Farnham: Ashgate, 2013), pp. 221–243.

Maltby, Judith, *Prayer Book and People in Elizabethan and Early Stuart England* (Cambridge: Cambridge University Press, 2009).

Manterfield, John B., *Newton's Grantham: The Hall Book and Life in a Puritan Town* (Grantham: Grantham Civic Society, 2014).

Marsh, Christopher, 'Order and Place in England, 1580–1640: The View from the Pew', *Journal of British Studies*, 44: 1 (2005), pp. 3–26.

Marshall, Peter, *Beliefs and the Dead in Reformation England* (Oxford: Oxford University Press, 2002).

Marshall, Peter, *Heretics and Believers: A History of the English Reformation* (London: Yale University Press, 2018).

Martin, Charles Trice (ed.), *Minutes of Parliament of the Middle Temple, Volume III: 1650–1703* (London: Butterworth & Co. Ltd., 1905).

Martin, Jessica, 'Early Modern English Piety' in Anthony Milton (ed.), *The Oxford History of Anglicanism, Volume 1: Reformation and Identity, c. 1520–1662* (Oxford: Oxford University Press, 2019), pp. 395–411.

Mayo, Charles, *A History of Wimborne Minster* (London: Bell and Daldy, 1860).

McCullough, Peter, 'Print, Publication, and Religious Politics in Caroline England', *The Historical Journal*, 51:2 (2008), pp. 285–313.

McGrath, Alister E., *Christian Theology: An Introduction*, 6th edition (Chichester: Wiley-Blackwell, 2017).

McGrath, Alister E., *Historical Theology: An Introduction to the History of Christian Thought*, 2nd edition (Oxford: Wiley-Blackwell, 2013).

McGrath, Alister E., *Reformation Thought: An Introduction*, 4th edition (Oxford: Wiley-Blackwell, 2012).

McKerrow, R. B. (ed.), *A Dictionary of Printers and Booksellers in England, Scotland and Ireland, and of Foreign Printers of English Books 1557–1640* (London: Blades, East & Blades, 1910).

McKitterick, David, 'University Printing at Oxford and Cambridge' in John Barnard, D. F. McKenzie and Maureen Bell (eds), *The Cambridge History of the Book in Britain, Volume IV: 1557–1695* (Cambridge: Cambridge University Press, 2002), pp. 189–205.

McLaren, Anne, 'Gender, Religion and Early Modern Nationalism: Elizabeth I, Mary Queen of Scots, and the Genesis of English Anti-Catholicism', *The American Historical Review*, 107:3 (2002), pp. 739–767.

McMullen, Norma, 'The Education of English Gentlewomen, 1540–1640', *History of Education*, 6 (1977), pp. 87–101.

McNulty, Robert, 'The Protestant Version of Robert Parsons' "*The First Booke of the Christian Exercise*"', *Huntington Library Quarterly*, 22:4 (1959), pp. 271–300.

Meyers, Thomas, *Commentaries on the Book of the Prophet Daniel by John Calvin* (Grand Rapids, MI: Christian Classics Ethereal Library, 1999).

Milton, Anthony, 'Introduction: Reformation, Identity and "Anglicanism"' in Anthony Milton (ed.), *The Oxford History of Anglicanism, Volume I: Reformation and Identity, c. 1520–1662* (Oxford: Oxford University Press, 2019), pp. 1–27.

Milton, Anthony, 'Unsettled Reformations, 1603–1662' in Anthony Milton (ed.), *The Oxford History of Anglicanism, Volume I: Reformation and Identity, c. 1520–1662* (Oxford: Oxford University Press, 2019), pp. 63–83.

Milton, Anthony, *Catholic and Reformed: The Roman and Protestant Churches in English Protestant Thought, 1600–1640* (Cambridge: Cambridge University Press, 1995).

Mitchell, Ian, '"Old Books – New Bound"? Selling Second-Hand Books in England, c. 1680–1850' in Jon Stobart and Ilja Van Damme (eds), *Modernity and the second-hand trade: European consumption cultures and practices, 1700–1900* (Basingstoke: Palgrave Macmillan, 2010), pp. 139–157.

Moore, Roger E., 'Sir Philp Sidney's Defense of Prophesying', *Studies in English Literature, 1500–1900*, 5:1 (2000), pp. 35–62.

Moran, Jo Ann Hoeppner, *The Growth of English Schooling, 1340–1548: Learning, Literacy and Laicization in Pre-Reformation York Diocese* (Princeton: Princeton University Press, 2014).

Morrissey, Mary, 'Sermons, Primers, and Prayerbooks' in Joad Raymond (ed.), *The Oxford History of Popular Print Culture: Volume One: Cheap Print in Britain and Ireland to 1660* (Oxford: Oxford University Press, 2011), pp. 491–509.

Mortimer, Jean E., *The Library Catalogue of Anthony Higgin: Dean of Ripon (1608–1624)* (Leeds: Chorley and Pickersgill, 1962).

Mumby, Frank A. and Ian Norrie, *Publishing and Bookselling*, 5th edition (London: Cape, 1974).

Murphy, G. Martin, 'Sherlock, Paul (1595–1646)', *Oxford Dictionary of National Biography*, (online, 2008).

Mynors, A. B., 'Kempsford', *Transactions of the Bristol and Gloucestershire Archaeological Society*, 57 (1935), pp. 192–233.

Newman, John and Nikolaus Pevsner, *The Buildings of England: Dorset* (London: Yale University Press, 2002).

Nicholson, William (ed.), *The Remains of Edmund Grindal* (Cambridge: Cambridge University Press, 1843).

Oates, Rosamund, "'Far Off from the Well's Head": The Production and Circulation of Books in Early Modern Yorkshire' in Rosamund Oates and Jessica G. Purdy (eds), *Communities of Print: Readers and their Books in Early Modern Europe* (Leiden: Brill, 2021).

Oates, Rosamund, 'Tobie Matthew and the Establishment of the Godly Commonwealth in England: 1560–1606', (Unpublished PhD Thesis, University of York, 2003).

Oates, Rosamund, *Moderate Radical: Tobie Matthew and the English Reformation* (Oxford: Oxford University Press, 2018).

Orr, Leah, 'Prices of English Books at Auction *c.* 1680', *The Library*, 20 (2019), pp. 501–526.

Owen, John (trans. and ed.), *Commentaries on the Catholic Epistles by John Calvin* (Edinburgh: T. Constable, 1855).

Pailin, David A., 'Herbert, Edward, first Baron Herbert of Cherbury and first Baron Herbert of Castle Ireland, (1582?–1648)', *Oxford Dictionary of National Biography*, (2009).

Palliser, D. M., *Tudor York* (Oxford: Oxford University Press, 1979).

Pantin, W. A., *The English Church in the Fourteenth Century* (Cambridge: Cambridge University Press, 2010).

Parkinson, Richard (ed.), *The Life of Adam Martindale* (Manchester: Charles Simms and Co. for the Chetham Society, 1845).

Parmalee, Lisa Ferraro, 'Printers, Patrons, Readers, and Spies: Importation of French Propaganda in Elizabethan England', *The Sixteenth Century Journal*, 25:4 (1994), pp. 853–872.

Patten, John, *English Towns, 1500–1700* (Folkestone: Dawson, 1978).

Patterson, W. B., *William Perkins and the Making of a Protestant England* (Oxford: Oxford University Press, 2014).

Peacock, Edward (ed.), *English Church Furniture, Ornaments and Decorations, at the Period of the Reformation* (London: John Camden Hotten, 1866).

Pearson, David, 'Patterns of Book Ownership in Late Seventeenth-Century England', *The Library*, 11 (2010), pp. 139–167.

Pearson, David, 'Scholars and bibliophiles: book collectors in Oxford, 1550–1650' in Robin Myers and Michael Harris (eds), *Antiquaries, Book Collectors and the Circles of Learning* (Winchester: St Paul's Bibliographies, 1996), pp. 1–26.

Pearson, David, 'The Libraries of English Bishops, 1600–1640', *The Library*, 14 (1992), pp. 221–257.

Pearson, David, *Provenance Research in Book History: A Handbook* (Oxford: The Bodleian Library, 2019).

Perkin, Michael, 'Parochial Libraries: Founders and Readers' in Peter Isaac and Barry McKay (eds), *The Reach of Print: Making, Selling and Using Books* (Winchester: St. Paul's Bibliographies, 1998), pp. 191–205.

Perkin, Michael, *A Directory of the Parochial Libraries of the Church of England and the Church in Wales* (London: Bibliographical Society, 2004).

Perkins, Thomas, 'Wimborne Minster' in Thomas Perkins and Herbert Pentin (eds), *Memorials of Old Dorset* (London: Bemrose & Sons Limited, 1907), pp. 117–130.

Perkins, Thomas, *Wimborne Minster and Christchurch Priory* (London: George Bell & Sons, 1902).

Peters, Robert, 'Erasmus and the Fathers: Their Practical Value', *Church History*, 36:3 (1967), pp. 254–261.

Peterson, Herman A., 'The Genesis of Monastic Libraries', *Libraries & the Cultural Record*, 45:3 (2010), pp. 320–332.

Pettegree, Andrew and Arthur der Weduwen, *The Bookshop of the World: Making and Trading Books in the Dutch Golden Age* (New Haven: Yale University Press, 2019).

Pettegree, Andrew and Matthew Hall, 'The Reformation and the Book: A Reconsideration', *The Historical Journal*, 47 (2004), pp. 785–808.

Pettegree, Andrew, 'Centre and Periphery in the European Book World', *Transactions of the Royal Historical Society*, 18 (2008), pp. 101–128.

Pettegree, Andrew, 'Printing in the Low Countries in the Early Sixteenth Century' in Malcolm Walsby and Graeme Kemp (eds), *The Book Triumphant: Print in Transition in the Sixteenth and Seventeenth Centuries* (Leiden: Brill, 2011), pp. 3–25.

Pettegree, Andrew, *Brand Luther: How an Unheralded Monk Turned His Small Town into a Center of Publishing, Made Himself the Most Famous Man in Europe – and Started the Protestant Reformation* (New York: Penguin Books, 2015).

Pettegree, Andrew, *The Book in the Renaissance* (New Haven and London: Yale University Press, 2010).

Pevsner, Nikolaus and John Harris, *The Buildings of England: Lincolnshire*, 2nd edition (New Haven and London: Yale University Press, 1989).

Pfaff, Richard W., 'Prescription and Reality in the Rubrics of Sarum Rite Service Books' in Lesley Smith and Benedicta Ward (eds), *Intellectual Life in the Middle Ages: Essays Presented to Margaret Gibson* (London: The Hambledon Press, 1992), pp. 197–205.

Pfander, H. G., 'The Medieval Friars and some Alphabetical Reference-Books for Sermons', *Medium Ævum*, 3:1 (1934), pp. 19–29.

Plomer, H. R., 'Books Mentioned in Wills', *The Library*, 7:1 (1902), pp. 99–121.

Plomer, Henry R., *A Dictionary of the Booksellers and Printers who were at work in England, Scotland and Ireland from 1641 to 1667* (London: Blades, East and Blades, 1907).

Prior, Charles W. A., 'Canons and Constitutions' in Charles W. A. Prior and Glenn Burgess (eds), *England's Wars of Religion, Revisited* (Farnham: Ashgate, 2011).

Quantin, Jean-Louis, *The Church of England and Christian Antiquity: The Construction of a Confessional Identity in the 17th Century* (Oxford: Oxford University Press, 2009).

Quehen, Hugh de, 'Pearson, John (1613–1686)', *Oxford Dictionary of National Biography*, (online, 2008).

Quehen, Hugh de, 'White, William (bap. 1604, d. 1678)', *Oxford Dictionary of National Biography*, (online, 2008).

Questier, Michael, 'Catholic Loyalism in Early Stuart England', *The English Historical Review*, 123:504 (2008).

Quintrell, Brian, 'Morton, Thomas (bap. 1564, d. 1659)', *Oxford Dictionary of National Biography*, (online, 2008).

Raine, James (ed.), *Testamenta Eboracensia or Wills Registered at York* (London: Surtees Society, 1836).

Raines, Francis Robert and Charles William Sutton, *Life of Humphrey Chetham, founder of the Chetham Hospital and Library, Manchester, Volume I*, printed for the Chetham Society (Manchester: James Stewart, 1903).

Raitt, Jill, *The Colloquy of Montbéliard: Religion and Politics in the Sixteenth Century* (Oxford: Oxford University Press, 1993).

Raven, James, 'Libraries for Sociability: the Advance of the Subscription Library' in Giles Mandelbrote and K. A. Manley (eds), *The Cambridge History of Libraries in Britain and Ireland, Volume II: 1640–1850* (Cambridge: Cambridge University Press, 2006), pp. 239–263.

Raven, James, *The Business of Books: Booksellers and the English Book Trade, 1450–1850* (New Haven: Yale University Press, 2007).

Raymond, Joad, 'The Development of the Book Trade in Britain' in Joad Raymond (ed.), *The Oxford History of Popular Print Culture: Volume One: Cheap Print in Britain and Ireland to 1660* (Oxford: Oxford University Press, 2011), pp. 59–75.

Reeve, David, 'Wimborne Minster, Dorset: a Study of a Small Town, 1620 to 1690' (Unpublished PhD Thesis, University of Exeter, 2000).

Reiser, Marius, 'The History of Catholic Exegesis, 1600–1800' in Ulrich L. Lehner, Richard A. Muller and A. G. Roeber (eds), *The Oxford Handbook of Early Modern Theology, 1600–1800* (Oxford: Oxford University Press, 2016), pp. 75–88.

Richards, Jennifer and Fred Schurink, 'Introduction: The Textuality and Materiality of Reading in Early Modern England', *Huntington Library Quarterly*, 73:3 (2010), pp. 345–361.

Richards, Jennifer, *Voices and Books in the English Renaissance: A New History of Reading* (Oxford: Oxford University Press, 2019).

Richards, Mary P., 'Texts and their Traditions in the Medieval Library of Rochester Cathedral', *Transactions of the American Philosophical Society*, 78:3 (1988), pp. i–xii, 1–129.

Richardson, R. C., *Puritanism in North-West England* (Manchester: Manchester University Press, 1972).

Richardson, William, 'Bilson, Thomas (1546/7–1616)', *Oxford Dictionary of National Biography*, (online, 2004).

Rigney, James, 'Sermons into Print' in Peter McCullough, Hugh Adlington and Emma Rhatigan (eds), *The Oxford Handbook of the Early Modern Sermon* (Oxford: Oxford University Press, 2011), pp. 198–212.

Riverso, Nicla, 'Paolo Sarpi: the Hunted Friar and his Popularity in England', *Annali d'Italianistica*, 34 (2016), pp. 297–318.

Roberts, Angela, 'The Chained Library, Grantham', *Library History*, 2 (1971), pp. 75–90.

Roberts, John, Águeda M. Rodriguez Cruz and Jurgen Herbst, 'Exporting Models' in H. de Ridder-Symoens (ed.), *A History of the University in Europe, Volume II: Universities in Early Modern Europe, 1500–1800* (Cambridge: Cambridge University Press), pp. 256–282.

Roberts, Julian, 'The Latin Trade' in John Barnard, D. F. McKenzie and Maureen Bell (eds), *The Cambridge History of the Book in Britain, Volume IV: 1557–1695* (Cambridge: Cambridge University Press, 2002), pp. 141–173.

Robertson, Archibald, Philip Schaff and Henry Wace (eds), *Against the Heathen (Contra Gentes)* (New York: The Christian Literature Company, 1892).

Robertson, Archibald, Philip Schaff and Henry Wace (eds), *On the Incarnation (De Incarnatione Verbi)* (New York: The Christian Literature Company, 1892).

Robertson, Scott, 'Queen Mary's responsibility for Parish Goods seized in 1553', *Archaeologia Cantiana*, 14 (1882), pp. 313–325.

Rose, Craig, 'The Origins and Ideals of the SPCK, 1699–1716' in John Walsh, Colin Haydon and Stephen Taylor (eds), *The Church of England, c. 1689–1833: From Toleration to Tractarianism* (Cambridge: Cambridge University Press, 1993), pp. 172–190.

Roussel, B. and R. E. Shillenn (trans.), 'Pagnini, Sante (1470–1536)', *The Oxford Encyclopedia of the Reformation*, (online, 2005).

Rozier, Charles C., 'Durham Cathedral Priory and its Library of History, c. 1090–c. 1150' in Laura Cleaver and Andrea Worm (eds), *Writing History in the Anglo-Norman World: Manuscripts, Makers and Readers, c. 1066–c. 1250* (Suffolk: Boydell and Brewer, 2018), pp. 133–148.

Ryrie, Alec, *Being Protestant in Reformation Britain* (Oxford: Oxford University Press, 2015).

Sacks, David Harris and Michael Lynch, 'Ports, 1540–1700' in Peter Clark (ed.), *The Cambridge Urban History of Britain, Volume II: 1540–1840* (Cambridge: Cambridge University Press, 2000), pp. 377–424.

Salter, H. E. and Mary D. Lobel (eds), 'St. Peter's Hall' in *The Victoria History of the County of Oxford: Volume 3, the University of Oxford* (London: Victoria County History, 1954), pp. 336–338.

Sargent, Clare, 'The Early Modern Library (to *c.* 1640)' in Elisabeth Leedham-Green and Teresa Webber (eds), *The Cambridge History of Libraries, Volume 1, to 1640* (Cambridge: Cambridge University Press, 2008), pp. 51–65.

Schaff, Philip (ed.) and Peter Holmes and Robert Ernest Wallis (trans.), *Nicene and Post-Nicene Fathers, Series 1, Volume V: St Augustine: Anti-Pelagian Writings* (New York: The Christian Literature Company, 1887).

Schaff, Philip and Henry Wade (trans.), *Contra Gentes by Saint Athanasius* (New York: The Christian Literature Company, 1892).

Schaff, Philip and Henry Wade (trans.), *De Incarnatione Verbi by Saint Athanasius* (New York: The Christian Literature Company, 1892).

Schaff, Philip and Henry Wade (trans.), *Statement of Faith by Saint Athanasius* (New York: The Christian Literature Company, 1892).

Schaff, Philip, *The Confessions and Letters of St. Augustin, with a Sketch of his Life and Work* (Edinburgh, T. & T. Clark, 1886).

Schurink, Fred, '"Like a Hand in the Margine of a Booke": William Blount's Marginalia and the Politics of Sidney's "Arcadia"', *The Review of English Studies*, 59:238 (2008), pp. 1–24.

Schurink, Fred, 'Manuscript Commonplace Books, Literature, and Reading in Early Modern England', *Huntington Library Quarterly*, 73:3 (2010), pp. 453–469.

Schwiebert, E. G., 'Chemnitz, Martin' in Berard L. Marthaler (general ed.), *New Catholic Encyclopedia, Volume III: Can-Col*, 2nd edition (Detroit: Thomson Gale, 2003), pp. 463–464.

Scott-Warren, Jason, 'Reading Graffiti in the Early Modern Book', *Huntington Library Quarterly*, 73:3 (2010), pp. 363–381.

Serjeantson, R. M. and H. Isham Longden, 'The Parish Churches and Religious Houses of Northamptonshire: their Dedications, Altars, Images and Lights', *The Archaeological Journal*, 70 (1913), pp. 217–452.

Sharpe, Kevin, *Reading Revolutions: The Politics of Reading in Early Modern England* (London: Yale University Press, 2000).

Shaw, David, 'Parochial Libraries in Kent', *Library & Information History*, 27:4 (2011), pp. 239–245.

Shaw, J. F. and S. D. Salmond (trans.) and Marcus Dods (ed.), *The Works of Aurelius Augustine, Bishop of Hippo, Volume IX: On Christian Doctrine; The Enchiridion; On Catechising; and On Faith and the Creed* (Edinburgh: T. & T. Clark, 1873).

Shaw, William A. (ed.), *Minutes of the Manchester Presbyterian Classis. Part 1*, printed for the Chetham Society (Manchester: Charles E. Sims, 1890).

Shearing, D. K., 'Education in Rutland in the sixteenth and seventeenth centuries', *Transactions of the Leicestershire Archaeological and Historical Society*, 55 (1979), pp. 38–48.

Sheehan, Jonathan, 'Sacred and Profane: Idolatry, Antiquarianism and the Polemics of Distinction in the Seventeenth Century', *Past & Present*, 192 (2006), pp. 35–66.

Sheils, W. J., 'Bishops and their dioceses: reform of visitation in the Anglican Church c. 1680–c. 1760', *CCEd Online Journal*, 1 (2007), <http://www.theclergydatabase.org.uk/cce_a1/>.

Sherman, William H., 'What Did Renaissance Readers Write in Their Books?' in Jennifer Andersen and Elizabeth Sauer (eds), *Books and Readers in Early Modern England: Material Studies* (Philadelphia: University of Pennsylvania Press, 2002), pp. 119–137.

Sherman, William H., *John Dee: The Politics of Reading and Writing in the English Renaissance* (Amherst: University of Massachusetts Press, 1995).

Sherman, William H., *Used Books: Marking Readers in Renaissance England* (Philadelphia: University of Pennsylvania Press, 2009).

Sherwood, Yvonne, 'Early Modern Davids: From Sin to Critique' in Kevin Killeen, Helen Smith and Rachel Willie (eds), *The Oxford Handbook of the Bible in Early Modern England, c. 1530–1700* (Oxford: Oxford University Press, 2018), pp. 640–658.

Shinners, John, 'Parish Libraries in Medieval England' in Jacqueline Brown and William P. Stoneman (eds), *A Distinct Voice: Medieval Studies in Honor of Leonard E. Boyle* (Notre Dame, Ind.: University of Notre Dame Press, 1997), pp. 207–230.

Slack, Paul, 'Great and Good Towns, 1540–1700' in Peter Clark (ed.), *The Cambridge Urban History of Britain, Volume II: 1540–1840* (Cambridge: Cambridge University Press, 2000), pp. 347–376.

Smith, David L., 'Spelman, Sir John (1594–1643)', *Oxford Dictionary of National Biography*, (online, 2008).

Smith, William, 'The Parochial Library of Steeple Ashton in Wiltshire', *Library History*, 6:4 (1983), pp. 97–113.

Snape, A. C., 'Seventeenth-century Book Purchasing in Chetham's Library, Manchester' *John Rylands University Library of Manchester Bulletin*, 67 (1985), pp. 783–796.

Speed, John, *Britain's Tudor Maps: County by County* (London: Batsford, 2016).

Spraggon, Julie, *Puritan Iconoclasm during the English Civil War* (Woodbridge: Boydell and Brewer, 2003).

Spurr, John, 'From Puritanism to Dissent, 1660–1700' in Christopher Durston and Jacqueline Eales (eds), *The Culture of English Puritanism, 1560–1700* (London: Macmillan Press, 1996), pp. 234–265.

Spurr, John, *The Post-Reformation: Religion, Politics and Society in Britain, 1603–1714* (Abingdon: Routledge, 2014).

Stanning, J. H. (ed.), *The Royalist Composition Papers, being the Proceedings of the Committee for Compounding, A.D. 1643–1660, so far as they relate to the County of Lancaster, Volume IV* (Manchester: The Record Society, 1898).

Stone, Lawrence, 'Literacy and Education in England, 1640–1900', *Past & Present*, 42 (1969), pp. 69–139.

Stone, Lawrence, 'The Educational Revolution in England, 1560–1640', *Past & Present*, 28 (1964), pp. 41–80.

Street, B., *Historical Notes on Grantham and Grantham Church* (Grantham: S. Ridge and Son, 1857).

Streeter, Burnett Hillman, *The Chained Library: A Survey of Four Centuries in the Evolution of the English Library* (New York: Burt Franklin, 1931).

Strickland, Forrest C., 'Teachers of Christ's Church: Protestant Ministers as Readers of the Church Fathers in the Dutch Golden Age' in Rosamund Oates and Jessica G. Purdy (eds), *Communities of Print: Readers and their Books in Early Modern Europe* (Leiden: Brill, 2021).

Sutton, C. W. and R. C. Richardson, 'Hollinworth, Richard (bap. 1607, d. 1656)', *Oxford Dictionary of National Biography*, (online, 2004).

Sutton, Dana F. (trans. and ed.), *Polydore Vergil, 'Anglica Historia'*, (2005), <http://www.philological.bham.ac.uk/polverg/>.

The Inner Temple, 'The Inner Temple Admissions', *The Inner Temple Admissions Database*, no date, <http://www.innertemplearchives.org.uk/>.

The Society of Lincoln's Inn, *The Records of the Honourable Society of Lincoln's Inn, Volume I: Admissions from A.D. 1420–A.D. 1799* (London: Lincoln's Inn, 1896).

Thomas, Andrea and Hilary Ely, 'The Cranston Library, Reigate: The First Three Hundred Years', *Library and Information History*, 27:4 (2011), pp. 246–254.

Thomas, Denise, 'Religious Polemic, Print Culture and Pastoral Ministry: Thomas Hall B.D. (1610–1665) and the Promotion of Presbyterian Orthodoxy in the English Revolution', Volume II, Appendix II (Unpublished PhD Thesis, University of Birmingham, 2011).

Thomas, Keith V., 'Women and the Civil War Sects', *Past & Present*, 13 (1958), pp. 42–62.

Thomas, Keith, *Religion and the Decline of Magic: Studies in Popular Beliefs in Sixteenth- and Seventeenth-Century England* (London: Penguin, 1991).

Tiffany, M. N. E., *The History of the Rev. Mr. William Stone and his Hospital together with that of other Almshouses in Oxford* (Headington: Tiffany Arts, 2000).

Todd, Margo, 'The Problem of Scotland's Puritans' in John Coffey and Paul C. H. Lim (eds), *The Cambridge Companion to Puritanism* (Cambridge: Cambridge University Press, 2008), pp. 174–188.

Towsey, Mark, *Reading the Scottish Enlightenment: Books and the Readers in Provincial Scotland, 1750–1820* (Leiden: Brill, 2010).

Trueman, Carl R., 'Scripture and Exegesis in Early Modern Reformed Theology' in Ulrich L. Lehner, Richard A. Muller and A. G. Roeber (eds), *The Oxford Handbook of Early Modern Theology, 1600–1800* (Oxford: Oxford University Press, 2016), pp. 179–194.

Turnor, Edmund, *Collections for the History of the Town and Soke of Grantham* (London: W. Bulmer and Co. for William Miller, 1806).

Tyacke, Nicholas, *Aspects of English Protestantism, c. 1530–1700* (Manchester: Manchester University Press, 2001).

Tymms, Samuel (ed.), *Wills and Inventories from the Registers of the Commissary of Bury St. Edmunds and the Archdeaconry of Sudbury* (London: Printed for the Camden Society, 1850).

Tyson, Moses, 'Handlist of Additions to the Collection of Latin Manuscripts in the John Rylands Library, 1908–28', *Bulletin of the John Rylands Library*, 12 (1928), pp. 581–609.

Unknown Author, 'Local Notes and Queries, Replies: Libraries', *Grantham Journal*, Saturday 26 October 1878.

Unknown Author, *Certain Sermons or Homilies Appointed to be Read in Churches in the Time of the Late Queen Elizabeth* (Oxford: Oxford University Press, 1844).

Unknown Author, *Memorials of the Church of ss. Peter and Wilfrid, Ripon, Volume II* (Durham: Andrews & Co. for the Surtees Society, 1886).

Unknown Author, *The Injunctions and other Ecclesiastical Proceedings of Richard Barnes, Bishop of Durham, from 1575 to 1587* (Durham: George Andrews for the Surtees Society, 1850).

Vanpaemel, Geert, 'Science for Sale: the Metropolitan Stimulus for Scientific Achievements in Sixteenth-Century Antwerp' in Hugh Kennedy (ed.), *Urban Achievement in Early Modern Europe: Golden Ages in Antwerp, Amsterdam and London* (Cambridge: Cambridge University Press, 2009), pp. 287–304.

Venn, John and J. A. Venn (eds), *Alumni Cantabrigienses, Part I, Volume I* (Cambridge: Cambridge University Press, 1922).

Venn, John and J. A. Venn (eds), *Alumni Cantabrigienses, Part I, Volume II* (Cambridge: Cambridge University Press, 1922).

Venn, John and J. A. Venn (eds), *Alumni Cantabrigienses, Part I, Volume IV* (Cambridge: Cambridge University Press, 1927).

Venning, Timothy, 'Thurloe, John (bap. 1616, d. 1668)', *Oxford Dictionary of National Biography*, (online, 2008).

Visser, Arnoud S. Q., *Reading Augustine in the Reformation: The Flexibility of Intellectual Authority in Europe, 1500–1620* (Oxford: Oxford University Press, 2011).

Visser, Arnoud, 'Reading Augustine through Erasmus' Eyes: Humanist Scholarship and Paratextual Guidance in the Wake of the Reformation', *Erasmus Studies*, 28 (2008), pp. 67–90.

Visser, Arnoud, 'Thirtieth Annual Erasmus Birthday Lecture: Erasmus, the Church Fathers and the Ideological Implications of Philology', *Erasmus of Rotterdam Society Yearbook*, 31:1 (2011), pp. 7–31.

Wabuda, Susan, '"A Day After Doomsday": Cranmer and the Bible Translations of the 1530s' in Kevin Killeen, Helen Smith, and Rachel Willie (eds), *The Oxford Handbook of the Bible in Early Modern England, c. 1530–1700* (Oxford: Oxford University Press, 2018), pp. 23–37.

Walbran, John Richard, *A Guide to Ripon, Fountains Abbey, Harrogate, Bolton Priory, and Several Places of Interest in their Vicinity*, 12th edition (Ripon: A. Johnson and Co., 1875).

Walker, R. B., 'The Growth of Puritanism in the County of Lincoln in the Reign of Queen Elizabeth I', *Journal of Religious History*, 1:3 (1961), pp. 148–159.

Wallace, Dewey D., Jr, 'Puritan Polemical Divinity and Doctrinal Controversy' in John Coffey and Paul C. H. Lim (eds), *The Cambridge Companion to Puritanism* (Cambridge: Cambridge University Press, 2008), pp. 206–222.

Wallis, P. J., 'The Library of William Crashawe', *Transactions of the Cambridge Bibliographical Society*, 2:3 (1956), pp. 213–228.

Wallis, Robert Ernest (trans.), Alexander Roberts and James Donaldson (eds), *The Writings of Cyprian, Bishop of Carthage, Volume I* (Edinburgh: T. & T. Clark, 1868).

Walsham, Alexandra, 'The Godly and Popular Culture' in John Coffey and Paul C. H. Lim (eds), *The Cambridge Companion to Puritanism* (Cambridge: Cambridge University Press, 2008), pp. 277–293.

Walsham, Alexandra, *Church Papists: Catholicism, Conformity and Confessional Polemic in Early Modern England* (Woodbridge: The Boydell Press, 1999).

Watkin, Dom Aelred, *Archdeaconry of Norwich, Inventory of Church Goods, temp. Edward III*, Volume XIX, Part I (Norfolk: Norfolk Record Society, 1947).

Watson, Paula and Andrew A. Hanham, 'Sydenham, Sir Philip, 3rd Bt. (c. 1676–1739)', *The History of Parliament Online*, (2002), <https://www.historyofparliamentonline.org/volume/1690-1715/member/sydenham-sir-philip-1676-1739>.

Watt, Jeffrey R., 'Calvin on Suicide', *Church History*, 66:3 (1997), pp. 463–476.

Watt, Tessa, *Cheap Print and Popular Piety, 1550–1640* (Cambridge: Cambridge University Press, 1991).

Watts, William (trans.) and T. E. Page and W. H. D. Rouse (eds), *Saint Augustine's Confessions* (London: William Heinemann, 1912).

Webster, Tom, 'Early Stuart Puritanism' in John Coffey and Paul C. H. Lim (eds), *The Cambridge Companion to Puritanism* (Cambridge: Cambridge University Press, 2008), pp. 48–66.

Weinandy, Thomas G., *Athanasius: A Theological Introduction* (Aldershot: Ashgate Publishing, 2007).

Whiting, Robert, *The Blind Devotion of the People: Popular Religion and the English Reformation* (Cambridge: Cambridge University Press, 1991).

Whitaker, Elaine, 'A Collaboration of Readers: Categorisation of the Annotations in Copies of Caxton's Royal Book', *Text*, 7 (1994), pp. 233–242.

Wiener, Carol Z., 'The Beleaguered Isle. A Study of Elizabethan and Early Jacobean Anti-Catholicism', *Past & Present*, 51 (1971), pp. 27–62.

Willen, Diane, 'Thomas Gataker and the Use of Print in the English Godly Community', *Huntington Library Quarterly*, 70:3 (2007), pp. 343–364.

Williams, David, 'English Parochial Libraries: A History of Changing Attitudes', *Antiquarian Book Monthly Review*, 5:4 (1978), pp. 138–147.

Williams, David, 'The Use and Abuse of a Pious Intention: Changing Attitudes to Parochial Libraries', *The Library Association and Study School and National Conference Proceedings*, Nottingham, 1979, pp. 21–28.

Williamson, J. Bruce, *The Middle Temple Bench Book*, 2nd edition (London: Chancery Lane Press, 1937).

Willis, Jonathan, *The Reformation of the Decalogue: Religious Identity and the Ten Commandments in England, c. 1485–1625* (Cambridge: Cambridge University Press, 2020).

Winship, Michael P., 'Weak Christians, Backsliders, and Carnal Gospelers: Assurance of Salvation and the Pastoral Origins of Puritan Practical Divinity in the 1580s', *Church History: Studies in Christianity and Culture*, 9 (2001), pp. 462–481.

Winters, Jennifer, 'The English Provincial Book Trade: Bookseller Stock-Lists, c. 1520–1640', Volume I (Unpublished PhD thesis, University of St Andrews, 2012).

Wooding, Lucy E. C., *Rethinking Catholicism in Reformation England* (Oxford: Clarendon Press, 2000).

Wooding, Lucy, 'Introduction: John Jewel and the Invention of the Church of England' in Angela Ranson, André A. Gazal and Sarah Bastow (eds), *Defending the Faith: John Jewel and the Elizabethan Church* (Philadelphia: University of Pennsylvania Press, 2018), pp. 1–17.

Woodward, William Harrison (ed.), *The Aim and Method of Education* by Desiderius Erasmus (Cambridge: Cambridge University Press, 1904).

Wright, Louis B., 'William Perkins: Elizabethan Apostle of "Practical Divinity"', *Huntingdon Library Quarterly*, 3 (1940), pp. 171–196.

Wright, Stephen, 'Alleine, Richard (1610/11–1681)', *Oxford Dictionary of National Biography*, (online, 2008).

Wright, Stephen, 'Alleine, William (1613/14–1677)', *Oxford Dictionary of National Biography*, (online, 2008).

Wright, Stephen, 'Bartlet, William (1609/10–1682)', *Oxford Dictionary of National Biography*, (online, 2008).

Wright, Stephen, 'Fisher, Samuel (1605/6–1681)', *Oxford Dictionary of National Biography*, (online, 2008).

Wrightson, Keith, '"Sorts of People" in Tudor and Stuart England' in Jonathan Barry and Christopher Brooks (eds), *The Middling Sort of People: Culture, Society and Politics in England, 1550–1800* (Basingstoke: Macmillan, 1994).

Yates, Nigel, 'The Parochial Library of All Saints, Maidstone, and Other Kentish Parochial Libraries', *Archaeologia Cantiana*, 99 (1983), pp. 159–173.

Yeo, Matthew, *The Acquisition of Books by Chetham's Library, 1655–1700* (Leiden: Brill, 2011).

Young, B. W., 'Theology in the Church of England' in Jeremy Gregory (ed.), *The Oxford History of Anglicanism, Volume II: Establishment and Empire, 1662–1829* (Oxford: Oxford University Press, 2017), pp. 392–428.

Zakai, Avihu, 'Thomas Brightman and English Apocalyptic Tradition' in Yosef Kaplan, Henry Méchoulan and Richard H. Popkin (eds), *Menasseh ben Israel and his World* (Leiden: Brill, 1989), pp. 31–44.

Index

Abbot, Robert, bishop of Salisbury 128
Act against Jesuits, seminary priests, and such other like disobedient persons (1584) 180
Act against Priests (1585) 180
Act Dissolving the Chantries (1547) 187
Act for the Advancement of True Religion (1543) 211
Act of Persuasions (1581) 180
Act of Ten Articles (1536) 186
Act of Thirty-Nine Articles (1571) 71
Admonitions Controversy (1570s) 147
Allen, William, English Catholic cardinal 93
Alston, Thomas, vicar of Assington 80
Ambrose, Isaac, Puritan divine 166, 214–216
Ambrose, saint 127
Andrewes, Lancelot, bishop of Winchester 63, 128, 158
Antichrist 166, 170, 178, 182–183, 197, 245
Antoninus of Florence, saint 108–109, 160
Antwerp 44, 141, 144–148
Apostolic Church 192, 197
  changes to 182–185
  corruption of 183, 196–198
  recognition of 196–198
Arminius, Jacob, Dutch Reformed minister and theologian 40
assurance of grace 163, 166, 199, 213, 218–222, 232, 240
Astesano, medieval Franciscan canon lawyer 137
Athanasius, saint 102, 118, 127, 181, 193, 195, 224–225
Augustine, saint 29, 77, 118–119, 127–128, 146, 169, 181, 193, 205, 208–210, 217, 232–233, 242, 247–249

Balbus, Johannes, Italian Dominican priest 108
Baronius, Caesar, Italian cardinal 108
Basel 118, 141, 144–146, 148–150
Basil of Caesarea, saint 127, 152
Baxter, Richard, nonconformist theologian 164, 166, 216, 228

Becanus, Martin, Jesuit priest and theologian 40, 126
Bede, medieval monk, author and scholar 40
Bell, Thomas, English Catholic priest 103
Bellarmine, Robert, Italian Jesuit and cardinal 62, 93, 124, 126, 146, 159
Beza, Theodore, French Reformed theologian 40, 93, 106, 136, 159
Bible, the 6, 27–28, 36–38, 75, 93, 124, 128, 141, 152, 155, 162, 168, 182, 186, 193, 198–209, 212, 216, 236
  accessibility of 200–201, 210–212
  commentaries on 3, 24, 27–29, 62, 79, 93–94, 99, 104, 110, 132, 154, 156, 158–159, 161–163, 168, 172, 208–209, 252
  reading 199–200, 203, 205, 208
Bilson, Thomas, bishop of Winchester 227
Binsfield, Peter, German bishop and theologian 126
Bolton School 69, 86
Bolton, Robert, clergyman and preacher 165–166
Bonner, Edmund, bishop of London 37
book trade
  continental 4–5, 22, 41–46, 55, 57, 105, 123, 140–146, 148–150, 162, 172
  English 42–47, 55, 57, 66, 92, 98, 105, 123, 135, 140–146, 156
  Latin 4, 57, 105, 140, 143, 146, 150
  second-hand 22, 55, 57, 66, 68, 92, 98, 123, 133–134, 138–140, 144, 172
Bray, Thomas, clergyman 6, 23, 32, 35, 47–48, 51, 108, 253
Brent, Nathaniel, college master and translator 170
Bright, Timothy, clergyman and physician 101
Brightman, Thomas, clergyman and biblical commentator 165–166, 181, 183, 185
Briskin, Griffin, prebendary of York 103
Bristol 49, 51
Bucer, Martin, German Protestant Reformer 60, 93, 189

Bullinger, Heinrich, Swiss Reformer and
  theologian   60, 93
Bunny, Edmund, rector of Bolton Percy   159
Burgess, Anthony, nonconformist clergyman
  and preacher   218, 228, 231, 235, 240, 244
Burkitt, William, rector of Milden   80–81
Burnet, Gilbert, Scottish historian and bishop
  of Salisbury   76, 170
Bury, Henry, clerk   89
Busby, Richard, Anglican priest   32

Caen   141
Calvin, John, French theologian and
  Reformer   4, 39–40, 60, 78, 93–94, 106,
  128, 159, 165, 171, 189, 192, 202, 206, 215–
  218, 220, 224–226, 232, 236, 238–239,
  242, 244–245, 247–249
Camborne, Stephen, rector of Lawshall   81
Cambridge   50, 66, 78, 91–92, 102–103, 105,
  134–135, 140–141, 148
  University of   29, 63, 66, 100–101, 109–110,
  135, 185
Camden, William, historian and antiquarian
  77, 170
Carlisle   23, 32, 51–52, 190
Cartwright, Thomas, Puritan preacher and
  theologian   147–148
Castell, Edmund, orientalist   155
catechisms   104, 141, 161–163, 172, 192, 204
Caxton, William, printer   252
Chamberlayne, Edward, writer   111
cheap print   42, 115, 138–139
Cheapside, English printing centre   98, 151
Chemnitz, Martin, German Lutheran
  theologian and reformer   181, 184–186,
  191–192, 195–196, 202–203, 206–208,
  220–221, 233, 241
Chetham, Humphrey, merchant and
  philanthropist   33, 39, 50, 56, 58, 67–70,
  78–79, 84, 89, 95–99, 108, 115, 117, 124,
  128–129, 138, 148, 163, 166–168, 171, 253
  will of   39, 58, 67–70, 78, 84, 94, 97, 129,
  138, 163, 168
Chetham, Margaret, niece of Humphrey   70,
  96
Chetham's Library, Manchester   68–69,
  94–95, 98, 163
Chetham's School of Music, Manchester   68

Chillingworth, William, controversial
  churchman   77, 111, 171, 182–183, 197, 204,
  226–227
Church Fathers   4, 29, 40, 57, 73, 101, 127–128,
  130–132, 140, 148, 154, 168–169
Church of England, the   3, 23, 32, 39, 65, 93,
  104, 106, 126, 128, 135, 158, 160, 162, 170,
  186, 197, 208, 226–227, 243, 248
Cicero, Roman scholar and philosopher   40,
  76
Cleaburne, William, clergyman   66, 82
Clement I, pope   127
Clement of Alexandria, saint   77, 169
Clungeon, John, London haberdasher   49,
  84
Cologne   44, 144, 148–150
continental books   41–46
Cooper, Thomas, bishop of Lincoln   207
cost of early modern books   42–43, 114–120,
  138
Cotton, Sir Robert, antiquarian and MP,
  founder of the Cotton Library   170
Council of Trent (1545–1563)   130, 159, 170,
  181–182, 189
Cox, Richard, bishop of Ely   42, 103
Cranmer, Thomas, archbishop of Canterbury
  194
Cranston, Andrew, vicar of Reigate   41,
  107–108
Crashawe, William, cleric and prebendary of
  Ripon Minster   65
Cromwell, Oliver, military leader and Lord
  Protector   50
Crowle, Eleanor, library founder   33, 99–100
Crowle, George, mayor of Kingston-upon-
  Hull   100
Cyprian, saint   234–235, 237
Cyril, saint   169

Danaeus, Lambertus, French Calvinist
  theologian   118
death   179, 229, 245–247, 249–250
  preparation for   1, 168, 179, 229–232,
  245–247, 250
despair   231–232, 236, 248–249
devil, the   214, 236, 249
Dod, John, nonconformist clergyman   185–
  186, 194, 203–204, 215–216, 234, 238–239

Dorman, Thomas, English Catholic theologian 126

Downame, George, bishop of Derry 128

Drusius, Joannes, the Elder, Flemish Protestant divine and exegetist 136

Dugdale, Sir William, antiquary 77, 111, 171

Dunscomb, George, rector of Wooton Wawen 50, 78

Durand, Guillaume, French liturgical writer 137

Edward VI, king of England 36–38, 187, 200

election 189, 238, 240
  signs of 163–166, 189–190, 213, 219, 222, 230–232, 239–245

Elizabeth I, queen of England 26, 36, 38, 48, 60, 63, 180, 196, 200, 207

English Civil War 7, 42, 47–49, 52, 58, 67, 70, 89, 94, 172, 212, 243

English Reformation 3, 21, 24, 26, 29–30, 31, 34, 49, 62, 76, 123, 133, 166, 188, 196–197, 200, 204, 213, 224, 237, 254

Epiphanius, saint 127

Erasmus, Desiderius, Dutch humanist and Catholic theologian 37–38, 106, 118, 128, 146, 171

Euripides, Ancient Greek tragedian 40

Eusebius, saint 77, 169

Favour, John, vicar of Halifax 103

Field, John, Puritan clergyman 147

Fisher, John, English Jesuit 226

Fleet Street, English printing centre 43, 151

Fleming, Roger, Lancashire library founder 122

Foster, John, bookseller 43–44

Fowler, Moses, dean of Ripon 64–65

Foxe, John, Protestant martyrologist 62, 108, 117

Fry, Dr Stephen 73

Fuller, Thomas, clergyman and historian 76–77, 170

Geree, John, clergyman and preacher 237

Gesner, Conrad, Swiss naturalist 101

Gillingham, Roger, gentleman and founder 35, 39, 59, 73–77, 83–85, 90, 111–113, 120, 122, 130–133, 139–141, 148–151, 154–155, 168–171, 181
  will of 35, 59, 73–75, 84, 111–112, 120, 140

Godfrey, Garrett, Dutch bookbinder 92

God
  correction of errors in the faithful 242–243
  image of 195, 198
  Word of 195–196, 198, 200–206, 212, 224, 233

godly living 1, 79, 104, 168, 178–179, 206, 229–245, 250–251, 254

good works 179, 189–190, 213, 221, 230–232, 238–241, 250, 254

Gorran, Nicolaus de, medieval French preacher and scriptural commentator 102

Gregory of Nyssa, saint 127

Grimeston, Edward, translator 111

Grindal, Edmund, archbishop of Canterbury 194, 199

Gunpowder Plot, the (1605) 180–181

Hammond, Henry, royalist cleric 76–77, 112

Harding, Thomas, English Catholic priest and controversialist 126, 146, 154

Harington, John, son of John, first baron Harington of Exton 100–101

Harington, John, first baron Harington of Exton 79, 100–101

Harington, Lady Anne, library founder 2, 33, 40, 79, 100–101

Harpsfield, Nicholas, English Catholic priest and apologist 126, 146

Harris, Robert, Puritan clergyman and preacher 206, 244

Harsnett, Samuel, archbishop of York 63, 158

Hartlib, Samuel, educational reformer 111

Henry VIII, king of England 26, 36, 143, 186, 201, 211

Herbert, Edward, historian and religious philosopher 76, 170, 188, 200–201, 211–212

Hesselszoon van Est, Willem, Dutch Catholic commentator 103, 136

Higgin, Anthony, clergyman and founder 58, 63–66, 82, 101–104, 118, 123, 126–128, 133, 135–137, 144–147, 152–154, 160–161, 171, 181
  will of 58, 66, 82, 133, 181

Higginbotham, James, Grantham donor 202

Higginbotham, William, annotating reader 202, 215–218, 220, 236, 238–239, 242, 245, 249

Hilary, saint 169

Hildersham, Arthur, Puritan clergyman and preacher 190, 220–221, 233, 246

Hippocrates, Ancient Greek physician 101

Hollinworth, Richard, Chetham's trustee 70, 94–99, 115, 128–129, 168

homilies 141, 156, 162, 233

Howell, William, historian and civil lawyer 76, 170

Hume, David, Scottish philosopher and historian 252

Hyde, Edward, 1st earl of Clarendon 226

idolatry 182, 192–198, 205

idols 179, 182, 192–198

images 160, 179, 182, 192–198

indulgences 179, 182, 185, 187–190, 198

Ingolstadt 141

Inns of Court 6, 71, 73–74
  Middle Temple 71, 74, 95, 98, 140, 151
  Inner Temple 71
  Lincoln's Inn 71
  Gray's Inn 71

Interregnum 5, 47–52, 58, 72, 172, 243

Ipswich Town Library 117

Isaacson, Henry, clergyman and biographer 170

Isocrates, Ancient Greek rhetorician 40

James I, king of England 64–65, 82, 160

Jerome, saint 169

Jesus Christ 166–167, 183, 185, 190, 192–196, 198, 203, 216, 223, 228, 235, 240, 245
  atonement 218, 222, 226
  dual nature of 225
  His sacrifice 213–214, 219, 222–229
  role in justification 222–227

Jewel, John, bishop of Salisbury 154, 187

John Chrysostom, saint 127–128, 169, 171

Johnson, Richard, Chetham's trustee, minister and Master of the Middle Temple 69–70, 94–98, 115, 128–129, 168

justification by faith alone 179, 189–192, 198, 213–214, 219, 222–225, 229

Kedermister, Sir John, library founder 80, 87

Kling, Conrad, Catholic theologian 102

Knox, John, Scottish Presbyterian Reformer 240

Lake, Arthur, bishop of Bath and Wells 63, 75, 111, 158, 171

Lancashire presbyterian experiment (1646) 95–96

Laud, William, archbishop of Canterbury 76, 112, 227, 243

Leaver, James, library founder 69, 86

Leiden 147–148
  University of 148

library accessibility
  intellectual 8, 57, 73, 79, 123, 151–155
  physical 21–22, 25, 29, 34, 42, 55–56, 62, 83–90

Lindt, Willem van der, Dutch churchman 102, 118

literacy 6–7, 21–22, 35, 44, 79, 83, 151

Little Britain, English printing centre 97–98, 140, 151

Littlebury, Robert, bookseller 70, 97–99, 138

Lombard, Peter, Italian scholastic theologian 160

London 4, 37, 42–47, 49, 66, 70–71, 73, 75, 92, 95, 97–99, 102–103, 105, 117, 136, 140–141, 144, 146–151, 164

Lumley, William, clergyman 66, 82

Luther, Martin, German priest and theologian 40, 181, 189–191, 195–196, 222–224, 228, 240–241

Magdeburg Centuriators, group of Lutheran scholars 117, 124

Manchester 28, 39, 49–50, 55–56, 58, 63, 67–70, 78, 89, 94–97, 99, 117, 122, 129, 163, 168

Mary I, queen of England 37–38, 143–144

Matthew, Tobie, archbishop of York 82, 93, 124, 126, 154

Mede, Joseph, biblical scholar and Hebraist 214, 219, 237

Melanchthon, Philipp, German Lutheran Reformer 40, 146

Montagu, Richard, cleric 128

Montano, Benitus Arias, Spanish orientalist
    and editor of the Antwerp polyglot   152
More, Henry, Platonist philosopher   109–110
More, Sir Richard, library founder   34, 40,
    80, 104–105
Morton, Thomas, bishop of Durham   64
Mothe le Vayer, Francois de la (alias Orosius
    Tubero), French writer   155

Napier, John, Scottish mathematician and
    astronomer   165
Naples   141
Newcome, John, college master and dean of
    Rochester   110–111
Newman Harrison, John, vicar of Reigate
    108
Norwich   26, 43–45, 49, 51

Oley, Barnabas, bishop of Ely   23, 32, 35,
    47–48, 51
Osorio da Fonseca, Jeronimo, Portuguese
    Catholic bishop   170
Overall, John, bishop of Coventry and
    Lichfield   128
Oxford   72–732, 89–90, 105, 131–132, 140,
    147–148
    University of   59, 71–72, 74, 105, 140

Pagnini, Sante, Italian Dominican friar   109
Paris   45, 141, 144–146, 148
Parochial Libraries Act (1709)   21, 48
Paternoster Row, English printing centre
    43, 151
Paul, saint   207
Payva de Andrada, Diego de, Portuguese
    theologian   159
Pearson, John, Restoration Anglican
    clergyman   106, 171
penance   187, 189–190, 213, 217, 219
Perkins, William, Puritan theologian   4,
    39–40, 78, 94, 166–167, 191, 205,
    208, 214–216, 219–220, 228, 231, 241,
    243–244, 246–247
Persons, Robert, English Jesuit priest   159
Pintus, Hector, Portuguese Catholic
    theologian   62, 93, 126, 159
Plato, Ancient Greek philosopher   76, 171
Pliny the Elder, Roman author and natural
    philosopher   124

Plutarch, Greek philosopher and historian
    76, 112
Polanus, Amandus, German theologian and
    Reformer   224
pope, the   180
    Corruption of   183
    Identification with Antichrist   182–183,
        197
Powel, Gabriel, Welsh Anglican priest
    128
practical divinity   21, 99, 104, 110, 161–166,
    172, 175, 178, 228, 231, 243, 251–253
prayer   25, 79, 179, 187, 202, 230, 233–236,
    250, 254
    as communication with God   233–234,
        250
    for the dead   25, 185–187, 245
    for the benefit of others   206, 235
    forms of   233, 236–238
predestination   159, 189, 218, 241, 245–246
Preston, John, college master and Anglican
    minister   78, 94
Prideaux, John, rector of Exeter College
    106, 170
prophesyings   207
purchase invoices   56, 78, 98–99, 115–117
purgatory   25,– 179, 182, 185–191, 198, 245

Rainolds, John, Puritan churchman and
    academic   124
Raleigh, Sir Walter, statesman, writer and
    explorer   76, 112
Ramesey, William, Scottish-English physician
    and astrologer   112
Recusancy Act (1587)   180
Regnans in Excelsis papal bull (1570)
    180–181
religious conversion   60, 124, 148, 160, 221,
    226–227, 231, 238–239, 250
repentance   1, 167, 178–179, 208, 212–213,
    218–222, 229–230, 242, 251, 254
Rhiems   148
Ribera, Francis, Spanish Jesuit theologian
    124, 159
righteousness   163, 179, 189, 205, 213, 219,
    222–224, 240
Roberts, Francis, Puritan clergyman   50, 208
Rogers, Richard, nonconformist clergyman
    166–167, 218, 238, 244

Rogers, Thomas, Anglican clergyman, theologian and controversialist   77
Roman Catholic Church   37, 106, 130, 154, 170–171, 181–182, 196, 198
   break with   36, 166, 186
   corruption of   106, 168–171, 178, 182–192, 197, 254
Rothwell, John, bookseller   70, 97–98
royal injunctions   26, 36–38, 45, 200
Russell, William, presbyter of Wimborne Minster   112

Salamanca   141
Salvard, Jean-François, Italian Reformed theologian   202, 227
salvation   168, 189–191, 204, 212–214, 216, 218–229, 231, 244–245, 250
   assurance of   218, 240
   hard times as a way to   214, 219, 228, 243–245
Sanderson, Robert, bishop of Lincoln   77, 171
Sarpi, Paolo, Venetian canon lawyer, historian and statesman   124, 129–130, 170–171
Savile, Sir Henry, manuscript and book collector   103
Scheibler, Christoph, German Lutheran theologian   111
Scott, Robert, bookseller   43–44
Scotus, John Duns, Scottish priest and Franciscan friar   62, 109
Scripture
   accessibility of   210–212
   as the Word of God   200–206, 208, 212
   containing everything necessary for faith   182, 184, 197, 200, 203–205, 212
   correct understanding of   200, 206–209, 212
   used for teaching and improvement   205–206, 212
Scudder, Henry, Presbyterian minister   243
Scultetus, Abraham, theologian and preacher   224
self-examination   162, 165, 219–222, 230
Seneca, Ancient Roman philosopher   124
sermons   21, 66, 70, 79, 81, 91, 93, 99, 110, 127, 154, 161–165, 168, 170, 172, 230, 232–233, 246
   travelling to   230, 232

sin   212–218, 223, 229, 236, 244, 246, 249
   avoidance of   213–214
   sinful actions   213, 217–218
   temptation   213–215, 236, 247, 249
Skipwith, Edward, merchant   81–82
Smarte, William, draper   34, 79, 83
Smith, Edward, vicar of Sleaford   85
Smith, Henry, lecturer at St Clement Danes   164
Society for Promoting Christian Knowledge (SPCK)   6, 23, 32, 35, 47–49, 51, 108, 253
sola fides   189, 225
Spanish Armada, the (1588)   180–181
Speed, John, cartographer and historian   51
Spelman, Clement, judge and library founder   45, 82–83
Spelman, Sir Henry, noted antiquary   45
Spelman, Sir John, historian and politician   45
St Paul's Churchyard, English printing centre   43, 97–98, 140, 151
Stationers' Company   144, 150, 158
Stone, William, clergyman and founder   35, 59, 70–74, 77, 83–85, 89–90, 105–106, 111–113, 120, 122, 128, 130–133, 139–140, 148–150, 154, 168–171, 181, 205, 208–210, 217
   will of   72–73
suicide   179, 232, 245, 247–250

Taylor, Jeremy, cleric   77, 187
Tertullian, Early Christian author   169, 171
Theodoret, bishop of Cyrus   102, 136
Thomas, Thomas, bookbinder   92
Thurloe, John, Secretary of State to Oliver Cromwell   50
Tildsley, John, Chetham's trustee and vicar   70, 94–99, 115, 128–129, 138, 168
Toledo, Francisco de, aristocrat and Viceroy of Peru   102
Trigge, Francis, clergyman and founder   34, 58–62, 67, 81, 83–84, 88, 91–94, 108–109, 117, 125, 133, 152, 156–160, 171, 253

Ussher, James, archbishop of Armagh   77, 111, 187, 201, 204

Venice   141

Vermigli, Peter Martyr, Italian Reformed theologian　4, 39, 194, 240
Viegas, Blasio, theologian　108
Volusianus, Roman emperor　210

Walker, Obadiah, college master　72
Wallington, Nehemiah, Puritan chronicler and diarist　248
Walsingham, Francis, Secretary of State to Elizabeth I　148
Walton, Brian, Anglian priest and scholar, editor of the Antwerp polyglot　75, 155
Watson, William, English Catholic priest　126
Weemes, John, Church of Scotland minister　193–194, 218, 246
White, Francis, bishop of Ely and controversialist　181–184, 190, 192, 197, 221
White, John, clergyman, royal chaplain and controversialist　184–185, 201

White, Thomas, bishop of Peterborough　34–35
White, William, clergyman and college master　80
Wilcox, Thomas, Puritan clergyman and controversialist　147
Willett, Andrew, clergyman and controversialist　62, 109
Wimborne Minster Grammar School　70–71
Winchelsey, Robert, archbishop of Canterbury　26–27

York　27, 43–44, 66, 102–103, 146

Zanchius, Hieronymus, Italian Reformed theologian　118, 159
Zwinger, Theodor, Renaissance humanist scholar　109
Zwingli, Huldrych, Swiss Reformer　189